The Federal Budget Process

A Description of the Federal and Congressional Budget Processes, Including Timelines

Compiled by TheCapitol.Net

TheCapitol.Net

For more than 40 years, TheCapitol.Net and its predecessor, Congressional Quarterly Executive Conferences, have been training professionals from government, military, business, and NGOs on the dynamics and operations of the legislative and executive branches and how to work with them.

Our training and publications include congressional operations, legislative and budget process, communication and advocacy, media and public relations, testifying before Congress, research skills, legislative drafting, critical thinking and writing, and more.

Our publications and courses, written and taught by current Washington insiders who are all independent subject matter experts, show how Washington works.™ Our products and services can be found on our web site at *<www.TheCapitol.Net>*.

TheCapitol.Net is a non-partisan firm.

Additional copies of *The Federal Budget Process* can be ordered online: *<TCNBooks.com>*.

Design and production by Zaccarine Design, Inc., Chicago, IL, *zacdesign@mac.com*.
Ebook conversion by Paula Reichwald *<igossi.com>*.
Index by Enid L. Zafran *<IndexingPartners.com>*.

∞ The paper used in this publication exceeds the requirements of the American National Standard for Information Sciences—Permanence of Paper for Printed Library Materials, ANSI Z39.48-1992.

v 2

The Federal Budget Process, softbound
ISBN: 1587332930
ISBN 13: 978-1-58733-293-7

Ebook ISBN:
Amazon Kindle ISBN: 978-1-58733-295-1
B&N nook ISBN: 978-1-58733-296-8
Google ISBN: 978-1-58733-294-4

The Federal Budget Process
A Description of the Federal and Congressional Budget Processes, Including Timelines

Introduction

Budgeting for the federal government is an enormously complex process. It entails dozens of subprocesses, countless rules and procedures, the efforts of tens of thousands of staff persons in the executive and legislative branches, and the active participation of the President, congressional leaders, Members of Congress, and members of the executive branch. This analysis shows the various elements of the federal budget process including the President's budget submission, framework, timetable, the budget resolution, reconciliation, the "Byrd Rule," appropriations, authorizations, and budget execution.

Congress is distinguished from nearly every other legislature in the world by the control it exercises over fashioning the government's budgetary policies. This power, referred to as "the power of the purse," ensures Congress' primary role in setting revenue and borrowing policies for the federal government and in determining how these resources are spent.

The congressional power of the purse derives from several key provisions in the Constitution.

- Article I, Section 8, Clause 1 declares in part that Congress shall have the power to raise (that is, "to lay and collect") revenues of various types, including taxes and duties, among other things.

- Article I, Section 8, Clause 2 declares that the power to borrow funds "on the credit of the United States" belongs to Congress. In addition to its powers regarding revenues and borrowing, Congress exerts control over the expenditure of funds.

- Article I, Section 9, Clause 7 declares in part that funds can be withdrawn from the Treasury only pursuant to laws that make appropriations.

Under the Constitution, revenue measures must originate in the House of Representatives. Beyond this requirement, however, the Constitution does not prescribe how the House and Senate should organize themselves, or the procedures they should use, to conduct budgeting. Over the years, however, both chambers have developed an extensive set of rules (some set forth in statute) and precedents that lay out complicated, multiple processes for making budgetary decisions. The House and Senate have also created an intricate committee system to support these processes.

As American society has grown and become ever more complex, and as the role of the federal government in the national economy has steadily expanded, Congress also has increasingly shared power over budgetary matters with the president and the executive branch. It has refashioned the president's role in budgeting by requiring him to submit to Congress each year a budget for the entire federal government and giving him responsibilities for monitoring agencies' implementation of spending and revenue laws. Accordingly, the president also exercises considerable influence over key budget decisions.

Summary Table of Contents

Introduction to the Federal Budget Process

Bill Heniff Jr., Coordinator
Analyst on Congress and the Legislative Process

Megan Suzanne Lynch
Analyst on Congress and the Legislative Process

Jessica Tollestrup
Analyst on Congress and the Legislative Process

December 3, 2012

Congressional Research Service
7-5700
www.crs.gov
98-721

CRS Report for Congress
Prepared for Members and Committees of Congress

Summary

Budgeting for the federal government is an enormously complex process. It entails dozens of subprocesses, countless rules and procedures, the efforts of tens of thousands of staff persons in the executive and legislative branches, millions of work hours each year, and the active participation of the President and congressional leaders, as well as other members of Congress and executive officials.

The enforcement of budgetary decisions involves a complex web of procedures that encompasses both congressional and executive actions. In the last four decades or so, these procedures have been rooted principally in two statutes—the Congressional Budget Act of 1974 and the Balanced Budget and Emergency Deficit Control Act of 1985. The 1974 act established a congressional budget process in which budget policies are enforced by Congress during the consideration of individual measures. The 1985 act embodies additional statutory enforcement procedures, substantially modified in 1990 and 1997, that have been used by the executive to enforce budget policies after the end of a congressional session. The 1997 iteration of these enforcement procedures were set aside in the latter years of their existence and effectively expired toward the end of the 107th Congress. Efforts to renew them in the 108th through 110th Congresses were not successful. In the 111th Congress, the pay-as-you-go procedures affecting direct spending and revenue legislation were restored in a modified version by the Statutory Pay-As-You-Go Act of 2010. More recently, in the 112th Congress, statutory limits on discretionary spending and a new automatic process to reduce spending were established by the Budget Control Act of 2011.

The President's budget is required by law to be submitted to Congress early in the legislative session. While the budget is only a request to Congress, the power to formulate and submit the budget is a vital tool in the President's direction of the executive branch and of national policy. The President's proposals often influence congressional revenue and spending decisions, though the extent of the influence varies from year to year and depends more on political and fiscal conditions than on the legal status of the budget.

The Congressional Budget Act of 1974 establishes the congressional budget process as the means by which Congress coordinates the various budget-related actions (such as the consideration of appropriations and revenue measures) taken by it during the course of the year. The process is centered on an annual concurrent resolution on the budget that sets aggregate budget policies and functional spending priorities for at least the next five fiscal years. Because a concurrent resolution is not a law—it cannot be signed or vetoed by the President—the budget resolution does not have statutory effect; no money can be raised or spent pursuant to it. Revenue and spending amounts set in the budget resolution establish the basis for the enforcement of congressional budget policies through points of order.

Congress implements budget resolution policies through action on individual revenue and debt-limit measures, annual appropriations acts, and direct spending legislation. In some years, Congress considers reconciliation legislation pursuant to reconciliation instructions in the budget resolution. Reconciliation legislation is used mainly to bring existing revenue and direct spending laws into conformity with budget resolution policies. Initially, reconciliation was a major tool for deficit reduction; in later years, reconciliation was used mainly to reduce revenues.

Contents

Tables

Contacts

The Evolution of Federal Budgeting

The "power of the purse" is a legislative power. The Constitution lists the power to lay and collect taxes and the power to borrow as powers of Congress; further, it provides that funds may be drawn from the Treasury only pursuant to appropriations made by law. The Constitution does not state how these legislative powers are to be exercised, nor does it expressly provide for the President to have a role in the management of the nation's finances.

During the nation's early years, the House and Senate devised procedures for the enactment of spending and revenue legislation. As these procedures evolved during the 19th century and the first decades of the 20th century, they led to highly fragmented legislative actions. In the course of each session, Congress passed many separate appropriations bills and other measures affecting the financial condition of the federal government. Neither the Constitution nor the procedures adopted by the House and Senate provided for a budget system—that is, for a coordinated set of actions covering all federal spending and revenues. As long as the federal government was small and its spending and revenues were stable, such a budget system was not considered necessary.

Early in the 20th century, the incessant rise in federal spending and the recurrence of deficits (spending exceeded revenues in half of the 20 years preceding FY1920) led Congress to seek a more coordinated means of making financial decisions. The key legislation was the Budget and Accounting Act of 1921, which established the executive budget process.

The 1921 act did not directly alter the procedures by which Congress makes revenue and spending decisions. The main impact was in the executive branch. The President was required to submit his budget recommendations to Congress each year, and the Bureau of the Budget— renamed the Office of Management and Budget (OMB) in 1970—was created to assist him in carrying out his budgetary responsibilities. Congress, it was expected, would be able to coordinate its revenue and spending decisions if it received comprehensive budget recommendations from the President. In line with this expectation, the House and Senate changed their rules to consolidate the jurisdiction of the Appropriations Committees over spending. The 1921 act also established the General Accounting Office (GAO), headed by the Comptroller General, and made it the principal auditing arm of the federal government. (The GAO recently was renamed the Government Accountability Office.) The 1921 act, as amended, remains the statutory basis for the presidential budget system.

After World War II, the belief that the presidential budget sufficed to maintain fiscal control gave way to the view that Congress needed its own budget process. Some members of Congress feared that dependence on the executive budget had bolstered the President's fiscal powers at the expense of Congress's; others felt that as long as its financial decisions were fragmented, Congress could not effectively control expenditures.

The Congressional Budget and Impoundment Control Act of 1974 established a congressional budget process centered on a concurrent resolution on the budget, scheduled for adoption prior to legislative consideration of revenue or spending bills. The congressional budget process initiated in the 1970s did not replace the preexisting revenue and spending processes. Instead, it provided an overall legislative framework within which the many separate measures affecting the budget would be considered. The central purpose of the budget process established by the 1974 act is to coordinate the various revenue and spending decisions which are made in separate revenue, appropriations, and other budgetary measures. To assist Congress in making budget decisions, the

1974 act established the Congressional Budget Office (CBO) and directed it to provide data on and analyses of the federal budget.

During the years that the congressional budget process has been in operation, its procedures have been adapted by Congress to changing circumstances. Following a decade of experience with the 1974 Congressional Budget Act, Congress made further changes in the budget process by enacting the Balanced Budget and Emergency Deficit Control Act of 1985 (also known as the Gramm-Rudman-Hollings Act), the Budget Enforcement Act of 1990 (BEA), the Line Item Veto Act in 1996, the Budget Enforcement Act of 1997, the Statutory Pay-As-You-Go Act of 2010, and the Budget Control Act of 2011, among other laws.

The 1985 act prescribed declining deficit targets intended to achieve balance in FY1991; the targets were enforced by sequestration, a process involving automatic, across-the-board cuts in nonexempt spending programs if the targets were expected to be exceeded. The 1990 act replaced the deficit targets with caps on discretionary spending and a pay-as-you-go (PAYGO) requirement for revenue and direct spending legislation; sequestration was retained as the means of enforcing the two new mechanisms. The 1996 act authorized the President to cancel discretionary spending in appropriation acts, as well as new direct spending and limited tax benefits in other legislation, subject to expedited legislative procedures by which Congress could overturn the cancellations. (The Supreme Court struck down the Line Item Veto Act in June 1998 as unconstitutional.) The 1997 act extended the BEA procedures for several more years. Without a consensus on extending the control mechanisms under the BEA, however, they expired at the end of FY2002. The Statutory Pay-As-You-Go Act of 2010 restored a modified version of the PAYGO requirement for direct spending and revenue legislation. More recently, as part of an agreement to increase the statutory limit on the public debt, the Budget Control Act of 2011 restored statutory limits on discretionary spending for each fiscal year through FY2021 and established an automatic process to reduce spending if subsequent legislation reducing the deficit by at least $1.2 trillion was not enacted, with spending reductions beginning in January 2013.

Basic Concepts of Federal Budgeting

The federal budget is a compilation of numbers about the revenues, spending, and borrowing and debt of the government. Revenues come largely from taxes, but stem from other sources as well (such as duties, fines, licenses, and gifts). Spending involves such concepts as budget authority, obligations, outlays, and offsetting collections. The numbers are computed according to rules and conventions that have accumulated over the years; they do not always conform to the way revenues and spending are accounted for in other processes.

Budget Authority and Outlays

When Congress appropriates money, it provides *budget authority*, that is, authority to enter into obligations. Budget authority also may be provided in legislation that does not go through the appropriations process (*direct spending* legislation). The key congressional spending decisions relate to the obligations that agencies are authorized to incur during a fiscal year, not to the outlays made during the year. (*Obligations* occur when agencies enter into contracts, submit purchase orders, employ personnel, and so forth; *outlays* occur when obligations are liquidated, primarily through the issuance of checks, electronic fund transfers, or the disbursement of cash.)

The provision of budget authority is the key point at which Congress exercises control over federal spending, although the outlay level often receives greater public attention because of its bearing on the deficit. Congress does not directly control outlays; each year's outlays derive in part from new budget authority and in part from "carryover" budget authority provided in prior years. For example, President Barack Obama's initial budget submission for FY2013 estimated that outlays would total $3,803 billion for that year. Approximately $2,833 billion of this amount was estimated to come from new budget authority for the fiscal year, while the remainder ($970 billion) was estimated to come from budget authority enacted in prior years.

The relation of budget authority to outlays varies from program to program and depends on *spendout rates*, the rates at which funds provided by Congress are obligated and payments disbursed. In a program with a high spendout rate, most new budget authority is expended during the fiscal year; if the spendout rate is low, however, most of the outlays occur in later years. Regardless of the spendout rate, the outlays in the budget are merely estimates of the amounts that will be disbursed during the year. If payments turn out to be higher than the budget estimate, outlays will be above the budgeted level. The President and Congress control outlays indirectly by deciding on the amount of budget authority to be provided or by limiting the amount of obligations to be incurred.

Certain receipts of the federal government are accounted for as "offsets" against outlays rather than as revenues. Various fees collected by government agencies are deducted from outlays; similarly, income from the sale of certain assets are treated as *offsetting receipts*. Most such receipts are offsets against the outlays of the agencies that collect the money, but in the case of offshore oil leases and certain other activities, the revenues are deducted from the total outlays of the government.

Scope of the Budget

The budget consists of two main groups of funds: *federal funds* and *trust funds*. Federal funds—which comprise mainly the general fund—largely derive from the general exercise of the taxing power and general borrowing and for the most part are not earmarked by law to any specific program or agency. One component of federal funds, called special funds, is earmarked as to source and purpose. The use of federal funds is determined largely by appropriations acts.

Trust funds are established, under the terms of statutes that designate them as trust funds, to account for funds earmarked by specific sources and purposes. The Social Security funds are the largest of the trust funds; revenues are collected under a Social Security payroll tax and are used to pay for Social Security benefits and related purposes. The *unified budget* includes both the federal funds and the trust funds. The balances in the trust funds are borrowed by the federal government; they are counted, therefore, in the federal debt. Because these balances offset a budget deficit but are included in the federal debt, the annual increase in the debt invariably exceeds the amount of the budget deficit. For the same reason, it is possible for the federal debt to rise when the federal government has a budget surplus.

Capital and operating expenses are not segregated in the budget. Hence, monies paid for the operations of government agencies as well as for the acquisition of long-life assets (such as buildings, roads, and weapons systems) are reported as budget outlays. Proposals have been made from time to time to divide the budget into capital and operating accounts. While these proposals have not been adopted, the budget provides information showing the investment and operating outlays of the government.

The budget totals do not include all the financial transactions of the federal government. The main exclusions fall into two categories—off-budget entities and government-sponsored enterprises. In addition, the budget includes direct and guaranteed loans on the basis of the accounting rules established by the Federal Credit Reform Act of 1990, which are discussed below.

Off-budget entities are excluded by law from the budget totals. The receipts and disbursements of the Social Security trust funds (the Old-Age and Survivors Insurance Fund and the Disability Insurance Fund), as well as spending for the Postal Service Fund, are excluded from the budget totals. These transactions are shown separately in the budget. Thus, the budget now reports two deficit or surplus amounts—one excluding the Social Security trust funds and the Postal Service Fund, and the other (on a unified basis) including these entities. The latter is the main focus of discussion in both the President's budget and the congressional budget process.

The transactions of government-owned corporations (excluding the Postal Service), as well as revolving funds, are included in the budget on a net basis. That is, the amount shown in the budget is the difference between receipts and outlays, not the total activity of the enterprise or revolving fund. If, for example, a revolving fund has annual income of $150 million and disbursements of $200 million, the budget would report $50 million as net outlays.

Government-sponsored enterprises (GSEs) historically have been excluded from the budget because they were deemed to be private rather than public entities. The federal government did not own any equity in these enterprises, most of which received their financing from private sources. Although they were established by the federal government, their budgets were not reviewed by the President or Congress in the same manner as other programs. Most of these enterprises engaged in credit activities. They borrowed funds in capital markets and lent money to homeowners, farmers, and others. In total, these enterprises had assets and liabilities measured in trillions of dollars. Financial statements of the government-sponsored enterprises were published in the President's budget.

Although some GSEs continue to operate on this basis, the economic downturn and credit instability that occurred in 2008 fundamentally changed the status of two GSEs that play a significant role in the home mortgage market, Fannie Mae and Freddie Mac. In September of 2008, the Federal Housing Finance Agency (FHFA) placed the two entities in conservatorship, thereby subjecting them to control by the Federal Government until the conservatorship eventually is brought to an end.

Deficit Reduction and the Rules of Congressional Budgeting

Between the early 1980s and the late 1990s, annual consideration of the budget was dominated by concern about the budget deficit. In the mid-1980s, the deficit exceeded $150 billion and amounted to about 6% of GDP at one point. In the early 1990s, the deficit approached the $300 billion level. Following four years of surpluses (FY1998-FY2001), the budget returned to deficit for FY2002. Current budget projections show sizeable deficits persisting over the coming years.

The size of the deficit depends on how it is measured. The unified budget deficit combines all on-budget federal funds and trust funds with the off-budget entities (the Social Security trust funds and the Postal Service Fund). The unified budget deficit generally is regarded as the most comprehensive measure of the impact of the budget on the economy. A narrower measure of the deficit is derived by excluding the Social Security trust funds from the totals. This exclusion is mandated by law, although Social Security is counted in the budget in reports on the deficit. Excluding Social Security from computations of the deficit or surplus results in higher deficit or lower surplus figures.

Regardless of the measure used, it is evident that the deficit was unusually high for an extended period of time. The chronic deficits of the 1980s prompted Congress to enact the Balanced Budget and Emergency Deficit Control Act of 1985. The 1985 act established deficit targets for each year through FY1991, when the budget was to be balanced, and a sequestration process under which budgetary resources would be canceled automatically (through largely across-the-board spending cuts) if the estimated deficit exceeded the amount allowed under the act.

Even with the targets, the actual deficit for the covered years was above the targeted level. Failure to achieve the deficit targets, and other problems, led Congress to revise the process in the Budget Enforcement Act (BEA) of 1990. Sequestration procedures were retained, but the fixed deficit targets were replaced by adjustable ones (which expired at the end of FY1995), adjustable limits were imposed on discretionary spending, and a pay-as-you-go (PAYGO) process was established for revenues and direct spending. The discretionary spending limits and PAYGO process were extended (through FY1998) by the Omnibus Budget Reconciliation of 1993 and again (through FY2002) by the BEA of 1997.

Under the discretionary spending limits, different categories of discretionary spending were used for different periods. Under the 1997 changes, discretionary spending limits applied separately to defense and nondefense spending for FY1998-FY1999 and to violent crime reduction spending for FY1998-FY2000; for the remaining fiscal years, the 1997 changes merged all discretionary spending into a single, general purpose category. In 1998, as part of the Transportation Equity Act for the 21st Century, Congress added separate categories for highway and mass transit spending. Finally, in 2000, Congress added a category for conservation spending; unlike the other categories, the conservation spending category had six subcategories.

The PAYGO process under the BEA required that the budgetary impact of revenue and direct spending legislation be recorded on a multiyear "PAYGO scorecard," and that in the net any such legislation not yield a negative balance for the upcoming fiscal year. Legislation reducing revenues or increasing direct spending for a fiscal year had to be offset (in the same or other legislation) by revenue increases or reductions in direct spending for that fiscal year so that the applicable balance on the PAYGO scorecard remained at or above zero.

Under the BEA procedures, violations of the discretionary spending limits or the PAYGO requirement were to be enforced by sequestration. However, sequestration was not used for more than a decade, either because Congress and the President enacted budgetary legislation consistent with the discretionary spending limits and PAYGO requirement, or, during the latter years under the BEA, effectively waived these enforcement requirements.

The BEA enforcement procedures effectively expired toward the end of the 107th Congress. As budget deficits persisted through the last decade, proposals to restore the BEA statutory procedures had been made from time to time by members of Congress and the President, but none of the proposals were enacted until 2010. The Statutory Pay-As-You-Go Act of 2010 (P.L. 111-139) restored in statute a modified version of the PAYGO requirement for direct spending and revenue legislation.[1] Subsequently, in 2011, the Budget Control Act (P.L. 112-25) established statutory limits on discretionary spending for each year through FY2021.

Like the previous statutory PAYGO requirement under the BEA, the new statutory PAYGO requirement is intended to discourage or prevent Congress from taking certain legislative action that would increase the on-budget deficit. It generally requires that legislation affecting direct spending or revenues not increase the deficit over a six-year period and an 11-year period. Likewise, the current statutory discretionary caps established under the Budget Control Act are similar to those under the BEA. The limits essentially cap the amount of spending provided and controlled through the annual appropriations process each year, with upward adjustments to these limits permitted for certain purposes, such as for Overseas Contingency Operations.

The statutory PAYGO requirement and the statutory discretionary spending limits are enforced by sequestration—the cancellation of budgetary resources provided by laws affecting direct spending. Further information on sequestration is provided in the "The Sequestration Process" section, below.

During the 1990s to the present, the Senate has supplemented the statutory PAYGO requirement with a special PAYGO rule included in annual budget resolutions; following the expiration of the BEA procedures, the Senate extended its PAYGO rule (currently through FY2017). The Senate PAYGO rule currently prohibits the consideration of any legislation that proposes changes in direct spending or revenue that increase the deficit over six-year and 11-year time periods (including the current fiscal year). The House adopted its own PAYGO rule for the first time at the beginning of the 110th Congress. At the beginning of the 112th Congress, however, the House modified this rule, renaming it CutGo, or cut-as-you-go, to prohibit the consideration of any legislation that would have the net effect of increasing direct spending over the same two time periods.

Budgeting for Discretionary and Direct Spending

The distinction drawn by the BEA and the congressional budget process between discretionary spending (which is controlled through the annual appropriations process) and direct spending (which is provided outside of the annual appropriations process) recognized that the federal government has somewhat different, though overlapping, means of dealing with these two types of spending. One set of procedures pertained to discretionary spending, another to direct spending.

Most of the direct spending subject to the PAYGO process under the BEA involved entitlement programs; the rest consisted of other forms of mandatory spending provided through authorizing legislation and interest payments. In fact, entitlements now account for about half of total federal spending (all direct spending, including net interest, accounts for about 60% of the total). The impressive feature of this trend is that most of the growth in spending and in the number of recipients has been built into existing law; for the most part, it has not been the result of new legislation.

---

[1] For more detailed information on the statutory PAYGO requirement, see CRS Report R41157, *The Statutory Pay-As-You-Go Act of 2010: Summary and Legislative History*, by Bill Heniff Jr.

The procedures for discretionary and direct spending converge at two critical points in federal budgeting: formulation of the President's budget and formulation of the congressional budget resolution. Both of these policy statements encompass discretionary and direct spending, but the procedures used in budgeting for these types of expenditure differ greatly. The distinctions have some notable exceptions. Some procedures associated with direct spending are applied to particular types of discretionary programs, and vice versa. Nevertheless, the generalizations presented here help to explain the complications of the budget process and explain how decisions are made.

(1) Budgetary Impact of Authorizing Legislation. An authorization for a discretionary spending program is only a license to enact an appropriation. The amount of budgetary resources available for spending is determined in annual appropriations acts. For direct spending programs (principally entitlements), on the other hand, the authorizing legislation either provides, or effectively mandates the appropriation of, budget authority. In those entitlement programs that are subject to annual appropriation, the Appropriations Committees have little or no discretion as to the amounts they provide.

(2) Committees That Provide or Mandate Budget Authority. The Appropriations Committees have jurisdiction and effective control over discretionary spending programs, while authorizing committees effectively control direct spending programs (including those funded in annual appropriations acts). In fact, committee jurisdiction determines whether a program is classified as discretionary or direct spending. All spending under the effective control of the Appropriations Committees is discretionary; everything else is direct spending. Accordingly, when legislation establishes a program as discretionary or direct spending, it not only determines the character of spending but the locus of congressional committee control as well.

(3) Frequency of Decision-Making. Discretionary appropriations are, with few exceptions, made annually for the current or next fiscal year. Direct spending programs typically are established in permanent law that continues in effect until such time as it is revised or terminated by another law. The fact that many entitlements have annual appropriations does not diminish the permanence of the laws governing the amounts spent. It should be noted, however, that some direct spending programs, such as Medicare, have been subject to frequent legislative changes. The purpose of such legislation has been to modify existing law, not to provide annual funding.

(4) Means of Enforcing the Budget Resolution. The procedures used by Congress to enforce the policies set forth in the annual budget resolution differ somewhat for discretionary and direct spending programs. For both types of spending, Congress relies on allocations made under Section 302 of the 1974 Congressional Budget Act to ensure that spending legislation reported by House and Senate committees conforms to established budget policies. But although this procedure is effective in controlling new legislation—both annual appropriations measures and new entitlement legislation—it is not an effective control on the spending that results from existing laws. Hence, Congress relies on reconciliation procedures to enforce budget policies with respect to existing spending and revenue laws. Reconciliation is not currently applied to discretionary programs funded in annual appropriations measures.

(5) Statutory Controls. Discretionary programs have been subject to the spending limits set in the BEA. Direct spending has not been capped, but has operated under the PAYGO process, which required that direct spending and revenue legislation enacted for a fiscal year not cause the deficit to rise or the surplus to decrease. The lack of caps was due to the fact that most direct spending

appropriate reference in the legislation or statement exists. The OMB and CBO scores on legislation sometimes differ.

In addition to enforcing PAYGO, baseline projections and scoring are used in computing the amount of deficit reduction agreed to in budget summit negotiations between the President and Congress and enacted in reconciliation acts.

Budgeting for Direct and Guaranteed Loans

The Federal Credit Reform Act of 1990 made fundamental changes in the budgetary treatment of direct loans and guaranteed loans. The reform, which first became effective for FY1992, shifted the accounting basis for federally provided or guaranteed credit from the amount of cash flowing into or out of the Treasury to the estimated subsidy cost of the loans. Credit reform entails complex procedures for estimating these subsidy costs and new accounting mechanisms for recording various loan transactions. The changes have had only a modest impact on budget totals but a substantial impact on budgeting for particular loan programs.

The new system requires that budget authority and outlays be budgeted for the estimated subsidy cost of direct and guaranteed loans. This cost is defined in the 1990 act as "the estimated long-term cost to the Government of a direct loan or a loan guarantee, calculated on a net present value basis, excluding administrative costs."

Under the new system, Congress appropriates budget authority or provides indefinite authority equal to the subsidy cost. This budget authority is placed in a program account from which funds are disbursed to a financing account.

The Budget Cycle

Federal budgeting is a cyclical activity that begins with the formulation of the President's annual budget and concludes with the audit and review of expenditures. The process spreads over a multi-year period. The main stages are formulation of the President's budget, congressional budget actions, implementation of the budget, and audit and review. While the basic steps continue from year to year, particular procedures often vary in accord with the style of the President, the economic and political considerations under which the budget is prepared and implemented, and other factors.

The activities related to a single fiscal year usually stretch over a period of two-and-a-half calendar years (or longer). As the budget is being considered, federal agencies must deal with three different fiscal years at the same time: implementing the budget for the current fiscal year; seeking funds from Congress for the next fiscal year; and planning for the fiscal year after that.

The Presidential Budget Process

The President's budget, officially referred to as the *Budget of the United States Government*, is required by law to be submitted to Congress early in the legislative session, no later than the first Monday in February. The budget consists of estimates of spending, revenues, borrowing, and debt; policy and legislative recommendations; detailed estimates of the financial operations of federal agencies and programs; data on the actual and projected performance of the economy; and other information supporting the President's recommendations.

The President's budget is only a request to Congress; Congress is not required to adopt his recommendations. Nevertheless, the power to formulate and submit the budget is a vital tool in the President's direction of the executive branch and of national policy. The President's proposals often influence congressional revenue and spending decisions, though the extent of the influence varies from year to year and depends more on political and fiscal conditions than on the legal status of the budget.

The Constitution does not provide for a budget, nor does it require the President to make recommendations concerning the revenues and spending of the federal government. Until 1921, the federal government operated without a comprehensive presidential budget process. The Budget and Accounting Act of 1921, as amended, provides for a national budget system. Its basic requirement is that the President should prepare and submit a budget to Congress each year. The 1921 act established the Bureau of the Budget, now named the Office of Management and Budget (OMB), to assist the President in preparing and implementing the executive budget. Although it has been amended many times, this statute provides the legal basis for the presidential budget, prescribes much of its content, and defines the roles of the President and the agencies in the process.

Formulation and Content of the President's Budget

Preparation of the President's budget typically begins in the spring (or earlier) each year, at least nine months before the budget is submitted to Congress, about 17 months before the start of the fiscal year to which it pertains, and about 29 months before the close of that fiscal year. The early stages of budget preparation occur in federal agencies. When they begin work on the budget for a fiscal year, agencies already are implementing the budget for the fiscal year in progress and awaiting final appropriations actions and other legislative decisions for the fiscal year after that. The long lead times and the fact that appropriations have not yet been made for the next year mean that the budget is prepared with a great deal of uncertainty about economic conditions, presidential policies, and congressional actions.

As agencies formulate their budgets, they maintain continuing contact with the OMB examiners assigned to them. These contacts provide agencies with guidance in preparing their budgets and also enable them to alert OMB to any needs or problems that may loom ahead. Agency requests are submitted to OMB in late summer or early fall; these are reviewed by OMB staff in consultation with the President and his aides. The 1921 Budget and Accounting Act bars agencies from submitting their budget requests directly to Congress. Moreover, OMB regulations provide for confidentiality in all budget requests and recommendations prior to the transmittal of the President's budget to Congress. However, it is quite common for internal budget documents to become public while the budget is still being formulated.

The format and content of the budget are partly determined by law, but the 1921 act authorizes the President to set forth the budget "in such form and detail" as he may determine. Over the years, there has been an increase in the types of information and explanatory material presented in the budget documents.

In most years, the budget is submitted as a multi-volume set consisting of a main document setting forth the President's message to Congress and an analysis and justification of his major proposals (the *Budget*) and supplementary documents providing account and program level details, historical information, and special budgetary analyses (the *Budget Appendix*, *Historical Tables*, and *Analytical Perspectives*), among other things.

Much of the budget is an estimate of requirements under existing law rather than a request for congressional action (more than half of the budget authority in the budget becomes available without congressional action). The President is required to submit a budget update (reflecting changed economic conditions, congressional actions, and other factors), referred to as the *Mid-Session Review*, by July 15 each year. The President may revise his recommendations any time during the year.

Executive Interaction with Congress

The President and his budget office have an important role once the budget is submitted to Congress. OMB officials and other presidential advisors appear before congressional committees to discuss overall policy and economic issues, but they generally leave formal discussions of specific programs to the affected agencies. Agencies thus bear the principal responsibility for defending the President's program recommendations at congressional hearings.

Agencies are supposed to justify the President's recommendations, not their own. OMB maintains an elaborate legislative clearance process to ensure that agency budget justifications, testimony, and other submissions are consistent with presidential policy. As the session unfolds, the President may formally signal his position on pending legislation through the issuance of a Statement of Administration Policy (SAP). These statements, which are maintained by OMB on its website, are sometimes used to convey a veto threat against legislation the President feels requires modifications to meet his approval.

Increasingly in recent years, the President and his chief budgetary aides have engaged in extensive negotiations with Congress over major budgetary legislation. These negotiations sometimes have occurred as formal budget "summits" and at other times as less visible, behind-the-scenes activities.

The Congressional Budget Process

The Congressional Budget and Impoundment Control Act of 1974 establishes the congressional budget process as the means by which Congress coordinates the various budget-related actions (such as the consideration of appropriations and revenue measures) taken by it during the course of the year. The process is centered around an annual concurrent resolution on the budget that sets aggregate budget policies and functional priorities for at least the next five fiscal years.

Because a concurrent resolution is not a law—it cannot be signed or vetoed by the President—the budget resolution does not have statutory effect; no money can be raised or spent pursuant to it. The main purpose of the budget resolution is to establish the framework within which Congress considers separate revenue, spending, and other budget-related legislation. Revenue and spending amounts set in the budget resolution establish the basis for the enforcement of congressional budget policies through points of order. The budget resolution also initiates the reconciliation process for conforming existing revenue and spending laws to congressional budget policies.

Formulation and Content of the Budget Resolution

The congressional budget process begins upon the presentation of the President's budget in January or February (see **Table 1**). The timetable set forth in the 1974 Congressional Budget Act calls for the final adoption of the budget resolution by April 15, well before the beginning of the new fiscal year on October 1. Although the House and Senate often pass the budget resolution separately before April 15, they often do not reach final agreement on it until after the deadline—sometimes months later. The 1974 act bars consideration of revenue, spending, and debt-limit measures for the upcoming fiscal year until the budget resolution for that year has been adopted, but certain exceptions are provided (such as the exception that allows the House to consider the regular appropriations bills after May 15, even if the budget resolution has not been adopted by then).

Table 1. Congressional Budget Process Timetable

Deadline	Action to be completed
First Monday in February	President submits budget to Congress.
February 15	CBO submits report on economic and budget outlook to Budget committees.
Six weeks after President's budget is submitted	Committees submit reports on views and estimates to respective Budget Committee.
April 1	Senate Budget Committee reports budget resolution.
April 15	Congress completes action on budget resolution.
June 10	House Appropriations Committee reports last regular appropriations bill.
June 30	House completes action on regular appropriations bills and any required reconciliation legislation.
July 15	President submits mid-session review of his budget to Congress.
October 1	Fiscal year begins.

Source: Compiled by the Congressional Research Service.

The 1974 Congressional Budget Act requires the budget resolution, for each fiscal year covered, to set forth budget aggregates and spending levels for each functional category of the budget. The aggregates included in the budget resolution are as follows:

- total revenues (and the amount by which the total is to be changed by legislative action);
- total new budget authority and outlays;
- the surplus or deficit; and
- the debt limit.

With regard to each of the functional categories, the budget resolution must indicate for each fiscal year the amounts of new budget authority and outlays, and they must add up to the corresponding spending or aggregates.

Aggregate amounts in the budget resolution do not reflect the revenues or spending of the Social Security trust funds, although these amounts are set forth separately in the budget resolution for purposes of Senate enforcement procedures.

The budget resolution does not allocate funds among specific programs or accounts, but the major program assumptions underlying the functional amounts are often discussed in the reports accompanying each resolution. Some recent reports have contained detailed information on the program levels assumed in the resolution. These assumptions are not binding on the affected committees. Finally, the 1974 act allows certain additional matters to be included in the budget resolution. The most important optional feature of a budget resolution is reconciliation directives (discussed below).

The House and Senate Budget Committees are responsible for marking up and reporting the budget resolution. In the course of developing the budget resolution, the Budget Committees hold hearings, receive "views and estimates" reports from other committees, and obtain information from CBO. These "views and estimates" reports of House and Senate committees provide the Budget Committees with information on the preferences and legislative plans of congressional committees regarding budgetary matters within their jurisdiction.

CBO assists the Budget Committees in developing the budget resolution by issuing, early each year, a report on the economic and budget outlook that includes baseline budget projections. The baseline projections presented in the report are supported by more detailed projections for accounts and programs; CBO usually revises the baseline projections one or more times before the Budget Committees mark up the budget resolution. In addition, CBO issues a report analyzing the President's budgetary proposals in light of CBO's own economic and technical assumptions. In past years, CBO also issued an annual report on spending and revenue options for reducing the deficit or maintaining the surplus.

The extent to which the Budget Committees (and the House and Senate) consider particular programs when they act on the budget resolution varies from year to year. Specific program decisions are supposed to be left to the Appropriations Committees and other committees of jurisdiction, but there is a strong likelihood that major issues will be discussed in markup, in the Budget Committees' reports, and during floor consideration of the budget resolution. Although any programmatic assumptions generated in this process are not binding on the committees of jurisdiction, they often influence the final outcome.

Floor consideration of the budget resolution is guided by House and Senate rules and practices. In the House, the Rules Committee usually reports a *special rule* (a simple House resolution), which, once approved, establishes the terms and conditions under which the budget resolution is considered. This special rule typically specifies which amendments may be considered and the sequence in which they are to be offered and voted on. It has been the practice in recent years to allow consideration of a few amendments (as substitutes for the entire resolution) that present broad policy choices. In the Senate, the amendment process is less structured, relying on agreements reached by the leadership through a broad consultative process. The amendments offered in the Senate may entail major policy choices or may be focused on a single issue.

Achievement of the policies set forth in the annual budget resolution depends on the legislative actions taken by Congress (and their approval or disapproval by the President), the performance of the economy, and technical considerations. Many of the factors that determine whether budgetary goals will be met are beyond the direct control of Congress. If economic conditions—

growth, employment levels, inflation, and so forth—vary significantly from projected levels, so too will actual levels of revenue and spending. Similarly, actual levels may differ substantially if the technical factors upon which estimates are based, such as the rate at which agencies spend their discretionary funds or participants become eligible for entitlement programs, prove faulty.

Budget Resolution Enforcement

Congress's regular tools for enforcing the budget resolution each year are overall spending ceilings and revenue floors and committee allocations and subdivisions of spending. In addition, the Senate in some years has enforced discretionary spending limits in the budget resolution, which paralleled the adjustable limits established in statute and enforced by the sequestration process, and both chambers have imposed additional rules on direct spending and revenue legislation. Finally, the House and Senate in recent years have included procedural features in budget resolutions to limit the use of advance appropriations.

In order for the enforcement procedures to work, Congress must have access to complete and up-to-date budgetary information so that it can relate individual measures to overall budget policies and determine whether adoption of a particular measure would be consistent with those policies. Substantive and procedural points of order are designed to obtain congressional compliance with budget rules. A point of order may bar House or Senate consideration of legislation that violates the spending ceilings and revenue floors in the budget resolution, committee subdivisions of spending, or congressional budget procedures.

Budget Resolution Aggregates

In the early years after the 1974 Congressional Budget Act, the principal enforcement mechanism was the ceiling on total budget authority and outlays and the floor under total revenues set forth in the budget resolution. The limitations inherent in this mechanism soon became apparent. For example, the issue of controlling breaches of the spending ceilings usually did not arise until Congress acted on supplemental appropriations acts, when the fiscal year was well underway. The emergency nature of the legislation often made it difficult to uphold the ceilings.

Changes sometimes are made in budget resolutions by virtue of the operation of reserve funds. Generally, reserve funds allow increases to be made in various spending levels associated with the budget resolution for legislation meeting criteria specified in the budget resolution, as long as any increases spending from the legislation is offset (e.g., by revenue increases) so as to be deficit neutral.

Allocations of Spending to Committees

In view of the inadequacies in the early years of congressional budgeting of relying on enforcement of the budget totals, Congress changed the focus of enforcement in the 1980s to the committee allocations and subdivisions of spending made pursuant to Section 302 of the act. The key to enforcing budget policy is to relate the budgetary impact of individual pieces of legislation to the overall budget policy. Because Congress operates through its committee system, an essential step in linking particular measures to the budget is to allocate the spending amounts set forth in the budget resolution among House and Senate committees.

Section 302(a) provides for allocations to committees to be made in the statement of managers accompanying the conference report on the budget resolution. A Section 302(a) allocation is made to each committee which has jurisdiction over spending, both for the budget year and the full period covered by the budget resolution—at least five fiscal years.

The committee allocations do not take into account jurisdiction over discretionary authorizations funded in annual appropriations acts. The amounts of new budget authority and outlays allocated to committees in the House or Senate may not exceed the aggregate amounts of budget authority and outlays set forth in the budget resolution. Although these allocations are made by the Budget Committees, they are not the unilateral preferences of these committees. They are based on assumptions and understandings developed in the course of formulating the budget resolution.

After the allocations are made under Section 302(a), the House and Senate Appropriations Committees subdivide the amounts they receive among their 12 subcommittees, as required by Section 302(b). The subcommittees' Section 302(b) subdivisions may not exceed the total amount allocated to the committee. Each Appropriations Committee reports its subdivisions to its respective chamber; the appropriations bills may not be considered until such a report has been filed.

Scoring and Cost Estimates

As mentioned previously, scoring (also called scorekeeping) is the process of measuring the budgetary effects of pending and enacted legislation and assessing its impact on a budget plan—in this case, the budget resolution. In the congressional budget process, scoring serves several broad purposes. First, scoring informs members of Congress and the public about the budgetary consequences of their actions. When a budgetary measure is under consideration, scoring information lets members know whether adopting the amendment or passing the bill at hand would breach the budget. Further, scoring information enables members to judge what must be done in upcoming legislative action to achieve the year's budgetary goals. Finally, scoring is designed to assist Congress in enforcing its budget plans. In this regard, scorekeeping is used largely to determine whether points of order under the 1974 act may be sustained against legislation violating budget resolution levels.

The principal scorekeepers for Congress are the House and Senate Budget Committees, which provide the presiding officers of their respective chambers with the estimates needed to determine if legislation violates the aggregate levels in the budget resolution or the committee subdivisions of spending. The Budget Committees make summary scoring reports available to members on a frequent basis, usually geared to the pace of legislative activity. CBO assists Congress in these activities by preparing cost estimates of legislation, which are included in committee reports, and scoring reports for the Budget committees. The Joint Committee on Taxation supports Congress by preparing estimates of the budgetary impact of revenue legislation.

Points of Order

The 1974 Congressional Budget Act provides for both substantive and procedural points of order to block violations of budget resolution policies and congressional budget procedures. One element of substantive enforcement is based on Section 311 of the act, which bars Congress from considering legislation that would cause total revenues to fall below the level set in the budget resolution or total new budget authority or total outlays to exceed the budgeted level. The House and Senate both enforce the spending ceilings for the first fiscal year only; the revenue floor, however, is enforced for the first fiscal year and the full number of fiscal years covered by the budget resolution.

In the House (but not the Senate), Section 311 does not apply to spending legislation if the committee reporting the measure has stayed within its allocation of new discretionary budget authority. Accordingly, the House may take up any spending measure that is within the appropriate committee allocations, even if it would cause total spending to be exceeded. Neither chamber bars spending legislation that would cause functional allocations in the budget resolution to be exceeded.

Section 302(f) of the 1974 act bars the House and Senate from considering any spending measure that would cause the relevant committee's spending allocations to be exceeded; in the House, the point of order applies only to violations of allocations of new discretionary budget authority. Further, the point of order also applies to suballocations of spending made by the Appropriations Committees.

In addition to points of order to enforce compliance with the budget resolution and the allocations and subdivisions made pursuant to it, the 1974 act contains points of order to ensure compliance with its procedures. Perhaps the most important of these is Section 303, which bars consideration of any revenue, spending, entitlement, or debt-limit measure prior to adoption of the budget resolution. However, the rules of the House permit it to consider regular appropriations bills after May 15, even if the budget resolution has not yet been adopted.

When the House or Senate considers a revenue or a spending measure, the chairman of the respective Budget Committee sometimes makes a statement advising the chamber as to whether the measure violates any of these points of order. If no point of order is made, or if the point of order is waived, the House or Senate may consider a measure despite any violations of the 1974 act. The House often waives points of order by adopting a special rule. The Senate may waive points of order by unanimous consent or by motion under Section 904 of the act. The Senate requires a three-fifths vote of the membership to waive certain provisions of the act.

In several past years, the House and Senate failed to reach agreement on a budget resolution. On these occasions, one or both houses agreed to their own "deeming resolutions," which established the basis for enforcing points of order under the 1974 act in that house only.

The Sequestration Process

Sequestration was the principle means used to enforce statutory budget enforcement policies in place from 1985 through 2002, and it is the principle means used to enforce the PAYGO requirement under the Statutory Pay-As-You-Go Act of 2010 and the statutory limits on discretionary spending under the Budget Control Act of 2011 (BCA). In addition, sequestration is used to achieve a portion of the spending reductions required as a result of the failure to enact deficit reduction legislation tied to the Joint Committee on Deficit Reduction, as provided by the BCA.[2]

---

[2] For further information on the BCA, see CRS Report R41965, *The Budget Control Act of 2011*, by Bill Heniff Jr., Elizabeth Rybicki, and Shannon M. Mahan.

Sequestration involves the issuance of a presidential order that permanently cancels budgetary resources (except for revolving funds, special funds, trust funds, and certain offsetting collections) for the purpose of achieving a required amount of outlay savings to reduce the deficit. Once sequestration is triggered by an executive determination, spending reductions are made automatically; this process, therefore, is regarded by many as providing a strong incentive for Congress and the President to reach agreement on legislation that would avoid a sequester.

From its inception in 1985 until its revision by the Budget Enforcement Act (BEA) in 1990, the process was tied solely to the enforcement of fixed deficit targets. The BEA changed the sequestration process substantially. First, it effectively eliminated the deficit targets as a factor in budget enforcement. Second, the BEA established adjustable limits on discretionary spending funded in the annual appropriations process. Third, the BEA created pay-as-you-go procedures to require that increases in direct spending (i.e., spending controlled outside of the annual appropriations process) or decreases in revenues due to legislative action were offset so that there was effectively no net increase in the deficit or reduction of the surplus.

The BEA established adjustable limits on discretionary spending for FY1991-FY1995. These limits were extended through FY1998 in 1993. The Budget Enforcement Act (BEA) of 1997 revised the limits for FY1998 and provided new limits through FY2002. The limits were established for the following categories of discretionary spending: defense and nondefense, for FY1998-FY1999; discretionary (a single, general purpose category), for FY2000-FY2002; and violent crime reduction, for FY1998-FY2000. In 1998, as part of the Transportation Equity Act for the 21st Century, separate categories were added for highway and mass transit spending. Finally, a spending conservation category was added in 2000. The limits expired at the end of FY2002. As noted above, the Budget Control Act of 2011 revived the statutory limits on discretionary spending by establishing them for each year through FY2021.

The original discretionary spending limits had to be adjusted periodically by the President for various factors, including (among others), changes in concepts and definitions, a special outlay allowance (to accommodate estimating differences between OMB and CBO), and the enactment of legislation providing emergency funding and funding for the International Monetary Fund, international arrearages, an earned income tax credit compliance initiative, and other specially designated purposes. The more recent limits, under the BCA, may be adjusted for spending designated for emergencies, Overseas Contingency Operations, and disaster relief, among other specified purposes.

Under the pay-as-you-go (PAYGO) process created by the BEA, legislation increasing direct spending or decreasing revenues for a fiscal year had to be offset so that the balance on the PAYGO scorecard for that year did not fall below zero. The PAYGO process did not require any offsetting action when the spending increase or revenue decrease was due to the operation of existing law, such as an increase in the number of persons participating in the Medicare program. Direct spending consists largely of spending for entitlement programs. Most direct spending and revenue programs are established under permanent law, so there is not necessarily any need for recurring legislative action on them (and the PAYGO process did not require such action).

The PAYGO process did not preclude Congress from enacting legislation to increase direct spending; it only required that the increase be offset by reductions in other direct spending programs (which could include increases in offsetting receipts), by increases in revenues, or by a combination of the two in order to avoid a sequester. If a sequester under this process was required, it would have had to offset the amount of any net deficit increase (or surplus reduction) for the fiscal year caused by the enactment of legislation in the current and prior sessions of Congress, and would have been applied to nonexempt direct spending programs.

Spending for Social Security benefits and federal deposit insurance commitments, as well as emergency direct spending and revenue legislation (so designated by both the President and by Congress), was exempted completely from the PAYGO sequestration process. All remaining direct spending programs were covered by the PAYGO process to the extent that legislation affecting their spending levels was counted in determining whether a net increase or decrease in the deficit has occurred for a fiscal year. If a PAYGO sequester had occurred, however, many direct spending programs would have been exempt from reduction.

In 1997, coverage of the PAYGO requirement was extended to legislation enacted through FY2002; however, the PAYGO process was slated to remain in effect through FY2006 to deal with the outyear effects of such measures. Consequently, a PAYGO sequester could have occurred in FY2003-FY2006 based on legislation enacted before the end of FY2002. At the end of the 107th Congress, legislation was enacted setting all of the remaining PAYGO balances to zero, effectively terminating the PAYGO requirement under the BEA.

The multiple sequestration procedures established by the BEA remained automatic, to be triggered by a report from the OMB director. For sequestration purposes generally, there was only one triggering report issued each year (just after the end of the congressional session), but preliminary and update sequestration reports were issued earlier in the session. Additionally, OMB reports triggering a sequester for discretionary spending could be issued during the following session if legislative developments so warranted (i.e., the enactment of supplemental appropriations). The CBO director was required to provide advisory sequestration reports, shortly before the OMB director's reports were due.

Sequestration procedures could be suspended in the event a declaration of war was enacted or if Congress enacted a special joint resolution triggered by the issuance of a CBO report indicating "low growth" in the economy. Also, there were several special procedures under the act by which the final sequestration order for a fiscal year could be modified or the implementation of the order affected.

As noted above, sequestration has been revived to enforce more recent statutory budget enforcement rules. First, the Statutory Pay-As-You-Go Act of 2010, enacted on February 12, 2010, restored the sequestration process to enforce the new PAYGO requirement for direct spending and revenue legislation. Generally, the new statutory PAYGO process provides that if the net effect of direct spending and revenue legislation enacted during a year increases the deficit, budgetary resources in certain direct spending programs are cut in order to eliminate the increase in the deficit. Specifically, the average budgetary effects (i.e., any increase or decrease in the deficit) over five- and 10-year periods[3] of each direct spending and revenue act are placed on five- and 10-year scorecards, respectively. Like the PAYGO process under the BEA, the sequestration process is triggered by a report from the OMB director issued 14 days after Congress adjourns at the end of a session. If either scorecard shows a positive balance (referred to as a debit) for the budget year, the President is required to issue a sequestration order cancelling

---

[3] The five-year period covers the budget year and four fiscal years thereafter, and the 10-year period covers the budget year and nine fiscal years thereafter. The statutory rule also requires that any budgetary effects for the current year must be added to the budgetary effects for the budget year.

budgetary resources in non-exempt direct spending programs sufficient to eliminate the balance (the larger balance if both scorecards show a positive balance).[4]

Second, the Budget Control Act of 2011 restored the sequestration process, including the reports and triggering mechanisms under the earlier BEA, to enforce the recently established statutory limits on discretionary spending for each fiscal year through FY2021. In addition, the BCA uses sequestration to achieve additional deficit reduction. Specifically, the BCA created a Joint Select Committee on Deficit Reduction, composed of an equal number of Senators and Members of the House, and instructed it to develop a proposal that would reduce the deficit by at least $1.5 trillion over the FY2012-FY2021 period. In the event that this Joint Committee was not successful, the BCA established the automatic process to reduce spending (a fallback mechanism to automatically reduce spending), beginning in 2013. If legislation developed by the Joint Committee did not reduce the deficit by at least $1.2 trillion through FY2021 and was not enacted by January 15, 2012, this automatic process would be triggered. The process presumably was intended to encourage agreement on such deficit reduction, either by enacting the Joint Committee proposal or possibly by enacting other legislation (through existing congressional procedures) prior to the beginning of 2013, when the automatic process would begin to make reductions. Given that the Joint Committee was not successful, this automatic process has been triggered. Therefore, at the time of this writing, spending reductions are scheduled to be made on January 2, 2013, with a sequester of $109 billion in budgetary resources equally divided between defense and nondefense spending, unless Congress and the President agree by statute to repeal or modify the automatic process. Additional spending reductions are also scheduled to be achieved in direct spending in each year through FY2021.

Spending Legislation

The spending policies of the budget resolution generally are implemented through two different types of spending legislation. Policies involving discretionary spending are implemented in the context of annual appropriations acts, whereas policies affecting direct or mandatory spending (which, for the most part, involves entitlement programs) are carried out in substantive legislation.

All discretionary spending is under the jurisdiction of the House and Senate Appropriations Committees. Direct spending is under the jurisdiction of the various legislative committees of the House and Senate; the House Ways and Means Committee and the Senate Finance Committee have the largest shares of direct spending jurisdiction. (Some entitlement programs, such as Medicaid, are funded in annual appropriations acts, but such spending is not considered to be discretionary.) The enforcement procedures under the congressional budget process, mentioned above, apply equally to discretionary and direct spending.

---

[4] Most direct spending programs and activities, including Social Security benefits, veterans' programs, retirement and disability benefits, and low-income programs, among others, are exempt from any sequestration. In addition, the amount of any sequestration is limited to 4% for Medicare and 2% for certain health and medical care activities.

Authorizing Measures

The rules of the House and (to a lesser extent) the Senate require that agencies and programs be authorized in law before an appropriation is made for them. An authorizing act is a law that (1) establishes a program or agency and the terms and conditions under which it operates; and (2) authorizes the enactment of appropriations for that program or agency. Authorizing legislation may originate in either the House or the Senate and may be considered any time during the year. Many agencies and programs have temporary authorizations that have to be renewed annually or every few years.

Action on appropriations measures sometimes is delayed by the failure of Congress to enact necessary authorizing legislation. The House and Senate often waive or disregard their rules against unauthorized appropriations for ongoing programs that have not yet been reauthorized.

The budgetary impact of authorizing legislation depends on whether it contains only discretionary authorizations (for which funding is provided in annual appropriations acts) or direct spending, which itself enables an agency to enter into obligations.

The Annual Appropriations Process

An appropriations act is a law passed by Congress that provides federal agencies legal authority to incur obligations and the Treasury Department authority to make payments for designated purposes. The power of appropriation derives from the Constitution, which in Article I, Section 9, provides that "[n]o money shall be drawn from the Treasury but in consequence of appropriations made by law." The power to appropriate is exclusively a legislative power; it functions as a limitation on the executive branch. An agency may not spend more than the amount appropriated to it, and it may use available funds only for the purposes and according to the conditions provided by Congress.

The Constitution does not require annual appropriations, but since the First Congress the practice has been to make appropriations for a single fiscal year. Appropriations must be used (obligated) in the fiscal year for which they are provided, unless the law provides that they shall be available for a longer period of time. All provisions in an appropriations act, such as limitations on the use of funds, expire at the end of the fiscal year, unless the language of the act extends their period of effectiveness.

The President requests annual appropriations in his budget submitted each year. In support of the President's appropriations requests, agencies submit justification materials to the House and Senate Appropriations Committees. These materials provide considerably more detail than is contained in the President's budget and are used in support of agency testimony during Appropriations subcommittee hearings on the President's budget.

Congress passes three main types of appropriations measures. *Regular appropriations* acts provide budget authority to agencies for the next fiscal year. *Supplemental appropriations* acts provide additional budget authority during the current fiscal year when the regular appropriation is insufficient or to finance activities not provided for in the regular appropriation. *Continuing appropriations* acts provide stop-gap (or full-year) funding for agencies that have not received a regular appropriation.

In a typical session, Congress acts on 12 regular appropriations bills and at least two supplemental appropriations measures. Because of recurring delays in the appropriations process, Congress also typically passes one or more continuing appropriations each year. The scope and duration of these measures depend on the status of the regular appropriations bills and the degree of budgetary conflict between the President and Congress. In recent years, Congress has merged two or more of the regular appropriations acts for a fiscal year into a single, omnibus appropriations act.

By precedent, appropriations originate in the House of Representatives. In the House, appropriations measures are originated by the Appropriations Committee (when it marks up or reports the measure) rather than being introduced by a member beforehand. Before the full Committee acts on the bill, it is considered in the relevant Appropriations subcommittee (the House and Senate Appropriations Committees have 12 parallel subcommittees). The House subcommittees typically hold extensive hearings on appropriations requests shortly after the President's budget is submitted. In marking up their appropriations bills, the various subcommittees are guided by the discretionary spending limits and the allocations made to them under Section 302 of the 1974 Congressional Budget Act.

The Senate usually considers appropriations measures after they have been passed by the House. When House action on appropriations bills is delayed, however, the Senate sometimes expedites its actions by considering a Senate-numbered bill up to the stage of final passage. Upon receipt of the House-passed bill in the Senate, it is amended with the text that the Senate already has agreed to (as a single amendment) and then passed by the Senate. Hearings in the Senate Appropriations subcommittees generally are not as extensive as those held by counterpart subcommittees in the House.

The basic unit of an appropriation is an account. A single unnumbered paragraph in an appropriations act comprises one account and all provisions of that paragraph pertain to that account and to no other, unless the text expressly gives them broader scope. Any provision limiting the use of funds enacted in that paragraph is a restriction on that account alone.

Over the years, appropriations have been consolidated into a relatively small number of accounts. It is typical for a federal agency to have a single account for all its expenses of operation and additional accounts for other purposes such as construction. Accordingly, most appropriation accounts encompass a number of activities or projects. The appropriation sometimes earmarks specific amounts to particular activities within the account, but the more common practice is to provide detailed information on the amounts intended for each activity in other sources (principally, the committee reports accompanying the measures).

In addition to the substantive limitations (and other provisions) associated with each account, each appropriations act has "general provisions" that apply to all of the accounts in a title or in the whole act. These general provisions appear as numbered sections, usually at the end of the title or the act.

The standard appropriation is for a single fiscal year—the funds have to be obligated during the fiscal year for which they are provided; they lapse if not obligated by the end of that year. An appropriation that does not mention the period during which the funds are to be available is a one-year appropriation. Congress also makes no-year appropriations by specifying that the funds shall remain available until expended. No-year funds are carried over to future years, even if they have not been obligated. Congress sometimes makes multiyear appropriations, which provide for funds to be available for two or more fiscal years.

Appropriations measures also contain other types of provisions that serve specialized purposes. These include provisions that liquidate (pay off) obligations made pursuant to certain contract authority; reappropriate funds provided in previous years; transfer funds from one account to another; rescind funds (or release deferred funds); or set ceilings on the amount of obligations that can be made under permanent appropriations, on the amount of direct or guaranteed loans that can be made, or on the amount of administrative expenses that can be incurred during the fiscal year. In addition to providing funds, appropriations acts often contain substantive limitations on government agencies.

Detailed information on how funds are to be spent, along with other directives or guidance, is provided in the reports accompanying the various appropriations measures. Agencies ordinarily abide by report language in spending the funds appropriated by Congress.

The appropriations reports do not comment on every item of expenditure. Report language is most likely when the Appropriations Committee prefers to spend more or less on a particular item than the President has requested or when the committee wants to earmark funds for a particular project or activity. When a particular item is mentioned by the committee, there is a strong expectation that the agency will adhere to the instructions.

Revenue Legislation

Article I, Section 8 of the Constitution gives Congress the power to levy "taxes, duties, imposts, and excises." Section 7 of this article requires that all revenue measures originate in the House of Representatives.

In the House, revenue legislation is under the jurisdiction of the Ways and Means Committee; in the Senate, jurisdiction is held by the Finance Committee. While House rules bar other committees from reporting revenue legislation, sometimes another committee will report legislation levying user fees on a class that benefits from a particular service or program or that is being regulated by a federal agency. In many of these cases, the user fee legislation is referred subsequently to the Ways and Means Committee.

Most revenues derive from existing provisions of the tax code or Social Security law, which continue in effect from year to year unless changed by Congress. This tax structure can be expected to produce increasing amounts of revenue in future years as the economy expands and incomes rise. Nevertheless, Congress usually makes some changes in the tax laws each year, either to raise or lower revenues or to redistribute the tax burden.

Congress typically acts on revenue legislation pursuant to proposals in the President's budget. An early step in congressional work on revenue legislation is publication by CBO of its own estimates (developed in consultation with the Joint Tax Committee) of the revenue impact of the President's budget proposals. The congressional estimates often differ significantly from those presented in the President's budget.

The revenue totals in the budget resolution establish the framework for subsequent action on revenue measures. The budget resolution contains only revenue totals and total recommended changes; it does not allocate these totals among revenue sources (although it does set out Medicare receipts separately), nor does it specify which provisions of the tax code are to be changed.

The House and Senate often consider major revenue measures, such as the Tax Reform Act of 1986, under their regular legislative procedures. However, as has been the case with direct spending programs, many of the most significant changes in revenue policy in recent years have been made in the context of the reconciliation process. Although revenue changes are usually incorporated into omnibus budget reconciliation measures, along with spending changes (and sometimes debt-limit increases), revenue reconciliation legislation may be considered on a separate legislative track (e.g., the Tax Equity and Fiscal Responsibility Act of 1982).

When the reconciliation process is used to advance revenue reductions (or spending increases) that would lead to a deficit, or would enlarge an existing deficit, Section 313 of the 1974 Congressional Budget Act (referred to as the Senate's "Byrd rule") limits the legislative changes to the period covered by the reconciliation directives. Accordingly, some recent tax cuts have been subject to sunset dates.

In enacting revenue legislation, Congress often establishes or alters tax expenditures. The term "tax expenditures" is defined in the 1974 Congressional Budget Act to include revenue losses due to deductions, exemptions, credits, and other exceptions to the basic tax structure. Tax expenditures are a means by which the federal government pursues public policy objectives and can be regarded as alternatives to other policy instruments such as grants or loans. The Joint Tax Committee estimates the revenue effects of legislation changing tax expenditures, and it also publishes five-year projections of these provisions as an annual committee print.

Debt-Limit Legislation

When the revenues collected by the federal government are not sufficient to cover its expenditures, it must finance the shortfall through borrowing. Federal borrowing is subject to a public debt limit established by statute. When the federal government operates with a budget deficit, the public debt limit must be increased periodically. The frequency of congressional action to raise the debt limit has ranged in the past from several times in one year to once in several years. When the federal government incurred large and growing surpluses in recent years, Congress did not have to increase the debt limit, but the enactment of increases in the debt limit has again become necessary with the recurrence of deficits.

Legislation to raise the public debt limit falls under the jurisdiction of the House Ways and Means Committee and the Senate Finance Committee. Although consideration of such measures in the House usually is constrained through the use of special rules, Senate action sometimes is far-ranging with regard to the issues covered. In the past, the Senate has added many non-germane provisions to debt-limit measures, such as the 1985 Balanced Budget Act.

In 1979, the House amended its rules to provide for the automatic engrossment of a measure increasing the debt limit upon final adoption of the conference report on the budget resolution. The rule, House Rule XLIX (commonly referred to as the Gephardt rule), was intended to facilitate quick action on debt increases. However, the Senate had no comparable rule. For years, the House and Senate could enact debt-limit legislation originating under the Gephardt rule or arising under conventional legislative procedures. During the past decade, Congress has enacted debt-limit increases as part of omnibus budget reconciliation measures, continuing appropriations acts, and other legislation. The House recodified the Gephardt rule as House Rule XXIII at the beginning of the 106th Congress, repealed it at the beginning of the 107th Congress, and reinstated it, as new Rule XXVII, at the beginning of the 108th Congress. At the beginning of the 112th Congress, the House once again repealed the rule, thereby requiring the House to vote directly on any legislation that changes the statutory limit on the public debt.

Reconciliation Legislation

Beginning in 1980, Congress has used reconciliation legislation to implement many of its most significant budget policies. Section 310 of the 1974 Congressional Budget Act sets forth a special procedure for the development and consideration of reconciliation legislation. Reconciliation legislation is used by Congress to bring existing revenue and spending law into conformity with the policies in the budget resolution. Reconciliation is an optional process, but Congress has used it more years than not; during the period covering 1980 through 2010, 20 reconciliation measures were enacted into law and three were vetoed.

The reconciliation process has two stages—the adoption of reconciliation instructions in the budget resolution and the enactment of reconciliation legislation that implements changes in revenue or spending laws. Although reconciliation has been used since 1980, specific procedures tend to vary from year to year.

Reconciliation is used to change the amount of revenues, budget authority, or outlays generated by existing law. In a few instances, reconciliation has been used to adjust the public debt limit. On the spending side, the process focuses on entitlement laws; it may not be used, however, to impel changes in Social Security law. Reconciliation sometimes has been applied to discretionary authorizations (which are funded in annual appropriations acts), but this is not the usual practice.

Reconciliation was used in the 1980s and into the 1990s as a deficit-reduction tool. Beginning in the latter part of the 1990s, some reconciliation measures were used principally to reduce revenues, thereby increasing the deficit. At the beginning of the 110th Congress, both chambers adopted rules requiring that reconciliation be used solely for deficit reduction.

Reconciliation Directives

Reconciliation begins with a directive in a budget resolution instructing designated committees to report legislation changing existing law or pending legislation. These instructions have three components: (1) they name the committee (or committees) that are directed to report legislation; (2) they specify the amounts by which existing laws are to be changed (but do not identify how these changes are to be made, which laws are to be altered, or the programs to be affected); and (3) they usually set a deadline by which the designated committees are to recommend the changes in law. The instructions typically cover the same fiscal years covered by the budget resolution. Sometimes, budget resolutions have provided for more than one reconciliation measure to be considered during a session.

The dollar amounts are computed with reference to the CBO baseline. Thus, a change represents the amount by which revenues or spending would decrease or increase from baseline levels as a result of changes made in existing law. This computation is itself based on assumptions about the future level of revenues or spending under current law (or policy) and about the dollar changes that would ensue from new legislation. Hence, the savings associated with the reconciliation process are assumed savings. The actual changes in revenues or spending may differ from those estimated when the reconciliation instructions are formulated.

Although the instructions do not mention the programs to be changed, they are based on assumptions as to the savings or deficit reduction (or, in some cases, increases) that would result from particular changes in revenue provisions or spending programs. These program assumptions are sometimes printed in the reports on the budget resolution. Even when the assumptions are not published, committees and members usually have a good idea of the specific program changes contemplated by the reconciliation instructions.

A committee has discretion to decide on the legislative changes to be recommended. It is not bound by the program changes recommended or assumed by the Budget Committees in the reports accompanying the budget resolution. Further, a committee has to recommend legislation estimated to produce dollar changes for each category delineated in the instructions to it.

When a budget resolution containing a reconciliation instruction has been approved by Congress, the instruction has the status of an order by the House and Senate to designated committees to recommend legislation, usually by a date certain. It is expected that committees will carry out the instructions of their parent chamber, but the 1974 Congressional Budget Act does not provide any sanctions against committees that fail to do so.

Development and Consideration of Reconciliation Measures

When more than one committee in the House and Senate is subject to reconciliation directives, the proposed legislative changes usually are consolidated by the Budget Committees into an omnibus bill. The 1974 Congressional Budget Act does not permit the Budget Committees to revise substantively the legislation recommended by the committees of jurisdiction. This restriction pertains even when the Budget Committees estimate that the proposed legislation will fall short of the dollar changes called for in the instructions. Sometimes, the Budget Committees, working with the leadership, develop alternatives to the committee recommendations, to be offered as floor amendments, so as to achieve greater compliance with the reconciliation directives.

The 1974 act requires that amendments offered to reconciliation legislation in either the House or the Senate be deficit neutral. To meet this requirement, an amendment reducing revenues or increasing spending must offset these deficit increases by equivalent revenue increases or spending cuts.

During the first several years' experience with reconciliation, the legislation contained many provisions that were extraneous to the purpose of reducing the deficit. The reconciliation submissions of committees included such things as provisions that had no budgetary effect, that increased spending or reduced revenues, or that violated another committee's jurisdiction.

In 1985, the Senate adopted a rule (commonly referred to as the Byrd rule) on a temporary basis as a means of curbing these practices. The Byrd rule has been extended and modified several times over the years. In 1990, the Byrd rule was incorporated into the 1974 Congressional Budget Act as Section 313 and made permanent.

Although the House has no rule comparable to the Senate's Byrd rule, it may use other devices to control the inclusion of extraneous matter in reconciliation legislation. In particular, the House may use special rules to make in order amendments that strike such matter.

House and Senate Earmark Disclosure Rules

In 2007, both the House and Senate adopted rules intended to bring more transparency to the process surrounding earmarks. Although the definitions vary, an earmark generally is considered to be an allocation of resources to specifically targeted beneficiaries, either through discretionary or direct spending, limited tax benefits, or limited tariff benefits.[5]

Concern about earmarking practices arose over such provisions being inserted into legislation or accompanying reports without any identification of the sponsor, and the belief that many earmarks were not subject to proper scrutiny and diverted resources to lesser-priority items or items without sufficient justification, thereby contributing to wasteful spending or revenue loss.

In response to this concern, earmark rules were adopted that vary by chamber, but include three main features. The first feature is a requirement that members requesting a congressional earmark provide a written statement to the chair and ranking minority member of the committee of jurisdiction that includes the member's name, the name and address of the intended earmark recipient, the purpose of the earmark, and a certification that the member or member's spouse has no financial interest in such an earmark. (The Senate rule applies not only to the spouse but the entire immediate family.)

The second feature is a general requirement that committees provide a list of all earmarks included in reported legislation. The third feature is a point of order against legislation that is not accompanied by a list of included earmarks. These vary by chamber.

House of Representatives

House Rule XXI, clause 9, generally requires that certain types of measures be accompanied by a list of earmarks or a statement that the measure contains no earmarks.[6] If the list of earmarks or the statement that no earmark exists in the measure is absent, a point of order may lie against the measure's floor consideration. The point of order applies to the absence of such a list or statement, and does not speak to the completeness or the accuracy of such document.

House earmark disclosure rules apply to any congressional earmark included in either the text of the measure or the committee report accompanying the measure, as well as the conference report and joint explanatory statement. The disclosure requirements apply to items in authorizing, appropriations, and revenue legislation. Furthermore, they apply not only to measures reported by committees, but also to unreported measures, "manager's amendments," Senate measures, and conference reports.

---

[5] For more information on House and Senate earmark rules, see CRS Report RL34462, *House and Senate Procedural Rules Concerning Earmark Disclosure*, by Sandy Streeter.

[6] Depending upon the type of measure, the list or statement is to be included either in the measure's accompanying report, or printed in the *Congressional Record*.

These earmark disclosure requirements, however, do not apply to all legislation at all times. Not subject to the rule are floor amendments (except a "manager's amendment"), amendments between the Houses, or amendments considered as adopted under a self-executing special rule, including a committee amendment in the nature of a substitute made in order as original text. The earmark rule, as with most House rules, is not self enforcing and relies instead on a member raising a point of order if the rule is violated. When a measure is considered under suspension of the rules, House rules are laid aside and earmark disclosure rules are, therefore, waived. It is not in order to consider a special rule that waives earmark requirements under the House rule.

The Senate

Senate Rule XLIV creates a point of order against a motion to proceed to consider a measure or a vote on adoption of a conference report, unless the chair of the committee or the Majority Leader (or designee) certifies that a complete list of earmarks and the name of each Senator requesting each earmark is available on a publicly accessible congressional website in a searchable form at least 48 hours before the vote. If a Senator proposes a floor amendment containing an earmark, those items must be printed in the *Congressional Record* as soon as "practicable."[7] If the earmark certification requirements have not been met, a point of order may lie against consideration of the measure or a vote on the conference report. The point of order applies only to the absence of such certification, and does not speak to its accuracy.

Senate earmark disclosure rules apply to any congressional earmark included in either the text of the bill or a committee report accompanying the bill, as well as a conference report and joint explanatory statement. The disclosure requirements apply to items in authorizing, appropriations, and revenue legislation. Furthermore, they apply not only to measures reported by committees, but also to unreported measures, amendments, House bills, and conference reports.

The earmark rule may be waived either by unanimous consent or by motion, which requires the affirmative vote of three-fifths of all Senators (60, if there are no vacancies).[8] The earmark rule, as with most Senate rules, is not self enforcing and relies instead on a Senator raising a point of order if the rule is violated.

While not embodied in either chamber's rules, an earmark "ban" or "moratorium" is currently in effect in both the House and Senate, enforced by committee and chamber leadership.[9]

---

[7] The rule does not apply to all earmarks in floor amendments, only those "not included in the bill or joint resolution as placed on the calendar or as reported by any committee, in a committee report on such a bill or joint resolution, or a committee report of the Senate on a companion measure," as stated in Rule XLIV, paragraph 4(a).

[8] These points of order may also be waived if the Majority and Minority Leaders jointly agree that "such a waiver is necessary as a result of a significant disruption to Senate facilities or to the availability of the Internet." Senate Rule XLIV, paragraph 12.

[9] The House Republican Conference Rules include a standing order, adopted December 8, 2010, stating that "It is the policy of the House Republican Conference that no Member shall request a congressional earmark, limited tax benefit, or limited tariff benefit, as such terms have been described in the Rules of the House," available at http://www.gop.gov/about/rules?standing-orders-for-the-112th. In the Senate, the chair of the Committee on Appropriations announced in a press release on February 1, 2011, and again on February 2, 2012, that an earmark moratorium would be enforced on all FY2011, FY2012, and FY2013 appropriations bills, available at http://www.appropriations.senate.gov/news.cfm?method=news.view&id=188dc791-4b0d-459e-b8d9-4ede5ca299e7 and http://www.appropriations.senate.gov/news.cfm?method=news.view&id=3883059e-7a0c-496e-8d51-440aa7c2d57c.

Impoundment and Line-Item Veto

Impoundment

Although an appropriation limits the amounts that can be spent, it also establishes the expectation that the available funds will be used to carry out authorized activities. Therefore, when an agency fails to use all or part of an appropriation, it deviates from the intentions of Congress. The Impoundment Control Act of 1974 prescribes rules and procedures for instances in which available funds are impounded.

An impoundment is an action or inaction by the President or a federal agency that delays or withholds the obligation or expenditure of budget authority provided in law. The 1974 Impoundment Control Act divides impoundments into two categories and establishes distinct procedures for each. A *deferral* delays the use of funds; a *rescission* is a presidential request that Congress rescind (cancel) an appropriation or other form of budget authority. Deferral and rescission are exclusive and comprehensive categories; an impoundment is either a rescission or a deferral—it cannot be both or something else.

Although impoundments are defined broadly by the 1974 act, in practice they are limited to major actions that affect the level or rate of expenditure. As a general practice, only deliberate curtailments of expenditure are reported as impoundments; actions having other purposes that incidently affect the rate of spending are not recorded as impoundments. For example, if an agency were to delay the award of a contract because of a dispute with a vendor, the delay would not be an impoundment; if the delay were for the purpose of reducing an expenditure, it would be an impoundment. The line between routine administrative actions and impoundments is not clear and controversy occasionally arises as to whether a particular action constitutes an impoundment.

Rescissions

To propose a rescission, the President must submit a message to Congress specifying the amount to be rescinded, the accounts and programs involved, the estimated fiscal and program effects, and the reasons for the rescission. Multiple rescissions can be grouped in a single message. After the message has been submitted to it, Congress has 45 days of "continuous session" (usually a larger number of calendar days) during which it can pass a rescission bill. Congress may rescind all, part, or none of the amount proposed by the President.

If Congress does not approve a rescission in legislation by the expiration of this period, the President must make the funds available for obligation and expenditure. If the President fails to release funds at the expiration of the 45-day period for proposed rescissions, the comptroller general may bring suit to compel their release. This has been a rare occurrence, however.

Deferrals

To defer funds, the President submits a message to Congress setting forth the amount, the affected account and program, the reasons for the deferral, the estimated fiscal and program effects, and the period of time during which the funds are to be deferred. The President may not propose a deferral for a period of time beyond the end of the fiscal year, nor may he propose a deferral that would cause the funds to lapse or otherwise prevent an agency from spending appropriated funds prudently. In accounts where unobligated funds remain available beyond the fiscal year, the President may defer the funds again in the next fiscal year.

At present, the President may defer only for the reasons set forth in the Antideficiency Act, including to provide for contingencies, to achieve savings made possible by or through changes in requirements or greater efficiency of operations, and as specifically provided by law. He may not defer funds for policy reasons (e.g., to curtail overall federal spending or because he is opposed to a particular program).

The comptroller general reviews all proposed rescissions and deferrals and advises Congress of their legality and possible budgetary and program effects. The comptroller general also notifies Congress of any rescission or deferral not reported by the President and may reclassify an improperly classified impoundment. In all cases, a notification to Congress by the comptroller general has the same legal effect as an impoundment message of the President.

The 1974 Impoundment Control Act provides for special types of legislation—rescission bills and deferral resolutions—for Congress to use in exercising its impoundment control powers. However, pursuant to court decisions that held the legislative veto to be unconstitutional, Congress may not use deferral resolutions to disapprove a deferral. Further, Congress has been reluctant to use rescission bills regularly. Congress, instead, usually acts on impoundment matters within the framework of the annual appropriations measures.

Line-Item Veto

During the 104th Congress, the Line Item Veto Act (P.L. 104-130) was enacted as an amendment to the 1974 Impoundment Control Act. The Supreme Court ruled the Line Item Veto Act unconstitutional in June 1998.

The authority granted to the President under the Line Item Veto Act differed markedly from the veto authority available to most chief executives at the state level. First, the President could not veto individual parts of legislation submitted for his approval. Under normal constitutional procedures, the President must approve or veto any measure in its entirety. His authority to use the line-item veto came into play only after a measure had been signed into law. Second, this authority applied not only to annual appropriations, but extended to new entitlement spending and targeted tax benefits as well. The line-item veto authority was intended to be in effect for eight years, from the beginning of 1997 through the end of 2004.

The Line Item Veto Act reversed the presumption underlying the process for the consideration of rescissions under the 1974 Impoundment Control Act. Under the Line Item Veto Act, presidential proposals would take effect unless overturned by legislative action. The act authorized the President to identify at enactment individual items in legislation that he proposed not go into effect. The identification was based not just upon the statutory language, but on the entire legislative history and documentation. The President had to notify Congress promptly of his proposals and provide supporting information. Congress had to respond within a limited period of time by enacting a law if it wanted to disapprove the President's proposals; otherwise, they would take effect permanently.

President Clinton exercised the line-item veto authority several times during the 1997 session before the act was declared unconstitutional.

Author Contact Information

Bill Heniff Jr., Coordinator
Analyst on Congress and the Legislative Process
wheniff@crs.loc.gov, 7-8646

Jessica Tollestrup
Analyst on Congress and the Legislative Process
jtollestrup@crs.loc.gov, 7-0941

Megan Suzanne Lynch
Analyst on Congress and the Legislative Process
mlynch@crs.loc.gov, 7-7853

Acknowledgments

This report was originally written by Robert Keith, formerly a Specialist in American National Government at CRS, and Allen Schick, formerly a Consultant at CRS. The analysts listed on the cover of this report, and under the "author contact information," updated portions of the report and are available to answer questions related to the federal budget process.

The Executive Budget Process: An Overview

Michelle D. Christensen

Analyst in Government Organization and Management

July 27, 2012

Congressional Research Service

7-5700

www.crs.gov

R42633

CRS Report for Congress ——————————————————————

Prepared for Members and Committees of Congress

Summary

The U.S. Constitution vests Congress with the power to raise revenue and borrow money. Those funds may only be drawn from the Treasury in consequence of appropriations made by law. The Constitution, however, is largely silent with respect to the President's role in the budget process. Instead, the current executive budget process is largely the result of statutes enacted by Congress.

The executive budget process consists of three main phases: development of the President's budget proposal, submission and justification of the President's budget proposal, and execution of enacted appropriations and other budgetary legislation. The purpose of this report is to provide an introduction to many elements of the executive budget process, highlighting the roles of the President, the Office of Management and Budget (OMB), and executive agencies.

The Budget and Accounting Act of 1921 established the modern executive budget process. It created a legal framework for a federal budget proposal to be developed by the President and submitted to Congress prior to the start of each fiscal year. In practice, development of the President's budget proposal begins approximately 18 months prior to the start of the fiscal year to which it applies. Executive agencies submit their requests and justification materials to OMB for examination and review. After final decisions have been made by the President, the budget proposal is compiled by OMB. Under current law, the President must submit the budget proposal to Congress no later than the first Monday in February.

Once the President has submitted the budget, OMB and agency officials explain and justify the request to Congress. Early in the congressional budget process, often in the week following the submission of the President's budget, the OMB director and other cabinet officials typically provide testimony regarding the President's broad budgetary objectives before congressional committees. In addition, agencies typically submit written justifications of their budget requests to Congress and agency officials often will testify before the committees of jurisdiction.

The President's budget, though not legally binding, provides Congress with recommended spending levels for programs, projects, and activities that are funded through appropriations and other budgetary legislation. Funds provided in appropriations and other budgetary legislation are not immediately available for obligation or expenditure. With certain exceptions, the Antideficiency Act requires that funds be apportioned (or divided), often by fiscal quarter, prior to obligation or expenditure. Agencies then allocate those funds to programs, projects, and activities.

Congress has recognized the need to permit agencies some flexibility during budget execution, and it has provided agencies with limited authority to make spending adjustments. For example, Congress may provide agencies with limited authority to reallocate funds from one appropriations account to another (i.e., transfers), or from one purpose to another *within* an appropriations account (i.e., reprogramming). Under the Impoundment Control Act (ICA) of 1974, the President may withhold appropriated funds temporarily (referred to as deferrals) or propose to Congress permanent cancellations of budget authority (referred to as rescissions).

Finally, certain executive budgetary procedures are triggered under limited, less common circumstances. For example, OMB and agencies have established procedures for implementing a shutdown of certain government operations in the event that their full-year or interim appropriations are not enacted by the start of the fiscal year. OMB and agencies may also be subject to additional procedures in the event of a statutorily prescribed sequestration.

Congressional Research Service

The Executive Budget Process: An Overview

Contents

Introduction

The U.S. Constitution vests Congress with the power to raise revenue and borrow money. Those funds may only by drawn from the Treasury in consequence of appropriations made by law.[1] The Constitution, however, is largely silent with respect to the President's role in the budget process. Instead, the executive budget process as it exists today is primarily the result of statutes enacted by Congress.

The Budget and Accounting Act of 1921 (P.L. 67-13; 42 Stat. 20-27) established the modern executive budget process. Prior to its enactment, executive budgeting was highly decentralized. At that time, agencies submitted their budget estimates to Congress individually, either directly or through the Secretary of the Treasury, with varying levels of involvement or direction by the President.[2] The Budget and Accounting Act altered this practice by establishing a legal framework for a consolidated federal budget proposal to be developed by the President and submitted to Congress prior to the start of each fiscal year.

This report outlines many of the budgetary procedures that are performed by the President, the Office of Management and Budget (OMB), and agencies. This report provides an overview of the development, submission, and justification of the President's budget proposal. This report also describes how the President, OMB, and agencies execute the federal budget following the enactment of appropriations and other budgetary legislation by Congress.[3]

Development of the President's Budget

The President's budget, or the *Budget of the United States Government* as it is referred to in 31 U.S.C. §1105(a), is a statement of the President's policy priorities and a unified plan for the allocation of federal budgetary resources. The President's budget is a set of recommendations. Congress is not required to adopt the recommendations contained within the President's budget. Nevertheless, the budget is one of the President's most important policy tools. Though it is not legally binding, the President's budget initiates the congressional budget process and provides Congress with recommended spending levels for agency programs, projects, and activities funded through the annual appropriations acts. The President's budget also includes budgetary projections based on existing law and provides Congress with estimations of the effects the President's revenue and direct spending proposals will have on those projections.

Under current law, the President is responsible for developing and submitting a consolidated budget to Congress no later than the first Monday in February prior to the start of the fiscal year.[4]

---

[1] U.S. Constitution, Article I, §9.

[2] Allen Schick, *The Federal Budget: Politics, Policy, Process*, 3rd ed. (Washington, D.C.: Brookings Institution Press, 2007), pp. 13-14.

[3] Appropriations legislation provides agencies with budget authority (i.e., the authority to enter into obligations such as contracts or the hiring of personnel) and the ability to make payments from the U.S. Treasury. Other budgetary legislation includes direct spending (i.e., budget authority provided outside the appropriations process, by authorizing statute, for example), as well as revenue and debt-limit legislation. For a broad overview of the federal budget process, see CRS Report 98-721, *Introduction to the Federal Budget Process*, coordinated by Bill Heniff Jr.

[4] 31 U.S.C. §1105. The President's budget includes budget requests for all executive departments and agencies, as well (continued...)

The development of the President's budget begins approximately 18 months prior to the start of the fiscal year that the budget will cover, which is about 10 months before the President must submit the proposal to Congress. To put this timeline in context, as Congress begins action on appropriations bills and other budgetary legislation for the upcoming fiscal year, OMB and agencies have already begun planning for the subsequent fiscal year.

Initial Preparation of Agency Budget Requests

In practice, the President has delegated to OMB certain budgetary tasks and authorities necessary for developing the budget. OMB coordinates the development of the President's budget proposal by issuing circulars, memoranda, and guidance documents to the heads of executive agencies. Executive agencies then prepare their budget requests in accordance with the instructions and guidance provided by OMB.

OMB Circular No. A-11 (hereafter Circular A-11) is an extensive document that contains instructions and schedules for agency submission of budget requests and justification materials to OMB.[5] Updated annually, Circular A-11 provides agencies with an overview of applicable budgetary laws, policies for the preparation and submission of budgetary estimates, and information on financial management and budget data systems. Circular A-11 also provides agencies with directions for budget execution and guidance regarding agency interaction with Congress and the public.

Early in the development phase, OMB issues a budget planning guidance memorandum, also referred to as the "Spring Guidance," which provides executive agencies with detailed instructions and deadlines for submitting their budget requests and supporting materials to OMB.[6] The guidance may also include specific instructions for how agency budget requests may help achieve the President's budgetary priorities and other policy goals. For example, the FY2013 Budget Guidance instructed,

> [u]nless your agency has been given explicit direction otherwise by OMB, your overall agency request for 2013 should be at least 5 percent below your 2011 enacted discretionary appropriation ... [and] should also identify additional discretionary funding reductions that would bring your request to a level that is at least 10 percent below your 2011 enacted discretionary appropriation.[7]

While the general contents and timeline for agency budget submissions are guided by OMB, agencies also have their own internal procedures for developing the requests they submit to

---

(...continued)

as budget requests for the legislative and judicial branches. Since the legislative and judicial branches are co-equal branches of government, the President and OMB play no role in the development of their requests. Instead, the legislative and judicial branches transmit their budget requests to the President, who then is required to include them in the budget submission to Congress without modification (31 U.S.C. §1105(b)).

[5] U.S. Office of Management and Budget, Circular No. A-11, "Preparation, Submission and Execution of the Budget," August 18, 2011, http://www.whitehouse.gov/omb/circulars_default.

[6] The budget planning guidance memorandum is usually issued in mid-to-late spring, nearly a year before the President submits the budget proposal to Congress. However, the memorandum has been issued as late as August.

[7] Memorandum from Jacob J. Lew, Director of OMB, M-11-30, "Fiscal Year 2013 Budget Guidance," August 17, 2011, http://www.whitehouse.gov/omb/memoranda_2011.

OMB. In practice, budget preparation is likely a time and data intensive process for agencies, involving detailed analysis and estimation of past and future budgetary resources.[8]

OMB Review of Agency Budget Requests

Agency budget requests are submitted to OMB in early fall, approximately four to five months before the President must submit the budget to Congress. OMB has been delegated the responsibility of reviewing executive agency requests and justification materials to ensure that they are consistent with the President's policy objectives.

Agency requests are first reviewed by the OMB program examiners who are responsible for the associated policy areas. Agency requests may also be reviewed by more senior OMB officials. Prior to making a recommendation, OMB program examiners may ask for additional information from agencies, either informally or by conducting formal hearings. Examiners' recommendations are reviewed by more senior OMB officials, culminating in review and approval by the OMB Director and the President.[9]

Agencies are notified of the President's decisions through a process known as "passback." During passback, OMB officials notify agencies of their approved budgetary levels, which may differ from the agencies' budget requests.[10] The passback process and the content of passback decisions has differed under each administration and each OMB Director. For example, passback decisions may also include program policy changes or personnel ceilings.[11] Agencies may appeal these decisions to the OMB Director, or in some cases, to the President directly, depending on the procedures established by the OMB Director.[12]

Submission and Justification of the President's Budget

The President's budget submission is a multi-volume set of documents, which may vary in size and composition from administration to administration. This section briefly discusses the components of the President's budget submission to Congress, and highlights some of the formal and informal interactions between Congress, the President, OMB, and agencies.[13]

---

[8] Allen Schick, *Federal Budget: Politics, Policy, and Process*, 3rd ed. (Washington, D.C.: The Brookings Institution, 2007), pp. 92-93.

[9] Shelley Lynne Tomkin, *Inside OMB: Politics and Process in the President's Budget Office* (New York: M.E. Sharpe, 1998), pp. 120-130. For additional information, see http://www.whitehouse.gov/omb/program_examiner.

[10] Ibid., pp. 131.

[11] U.S. Government Accountability Office, *A Glossary of Terms Used in the Federal Budget Process*, GAO-05-734SP, September 2005, pp. 105, http://gao.gov/assets/80/76911.pdf.

[12] Shelley Lynne Tomkin, *Inside OMB: Politics and Process in the President's Budget Office* (New York: M.E. Sharpe, 1998), pp. 131-134.

[13] The details of the congressional budget process are outside the scope of this report. For discussion of congressional budgetary procedures, see CRS Report RS20095, *The Congressional Budget Process: A Brief Overview*, by James V. Saturno and CRS Report R42388, *The Congressional Appropriations Process: An Introduction*, by Jessica Tollestrup.

Composition of the President's Budget Submission to Congress

Under 31 U.S.C. §1105, the President is required to provide certain information in the budget submission to Congress. The complete list of content the President is required to submit as part of the budget proposal is extensive, and includes (1) estimated receipts, expenditures, and proposed appropriations for the next five fiscal years; (2) actual receipts, expenditures, and appropriations for the previous fiscal year; (3) information on the public debt; and (4) separate statements of amounts for specified appropriations accounts and trust funds, among other things.[14]

The budget submissions of the past three Presidents have each included the following volumes:

- *Budget of the U.S. Government* - includes a short budget message summarizing the President's policy priorities, summary tables of budgetary aggregates, and a detailed narrative description of proposed government activities, organized by issue and agency;

- *Historical Tables* - provides a historical overview of federal government finances, including time series statistics on budget authority, government receipts, outlays, government employment, gross domestic product (GDP), and the federal debt going back several decades and in some cases as far back as 1789;[15]

- *Analytical Perspectives* - contains in-depth analysis of government programs, including credit and insurance programs, discussion of crosscut budgets that span two or more agencies, and technical explanation of the budget baselines used in the analyses and estimates contained in the President's budget proposal; and

- *Appendix* - includes detailed budget estimates and financial information on individual programs and appropriations accounts, proposed text of appropriations language, and information on the legislative and judicial branch appropriations that are not included in other volumes of the President's budget proposal.[16]

Presidents have also included supplemental materials, such as legislative proposals for budget process reform, a brief guide to the budget that is intended for members of the public, or a summary of proposed spending reductions or program consolidations.

Supplements and Revisions to the President's Budget Request

The President may also update the budget by submitting supplemental requests and revisions to Congress. Under current law, the President is required to submit a supplemental summary of the budget, commonly referred to as the Mid-Session Review (MSR), before July 16 of each year.

---

[14] 31 U.S.C. §1105.

[15] The time frame for the information contained in the *Historical Tables* volume varies from table to table, presumably due to the availability of data. For example, information on aggregate levels of receipts and outlays is provided for all years starting with 1789, while information on total levels of federal government employment is only provided as far back as 1962.

[16] CRS Report R42384, *FY2013 Budget Documents: Internet and GPO Availability*, by Jared Conrad Nagel.

The MSR is required to include any substantial changes in estimates of expenditures, receipts, or substantial changes to obligations plus any changes in outlays or budget authority requested.[17] The MSR may reflect changes in economic conditions, budgetary actions taken by Congress, or other factors that have led the President to make adjustments to the initial budget submission.

Agency Budget Requests and Justifications

Once the President has submitted the budget, OMB and agency officials explain and justify the request to Congress. This frequently involves both formal and informal interactions. Early in the congressional budget process, often in the week following the submission of the President's budget, the OMB Director and other cabinet officials usually provide testimony regarding the President's broad budgetary objectives before congressional committees. For example, in February of 2012, acting OMB Director Jeffrey Zients and Treasury Secretary Timothy Geithner each testified before the House and Senate Budget Committees.

Agencies also submit written justification of their budget requests to the appropriations committee and subcommittees of jurisdiction in each chamber.[18] As budgetary legislation is being formulated by Congress, agency officials are often called before the appropriations subcommittees to justify and explain their budget requests to Congress. To ensure that all testimony and written justification materials are consistent with the President's policy objectives, OMB may review materials before agencies provide them to Congress.[19]

Agency testimony and written justification materials facilitate dialogue and information sharing between federal agencies and congressional committees. Justification materials are often the starting point for language contained in the committee reports that accompany each appropriations bill. Agency justification materials also provide program details that Congress may use when determining the amounts to be appropriated and the language to be included in reports accompanying appropriations acts.

Finally, agencies and other administration officials may interact with Members of Congress informally. While the specifics of these informal communications are not public, committees may seek to develop ongoing relationships with the agencies within their jurisdiction.

Statements of Administration Policy and Other Presidential Actions

As Congress is considering budgetary legislation, formal and informal communications may be used to clarify and reiterate the President's policy positions. For example, OMB may formally communicate the President's position on proposed or pending legislation by issuing Statements of Administration Policy (SAPs), which are brief documents expressing support or opposition to pending legislation. The President and his or her administration may also negotiate with Congress

---

[17] 31 U.S.C. §1106.

[18] Federal agencies also make their justification materials available electronically. For a list of links to the justification materials for all 15 executive branch departments and selected independent agencies, please see CRS Report R42453, *Selected Agency Budget Justifications for FY2013*, by Justin Murray.

[19] For example, Circular A-11 §22 establishes guidelines regarding agency conversations with Congress or the public and emphasizes statutory restrictions on attempts to influence legislation outside of official channels.

informally at any time during the congressional budget process by holding summits or private meetings with Members of Congress. The President may also attempt to influence Congress indirectly by promoting his or her policy priorities through direct appeals to the public.[20]

Finally, the President may veto, or threaten to veto, any budgetary legislation passed by Congress. Between 1973 and 2012, for example, Presidents have successfully vetoed appropriations acts on at least 33 occasions.[21]

Execution of Appropriations and Other Enacted Budgetary Legislation

Once appropriations and other budgetary legislation have become law, federal agencies are responsible for executing the budget.[22] The President, OMB, and agencies execute the budget by collecting, obligating, and expending federal resources in accordance with the budgetary laws that have been enacted. The President, OMB, and agencies also possess limited authority to make spending adjustments after appropriations and other spending legislation have been enacted.

Apportionment and Allocation of Budget Authority

Appropriations and other budgetary legislation provide agencies with budget authority, which allows agencies to enter into obligations, such as contracts or employment of new personnel. The budget authority provided to agencies may not be automatically available for obligation or expenditure. With certain exceptions, the Antideficiency Act requires that appropriated funds be apportioned (or divided)—by time period, function, or program—in order to prevent agencies from exhausting their appropriated funds prematurely.[23]

Under the Antideficiency Act, funds appropriated for a definite period of time shall be apportioned "to prevent obligation or expenditure at a rate that would indicate a necessity for a deficiency or supplemental appropriation," while funds appropriated for an indefinite amount of time shall be apportioned "to achieve the most effective and economical use."[24] Appropriations must be apportioned no later than (1) 30 days prior to the start of the fiscal year for which the appropriations were provided, or (2) 30 days after the date of enactment of the appropriations act.[25]

---

[20] Samuel Kernell, *Going Public: New Strategies of Presidential Leadership*, 4th ed. (Washington: CQ Press, 2006).

[21] CRS Report RS22188, *Regular Vetoes and Pocket Vetoes: An Overview*, by Kevin R. Kosar.

[22] In the event that an agency's regular appropriations act has not become law prior to the start of the fiscal year, a temporary continuing appropriations act (i.e., a continuing resolution or CR) may be enacted. This allows the agency to continue operating for the period of time covered by the CR. See CRS Report RL30343, *Continuing Resolutions: Latest Action and Brief Overview of Recent Practices*, by Sandy Streeter and CRS Report RL32614, *Duration of Continuing Resolutions in Recent Years*, by Jessica Tollestrup.

[23] The collection of statutes commonly referred to as the Antideficiency Act have been codified in multiple sections of Title 31 (31 U.S.C. §§1341-1342, 1349-1350, 1511-1519). Select government entities are exempted from the apportionment requirements of the Antideficiency Act, including the Senate, the House of Representatives, congressional committees, and the Office of the Architect of the Capitol (31 U.S.C. §1511 (b)(3)).

[24] 31 U.S.C. §1512(a).

[25] 31 U.S.C. §1513(a).

Funds appropriated to executive agencies are apportioned by OMB.[26] Executive agencies must submit an apportionment request to OMB at least 40 days before the start of the fiscal year or within 15 days of the enactment of the appropriations act.[27] OMB then determines how executive agency funds will be apportioned, generally by fiscal quarter or by project.[28] OMB may also apportion multi-year and no-year funds for a period longer than one fiscal year, provided that an apportionment is made at the beginning of each fiscal year.[29]

Once funds are apportioned by OMB, executive agencies determine how to allocate and sub-allocate those funds amongst the programs, projects, and activities that fall within the scope of each apportionment. While executive agencies may have legal discretion to determine how to allocate the funds available to them, they are also legally obligated to execute spending legislation as enacted. In practice, executive agencies may come to informal arrangements with appropriations committees and subcommittees to ensure that they allocate funds in a manner consistent with both the text of appropriations and the details contained within reports accompanying appropriations acts.

Under the Antideficiency Act, executive agencies are responsible for ensuring that their obligations and expenditures stay within the allowable limits throughout the fiscal year. Agency heads must report any Antideficiency Act violations to the President (through the Director of OMB), to Congress, and to the Comptroller General. In the event that an agency's budgetary needs exceed their funding resources, the agency must request additional funding if it wants to spend more than it has available. OMB is responsible for reviewing requests for supplemental appropriations prior to the President's transmittal of those requests to Congress.

---

[26] Under 31 U.S.C. §1513(b)(1), the President is statutorily responsible for apportioning funds for executive branch agencies. This responsibility has been delegated to OMB. For the legislative and judicial branches, apportionments are made by the officials who maintain administrative control of each appropriations account. For example, the appropriations bill for the judicial branch is currently comprised of 12 accounts. According to an official at the Administrative Office of the U.S. Courts, eight of those accounts—including accounts that provide funds for federal court jurors, court security, federal judicial salaries (excluding salaries of the Supreme Court) and retirement funds— are administered by the Director of the Administrative Office of the U.S. Courts, who also serves as the Secretary of the U.S. Judicial Conference. The remaining four accounts provide funds for Supreme Court salaries and expenses and for judicial organizations such as the U.S. Sentencing Commission and the Court of International Trade. These accounts are administered by the organizations they fund. Each of those organizations is responsible for apportioning the funds that they have been appropriated. (Telephone and email conversations with an official at the Administrative Office of the U.S. Courts, May 17, 2012 and June 12, 2012).

[27] 31 U.S.C. §1513(b)(1) states that agencies must submit "information required for the apportionment" to the President. Circular A-11 §120.26 has further specified that agencies should submit their apportionment requests by August 21, or "within 10 calendar days after the approval of the appropriation or substantive acts providing new budget authority, whichever is later."

[28] Circular A-11 §120 defines an apportionment as "a plan, approved by OMB, to spend resources provided by one of the annual appropriations acts, a supplemental appropriations act, a continuing resolution, or a permanent law (mandatory appropriations)." OMB may also apportion non-financial resources, such as personnel and motor vehicles. In addition to apportioning appropriated funds, OMB may also provide agencies with guidance regarding the implementation of laws related to mandatory spending (i.e., spending provided in acts other than appropriations), such as laws authorizing certain entitlement programs. For additional information, see CRS Report R41375, *OMB Controls on Agency Mandatory Spending Programs: "Administrative PAYGO" and Related Issues for Congress*, by Clinton T. Brass and Jim Monke.

[29] Multi-year funds are appropriations that remain available for obligation for more than one year. No-year funds are appropriations that remain available until expended. Unobligated balances from each quarter remain available until the end of the fiscal year without reapportionment. U.S. Government Accountability Office, *A Glossary of Terms Used in the Federal Budget Process*, GAO-05-734SP, September 2005, http://gao.gov/assets/80/76911.pdf.

Reallocation of Budget Authority: Transfers and Reprogramming

Agencies may also possess limited authority to reallocate funds during budget execution, either by transfers or by reprogramming. Transfers typically involve a shift of budgetary resources from one appropriations account to another, while reprogramming involves a shift of budgetary resources from one project or purpose to another *within* an appropriations account.[30]

Transfers

There are two types of transfers: "expenditure" and "non-expenditure" transfers. Expenditure transfers occur when one agency or program "purchases" goods or services from another agency or program.[31] Non-expenditure transfers are all other transfers, including movement of funds from one account to another for the purpose of increasing the budgetary resources available to a specific program or activity. Both types require prior statutory authorization.

A general restriction against transfers may be found in 31 U.S.C. §1532, which reads, "An amount available under law may be withdrawn from one appropriation account and credited to another or to a working fund only when authorized by law."[32] There are statutory exceptions to this general restriction, and Congress may provide agencies with transfer authority either in authorizing statutes or within appropriations.

Appropriations or authorizing statutes that provide agencies with transfer authority will frequently include language establishing limitations on that authority. For example, transfers may be limited to a specific dollar amount. Alternatively, transfers may be limited to a certain percentage of the total amount appropriated. In addition, statutes may include language limiting the use of the transferred funds to specific purposes. In many of these instances, such transfer authority is governed by provisions requiring notification to Congress, either prior to the transfer or within a certain time period following the transfer.[33]

Reprogramming[34]

Reprogramming is the use of funds for a project or purpose other than that for which they were originally provided.[35] An agency's authority to reprogram "is implicit in an agency's

---

[30] An "appropriations account" is the basic unit of an appropriation. In the case of funds provided in appropriations acts, each "account" reflects an unnumbered paragraph in an appropriations act, which may encompass a number of related programs, projects, and activities.

[31] Such transfers are subject to the procedures established by the Economy Act (31 U.S.C. §1535). The act established guidelines and procedures allowing agencies to perform work and provide goods and services to one another. Transfers to and from federal funds, (e.g., revolving, trust, or other special funds) are also considered expenditure transfers as are transfers between budget accounts and off-budget deposit accounts. For discussion of Economy Act transactions and other interagency procurement, see CRS Report R40814, *Interagency Contracting: An Overview of Federal Procurement and Appropriations Law*, by Kate M. Manuel and Brian T. Yeh.

[32] 31 U.S.C. §1532.

[33] CRS Report RL33151, *Committee Controls of Agency Decisions*, by Louis Fisher.

[34] It should be noted that the Department of Defense uses the term "reprogramming" to refer to both reprogramming and transfers.

[35] U.S. Government Accountability Office, *A Glossary of Terms Used in the Federal Budget Process*, GAO-05-734SP, September 2005, http://gao.gov/assets/80/76911.pdf.

responsibility to manage its funds."[36] Though agencies are not statutorily prohibited from reprogramming funds, Congress may limit an agency's ability to reprogram by including limiting language within appropriations bills. Alternatively, Congress may require agencies to notify committees within a specific time frame either before or after they reprogram funds.

Reprogramming of funds may require an agency to adjust its apportionments. For executive agencies, reapportionments are generally prohibited without prior approval from OMB. Under Circular A-11, executive agencies are generally allowed to adjust apportioned amounts by up to $400,000 or 2% of their total budgetary resources, whichever is lower, without obtaining prior approval from OMB.[37] In addition, agencies may have additional procedures governing the reprogramming of certain funds. For example, executive agencies are required to submit a request to the Office of National Drug Control Policy prior to reprogramming any drug-related budgetary resources.[38]

Congressional Notification and Holds

Congress may exercise oversight over agency budget execution by requiring congressional notification before certain expenditures take place. For example, under certain provisions of the Foreign Assistance Act of 1961 and the International Development and Food Assistance Act of 1978 (22 U.S.C. §2151, et seq.) the Secretary of Defense, and in some cases the Secretary of State, is required to submit a congressional notification (CN) to specified congressional committees at least 15 days before the obligation or expenditure of select foreign aid funds.[39]

Similar notification requirements may also be included in appropriations and authorization acts. For example, the National Defense Authorization Act for Fiscal Year 2012 (P.L. 112-81) included multiple provisions requiring a CN at least 15 days prior to the obligation or expenditure of specified funds, including certain funds for the Commanders' Emergency Response Program in Afghanistan and the Global Security Contingency Fund.[40]

Following receipt of a CN, one or more of the committees may issue a hold instructing agencies not to obligate the specified funds until the hold is released by the issuing committee. While the congressional notification requirement is statutory, the hold on the obligation or expenditure of funds is a non-statutory understanding between congressional committees and the agencies under their jurisdiction.[41]

[36] U.S. Government Accountability Office (then the U.S. General Accounting Office), *Principles of Federal Appropriations Law, Volume I*, GAO-04-261SP, January 2004, p. 30, http://www.gao.gov/products/GAO-04-261SP.

[37] Circular A-11 §120.37.

[38] R. Gil Kerlikowske, Director of the Office of Drug Control Policy, *Fiscal Year 2010 Accounting of Drug Control Funds*, Executive Office of the President, Office of Drug Control Policy, June 13, 2011, http://www.whitehouse.gov/sites/default/files/ondcp/Fact_Sheets/fy2010_accounting_of_drug_control_funds_report_and_letters_june_2011.pdf.

[39] The specified committees include the House Committee on Foreign Affairs, the Senate Committee on Foreign Relations, and the House and Senate Appropriations Committees. In cases involving funds for military assistance, the Secretaries may also be required to submit CNs to the House and Senate Armed Services Committees.

[40] P.L. 112-81, §1201(g) and §1207 (l)(1).

[41] Agencies maintain the authority to obligate funds despite a congressional hold. For further discussion of non-statutory understandings, see CRS Report RL33151, *Committee Controls of Agency Decisions*, by Louis Fisher.

Impoundment of Appropriated Funds: Rescissions and Deferrals

Impoundment is a process by which budgetary authority is reduced (either permanently or temporarily) subsequent to the enactment of appropriations and other budgetary legislation.[42] Under the procedures established by the Impoundment Control Act (ICA) of 1974 (Title X of P.L. 93-344, 2 U.S.C. §681 et seq.), the President has limited authority to reduce or withhold agency funding by impoundment (i.e., an executive action or inaction that prevents the obligation and expenditure of budget authority). The act distinguishes between two types of impoundments: rescissions, which permanently cancel budget authority, and deferrals, which temporarily delay the spending of funds.

Rescissions

Rescissions permanently cancel a specified portion of the budget authority available to an agency. The President may initiate rescissions by submitting a special message to Congress requesting that the specified budget authority be rescinded.[43]

Under the ICA, if the President determines that the total amount of budget authority is no longer required to carry out the objectives for which it was provided, he or she may submit one or more rescission requests to Congress. If a President's rescission request is approved by Congress and enacted into law, the funds are no longer available for obligation and expenditure. However, if after 45 days Congress has not approved the rescission request, the funds must be reapportioned and made available for obligation and expenditure.

Deferrals

Deferrals are the temporary delay in the obligation or expenditure of appropriated funds, generally for no longer than 45 days. Deferrals allow agencies to adjust the timing of their obligations and expenditures in response to changing circumstances, such as a reduction or delay in expenses.

Under the ICA, funds may only be deferred (1) to provide for contingencies, (2) to achieve savings made possible by changes in requirements or greater efficiency of operations, or (3) as specifically provided by law. Funds may also be deferred pending congressional action on a rescission request from the President, but must be released if that request is not approved.[44] Funds may be deferred without prior approval of Congress. However, the President must inform Congress and the Comptroller General of all deferrals, including those initiated by legislative and judicial branch agencies.[45]

---

[42] Budget authority may also be reduced by sequestration. Sequestration involves the cancellation of budgetary authority after a statutorily prescribed sequester order.

[43] Rescissions may also be initiated by Congress by introducing legislation that would cancel budget authority previously enacted.

[44] 2 U.S.C. §684.

[45] 2 U.S.C. §684(a).

Occasional Procedures During Budget Execution

The previous section provided an overview of the budget execution procedures that the President, OMB, and agencies utilize under normal conditions. Under existing law, there are additional executive budgetary procedures that are triggered under specific, less common circumstances.

Budget Execution During Federal Funding Gaps and Government Shutdowns

Under the Antideficiency Act, agencies are generally prohibited from obligating or spending funds prior to the enactment of their appropriations. A funding gap occurs when full-year or interim appropriations are not enacted by the start of the fiscal year.[46] A funding gap may also occur at other times during the fiscal year if an agency's interim appropriations (i.e., a continuing resolution or CR), expires and an additional CR is not subsequently enacted.[47] During a funding gap, the only budgetary resources that may be obligated or expended are those that will be used to provide for excepted activities, such as those involving "the safety of human life or the protection of property."[48]

During periods when enactment of full-year or interim appropriates seems uncertain, OMB may instruct executive agencies to prepare for funding gaps and government shutdowns.[49] Circular A-11 provides general guidance on how executive agencies should proceed if their regular appropriations or CRs are not enacted or if their existing CRs have expired.[50] For example, Circular A-11 instructs agencies to develop shutdown plans that identify "excepted" activities which will continue and "non-excepted" activities which will be terminated in the event of a funding gap. In addition, the circular instructs agencies to determine which of their employees will be subject to furlough and which will be retained. If a funding gap is imminent, OMB may issue additional guidance to agency heads.[51]

Budget Execution in the Event of Sequestration

Sequestration involves the cancellation of budgetary resources under a statutorily prescribed presidential sequester order. A sequester order identifies the specific budgetary resources that can no longer be obligated or expended despite their being enacted into law. Under the provisions of the Balanced Budget and Emergency Deficit Control Act of 1985 (BBEDCA; P.L. 99-177), as

---

[46] 31 U.S.C. §1341(a)(1)(A).

[47] For historical information on previous federal funding gaps, see CRS Report RS20348, *Federal Funding Gaps: A Brief Overview*, by Jessica Tollestrup. For discussion of the potential impact of CRs, see CRS Report RL34700, *Interim Continuing Resolutions (CRs): Potential Impacts on Agency Operations*, by Clinton T. Brass.

[48] 31 U.S.C §1342.

[49] CRS Report RL34680, *Shutdown of the Federal Government: Causes, Processes, and Effects*, by Clinton T. Brass.

[50] Circular A-11 §124.

[51] For example, on December 15, 2011, one day prior to the expiration of the third FY2012 Continuing Resolution, OMB Director Jacob J. Lew issued a memorandum instructing agencies on how to prepare for operations in the event of a funding gap and subsequent shutdown of the federal government. Memorandum from Jacob J. Lew, Director of the Office of Management and Budget, M-12-03, "Planning for Agency Operations During a Lapse in Government Funding," December 15, 2011, http://www.whitehouse.gov/sites/default/files/omb/memoranda/2012/m-12-03.pdf.

amended by the Statutory Pay-As-You-Go Act of 2010 (Statutory PAYGO Act; P.L. 111-139), a sequestration of nonexempt direct spending may be triggered if the new revenue and new direct spending legislation enacted during a congressional session are not "deficit neutral."[52] Under the BBEDCA and Statutory PAYGO, OMB is responsible for tracking the cumulative deficit impact of enacted budgetary legislation. If a sequestration is triggered, OMB is responsible for calculating the uniform percentage by which the budgetary resources of nonexempt programs will be reduced.

Under the provisions of the Budget Control Act of 2011 (BCA; P.L. 112-25) automatic spending reductions, including sequestration of nonexempt discretionary and direct spending, are triggered if legislation to reduce the deficit by $1.2 trillion by the end of FY2021 is not enacted by January 15, 2012.[53] The BCA also includes provisions requiring sequestration in the event that the statutory discretionary spending caps established by the BCA are exceeded.[54] Under the BCA, OMB is responsible for calculating and preparing the sequestration order using the formula provided in the BCA and following the same procedures as those specified in the BBEDCA. Once prepared, the sequestration order is to be issued by the President.

Under both the BCA and the BBEDCA, once issued, the implementation of a sequestration (and execution of the resulting spending cuts) are the responsibility of OMB and each agency, respectively.[55] Circular A-11 summarizes the requirements of the BBEDCA and the Statutory PAYGO Act, and briefly discusses how agencies should manage and record sequestrations issued under those statutes, in order to avoid potential Antideficiency Act violations.[56] However, the circular does not specifically discuss how agencies might manage sequestrations that may be issued under the provisions of the BCA.[57]

---

[52] For additional information on sequestration under the BBEDCA and the Statutory PAYGO Act, see CRS Report R41157, *The Statutory Pay-As-You-Go Act of 2010: Summary and Legislative History*, by Bill Heniff Jr.

[53] The necessary deficit reduction legislation was not enacted by the January 15, 2012, deadline. Consequently, the reductions, including sequestration, are scheduled to take effect in January 2013.

[54] For additional information on the BCA, see CRS Report R41965, *The Budget Control Act of 2011*, by Bill Heniff Jr., Elizabeth Rybicki, and Shannon M. Mahan and CRS Report R42050, *Budget "Sequestration" and Selected Program Exemptions and Special Rules*, coordinated by Karen Spar. For discussion of the potential impact of sequestration, see CRS Report R42506, *The Budget Control Act of 2011: The Effects on Spending and the Budget Deficit When the Automatic Spending Cuts Are Implemented*, by Mindy R. Levit and Marc Labonte and CRS Report R42051, *Budget Control Act: Potential Impact of Automatic Spending Reduction Procedures on Health Reform Spending*, by C. Stephen Redhead.

[55] According to GAO, under the BCA "the execution and impact of any spending reductions will depend on the legal interpretations and actions taken by the Office of Management and Budget, which is vested with implementing the Budget Control Act." See U.S. Government Accountability Office, *The Budget Control Act and the Department of Veterans Affairs' Programs*, B-323157, May 21, 2012, pp. 4-5, http://gao.gov/assets/600/591052.pdf.

[56] Circular A-11 §20 and §81. The Antideficiency Act prohibits agencies from obligating or expending funds required to be sequestered under the BBEDCA (31 U.S.C. §1341(a)(1)).

[57] Circular A-11, Appendix F. The circular does, however, provide agencies with guidance for reporting budgetary information in a manner consistent with the new discretionary spending subcategories established by the BCA. These reporting guidelines may help facilitate agency identification of accounts that would be subject to sequestration.

Author Contact Information

Michelle D. Christensen
Analyst in Government Organization and
Management
mchristensen@crs.loc.gov, 7-0764

Congressional
Research
Service

The Executive Budget Process Timetable

Michelle D. Christensen
Analyst in Government Organization and Management

December 5, 2012

Congressional Research Service

7-5700

www.crs.gov

RS20152

CRS Report for Congress
Prepared for Members and Committees of Congress

The executive budget process is a complex set of activities that includes (1) development of the President's budget proposal, (2) submission and justification of the President's budget proposal, and (3) execution of enacted appropriations and other budgetary legislation. While some of the activities must be completed by specific dates, many follow a more flexible schedule established by formal and informal rules and procedures. This report provides a brief overview of the phases the executive budget process.[1] In addition, this report provides an illustrative example of the budget development timeline (see **Table 1**) and the executive budget process timetable that has generally been followed by Presidents in recent years (see **Table 2**).

The Budget and Accounting Act of 1921 (P.L. 67-13; 42 Stat. 20) established the modern executive budget process. Now codified in Title 31 of the *U.S. Code*, the act requires the President to develop and submit a consolidated budget proposal to Congress prior to the start of each fiscal year.[2] The President is also required to submit an update of the budget proposal to Congress in the middle of the legislative session. Section 221(b) of the Legislative Reorganization Act of 1970,[3] also codified in Title 31 of the *U.S. Code*, requires the President to submit a supplemental summary of the budget, commonly referred to as the *mid-session review* (or MSR), on or before July 15 each year.[4] In addition, the President may submit revisions to the budget submission at any time during the legislative session.

Development of the President's Budget Proposal

The developmental phase of the executive budget process is largely coordinated through the Office of Management and Budget (OMB), which assists the President in the preparation of the budget proposal and the execution of enacted appropriations and other budgetary legislation. OMB budget guidelines are communicated formally to executive agencies through circulars, memoranda, and other publications.[5]

Generally, development of the President's budget proposal begins approximately 10 months before the President must submit the proposal to Congress, which is about 18 months prior to the start of the fiscal year that the budget will cover. Early in the development phase, the Office of Management and Budget (OMB) issues a budget planning guidance memorandum, also referred to as the "Spring Guidance."[6] In accordance with this guidance, executive agencies submit their budget requests and supporting materials to OMB for review in early fall, culminating in final approval by the OMB Director and the President in late November or early December. Under

---

[1] For more information on the executive budget process, see CRS Report R42633, *The Executive Budget Process: An Overview*, by Michelle D. Christensen.

[2] 31 U.S.C. §1105.

[3] P.L. 91-510; 84 Stat. 1140.

[4] 31 U.S.C. §1106. The mid-session review reflects changed economic conditions, any legislative actions taken by Congress, and other factors affecting the President's budget submission. For more information on the mid-session review, see CRS Report RL32509, *The President's Budget Request: Overview and Timing of the Mid-Session Review*, by Michelle D. Christensen.

[5] For example, see Office of Management and Budget, Circular No. A-11, "Preparation, Submission and Execution of the Budget," August 3, 2012, http://www.whitehouse.gov/omb/circulars_default. Updated annually, OMB Circular No. A-11 is an extensive document that contains instructions and schedules for agency submission of budget requests and justification materials to OMB.

[6] For example, see Memorandum from Jeffrey D. Zients, Acting Director of OMB, M-12-13, "Fiscal Year 2014 Budget Guidance," May 18, 2012, http://www.whitehouse.gov/sites/default/files/omb/memoranda/2012/m-12-13.pdf.

---

current law (31 U.S.C. §1105(a)), the President is responsible for developing and submitting a consolidated budget to Congress no later than the first Monday in February prior to the start of the fiscal year.[7] An illustrative example of the FY2013 timeline, including the submission dates of select executive budget documents, is shown in **Table 1**.[8]

Table 1. Development of the President's Budget Proposal

Illustrative Example of FY2013 Timeline	
August 17, 2011	OMB issues "FY2013 Budget Guidance" memorandum
August 18, 2011	OMB issues annual update to Circular A-11
September 12, 2011	Deadline for agencies to submit FY2013 budget requests to OMB
February 13, 2012	President submits FY2013 budget proposal to Congress
July 27, 2012	President submits FY2013 mid-session review to Congress
October 1, 2012	Start of FY2013

Submission and Justification to Congress of the President's Budget Proposal

Although it is not legally binding, the President's budget proposal initiates the congressional budget process and provides Congress with recommended spending levels for agency programs, projects, and activities funded through the annual appropriations acts and other budgetary measures.[9]

During what OMB refers to as the "congressional phase" of the budget process, executive branch activities concerning the budget year typically involve negotiations with Congress about budgetary legislation. Shortly after the President submits the budget proposal to Congress, agencies submit written justifications of their budget requests to each chamber's appropriations committee and subcommittees of jurisdiction.[10] In addition, Administration and agency officials are often called before the appropriations subcommittees to justify and explain the budget requests to Congress.

---

[7] Occasionally, however, the President's budget proposal is submitted after the deadline. For example, during presidential transition years, the budget proposal of the newly elected President is frequently submitted after the deadline. See CRS Report RS20752, *Submission of the President's Budget in Transition Years*, by Michelle D. Christensen.

[8] See Memorandum from Jacob J. Lew, Director of OMB, M-11-30, "Fiscal Year 2013 Budget Guidance," August 17, 2011, http://www.whitehouse.gov/sites/default/files/omb/memoranda/2011/m11-30.pdf; Office of Management and Budget, Circular No. A-11 [2011 update], "Preparation, Submission and Execution of the Budget," August 18, 2011; Office of Management and Budget, *Fiscal Year 2013 Budget of the United States Government*, February 13, 2012, http://www.whitehouse.gov/sites/default/files/omb/budget/fy2013/assets/budget.pdf; and Office of Management and Budget, *Fiscal Year 2013 Mid-Session Review, Budget of the U.S. Government*, July 27, 2012, http://www.whitehouse.gov/sites/default/files/omb/budget/fy2013/assets/13msr.pdf.

[9] For information on the congressional budget process, see CRS Report RS20095, *The Congressional Budget Process: A Brief Overview*, by James V. Saturno and CRS Report R42388, *The Congressional Appropriations Process: An Introduction*, by Jessica Tollestrup. For a broad overview of the federal budget process, see CRS Report 98-721, *Introduction to the Federal Budget Process*, coordinated by Bill Heniff Jr.

[10] For examples of agency budget justifications see CRS Report R42453, *Selected Agency Budget Justifications for FY2013*, by Justin Murray.

Execution of Enacted Appropriations and Other Budgetary Legislation

Once appropriations and other budgetary legislation have been enacted, OMB apportions available funds to executive agencies by time period, program, project, or activity. Throughout the fiscal year, agencies allocate, obligate, and expend funds. If necessary, agencies may request supplemental appropriations, and the President may propose supplemental appropriations or other budgetary adjustments to Congress.

At any given time, agencies are likely working on the budgets for three fiscal years simultaneously. For example, in May 2012, agencies were implementing the FY2012 budget, justifying their requests for the FY2013 budget, and developing their requests for the FY2014 budget. To put this timeline in context, as Congress began action on appropriations bills and other budgetary legislation for FY2013, OMB and agencies were already planning for FY2014.

Table 2 illustrates the full budgetary cycle for a single fiscal year organized by phase of the executive budget process. The timetable begins with the issuance of planning guidance by OMB and culminates in the end of the fiscal year. Typically, the full budgetary cycle takes more than two calendar years to complete. For example, OMB issued the FY2013 planning guidance on August 17, 2011 and FY2013 will end on September 30, 2013—a period lasting approximately two years and one month.

The Executive Budget Process Timetable

Table 2. The Executive Budget Process Timetable for a Typical, Single Fiscal Year

Dates	Activities
Calendar Year Prior to the Year in Which Fiscal Year Begins	**Development of the President's Budget Proposal**
Spring	OMB issues budget planning guidance to executive agencies for the fiscal year that begins in approximately 18 months (on October 1).
Spring and Summer	All agencies begin development of budget requests.
Summer	OMB issues annual update to Circular A-11, providing detailed instructions for submitting budget data and material for executive agency budget requests.
September	Executive agencies submit initial budget requests to OMB, typically by the deadline set in OMB's budget planning guidance.ª
October-November	OMB staff review executive agency budget requests in relation to President's priorities, program performance, budget constraints, and other criteria.
November-December	President, based on recommendations by the OMB director, makes decisions on executive agency requests. OMB informs executive agencies of decisions, a practice commonly referred to as OMB "passback."
December	Executive agencies may appeal these decisions to the OMB director and in some cases directly to the President.
Calendar Year in Which Fiscal Year Begins	**Submission and Justification of the President's Budget Proposal**
By first Monday in February	President submits consolidated budget proposal to Congress.
February-September	Administration and agency officials interact with Congress, justifying and explaining the President's budget proposal and agencies' budget requests.
On or before July 15	President submits mid-session review to Congress.
August 21 (or within 10 days after approval of a spending bill)	Executive agencies submit apportionment requests to OMB for each budget account.
September 10 (or within 30 days after approval of a spending bill)	OMB apportions available funds to executive agencies by time period, program, project, or activity.
Calendar Years in Which Fiscal Year Begins and Ends	**Execution of Appropriations and Other Budgetary Legislation**
October 1	Fiscal year begins.
October-September	Agencies make allotments, obligate funds, conduct activities, and may request supplemental appropriations, if necessary. President may propose supplemental appropriations and impoundments (i.e., deferrals or rescissions) to Congress.
September 30	Fiscal year ends.

Source: Prepared by CRS, drawing from Office of Management and Budget, *Circular No. A-11*, Section 10.5, August 3, 2012, http://www.whitehouse.gov/omb/circulars_default.

a. The budgets of certain agencies, including those within the legislative branch and the judicial branch, are not subject to presidential or OMB review. Those agencies transmit their budget requests to the President, who is then required to include the requests, without modification, in the budget submission to Congress (31 U.S.C. §1105(b)).

Author Contact Information

Michelle D. Christensen
Analyst in Government Organization and
Management
mchristensen@crs.loc.gov, 7-0764

Acknowledgments

This report was originally authored by Bill Heniff Jr., Analyst on Congress and the Legislative Process at CRS. The analyst listed on the cover has updated this report and is available to answer questions concerning the report's subject matter.

The Congressional Budget Process:
A Brief Overview

James V. Saturno
Section Research Manager

August 22, 2011

Congressional Research Service

7-5700

www.crs.gov

RS20095

CRS Report for Congress
Prepared for Members and Committees of Congress

Summary

The term "budget process," when applied to the federal government, actually refers to a number of processes that have evolved separately and that occur with varying degrees of coordination. This overview, and the accompanying flow chart, are intended to describe in brief each of the parts of the budget process that involve Congress, clarify the role played by each, and explain how they operate together. They include the President's budget submission, the budget resolution, reconciliation, sequestration, authorizations, and appropriations.

This report will be updated to reflect any changes in the budget process.

Contents

Figures

Contacts

The Basic Framework

The Constitution grants the "power of the purse" to Congress,[1] but does not establish any specific procedure for the consideration of budgetary legislation. Instead, a number of laws and congressional rules contribute to the federal budget process, with two statutes in particular forming the basic framework.[2]

The Budget and Accounting Act of 1921, as codified in Title 31 of the *United States Code*, established the statutory basis for an executive budget process by requiring the President to submit to Congress annually a proposed budget for the federal government. It also created the Bureau of the Budget (reorganized as the Office of Management and Budget (OMB) in 1970) to assist him in carrying out his responsibilities, and the General Accounting Office (GAO, renamed the Government Accountability Office in 2004) to assist Congress as the principal auditing agency of the federal government.

The Congressional Budget and Impoundment Control Act of 1974 (P.L. 93-344, 88 Stat. 297) established the statutory basis for a congressional budget process, and provided for the annual adoption of a concurrent resolution on the budget as a mechanism for facilitating congressional budgetary decision making. It also established the House and Senate Budget Committees, and created the Congressional Budget Office (CBO) to provide budgetary information to Congress independent of the executive branch.

The Budget Cycle

The President is required to submit to Congress a proposed budget by the first Monday in February. Although this budget does not have the force of law, it is a comprehensive examination of federal revenues and spending, including any initiatives recommended by the President, and is the start of extensive interaction with Congress.

Within six weeks of the President's budget submission, congressional committees are required to submit their "views and estimates" of spending and revenues within their respective jurisdictions to the House and Senate Budget Committees. These views and estimates, along with information from other sources, are then used by each Budget Committee in drafting and reporting a concurrent resolution on the budget to its respective house. Other information is gathered by the Budget Committees in reports and hearing testimony. That information includes budget and economic projections, programmatic information, and budget priorities, and comes from a variety of sources, such as CBO, OMB, the Federal Reserve, executive branch agencies, and congressional leadership.

---

[1] Article I, Section 8 provides that "The Congress shall have Power To lay and collect Taxes, Duties, Imposts and Excises," and Section 9 provides that "No Money shall be drawn from the Treasury, but in Consequence of Appropriations made by Law."

[2] For a more extensive overview of the federal budget process, see CRS Report 98-721, *Introduction to the Federal Budget Process*, coordinated by Bill Heniff Jr.

Although it also does not have the force of law, the budget resolution is a central part of the budget process in Congress. As a concurrent resolution, it represents an agreement between the House and Senate that establishes budget priorities, and defines the parameters for all subsequent budgetary actions. The spending, revenue, and public debt legislation necessary to implement decisions agreed to in the budget resolution are subsequently enacted separately.

Discretionary spending,[3] in the form of appropriation bills, involves annual actions that must be completed before the beginning of a new fiscal year on October 1. Changes in direct spending[4] or revenue laws may also be a part of budgetary actions in any given year. When these changes are directly tied to implementing the fiscal policies in the budget resolution for that year, the reconciliation process may be used. Reconciliation typically follows a timetable established in the budget resolution. Other budgetary legislation, such as changes in direct spending or revenue laws separate from the reconciliation process, changes in the public debt limit, or authorizing legislation, are not tied directly to the annual budget cycle. However, such legislation may be a necessary part of budgetary actions in any given year.

The Budget Resolution and Reconciliation

The budget resolution represents an agreement between the House and Senate concerning the overall size of the federal budget, and the general composition of the budget in terms of functional categories. The amounts in functional categories are translated into allocations to each committee with jurisdiction over spending in a process called "crosswalking" under Section 302(a) of the Congressional Budget Act. Legislation considered by the House and Senate must be consistent with these allocations, as well as with the aggregate levels of spending and revenues. Both the allocations and aggregates are enforceable through points of order that may be made during House or Senate floor consideration of such legislation. These allocations are supplemented by nonbinding assumptions concerning the substance of possible budgetary legislation that are included in the reports from the Budget Committees that accompany the budget resolution in each house.

In some years, the budget resolution includes reconciliation instructions. Reconciliation instructions identify the committees that must recommend changes in laws affecting revenues or direct spending programs within their jurisdiction in order to implement the priorities agreed to in the budget resolution.[5] All committees receiving such instructions must submit recommended legislative language to the Budget Committee in their respective chamber, which packages the recommended language as an omnibus measure and reports the measure without substantive revision. A reconciliation bill would then be considered, and possibly amended, by the full House or Senate. In the House, reconciliation bills are typically considered under the terms of a special rule. In the Senate, reconciliation bills are considered under limitations imposed by Sections 305, 310, and 313 of the Congressional Budget Act. These sections limit debate on a reconciliation bill to 20 hours, and limit the types of amendments that may be considered.

---

[3] Discretionary spending is that spending not mandated by existing law, and therefore is made available in such amounts as Congress chooses through the appropriations process.

[4] Direct spending, also referred to as mandatory or entitlement spending, is that spending directly controlled through eligibility requirements and benefit payments mandated in laws other than appropriations.

[5] CRS Report R41186, *Reconciliation Directives: Components and Enforcement*, by Megan Suzanne Lynch.

The Appropriations Process

The annual appropriations process provides funding for discretionary spending programs through regular annual appropriations bills.[6] Congress must enact these measures prior to the beginning of each fiscal year (October 1) or provide interim funding for the affected programs through a "continuing resolution." By custom, appropriations bills originate in the House, but may be amended by the Senate, as other legislation.

The House and Senate Appropriations Committees are organized into subcommittees, each of which is responsible for developing an appropriations bill. Appropriations bills are constrained in terms of both their purpose and the amount of funding they provide. Appropriations are constrained in terms of purpose because the rules of both the House (Rule XXI) and the Senate (Rule XVI) generally require authorization prior to consideration of appropriations for an agency or program.[7]

Constraints in terms of the amount of funding exist on several levels. For individual items or programs, funding may be limited to the level recommended in authorizing legislation. The overall level of discretionary spending provided in appropriations acts is limited by the allocations from the budget resolution made to the Appropriations Committees under Section 302(a) of the Budget Act. These allocations provide limits that may be enforced procedurally through points of order in the House and Senate during consideration of legislation. In the absence of a final agreement on a concurrent resolution on the budget, the House or Senate may adopt a "deeming resolution" to establish provisional enforcement levels.[8]

Section 302(b) of the Budget Act further requires the House and Senate Appropriations Committees to subdivide the amounts allocated to them under the budget resolution among their subcommittees. These suballocations are to be made "as soon as practicable after a concurrent resolution on the budget is agreed to." Because each subcommittee is responsible for developing a single general appropriations bill, the process of making suballocations effectively determines the spending level for each of the regular annual appropriations bills. Legislation (or amendments) that would cause the suballocations made under 302(b) to be exceeded is subject to a point of order. The Appropriations Committees can (and do) issue revised subdivisions over the course of appropriations actions to reflect changes in spending priorities effected during floor consideration or in conference.

Revenue and Public Debt Legislation

The budget resolution provides a guideline for the overall level of revenues, but not for their composition. Legislative language controlling revenues is reported by the committees of

---

[6] CRS Report 97-684, *The Congressional Appropriations Process: An Introduction*, by Sandy Streeter.

[7] Authorizations are legislation that establish, continue, or modify an agency or program, and authorize the enactment of appropriations to carry out such purposes. Authorizations may be temporary or permanent, and their provisions may be general or specific, but they do not themselves provide funding in the absence of appropriations actions. Although House and Senate rules generally prohibit unauthorized appropriations, both provide exceptions in their respective rules, and the prohibition itself may be waived.

[8] CRS Report RL31443, *The "Deeming Resolution": A Budget Enforcement Tool*, by Megan Suzanne Lynch.

---

jurisdiction (the House Ways and Means Committee and the Senate Finance Committee). The revenue level agreed to in the budget resolution acts as a minimum, limiting consideration of revenue legislation that would decrease revenue below that level. In addition, Article I, Section 7 of the Constitution requires that all revenue measures originate in the House of Representatives, although the Senate may amend them, as other legislation. Revenue legislation may be considered at any time, although revenue provisions are often included in reconciliation legislation.[9]

The budget resolution also specifies an appropriate level for the public debt that reflects the budgetary policies agreed to in the resolution. Any change in the authorized level of the public debt must be implemented through a statutory enactment.[10]

Budget Enforcement and Sequestration

The Balanced Budget and Emergency Deficit Control Act of 1985 (P.L. 99-177, 99 Stat. 1037) established the sequester[11] as a means to enforce statutory budget limits. Amendments to this act were designed to use sequesters to control direct spending and revenues (through the pay-as-you-go, or PAYGO, process) and discretionary spending (through spending caps). Under these mechanisms, the budgetary impact of all legislation was scored by OMB, and reported three times each year (a preview with the President's budget submission, an update with the Mid-Session Review of the Budget, and a final report 15 days after Congress adjourned). If the final report on either the PAYGO or spending caps mechanism indicated that the statutory limitations within that category had been violated, the President was required to issue an order making across-the-board cuts of nonexempt spending programs within that category. Those mechanisms expired October 1, 2002.[12]

Although formal enforcement of these mechanisms was through a presidential order, by enforcing the allocations and aggregates for spending and revenues provided in the budget resolution consistent with these limits, Congress was able to use points of order to enforce them as well. Although these statutory limits expired at the end of FY2002, Congress has continued to use the concurrent resolution on the budget and points of order to establish and enforce budgetary limits.[13]

---

[9] CRS Report R41408, *Rules and Practices Governing Consideration of Revenue Legislation in the House and Senate*, by Megan Suzanne Lynch.

[10] CRS Report RS21519, *Legislative Procedures for Adjusting the Public Debt Limit: A Brief Overview*, by Bill Heniff Jr.

[11] A sequester was an executive order canceling budgetary resources in accordance with the provisions of the Balanced Budget and Emergency Deficit Control Act of 1985, as amended.

[12] These mechanisms were first established under the Budget Enforcement Act of 1990 (Title XIII of P.L. 101-508, Omnibus Budget Reconciliation Act of 1990). Originally enacted with a sunset date of FY1995, they were extended twice, through FY1998 (Title XIV of P.L. 103-66, Omnibus Budget Reconciliation Act of 1993) and through FY2002 (Budget Enforcement Act of 1997, Title X of P.L. 105-33, Balanced Budget Act of 1997). See CRS Report R41005, *The Statutory PAYGO Process for Budget Enforcement: 1991-2002*, by Robert Keith.

[13] CRS Report 97-865, *Points of Order in the Congressional Budget Process*, by James V. Saturno.

More recently, new statutory control mechanisms have been established. The first was the Statutory PAYGO Act of 2010 to limit increases in the deficit caused by new direct spending or revenue legislation.[14] Like its predecessor, it uses sequestration as its enforcement mechanism.

On August 2, 2011, the Budget Control Act of 2011 was signed into law.[15] This law reestablished discretionary spending caps to apply to FY2012-FY2021 as well as parameters for further deficit reduction to be achieved over the same period. It includes two separate sequester mechanisms to enforce its requirements. These sequesters would enforce (1) the discretionary spending limit and (2) any amounts of the additional deficit reduction required under the act not achieved through a privileged measure to be authored by a Joint Select Committee on Deficit Reduction.

Although the primary enforcement of these limits is through sequestration, the Budget Control Act also established a point of order against the consideration of legislation that would exceed the discretionary spending caps. In addition, by enforcing allocations and aggregates in the budget resolution consistent with these limits, Congress can enforce them through existing points of order as well.

---

[14] P.L. 111-139. For detailed information see CRS Report R41157, *The Statutory Pay-As-You-Go Act of 2010: Summary and Legislative History*, by Bill Heniff Jr.

[15] P.L. 112-25. For detailed information see CRS Report R41965, *The Budget Control Act of 2011*, by Bill Heniff Jr., Elizabeth Rybicki, and Shannon M. Mahan.

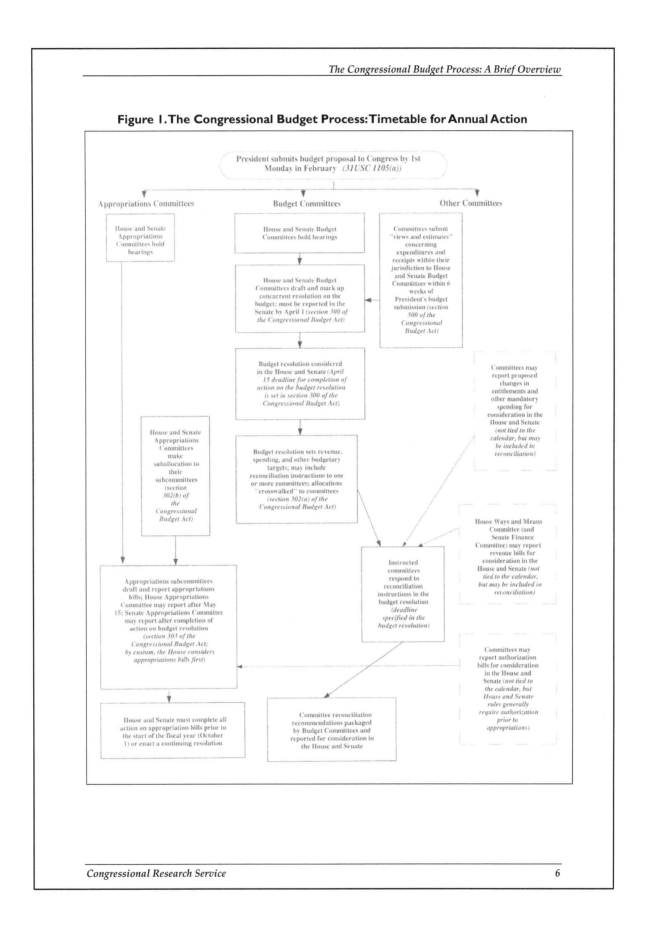

Author Contact Information

James V. Saturno
Section Research Manager
jsaturno@crs.loc.gov, 7-2381

Budget Resolution Enforcement

Bill Heniff Jr.
Analyst on the Congress and Legislative Process

August 12, 2008

Congressional Research Service

7-5700

www.crs.gov

98-815

CRS Report for Congress
Prepared for Members and Committees of Congress

Summary

The annual budget resolution sets forth Congress's budget plan for a period of at least five fiscal years. It includes total levels of new budget authority, outlays, revenues, the deficit, and the public debt for each of the fiscal years covered. While the budget resolution does not become law, the Congressional Budget Act of 1974 (Titles I-IX of P.L. 93-344, 2 U.S.C. 601-688), as amended, provides for the enforcement of its provisions as they are implemented in subsequent annual appropriations bills, revenue measures, and other budgetary legislation. For more information on the budget process, see the CRS Guides to Congressional Processes at http://www.crs.gov/products/guides/guidehome.shtml.

Contents

Contacts

The annual budget resolution sets forth Congress's budget plan for a period of at least five fiscal years. It includes total levels of new budget authority, outlays, revenues, the deficit, and the public debt for each of the fiscal years covered. While the budget resolution does not become law, the Congressional Budget Act of 1974 (Titles I-IX of P.L. 93-344, 2 U.S.C. 601-688), as amended, provides for the enforcement of its provisions as they are implemented in subsequent annual appropriations bills, revenue measures, and other budgetary legislation. For more information on the budget process, see the CRS Guides to Congressional Processes at http://www.crs.gov/products/guides/guidehome.shtml.

Once a budget resolution is adopted, Congress may enforce its provisions, through points of order, at several levels: the total levels of spending and revenues, the level of resources allocated to committees, and the level of resources allocated to the appropriations subcommittees. Congress also may use reconciliation legislation to enforce the direct spending, revenue, and debt limit provisions of a budget resolution (see CRS Report 98-814, *Budget Reconciliation Legislation: Development and Consideration*, by Bill Heniff Jr.).

At the aggregate level, Section 311(a) of the Budget Act prohibits the House and Senate from considering any measure that would cause the spending or revenue totals for the first fiscal year, or the revenue totals for the full period, covered by the budget resolution to be breached. In the House, however, any measure that would not also cause the relevant committee allocation to be exceeded is exempt from this point of order by Section 311(c) of the Budget Act.

Although Congress sets budget priorities by allocating spending among each major functional category in a budget resolution, these amounts are not binding or enforceable in subsequent budgetary legislation. The functional category amounts instead are translated into allocations to the relevant House and Senate committees with jurisdiction over spending under Section 302(a) of the Budget Act. It is these committee spending allocations, commonly referred to as 302(a) allocations and published in the joint explanatory statement accompanying the conference report on a budget resolution, that are enforceable by a point of order on the floor of each chamber. Section 302(f) of the Budget Act prohibits the consideration of any measure, including any amendment, that would cause a committee's 302(a) allocations for the first fiscal year and for the full period covered by the budget resolution to be exceeded.

The chairs of the Budget Committees may make adjustments to the total levels set forth in a budget resolution, and the associated committee spending allocations, after the budget resolution has been agreed to by Congress, under the terms of certain provisions, such as a reserve fund, contained in the budget resolution.

Soon after the budget resolution is adopted by Congress, the House and Senate Appropriations Committees, under Section 302(b) of the Budget Act, subdivide their committee spending allocations among their subcommittees and formally report these subcommittee allocations to their respective chambers. The Appropriations Committees may revise the subcommittee allocations, commonly referred to as Section 302(b) allocations, during the appropriations process. Section 302(c) prohibits the consideration of any appropriations measure in the House or Senate before each respective committee has made the required subcommittee allocations. Once reported, the 302(b) allocations effectively represent spending ceilings on each of the regular appropriations acts. Section 302(f) of the Budget Act prohibits the consideration of an appropriations measure, or an amendment, that would cause a 302(b) allocation to be exceeded.

Congressional Research Service

1

The Budget Act also provides for Senate enforcement of the Social Security levels set forth in a budget resolution. Section 311(a)(3) of the Budget Act prohibits from being considered in the Senate any measure that would cause a decrease in Social Security surpluses or an increase in Social Security deficits relative to the levels included in the applicable budget resolution for the first fiscal year or for the full period covered by the budget resolution.

In each case, a point of order is the procedural mechanism for enforcing the provisions set forth in the budget resolution. Points of order, however, are not self-enforcing: a Member must raise a point of order to enforce the spending and revenue amounts included in a budget resolution. Budget enforcement points of order also may be waived. In the House, a point of order may be waived by unanimous consent, by suspension of the rules, or by a special rule reported by the Rules Committee and adopted by the full House. In the Senate, Budget Act points of order may be waived by unanimous consent or by motion as provided under Section 904 of the Budget Act. A motion to waive most Budget Act points of order requires an affirmative vote of three-fifths of all Senators duly chosen and sworn (60 votes if there are no vacancies). Congress may consider and pass legislation even if it violates the provisions of a budget resolution if no point of order is made or an applicable point of order is waived.

An integral part of enforcing the spending and revenue levels of a budget resolution is scorekeeping. Generally, scorekeeping is the process of measuring the budgetary impact of pending legislation and is used to determine whether or not such legislation violates budget resolution levels (see CRS Report 98-560, *Baselines and Scorekeeping in the Federal Budget Process*, by Bill Heniff Jr.). The House and Senate Budget Committees, acting with the assistance of the Congressional Budget Office and the Joint Committee on Taxation (for revenue measures), are responsible for scorekeeping in Congress. Section 312 of the Budget Act requires that the determination of budget resolution violations be based on estimates made by the Budget Committees.

Author Contact Information

Bill Heniff Jr.
Analyst on the Congress and Legislative Process
wheniff@crs.loc.gov, 7-8646

Congressional
Research Service
Informing the legislative debate since 1914

Deeming Resolutions: Budget Enforcement in the Absence of a Budget Resolution

Megan S. Lynch
Specialist on Congress and the Legislative Process

June 26, 2017

Congressional Research Service

7-5700

www.crs.gov

R44296

Summary

The budget resolution reflects an agreement between the House and Senate on a budgetary plan for the upcoming fiscal year. When the House and Senate do not reach final agreement on this plan, it may be more difficult for Congress to reach agreement on subsequent budgetary legislation, both within each chamber and between the chambers.

In the absence of agreement on a budget resolution, Congress may employ alternative legislative tools to serve as a substitute for a budget resolution. These substitutes are typically referred to as "deeming resolutions," because they are deemed to serve in place of an annual budget resolution for the purposes of establishing enforceable budget levels for the upcoming fiscal year.

Since the creation of the budget resolution, there have been nine years in which Congress did not come to agreement on a budget resolution. In each of those years, one or both chambers employed at least one deeming resolution to serve as a substitute for a budget resolution.

While referred to as deeming resolutions, such mechanisms are not formally defined and have no specifically prescribed content. Instead, they simply denote the House and Senate, often separately, engaging legislative procedures to deal with enforcement issues on an ad hoc basis. As described below, the mechanisms can vary significantly in content and timing. This report covers the use of deeming resolutions pertaining to fiscal years for which the House and Senate did not agree on a budget resolution.

The House and Senate ultimately agreed to a budget resolution for FY2017, and so data pertaining to FY2017 is not included in this report. It may be of interest, however, that the appropriations process for FY2017 moved forward even without agreement on a budget resolution. For the Senate, the Bipartisan Budget Act of 2015 (P.L. 114-74) included a provision directing the Senate Budget Committee chair to file levels in the *Congressional Record* that would be enforceable in the Senate as if they had been included in a budget resolution for FY2017. On April 18, 2016, Senate Budget Committee Chairman Enzi filed such levels.

No such provision was included for the House. In the absence of any such enforceable levels, the House Appropriations Committee adopted "interim 302(b) sub-allocations" for some individual appropriations bills. Such levels did not act as an enforceable cap on appropriations measures when they were considered on the floor. A separate House rule, however, prohibited floor amendments that would increase spending in a general appropriations bill, effectively creating a cap on individual appropriations bills when they were considered on the floor.

Contents

Figures

Tables

Contacts

What Is the Budget Resolution and How Is It Enforced?

The Congressional Budget Act of 1974 (hereinafter referred to as the Budget Act) provides for the annual adoption of a budget resolution.[1] The budget resolution reflects an agreement between the House and Senate on a budgetary framework designed to establish parameters within which Congress will consider subsequent budgetary legislation.

The budget resolution does not become law; therefore no money is spent or collected as a result of its adoption. Instead, it is meant to assist Congress in considering an overall budget plan. Once agreed to by both chambers, the budget resolution creates parameters that may be enforced in two primary ways: (1) by points of order, and (2) by using the budget reconciliation process.

Enforcement Through Points of Order

Once the budget resolution has been agreed to by both chambers, certain levels contained in it are enforceable through points of order. This means that if legislation is being considered on the House or Senate floor that would violate certain levels contained in the budget resolution, a Member may raise a point of order against the consideration of that legislation. Points of order can be raised against bills, resolutions, amendments, or conference reports. If such a point of order is raised against legislation for violating levels in the budget resolution, the presiding officer makes a ruling on the point of order based on estimates provided by the relevant Budget Committee.[2]

Points of order are not self-enforcing, meaning that if no Member raises a point of order, a chamber may consider and pass legislation that would violate levels established in the budget resolution. In addition, either chamber may waive the point of order. The process for waiving points of order, and the number of Members required to waive points of order, varies by chamber. Generally, such points of order can be waived in the House by a simple majority of Members[3] and in the Senate by three-fifths of all Senators.[4]

The Budget Act requires that the budget resolution include the following budgetary levels for the upcoming fiscal year and at least four out years: total spending, total revenues, the surplus/deficit, new spending for each major functional category, the public debt, and (in the Senate only) Social Security spending and revenue levels. The Budget Act also requires that the aggregate amounts of

---

[1] Titles I-IX of P.L. 93-344, as amended; 2 U.S.C. 601-688.

[2] §312 of the Budget Act.

[3] In the House, most measures are considered in one of two ways, both of which routinely waive points of order. First, a measure may be considered under terms specified in a resolution (referred to as a special rule) reported from the House Rules Committee. Such resolutions often include language waiving points of order against the underlying legislation as well as certain specified amendments. A special rule requires for adoption a simple majority of those voting, assuming a quorum is present. The second common way that measures are considered in the House is under the suspension of the rules procedure. When measures are considered under this procedure, such points of order are automatically waived. Measures considered under this procedure require for passage a two-thirds vote of those voting, assuming a quorum is present.

[4] In the Senate, such points of order can be waived with the support of three-fifths of Senators duly chosen and sworn. In such a situation, a Senator may make a motion to waive the point of order either after one has been raised or before it has been raised (in anticipation of the point of order). The waiver motion may apply to one or more points of order, as specified by the Senator making the motion.

spending recommended in the budget resolution be allocated among committees.[5] The Budget Act provides that the House and Senate Appropriations Committees receive an allocation for only the upcoming fiscal year (referred to as the budget year), but the remaining House and Senate committees receive allocations for the entire period covered by the budget resolution. The Budget Act requires that the House and Senate Appropriations Committees subdivide their allocations by subcommittee and report these sub-allocations to their respective chambers.

While the Budget Act requires that the budget resolutions include the levels described above, it does not require that all of these levels be enforceable by points of order. (Some levels in the budget resolution are, therefore, included only for informational purposes.)

Budgetary levels that *are* enforceable include spending and revenue aggregates and committee spending allocations. The Budget Act prohibits the consideration of (1) any measure that would cause spending to exceed levels in the budget resolution,[6] or (2) any measure that would cause total revenue levels to fall below the levels in the budget resolution.[7]

Likewise, the Budget Act prohibits the consideration of legislation that would violate the committee spending allocations.[8] Similarly, once the Appropriations Committees report their sub-allocations to their respective chambers, the Budget Act bars the consideration of any spending measures that would cause those sub-allocations to be violated.

Enforcement Through the Budget Reconciliation Process

While points of order can be effective in enforcing the budgetary goals outlined in the budget resolution, they can be raised against legislation only when it is pending on the House or Senate floor. This can be effective for legislation such as appropriations measures, which typically provide funding for one year and are therefore considered on the House and Senate floor annually. Points of order cannot, however, limit direct spending or revenue levels resulting from current law.

Often, for the budgetary levels in the budget resolution to be achieved, Congress must pass legislation to alter the levels of revenue and/or direct spending resulting from current law. In this situation, Congress seeks to *reconcile* the levels resulting from existing law with the budgetary levels expressed in the budget resolution. To assist in this process, the budget reconciliation process allows the expedited consideration of such legislation.

If Congress intends to use the reconciliation process, reconciliation directives (also referred to as reconciliation instructions) must be included in the annual budget resolution. These directives instruct individual committees to develop and report legislation that would change laws within their respective jurisdictions related to direct spending, revenue, or the debt limit. Once a specified committee develops legislation, the reconciliation directive may direct it to report the

---

[5] These committee spending allocations are required to be included in the joint explanatory statement accompanying the conference report on the budget resolution. The report accompanying the budget resolution is also required to include other components (§301(e)(2) of the Budget Act).

[6] Specifically, in the Senate the Budget Act prohibits consideration of spending legislation that would cause new budget authority or outlays to exceed the levels set forth in the budget resolution for the first fiscal year. In the House, the Budget Act prohibits consideration of legislation that would cause new budget authority or outlays to exceed the levels set forth in the budget resolution for the first fiscal year (§§311(a)(2) and 311(a)(1)).

[7] Specifically, the Budget Act prohibits consideration in the House and the Senate of legislation that would cause revenues to fall below the levels set forth in the budget resolution for the first fiscal year or for the total of all fiscal years covered in the budget resolution (§§311(a)(1) and 311(a)(2)).

[8] §302(f) of the Budget Act.

---

legislation for consideration in its chamber or submit it to the Budget Committee to be included in an omnibus reconciliation measure. Such reconciliation legislation is then eligible to be considered under special expedited procedures in both the House and Senate.[9]

What Complications Arise When the House and Senate Do Not Reach Agreement on a Budget Resolution?

The budget resolution reflects an agreement between the House and Senate on a budgetary plan for the upcoming fiscal year. When the House and Senate do not reach final agreement on this plan, the budget process for the upcoming fiscal year may become complicated. Without an agreement on budgetary parameters, it may be more difficult for Congress to reach agreement on subsequent budgetary legislation, both within each chamber and between the chambers.

If Congress agreed upon a budget resolution for the prior fiscal year, that resolution remains in effect and may provide some operative parameters, since a resolution includes multi-year enforceable levels.[10] The usefulness of such levels may be limited, however, due to altered economic conditions and technical factors, not to mention any changes in congressional budgetary goals.

Furthermore, since a committee allocation to the Appropriations Committee is made for only the upcoming fiscal year, the House and Senate cannot rely on a prior year's budget resolution. This means that there is no allocation of spending made to the Appropriations Committees and no formal basis for them to make the required spending sub-allocations.[11] Without such enforceable budgetary levels, the development and consideration of individual appropriations measures may encounter difficulties.

Further, the Budget Act sought to require adoption of a budget resolution before Congress could consider budgetary legislation for the upcoming year. Under Section 303(a) of the Budget Act, the House and Senate generally may not consider spending, revenue, or debt limit legislation for a fiscal year until the budget resolution for that fiscal year has been adopted. The Budget Act provides for exceptions, however, and in addition allows the point of order to be waived in both chambers by a simple majority.

Without agreement on a budget resolution, Congress also may not use the budget reconciliation process. This means that any budgetary changes to revenue or mandatory spending may not be considered under the special expedited procedures provided by the budget reconciliation process.

---

[9] For more information on the budget reconciliation process, see CRS Report R41186, *Reconciliation Directives: Components and Enforcement*, by Megan S. Lynch.

[10] In the event that a new Congress has begun, the prior year's budget resolution is still in effect in the Senate but not in the House. The House, however, often renews a prior year's budget resolution (or deeming resolution) as part of the opening-days rules package. See for example, Section 3(e) of H.Res. 5 (114th Congress).

[11] As described below, statutory limits on discretionary spending currently exist through FY2021 and may provide a basis for discretionary spending levels for defense and non-defense while they are in effect, but they generally do not provide enforceable limits on individual appropriations measures in a way comparable to committee sub-allocations. Section 302(a)(5) of the Budget Act authorizes the chairman of the House Budget Committee to issue a provisional spending allocation to the House Appropriations Committee consistent with the most recently agreed to budget resolution, although the House has often used deeming resolutions (described below) so that consideration of regular appropriations acts can proceed under more updated spending allocations.

Deeming Resolutions: Budget Enforcement in the Absence of a Budget Resolution

What Can Be Used for Budget Enforcement in the Absence of a Budget Resolution?

In the absence of a budget resolution, other budget enforcement mechanisms are available to Congress comprising two general categories. First, there are types of budget enforcement that are entirely separate from the budget resolution, such as chamber rules and statutory spending caps. These mechanisms remain in effect in the absence of a budget resolution and place restrictions on certain types of budgetary legislation. Such enforcement is briefly described below in the section titled "What Types of Budgetary Enforcement Exist Outside of the Budget Resolution?"

Second, in the absence of agreement on a budget resolution, Congress may employ alternative legislative tools to serve as a substitute for a budget resolution. When Congress has been late in reaching final agreement on a budget resolution, or has not reached agreement at all, it has relied on such substitutes. These substitutes are typically referred to as "deeming resolutions," because they are *deemed* to serve in place of an agreement between the two chambers on an annual budget resolution for the purposes of establishing enforceable budget levels for the upcoming fiscal year (or multiple fiscal years). Employing a deeming resolution, however, does not preclude Congress from subsequently agreeing to a budget resolution.

While referred to as deeming resolutions, such mechanisms are not formally defined and have no specifically prescribed content. Instead, they simply denote the House and Senate, often separately, engaging legislative procedures to deal with enforcement issues on an ad hoc basis. As described below, the mechanisms vary in form and function, but they always (1) include or reference certain budgetary levels (e.g., aggregate spending limits and committee spending allocations) and (2) contain language stipulating that such levels are to be enforceable by points of order as if they had been included in a budget resolution.[12]

In Which Years Did Congress Rely on Deeming Resolutions in the Absence of Agreement on a Budget Resolution?

As shown in **Table 1**, since the creation of the budget resolution, dates of adoption have varied, and there have been nine years in which Congress did not come to agreement on a budget resolution. As shown in **Table 2**, in each of those years, one or both chambers employed at least one deeming resolution to serve as a substitute for a budget resolution.

Table 1. Dates of Final Adoption of Budget Resolutions: FY1976-FY2017

Fiscal Year	Date Adopted	Fiscal Year	Date Adopted
1976	05-14-1975	1997	06-13-1996
1977	05-13-1976	1998	06-05-1997
1978	05-17-1977	1999	[none]

---

[12] Because a deeming resolution typically provides enforcement for only one chamber, it may be not be possible to trigger the budget reconciliation process allowing expedited consideration of reconciliation legislation in both chambers of Congress.

Deeming Resolutions: Budget Enforcement in the Absence of a Budget Resolution

Fiscal Year	Date Adopted	Fiscal Year	Date Adopted
1979	05-17-1978	2000	04-15-1999
1980	05-24-1979	2001	04-13-2000
1981	06-12-1980	2002	05-10-2001
1982	05-21-1981	2003	[none]
1983	06-23-1982	2004	04-11-2003
1984	06-23-1983	2005	[none]
1985	10-01-1984	2006	04-28-2005
1986	08-01-1985	2007	[none]
1987	06-27-1986	2008	05-17-2007
1988	06-24-1987	2009	06-05-2008
1989	06-06-1988	2010	04-29-2009
1990	05-18-1989	2011	[none]
1991	10-09-1990	2012	[none]
1992	05-22-1991	2013	[none]
1993	05-21-1992	2014	[none]
1994	04-01-1993	2015	[none]
1995	05-12-1994	2016	05-05-2015
1996	06-29-1995	2017	01-13-2017

Source: Legislative Information Service.

Table 2. Deeming Resolutions Pertaining to Those Fiscal Years for Which Congress Did Not Agree on a Budget Resolution

Legislative Vehicles and Dates of Adoption

Fiscal Year (Congress)	House	Senate
FY1999 (105th)	• H.Res. 477: a resolution also providing for the consideration of the FY1999 Military Construction Appropriations Act. Adopted 6-19-1998.	• S.Res. 209: a resolution solely for deeming purposes. Adopted 4-2-1998. • S.Res. 312: a resolution solely for deeming purposes. Adopted 10-21-1998.
FY2003 (107th)	• H.Res. 428: a resolution also providing for the consideration of a FY2002 supplemental appropriations act. Adopted 5-22-2002.	• The Senate did not adopt a deeming resolution.
FY2005 (108th)	• H.Res. 649: a resolution also providing for the consideration of the conference report on the FY2005 budget resolution. Adopted 5-19-2004.	• H.R. 4613: the Defense Appropriations Act for FY2005, Section 14007 (P.L. 108-287). Enacted 8-5-2004.
FY2007 (109th)	• H.Res. 818: a resolution also providing for the consideration of the FY2007 Department of Interior Appropriations Act. Adopted 5-18-2006.	• H.R. 4939: the Emergency Supplemental Appropriations Act for Defense, the Global War on Terror, and Hurricane Recovery for FY2006, Section 7035 (P.L. 109-234). Enacted 6-15-2006.
FY2011 (111th)	• H.Res. 1493: A resolution solely for deeming purposes (referred to as a budget enforcement resolution) was adopted as part of H.Res. 1500, a resolution also providing for consideration of a Senate amendment to an FY2010 Supplemental Appropriations Act. Adopted 7-1-2010.	• The Senate did not adopt a deeming resolution.
FY2012 (112th)	• H.Res. 287: a resolution also providing for providing for the consideration of the FY2012 Department of Homeland Security Appropriations Act. Adopted 6-1-2011.	• S. 365: The Budget Control Act of 2011, Section 106, requires the chair of the Senate Budget Committee to file enforceable budgetary levels for FY2012 (P.L. 112-25). Enacted 8-2-2011.
FY2013 (112th)	• H.Res. 614: a resolution also providing for the consideration of the Sportsmen's Heritage Act. Adopted 4-17-2012. • H.Res. 643: a resolution also providing for the consideration of the FY 2013 Commerce, Justice, Science Appropriations Act. Adopted 5-8-2012.	• S. 365: The Budget Control Act of 2011, Section 106, requires the chair of the Senate Budget Committee to file enforceable budgetary levels for FY2013 by April 15, 2012 (P.L. 112-25). Enacted 8-2-2011.

Deeming Resolutions: Budget Enforcement in the Absence of a Budget Resolution

Fiscal Year (Congress)	House	Senate
FY2014 (113th)	• H.Res. 243: a resolution also providing for consideration of the FY2014 Military Constructions and Veterans Affairs Appropriations Act and the FY2014 Homeland Security Appropriations act. Adopted 6-4-2013. • H.J.Res. 59: The Bipartisan Budget Act of 2013. Section 111, requires the chair of the House Budget Committee to file enforceable budgetary levels for FY2014 (P.L. 113-67). Enacted 12-26-2013.	• H.J.Res. 59: The Bipartisan Budget Act of 2013, Section 111, requires the chair of the Senate Budget Committee to file enforceable budgetary levels for FY2014 (P.L. 113-67). Enacted 12-26-2013.
FY2015 (113th)	• H.J.Res 59: The Bipartisan Budget Act of 2013, Section 115, requires the chair of the House Budget Committee to file enforceable budgetary levels for FY2015 if Congress has not agreed to a budget resolution by 4-15-2014 (P.L. 113-67). Enacted 12-26-2013.	• H.J.Res 59: The Bipartisan Budget Act of 2013, Section 115, requires the chair of the Senate Budget Committee to file enforceable budgetary levels for FY2015 if Congress has not agreed to a budget resolution by 4-15-2014 (P.L. 113-67). Enacted 12-26-2013.

Notes: The Bipartisan Budget Act of 2015, Section 102 (P.L. 114-74) included a provision directing the Senate Budget Committee chair to file in the *Congressional Record* levels that would then become enforceable in the Senate as if they had been included in a budget resolution for FY2017. The Senate Budget Committee chair was directed to file such levels after April 15, 2016, but not later than May 15, 2016. Senate Budget Committee Chairman Enzi filed such levels on April 18, 2016. This provision did not prohibit the Senate from considering and adopting a traditional budget resolution for FY2017.

In What Ways Have Deeming Resolutions Varied?

As described below, deeming resolutions have varied in several ways.

Variations in Legislative Vehicle

Congress initially used simple resolutions as the legislative vehicle for deeming resolutions (which is why they are referred to as resolutions). As shown in **Table 2**, however, deeming resolutions have also been included as provisions in lawmaking vehicles, such as appropriations bills.[13]

Questions sometimes arise regarding whether the use of an alternative legislative vehicle has any impact on the enforceability of the budgetary levels. Article I of the Constitution, however, gives each house of Congress broad authority to determine its rules of procedure. The House and the Senate may include rulemaking provisions, such as enforceable budgetary levels, in any type of legislative vehicle. In each case, the rulemaking provisions have equal standing and effect. Further, under this constitutional rulemaking principle, each house has the authority to take

---

[13] Variations in legislative vehicle affect when the budgetary levels will become enforceable. For example, budgetary levels included in a simple resolution may be enforceable as soon as the resolution is agreed to by the chamber. On the other hand, if such provisions were included in a lawmaking vehicle, such levels would not be enforceable until that measure was enacted. If, as described below, the deeming resolution requires certain budgetary levels to be filed by the Budget Committee chair, levels would not be enforceable until filed.

parliamentary action that waives its own rules in certain circumstances if it sees fit. This power is not compromised by the fact that the rulemaking provision may be established in statute.

Variations in Timing

As shown in **Figure 1**, timing of congressional action on deeming resolutions has varied, since deeming resolutions may be initiated any time Congress regards it as necessary. Chambers have often agreed to deeming resolutions several months after they have separately agreed to a budget resolution but have not come to agreement with each other. Also, chambers have agreed to a deeming resolution on the same day as agreeing to a budget resolution in situations when one chamber foresees difficulty resolving differences with the other chamber. For example, the Senate agreed to a budget resolution for FY1999 on April 2, 1998, and, anticipating an impasse with the House, agreed to a deeming resolution the same day. Similarly, the House passed a budget resolution for FY2007 on May 18, 2006, and agreed to a deeming resolution the same day. Further, deeming resolutions have been provided for far in advance of potential action on a budget resolution. For example, the Bipartisan Budget Act of 2015 (P.L. 114-74, enacted in November of 2015) included a provision directing the Senate Budget Committee chair to file in the *Congressional Record* levels that would then become enforceable in the Senate as if they had been included in a budget resolution for FY2017.

Often, a chamber initiates action on a deeming resolution so that it can subsequently begin consideration of appropriations measures. In the House deeming resolutions are often included in the same resolution providing for consideration of the first appropriations measure for the upcoming fiscal year.[14]

Just as employing a deeming resolution does not preclude Congress from subsequently agreeing to a budget resolution, it also does not preclude Congress from acting on another deeming resolution that either expands or replaces the first deeming resolution. For example, in FY1999 the Senate agreed to a deeming resolution in April, and in October it agreed to a further deeming resolution that amended the previous deeming resolution. Likewise, the House agreed to a deeming resolution for FY2014 in June but in December passed the Bipartisan Budget Act, which included a deeming resolution that superseded parts of the initial deeming resolution.

---

[14] For example, deeming resolutions were included in the resolutions providing for consideration of the first appropriations measure for FY1999, FY2007, and FY2012.

Figure 1. Timing of Agreement on Deeming Resolutions

Compared to Agreement on Budget Resolutions

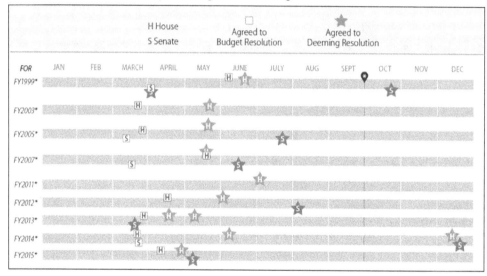

Source: Legislative Information Service.

Notes: Asterisks denote that the information provided references the upcoming fiscal year and not the calendar year.

Variations in Content

Deeming resolutions always include at least two things: (1) language setting forth or referencing specific budgetary levels (e.g., aggregate spending limits and/or committee spending allocations), and (2) language stipulating that such levels are to be enforceable as if they had been included in a budget resolution. Even so, significant variations exist in their content, as shown in **Table 3**.

Budget resolutions include budgetary levels in the form of explicit dollar amounts, and in some instances deeming resolutions have done the same. For example:

> Pending the adoption by the Congress of a concurrent resolution on the budget for FY1999, the following allocations contemplated by section 302(a) of the Congressional Budget Act of 1974 shall be considered as made to the Committee on Appropriations: (1) New discretionary budget authority: $531,961,000,000. (2) Discretionary outlays: $562,277,000,000.[15]

Some deeming resolutions, however, have not included the budgetary levels themselves but have incorporated them by reference, particularly in situations when that chamber has already passed a budget resolution but has not come to agreement with the other chamber. For example:

> Pending the adoption of a concurrent resolution on the budget for fiscal year 2003, the provisions of House Concurrent Resolution 353, as adopted by the House, shall have force and effect in the House as though Congress has adopted such concurrent resolution.[16]

---

[15] H.Res. 477, §2 (105th Congress).

[16] H.Res. 428, §2 (107th Congress).

In some cases, the deeming resolution has stated that the chairs of the House and Senate Budget Committees shall subsequently file in the *Congressional Record* levels that will then become enforceable as if they had been included in a budget resolution. The committee chairs are typically directed to file particular levels, such as those consistent with discretionary spending caps or those consistent with the baseline projections of the Congressional Budget Office. Such provisions have been used recently in both the Budget Control Act of 2011 and the Bipartisan Budget Act of 2013. For example:

> For the purpose of enforcing the Congressional Budget Act of 1974 for fiscal year 2014... the ... levels provided for in subsection (b) shall apply in the same manner as for a concurrent resolution on the budget for fiscal year 2014.... The Chairmen of the Committee on the Budget of the House of Representatives and the Senate shall each submit a statement for publication in the Congressional Record as soon as practicable after the date of enactment of this Act that includes ... committee allocations for fiscal year 2014 consistent with the discretionary spending limits set forth in this Act.[17]

As stated above, deeming resolutions will sometimes reference a budget resolution that has been previously adopted by that chamber and will deem that budget resolution to be enforceable. Alternatively, mechanisms may include or reference only certain levels normally included in a budget resolution. For example, in some cases deeming resolutions have included only committee allocations to the Appropriations Committee, while in other cases they have included allocations for all committees, as well as aggregate spending and revenue levels. While content has varied, deeming resolutions that have not referenced a previously passed budget resolution have typically included only levels to be enforced by points of order, such as aggregate spending and revenue levels as well as spending allocations for each committee. Deeming resolutions generally do not include *all* of the levels required to be in a budget resolution by the Budget Act. For example, the Budget Act requires that the budget resolution include the corresponding deficit level and public debt level under the enforceable budgetary framework. These have not typically been included in deeming resolutions. In addition, deeming resolutions have often included other matter, such as points of order.

---

[17] Section 111 of the Bipartisan Budget Act, also referred to as the Murray-Ryan agreement (Division A of P.L. 113-67).

Table 3. Provisions Included in Deeming Resolutions Pertaining to Those Fiscal Years for Which Congress Did Not Agree on a Budget Resolution

Fiscal Year (Congress)	Chamber	Deeming Resolution	Standard Provisions	Other Provisions
FY1999 (105th)	House	H.Res. 477	Provides committee spending allocation to the House Appropriations Committee.	—
	Senate	S.Res. 209	Provides committee spending allocation to the Senate Appropriations Committee.	—
		S.Res. 312	Provides aggregate spending levels, aggregate revenue levels, and Social Security spending and revenue levels. Directs the Senate Budget Committee chair to file committee spending allocations.	Strikes the text in S.Res. 209 (the deeming resolution previously agreed to). Allows the Senate Budget Committee chair to make revisions to levels in the resolution reflecting legislation enacted in the 105th Congress. Directs the Senate Budget Committee chair to make revisions to the congressional PAYGO. Includes effective date and expiration date.
FY2003 (107th)	House	H.Res. 428	References H.Con.Res. 353, the budget resolution for FY2003, as adopted by the House. Directs the House Budget Committee chair to file committee spending allocations.	Provides that accounts identified for advance appropriations shall be those referred to in H.Con.Res. 353 (to be filed by the House Budget Committee chair). Provides estimated surplus in reference to the Contingency Fund for Additional Surpluses included in H.Con.Res. 353 (to be filed by the House Budget Committee chair). Provides committee allocations for Medicare, as required in H.Con.Res. 353 (to be filed by the House Budget Committee chair).
	Senate	—	—	—

Fiscal Year (Congress)	Chamber	Deeming Resolution	Standard Provisions	Other Provisions
FY2005 (108th)	House	H.Res. 649	References the conference report for S.Con.Res. 95, the budget resolution for FY2005, as adopted by the House.	Notes that the deeming resolution shall not be construed to engage Rule XXVII (the former House rule known as the Gephardt rule that required the House clerk to engross and transmit public debt limit legislation to the Senate upon adoption of the budget resolution).
	Senate	H.R. 4613	Provides committee spending allocation to the Senate Appropriations Committee.	References certain adjustments and limits in S.Con.Res. 95 related to contingency procedures for surface transportation, discretionary spending limits in the Senate, supplemental appropriations for Iraq and related activities, and the extension of the emergency rule in the Senate. Revokes the budget resolution for FY2004. Includes definitions and effective date.
FY2007 (109th)	House	H.Res. 818	References H.Con.Res. 376, the budget resolution for FY2007, as adopted by the House.	Notes that the deeming resolution shall not be construed to engage the Gephardt rule.
	Senate	H.R. 4939	Provides committee spending allocation to the Senate Appropriations Committee.	References certain adjustments and limits in S.Con.Res. 83—the budget resolution for FY2007, as passed by the Senate—related to emergency legislation. Alters certain sections of the budget resolution for FY2006 related to Senate discretionary spending limits and the unfunded mandates point of order. Includes effective date.
FY2011 (111th)	House	H.Res. 1493	Provides committee spending allocation to the House Appropriations Committee.	Extends provisions of the FY2010 budget resolution. Alters provisions of the FY2010 budget resolution and includes new provisions to reflect policies enacted in the Statutory Pay-As-You-Go Act of 2010. Includes "sense of the House" provisions related to the economy, investment, and deficit reduction. Includes a deficit-neutral reserve fund related to the recommendations of the National Commission on Fiscal Responsibility and Reform. Notes that the deeming resolution shall not be construed to engage the Gephardt rule.

CRS-12

Deeming Resolutions: Budget Enforcement in the Absence of a Budget Resolution

Fiscal Year (Congress)	Chamber	Deeming Resolution	Standard Provisions	Other Provisions
	Senate	—	—	—
FY2012 (112th)	House	H.Res. 287	References H.Con.Res. 34, the budget resolution for FY2012, as adopted by the House. Provides committee spending allocations (in the committee report of H.Res. 287).	Directs the House Budget Committee chair to adjust allocations to accommodate enactment of certain legislation. Includes expiration.
	Senate	S. 365	Directs the Senate Budget Committee chair to file committee spending allocations, aggregate spending levels, aggregate revenue levels, and Social Security spending and revenue levels.	Directs the Senate Budget chair to make revisions to the congressional PAYGO scorecard. Includes expiration.
FY2013 (112th)	House	H.Res. 614	References H.Con.Res. 112, the budget resolution for FY2013 as adopted by the House, with modifications.	—
		H.Res. 643	Amends H.Res. 614 (the previously agreed-to deeming resolution) by inserting committee spending allocations as included in the committee report of the budget resolution.	—
	Senate	S. 365	Directs the Senate Budget Committee chair to file committee spending allocations, aggregate spending levels, aggregate revenue levels, and Social Security spending and revenue levels.	Directs the Senate Budget Committee chair to make revisions to the Senate PAYGO scorecard. Includes expiration.
FY2014 (113th)	House	H.Res. 243	References H.Con.Res. 25, the budget resolution for FY2014, as adopted by the House, with committee allocations as included in the committee report of the budget resolution.	—
		H.J.Res 59	Directs the House Budget Committee chair to file committee spending allocations, aggregate spending levels, and aggregate revenue levels.	States that H.Con.Res. 25, the budget resolution for FY2014 as passed by the House, shall be enforceable to the extent that its levels are not superseded by the levels filed by the House Budget Committee chair. Allows the House Budget Committee chair to reduce levels to reflect enactment of legislation reducing the deficit.

Fiscal Year (Congress)	Chamber	Deeming Resolution	Standard Provisions	Other Provisions
	Senate	H.J.Res 59	Directs the Senate Budget Committee chair to file committee spending allocations, aggregate spending levels, aggregate revenue levels, and Social Security spending and revenue levels.	Allows the Senate Budget Committee chair to reduce levels to reflect enactment of legislation reducing the deficit.
				Creates a point of order for advance appropriations.
				Directs the Senate Budget Committee chair to make revisions to the Senate PAYGO scorecard.
				References provisions from S.Con.Res. 13, the budget resolution for FY2010 as passed by the Senate, that shall remain in effect (related to budgetary treatment of certain discretionary administrative expenses, application and effect of changes in allocations and aggregates, and adjustments to reflect changes in concepts and definitions).
				Includes a deficit-neutral reserve fund to replace sequestration and incorporates by reference many reserve funds included in S.Con.Res. 8, the budget resolution for FY2014 as adopted by the Senate.
				Notes that certain provisions shall expire if a budget resolution for FY2015 is agreed to by the House and Senate.
FY2015 (113th)	House	H.J.Res 59	Directs the House Budget Committee chair to file committee spending allocations, aggregate spending levels, and aggregate revenue levels (if a budget resolution for FY2015 has not been agreed upon by April 15, 2014).	Allows the House Budget Committee chair to also file updated versions of certain provisions included in H.Con.Res. 25, the budget resolution for FY2014 (related to reserve funds, limits on advance appropriations, adjustments of discretionary spending levels, budgetary treatment of certain transactions, and a separate allocation for overseas contingency operations/global war on terrorism).
				Allows the House Budget Committee chair to reduce levels to reflect enactment of legislation reducing the deficit.
				Notes that if all levels have not been filed by the House Budget Committee chair by May 15, then on the next day of House session, the Budget Committee chair shall file a committee spending allocation for the House Appropriations Committee.
				Notes that certain provisions shall expire if a budget resolution for FY2015 is agreed to by the House and Senate.

Deeming Resolutions: Budget Enforcement in the Absence of a Budget Resolution

Fiscal Year (Congress)	Chamber	Deeming Resolution	Standard Provisions	Other Provisions
	Senate	H.J.Res 59	Directs the Senate Budget Committee chair to file committee spending allocations, aggregate spending levels, aggregate revenue levels, and Social Security spending and revenue levels (if a budget resolution for FY2015 has not been agreed upon by April 15, 2014).	Allows Senate Budget Committee chair to also file updated versions of a reserve fund to replace sequestration and those reserve funds incorporated by reference from S.Con.Res. 8, the budget resolution for FY2014 as adopted by the Senate. Notes that the levels filed will supersede levels filed for FY2014 (described above). Notes that certain provisions shall expire if a budget resolution for FY2015 is agreed to by the House and Senate.

Source: Legislative Information Service.

CRS-15

What Types of Budgetary Enforcement Exist Outside of the Budget Resolution?

In addition to the budget resolution, Congress employs other types of budget enforcement. Some of these enforcement mechanisms are procedural (which are enforced through points of order), and some are statutory (which are enforced through sequestration). In the absence of a budget resolution, these additional budget enforcement mechanisms remain intact. This means that even without a budget resolution, there are still prohibitions and restrictions on different types of budgetary legislation. For example, a limit on defense and non-defense discretionary spending currently exists in the form of annual discretionary spending caps and in addition can act as a guide to appropriators in crafting appropriations measures. In addition, limits on new direct spending and revenue legislation exist through points of order and statutory enforcement such as Senate PAYGO, House CUTGO, and Statutory PAYGO.

Budget Enforcement Through Points of Order

The House and Senate have many budget-related points of order that seek to restrict or prohibit consideration of different types of budgetary legislation. These points of order are found in various places such as the Budget Act, House and Senate standing rules, and past budget resolutions.

For example, for FY2017, Congress moved forward with appropriations in the absence of a budget resolution or deeming resolution. The House Appropriations Committee adopted "interim 302(b) sub-allocations" for some individual appropriations bills.[18] Such levels did not act as an enforceable cap on appropriations measures when they were considered on the floor. A separate order adopted by the House as a part of H.Res. 5 (114th Congress), however, prohibited floor amendments that would increase spending in a general appropriations bill, effectively creating a cap on individual appropriations bills when they were considered on the floor.[19]

In addition, in the Senate there exists a pay-as-you-go (PAYGO) rule that prohibits the consideration of direct spending or revenue legislation that is projected to increase the deficit.[20]

---

[18] These levels were made available on the House Appropriations Committee website. The most recent version was released July 14, 2016, and can be accessed at http://appropriations.house.gov/uploadedfiles/ 07.14.16_revised_suballocation_of_budget_allocations_for_fy_2017.pdf.

[19] Specifically, H.Res. 5, Section 3(d)(3), stated, "It shall not be in order to consider an amendment to a general appropriation bill proposing a net increase in budget authority in the bill (unless considered en bloc with another amendment or amendments proposing an equal or greater decrease in such budget authority pursuant to clause 2(f) of rule XXI)." This standing order, which was in effect as a separate order in the 112th, 113th, and 114th Congresses, was incorporated into House Rule XXI by H.Res. 5 (115th Congress). This provision prohibits amendments to general appropriations bills that would result in a net increase in the level of budget authority in the bill. This does not, however, prohibit amendments that would increase budget authority in the bill if the amendment also includes an equal or greater decrease in budget authority.

[20] In either of two time periods: (1) the period consisting of the current fiscal year, the budget year, and the four ensuing fiscal years following the budget year; and (2) the period consisting of the current year, the budget year, and the ensuing nine fiscal years following the budget year. This applies to the on-budget deficit, which excludes the off-budget entities (Social Security trust funds and the Postal Service fund). This rule may be waived by three-fifths of Senators chosen and sworn. This rule has been articulated in past budget resolutions dating back to the 104th Congress and has no expiration per S.Con.Res. 11 (114th Congress).

Another example is the House cut-as-you-go (CUTGO) rule that prohibits the consideration of direct spending legislation that is projected to increase the deficit.[21]

Numerous other points of order exist. A summary of many of these can be found in CRS Report 97-865, *Points of Order in the Congressional Budget Process*, by James V. Saturno.

Budget Enforcement Through Statutory Means

In addition to points of order, there are other types of budget enforcement mechanisms that employ statutory enforcement known as a sequester. A sequester provides for the automatic cancellation of previously enacted spending, making largely across-the-board reductions to non-exempt programs, activities, and accounts. A sequester is implemented through a sequestration order issued by the President as required by law.[22]

The purpose of a sequester is to enforce certain statutory budget requirements, such as enforcing statutory limits on discretionary spending or ensuring that new revenue and direct spending laws do not have the net effect of increasing the deficit. Generally, sequesters have been used as an enforcement mechanism that would either discourage Congress from enacting legislation violating a specific budgetary goal or encourage Congress to enact legislation that would fulfill a specific budgetary goal.

Sequestration is currently employed as the enforcement mechanism for three budgetary policies:

1. The Budget Control Act of 2011 (BCA; P.L. 112-25) established annual statutory limits on each defense discretionary and non-defense discretionary spending that are in effect through 2021. If legislation is enacted breaching either the defense or non-defense discretionary spending cap, then a sequester will occur, making cuts to non-exempt programs within the corresponding category to make up for the breach. In this situation, the sequester will either deter enactment of legislation violating the spending limits or—in the event that legislation is enacted violating these limits—automatically reduce discretionary spending to the limit specified in law.[23]

2. The BCA also created a Joint Select Committee on Deficit Reduction instructed to develop legislation to reduce the budget deficit by at least $1.5 trillion over the 10-year period FY2012-FY2021. The BCA stipulated that if a measure meeting specific requirements was not enacted by January 15, 2012, then a sequester would be triggered to enforce the budgetary goal established for the committee. In this situation the sequester was meant to either encourage agreement on deficit reduction legislation or, in the event that such agreement was not reached, automatically reduce spending so that an equivalent budgetary goal would be achieved. Because the agreement was not reached, this sequester is now in effect through 2024.[24]

---

[21] In either of two time periods: (1) the period consisting of the current fiscal year, the budget year, and the four ensuing fiscal years following the budget year; and (2) the period consisting of the current year, the budget year, and the ensuing nine fiscal years following the budget year (House rule XXI, clause 10).

[22] For more information on sequester, see CRS Report R42972, *Sequestration as a Budget Enforcement Process: Frequently Asked Questions*, by Megan S. Lynch.

[23] The BCA specified that the statutory limits may be adjusted for specific purposes, such as to provide for disaster relief and the global war on terrorism. For more information on discretionary spending caps, see CRS Report R44874, *The Budget Control Act: Frequently Asked Questions*, by Grant A. Driessen and Megan S. Lynch.

[24] While the committee was directed to report $1.5 trillion in savings, the BCA required the relevant sequester to (continued...)

3. Another enforcement mechanism was created by the Statutory Pay-As-You-Go Act of 2010 (P.L. 111-139). The budgetary goal of Statutory PAYGO is to ensure that new revenue and direct spending legislation enacted during a session of Congress does not have the net effect of increasing the deficit (or reducing a surplus) over either a 6- or 11-year period. The sequester enforces this requirement by either deterring enactment of such legislation or, in the event that legislation has such an effect, automatically reducing spending to achieve the required deficit neutrality.[25]

Author Contact Information

Megan S. Lynch
Specialist on Congress and the Legislative Process
mlynch@crs.loc.gov, 7-7853

Acknowledgments

This report draws on CRS Report RL31443, *The "Deeming Resolution": A Budget Enforcement Tool*, authored by former CRS Senior Specialist Robert Keith. Keith performed extensive analysis and recordkeeping, and his work contributed significantly to this and many other CRS products.

(...continued)

achieve a total savings of $1.2 trillion over a nine-year period, including $216 billion of assumed savings due to debt service costs. The remaining $984 billion of required savings was divided equally across each of the nine years, resulting in annual required spending reductions of approximately $109 billion, which is approximately $55 billion for each of defense and non-defense spending. Generally, the spending reductions are to be made equally from the categories of defense spending and non-defense spending. The reductions required in each of these categories are then divided proportionally between discretionary spending and mandatory spending.

[25] For more information on Statutory PAYGO, see CRS Report R41157, *The Statutory Pay-As-You-Go Act of 2010: Summary and Legislative History*, by Bill Heniff Jr.

Chapter Seven

Legislating in Congress: Federal Budget Process

Contributing Author

Bill Heniff Jr.

with updates by

Robert Keith and Megan Lynch

Analysis

§ 7.00 Introduction: Congress' "Power of the Purse"

Congress is distinguished from nearly every other legislature in the world by the control it exercises over fashioning the government's budgetary policies. This power, referred to as "the power of the purse," ensures Congress' primary role in setting revenue and borrowing policies for the federal government and in determining how these resources are spent.

The congressional power of the purse derives from several key provisions in the Constitution. (*See § 7.01, Congress' Constitutional "Power of the Purse."*) Article I, Section 8, Clause 1 declares in part that Congress shall have the power to raise (that is, "to lay and collect") revenues of various types, including taxes and duties, among other things. Section 8, Clause 2 declares that the power to borrow funds "on the credit of the United States" belongs to Congress. In addition to its powers regarding revenues and borrowing, Congress exerts control over the expenditure of funds. Article I, Section 9, Clause 7 declares in part that funds can be withdrawn from the Treasury only pursuant to laws that make appropriations.

Under the Constitution, revenue measures must originate in the House of Representatives. Beyond this requirement, however, the Constitution does not prescribe how the House and Senate should organize themselves, or the procedures they should use, to conduct budgeting. Over the years, however, both chambers have developed an extensive set of rules (some set forth in statute) and precedents that lay out complicated, multiple processes for making budgetary decisions. The House and Senate have also created an intricate committee system to support these processes. (*See § 7.02, Federal Budgeting Concepts and Terminology.*)

As American society has grown and become ever more complex, and as the role of the federal government in the national economy has steadily expanded, Congress also has increasingly shared power over budgetary matters with the president and the executive branch. It has refashioned the president's role in budgeting by requiring him to submit to Congress each year a budget for the entire federal government and giving him responsibilities for monitoring agencies' implementation of spending and revenue laws. Accordingly, the president also exercises considerable influence over key budget decisions.

§ 7.01

Congress' Constitutional "Power of the Purse"

Revenues and Borrowing
The Congress shall have the Power

[1] To lay and collect Taxes, Duties, Imposts, and Excises . . .

[2] To borrow Money on the credit of the United States . . .

(*Art. I, sec. 8.*)

Spending
No Money shall be drawn from the Treasury, but in Consequence of Appropriations made by Law . . .

(*Art. I, sec. 9, cl. 7.*)

§ 7.10 Key Budget Process Laws

Many different statutes lay the foundation for the modern budget process used by the federal government, but five laws are key: the Budget and Accounting Act of 1921, the Congressional Budget and Impoundment Control Act of 1974, the Balanced Budget and Emergency Deficit Control Act of 1985, the Statutory PAYGO Act of 2010, and the Budget Control Act of 2011. Each of the laws has been amended, some on numerous occasions.

Except for the 1921 act, these laws also contain provisions that set forth significant congressional budget procedures. The provisions dealing with congressional procedure were enacted as an exercise

§7.02

Federal Budgeting Concepts and Terminology

Federal budgeting involves a complex web of legislative and executive procedures, categories of budgetary legislation, and types of financial transactions. Some concepts and terms fundamental to understanding federal budgeting include those that follow.

Revenues

Income received by the federal government is referred to as *revenues* or *receipts.* (Congress tends to use the former term and the executive branch tends to use the latter.) Revenues are raised from several different sources. In recent decades, revenues have stemmed mainly from individual income taxes, social insurance taxes, corporate income taxes, and excise taxes. Revenues also are raised by tariffs, fees, fines, gifts and bequests, and other means.

A *tax expenditure* is revenue forgone due to an exemption, deduction, or other exception to an underlying tax law. A tax expenditure represents a means of pursuing federal policy that is an alternative to a spending program. For example, home ownership is encouraged by allowing deductions from individual income taxes for mortgage interest paid during the year; the same goal could be promoted on the spending side of the budget by issuing grants or loans for home ownership to individuals.

Spending

When Congress enacts legislation providing legal authority for an agency to spend money, it provides *budget authority*. The most well-known type of legislation that provides budget authority is an annual appropriations act. Budget authority authorizes agencies to enter into *obligations*. An obligation is any type of action that creates a financial liability on the part of the federal government, such as entering into a contract, submitting a purchase order for goods, or employing personnel. When the obligation is liquidated, an outlay ensues. *Outlays* represent the actual payment of obligations, and usually take the form of electronic fund transfers, the issuance of checks, or the disbursement of cash. The stages of spending involving the enactment of budget authority and the incurring of obligations and outlays are referred to informally as the "spending pipeline."

The rate at which funds are spent (that is, converted from budget authority into outlays) is known as the *spendout rate*. Spendout rates vary from account to account, and from program to program within accounts. An account that involves personnel-intensive activities may have a high spendout rate, obligating and expending 90 percent or more of its budget authority during the fiscal year. Conversely, an account that involves the procurement of major weapons systems may have a low spendout rate, with only 5 or 10 percent of its budget authority being disbursed, or converted to outlays, in the first year.

Congress exercises direct control over the enactment of budget authority, but its influence over obligations—and, to a greater degree, outlays—is indirect. Ultimately, federal agencies determine the outlay levels for a particular year through thousands of discrete actions.

Some income to the federal government is not treated as revenue. Rather, it is offset against spending. *Offsetting collections and receipts* arise from fees collected by the federal government for its business-type operations, from the sale of assets, and from other sources. Most such receipts are offsets against the outlays of the agencies that collect the money, but in the case of offshore oil leases and certain other activities, the revenues are deducted from the total outlays of the federal government.

Surplus and Deficit

The relationship between spending and revenues is reflected in the surplus or deficit figure. A *surplus* is an excess of revenues over outlays, while a *deficit* is an excess of outlays over revenues. Congress controls the enactment of legislation providing budget authority and raising revenues, but not the occurrence of outlays. Because of this, Congress' efforts to control the level of the surplus or the deficit are less effective over the short run compared to the long run.

Baseline Budgeting

Congress and the president employ baseline budgeting as a tool to analyze the context in which budget policy choices are made and to assess the impact of particular proposals. In the simplest terms, a *baseline* is a set of projections of future spending and revenues, and the resulting surplus or deficit, based on assumptions about the state of the economy and the continuation of current policies without change. Overall revenue and spending levels usually increase from year to year under the baseline because of demographic trends, workload changes, and other factors. Following the late-2000s recession, however, baseline projections showed declining revenues due to the economic recession.

The Office of Management and Budget develops a budget baseline, referred to as the *current services estimates*, to support the president's budget, while the Congressional Budget Office develops its own baseline, referred to as *baseline budget projections,* to aid the congressional budget process. Although, for the most part, the two agencies share a common approach to constructing budget baselines, differences in projected economic growth and estimates for particular accounts and programs are inevitable. Sometimes the differences may be significant enough to complicate the process of resolving policy differences.

The national economy can exert a significant influence on the federal budget. If projections about economic growth, unemployment levels, inflation, and other economic factors prove to be significantly inaccurate, projected budgetary levels may change by billions of dollars during the course of a year. For this reason, the economic assumptions that underlie the budget baseline are crucially important. Congress and the president usually require that economic assumptions be revised only once or twice a year, to avoid complicating the decisionmaking process.

Statutory Limit on the Debt

When the federal government needs to borrow funds, it issues debt to the public. In addition, the federal government is compelled to incur debt because of requirements that trust fund surpluses be invested in federal securities. As a consequence, the federal government owes debt to the public and to itself. As a general matter, the amount of money that the federal government is able to borrow is constrained by a limit in statute. As long as the federal government incurs annual deficits and trust funds incur annual surpluses, Congress and the president from time to time must enact legislation to raise the statutory limit on the debt.

Federal Funds and Trust Funds

The budget consists of two main groups of funds: *federal funds* and *trust funds*. Federal funds—which comprise mainly the general fund—largely derive from the general exercise of the taxing power and general borrowing. For the most part, they are not earmarked by law to any specific program or agency. One component of federal funds, called *special funds*, is earmarked according to source and purpose. The use of federal funds is determined largely by annual appropriations acts.

Trust funds are established, under the terms of statutes that designate them as trust funds, to account for funds earmarked by specific sources and purposes. The Social Security trust funds (the Old-Age and Survivors Insurance Fund and the Disability Insurance Fund) are the largest of the trust funds; revenues are collected under a Social Security payroll tax and are used to pay for Social Security benefits and related purposes. The use of trust funds is controlled primarily by entitlement laws and other substantive legislation.

The total budget includes both the federal funds and the trust funds. The merging together of federal funds and trust funds into a single budget sometimes is referred to as the "unified budget approach."

Continued on page 7-6

§ 7.02 (continued)

On-Budget and Off-Budget Entities

On-budget entities are federal agencies and programs that are fully reflected in the totals of the president's budget and the congressional budget resolution. *Off-budget entities*, on the other hand, specifically are excluded by law from these totals. The revenues and spending of the Social Security trust funds, as well as the financial transactions of the Postal Service Fund, are at present the only off-budget entities. These transactions are shown separately in the budget. Thus, the budget reports two deficit or surplus amounts— one excluding the Social Security trust funds and the Postal Service Fund and the other including these entities.

Further, off-budget entities are excluded from the budget enforcement procedures applicable to federal programs generally. Congress has established special procedures for the consideration of measures affecting Social Security revenues and spending.

of Congress' *rule-making authority*, and effectively serve as rules of the House and Senate. As such, either chamber may modify the provisions that affect its operations without the concurrence of the other chamber and without the enactment of a law.

Budget and Accounting Act of 1921

The Budget and Accounting Act of 1921 (*P.L. 13, 67th Congress; 42 Stat. 20–27*) required for the first time that the president submit to Congress each year a *budget* for the entire federal government. The president is free to submit the budget in the form and detail he deems appropriate, but certain information is required. In addition, the estimates of the legislative and judicial branches must be incorporated in his budget, as submitted by those branches, without change. (*See § 7.40, Presidential Budget Process.*)

The 1921 Budget and Accounting Act also established the Bureau of the Budget, now called the Office of Management and Budget (OMB) and headed by a director subject to Senate confirmation, to assist the president in formulating the budget, in presenting it to Congress, and in monitoring the execution of the enacted budget by agencies. In addition, the 1921 act established the General Accounting Office, later renamed the Government Accountability Office, a congressional agency, headed by the *comptroller general*, to audit and evaluate federal programs and perform other budgetary duties. (*See § 4.130, Legislative-Branch Support Agencies.*)

Congressional Budget and Impoundment Control Act of 1974

The 1974 Congressional Budget and Impoundment Control Act (*P.L. 93-344; 88 Stat. 297–339*) requires the House and Senate each year to adopt a *concurrent resolution on the budget*, which serves as a guide for the subsequent consideration of spending, revenue, and debt-limit legislation. (*See § 7.50, Congressional Budget Process.*) The 1974 act created the House and Senate Budget Committees to develop the budget resolution and monitor compliance with its policies, and the Congressional Budget Office to serve as an independent, nonpartisan agency to provide budgetary information and analysis for Congress. New procedures were established for congressional review of *impoundments* by the president; the comptroller general was given an oversight role in this process. (*See § 7.150, Impoundment: Deferrals and Rescissions.*)

§7.11

Budget Enforcement Act Procedures:
1990–2002

Between 1990 and 2002, Congress and the president were constrained by *statutory* limits on discretionary spending and a pay-as-you-go (PAYGO) requirement on new direct spending and revenue legislation established by the Budget Enforcement Act of 1990 and extended by other laws. These mechanisms supplemented the enforcement procedures associated with the annual budget resolution under the 1974 Congressional Budget Act. However, while the budget resolution is enforced by points of order when legislation is considered on the floor of each chamber, the discretionary-spending limits and PAYGO requirement were enforced by a sequestration process after legislative action for a session of Congress ended. Under the sequestration process, if legislative action was determined to violate the budget constraints, the president was required to issue a sequestration order canceling budgetary resources, on a largely across-the-board basis, in non-exempt programs in the category in which the violation occurred.

Initially, these budget enforcement controls applied to FY1991–1995. In 1993, they were modified and extended through FY1998. Finally, the controls were extended again in 1997 to apply to legislation enacted through FY2002 (and, in the case of PAYGO, to the effects of such legislation through FY2006). In each case, the controls were designed to enforce multiyear budget agreements between Congress and the president. Without any legislative action by Congress and the president to extend them, the discretionary spending limits expired on September 30, 2002 (the end of FY2002), and PAYGO effectively was terminated in December of that year by the enactment of P.L. 107-312. (*See § 7.50, Congressional Budget Process, Points of Order.*)

Beginning in 2002, some members of Congress, as well as President George W. Bush, proposed restoring and modifying these budget enforcement procedures. In 2010, a statutory PAYGO process was reinstituted based largely on a proposal submitted by President Obama in the previous year (*see § 7.12, Statutory PAYGO Act of 2010*). Likewise, Statutory limits on discretionary spending for FY2012–2021 were imposed by the Budget Control Act of 2011.

Balanced Budget and Emergency Deficit Control Act of 1985

To strengthen control over spending and *deficit* levels, and to promote more efficient legislative action on budgetary issues, Congress and the president enacted the Balanced Budget and Emergency Deficit Control Act of 1985 (*P.L. 99-177, title II; 99 Stat. 1038–1101*). At the time, the measure was commonly known as the Gramm-Rudman-Hollings Act, after its three primary sponsors in the Senate (then-Senators Phil Gramm, R-TX, Warren Rudman, R-NH, and Ernest Hollings, D-SC).

The 1985 Balanced Budget Act sought to drive the deficit downward, from nearly $200 billion in fiscal year (FY) 1986 to zero in FY1991. *Sequestration*, a process involving largely automatic across-the-board spending cuts made toward the beginning of a fiscal year, was established as the means of enforcing deficit targets. The sequestration process was designed to trigger automatically if the deficit exceeded prescribed levels, as determined by a report issued by the comptroller general.

The 1985 act was revised in 1987 to meet a constitutional challenge and to modify the timetable for achieving a balanced budget (*P.L. 100-119, 101 Stat. 754*). The Supreme Court, in *Bowsher v. Synar*, 478 U.S. 714 (1986), ruled that the comptroller general, as a legislative-branch official, could not be involved in the execution of laws. Accordingly, the authority to trigger a sequester (based upon conditions carefully set forth in law) was placed in the hands of the OMB director. Also, the target for bringing the budget into balance was shifted to FY1993.

The Budget Enforcement Act of 1990 (*P.L. 101-508, title XIII; 104 Stat. 1388–628*) amended the 1985 Act, fundamentally revising the process. The deficit targets effectively were replaced by two new mechanisms: statutory limits on *discretionary spending* and a *pay-as-you-go* (PAYGO) requirement aimed at keeping the projected effect of *revenue* and *direct-spending* legislation enacted during a session deficit-neutral. Sequestration was retained as the means of enforcing the new mechanisms. Congress and the president enacted several measures after 1990 that extended the discretionary-spending limits and the PAYGO requirement. (*See § 7.30, Budget Enforcement Framework.*) The most recent of these extensions, the Budget Enforcement Act of 1997 (*P.L. 105-33, title X; 111 Stat. 677–712*), extended these budget control mechanisms through 2002. At that time, they were allowed to expire or effectively were terminated.

Statutory PAYGO Act of 2010

In 2009, President Barack Obama proposed that a statutory pay-as-you-go (PAYGO) process be reinstituted, but in significantly modified form compared to the statutory PAYGO process that had existed earlier and was terminated in 2002. The president's proposal, as modified by the House and Senate, was enacted into law on February 12, 2010, as the Statutory Pay-As-You-Go Act of 2010 (*P.L. 111-139, title I, 124 Stat. 8-29*). The goal of the act is to encourage the enactment of revenue and direct spending legislation in a deficit-neutral manner.

Under the new process, the budgetary effects of revenue and direct spending provisions enacted into law, including both costs and savings, are recorded by the Office of Management and Budget (OMB) on two PAYGO scorecards covering rolling five-year and ten-year periods. These effects may be determined by statements inserted into the *Congressional Record* by the chairmen of the House and Senate Budget Committees and referenced in the measures. As a general matter, the statements are expected to reflect cost estimates prepared by the Congressional Budget Office. If this procedure is not followed for a PAYGO measure, then the budgetary effects of the measure are determined by OMB. It should be noted that legislation has sometimes included a provision stating that the legislation's budgetary effects should not be recorded on the PAYGO scorecards.

Shortly after a congressional session ends, OMB finalizes the two PAYGO scorecards and determines whether a violation of the PAYGO requirement has occurred (if a debit has been recorded for the budget year on either scorecard). If so, the president issues a sequestration order that implements largely across-the-board cuts in nonexempt direct spending programs sufficient to remedy the violation by eliminating the debit. Many direct spending programs and activities are exempt from sequestration. If no PAYGO violation is found, no further action occurs and the process is repeated during the next session.

The new statutory PAYGO process was created on a permanent basis; there are no expiration dates in the act.

Budget Control Act of 2011

A key issue confronting President Barack Obama and Congress toward the beginning of 2011 was the need to raise the statutory limit on the public debt by a significant amount to accommodate the persistent, high deficits projected by the Office of Management and Budget (OMB) and the Congressional Budget Office (CBO). The president wanted Congress to raise the debt limit by more than $2 trillion, which was the amount judged necessary to last beyond the November 2012 elections.

Members of both parties in the House and Senate were concerned that the public would not accept such an increase, given that the debt limit already stood at the record level of $14.3 trillion, without a strengthened commitment also being made to control spending and curb the deficit.

The Simpson-Bowles Commission (officially known as the National Commission on Fiscal Responsibility and Reform) and various other groups, such as the "Gang of Six" in the Senate, made recommendations to reduce the deficit over the coming decade by as much as $4 trillion. In an effort to reach a "grand bargain" on the federal budget, in which the deficit would be reduced by amounts comparable to what others had proposed, President Obama and Speaker of the House John Boehner carried out negotiations but could not conclude such a deal.

With Treasury Secretary Timothy Geithner issuing dire warnings about economic catastrophe if the debt limit was not raised in a timely way, Standard and Poor's downgrading the federal government's credit rating, turbulence in the stock market, and other factors adding to the urgency of the situation, the president and Congress finally reached a scaled-back agreement. The president signed the compromise measure, the Budget Control Act of 2011, into law on August 2, 2011, as P.L. 112-25 (*125 Stat. 240-267*).

The BCA contains several elements related to the federal budget, some of which are no longer in effect. There are five primary elements:

1. An authorization to the executive branch to increase the debt limit in three installments, subject to disapproval by Congress. (The authorization was temporary and is no longer in effect.)

2. A one-time requirement for Congress to vote on a Constitutional amendment to require a balanced budget. The House and Senate each satisfied the one-time requirement. The Senate rejected two balanced budget amendments, while the House failed to achieve the necessary two-thirds vote needed for passage.

3. The establishment of limits on discretionary spending (which are currently separate limits on defense discretionary spending and nondefense discretionary spending). These discretionary spending limits are enforced by sequestration (automatic, across-the-board reductions) in effect through FY2021. Under this mechanism, sequestration is intended to deter enactment of legislation violating the spending limits or, in the event that legislation is enacted violating these limits, to automatically reduce discretionary spending to the limits specified in law.

4. The establishment of the Joint Select Committee on Deficit Reduction (commonly referred to as "the Joint Committee" or "the super committee"), which was directed to develop a proposal that would reduce the deficit by at least $1.5 trillion over FY2012 to FY2021.

5. The establishment of an automatic process to reduce spending, beginning in 2013, in the event that Congress and the President did not enact a bill reported by the Joint Committee reducing the deficit by at least $1.2 trillion. (Such a bill was not enacted.) This automatic process requires annual downward adjustments of the discretionary spending limits (mentioned above), as well as a sequester (automatic, across-the-board reduction) of nonexempt mandatory spending programs. In this case, sequestration was included to encourage the Joint

Committee to agree on deficit reduction legislation or, in the event that such agreement was not reached, to automatically reduce spending so that an equivalent budgetary goal would be achieved. (*See § 16, Budget Control Act: Frequently Asked Questions.*)

§ 7.20 The Budget Cycle

Federal budgeting is a cyclical activity that begins with the formulation of the president's annual budget and concludes with the audit and review of expenditures. The process spreads over a multiyear period. The first stage is the formulation of the president's budget and its presentation to Congress. The next stage is congressional action on the budget resolution and subsequent spending, revenue, and debt-limit legislation. The third stage is implementation of the budget by executive agencies. The final stage is *audit* and *review*. While the basic steps continue from year to year, particular procedures often vary in accord with the style of the president, the economic and political considerations under which the budget is prepared and implemented, and other factors.

Budget decisions are made on the basis of the *fiscal year*. Originally, the fiscal year used by the federal government coincided with the calendar year. In the 1840s, the fiscal year was changed to a July 1 through June 30 cycle. Finally, the 1974 Congressional Budget Act pushed back the start of the fiscal year by three months, to October 1, to give Congress more time to finish legislative action during a session. Under current procedures, for example, fiscal year 2018 began on October 1, 2017, and ends September 30, 2018. During the 2017 session, Congress considered regular appropriations and other budgetary legislation for fiscal year 2018, as well as supplemental appropriations for fiscal year 2017.

The activities related to a single fiscal year usually stretch over a period of at least two-and-a-half calendar years. As the budget is being considered, federal agencies must deal with three different fiscal years at the same time: implementing the budget for the current fiscal year; seeking funds from Congress for the next fiscal year; and planning for the fiscal year after that.

§ 7.30 Budget Enforcement Framework

Congress considers budgetary legislation within the framework of budget enforcement procedures established under the 1974 Congressional Budget Act, which are intended generally to uphold the policies underlying the annual budget resolution. Enforcement relies principally on the reconciliation process and, while legislation is under consideration, on points of order to prevent the passage of legislation that would violate established policies (both are discussed in more detail later in this chapter). The House and Senate Budget Committees have primary responsibility for enforcement.

In addition to provisions in the 1974 act, the House and Senate also incorporate enforcement provisions into annual budget resolutions and their standing rules. Internal PAYGO procedures affecting the consideration of direct spending and revenue legislation, for example, were established by the Senate in 1993 as a provision in an annual budget resolution (and modified by subsequent budget resolutions).

The availability of information is crucial to the effective operation of enforcement procedures. The Budget Committees rely on *cost estimates* on legislation prepared by the Congressional Budget Office (and the Joint Committee on Taxation in the case of revenue measures) and integrates them into a *scorekeeping system*, which shows the impact of budgetary legislation compared to budget resolution levels.

As indicated previously, congressional procedures for budget enforcement may be linked to, or reinforced by, statutory procedures that involve the president and the OMB director. The most recent example in this regard is the Budget Control Act of 2011 (*discussed in § 7.10*).

§ 7.40 Presidential Budget Process

The president's budget, officially referred to as the *Budget of the United States Government*, is required by law to be submitted to Congress early in the legislative session, no later than the first Monday in February. The budget consists of estimates of spending, revenues, borrowing, and debt; policy and legislative recommendations; detailed estimates of the financial operations of federal agencies and programs; data on the actual and projected performance of the economy; and other information supporting the president's recommendations.

Before the deadline for submission of the budget was changed in 1990, presidents usually had to submit their budgets in January. In years in which a new president was inaugurated (which occurs on January 20), the outgoing president usually submitted a budget before the inauguration. Later in the session, the new president submitted revisions to this budget that reflected his priorities and initiatives. In the transition years since 1990, however, the incoming president rather than the outgoing president has submitted the budget.

The president's budget is only a request to Congress; Congress is not required to adopt or even consider the president's recommendations. Nevertheless, the power to formulate and submit a budget is a vital tool in the president's direction of the executive branch and of national policy. The president's proposals often influence congressional revenue and spending decisions, though the extent of the influence varies from year to year and depends more on political and fiscal conditions than on the legal status of the budget.

The Constitution does not provide for a budget, nor does it require the president to make recommendations concerning the revenues and spending of the federal government. Until 1921, the federal government operated without a comprehensive presidential budget process. As stated previously, the Budget and Accounting Act of 1921 provided for an executive budget process, requiring the president to prepare and submit a budget to Congress each year (beginning with FY1923). Although it has been amended many times, this statute provides the legal basis for the presidential budget, prescribes much of its content, and defines the roles of the president and the agencies in the process.

Formulation and Content of the President's Budget

Preparation of the president's budget typically begins in the spring each year, about nine months before the budget is submitted to Congress, about seventeen months before the start of the fiscal year to which it pertains, and about twenty-nine months before the close of that fiscal year. (*See § 7.41, Executive Budget Process Timetable.*) The early stages of budget preparation occur in federal agencies. When they begin work on the budget for a fiscal year, agencies already are implementing the budget for the fiscal year in progress and awaiting final appropriations actions and other legislative decisions for the fiscal year after that. The long lead times and the fact that appropriations have not yet been made for the next year mean that the budget is prepared with a great deal of uncertainty about economic conditions, presidential policies, and congressional actions.

As agencies formulate their budgets, they maintain continuing contact with the Office of Manage-

§7.41

Executive Budget Process Timetable

Calendar Year Prior to the Year in Which Fiscal Year Begins

Date	Activities
Spring	Agencies begin the formulation of budget requests, under guidance from OMB, for the budget that will begin October 1 of the following year.
Spring and Summer	OMB and executive branch agencies discuss budget issues and options.
September	Agencies submit budget requests to OMB.
October–November	OMB conducts its fall review, analyzing agency proposals and briefing the president and senior advisors.
November–December	OMB makes decisions on agencies' requests, referred to as the "passback." Agencies may appeal these decisions to the OMB director and to the president.

Calendar Year in Which Fiscal Year Begins

Date	Activities
By first Monday in February	President submits budget to Congress.
February–September	Congressional phase. Agencies interact with Congress, justifying and explaining president's budget.
By July 15	President submits mid-session review to Congress.
October 1	Fiscal year begins.
October–September (the fiscal year)	OMB apportions enacted funds to agencies. Agencies execute the enacted budget, incurring obligations, and the Treasury makes payments to liquidate obligations, resulting in outlays.

ment and Budget (OMB) budget examiners assigned to them. These contacts provide agencies with guidance in preparing their budgets and also enable them to alert OMB to any needs or problems that may loom ahead. (*See § 7.42, Office of Management and Budget Publications for Agencies.*) Agency requests are submitted to OMB in September, and are reviewed by OMB staff in consultation with the president and his senior advisors during September–October. OMB informs agencies of approved budget levels in the "passback"; agencies may appeal these results to OMB or the president. The 1921 Budget and Accounting Act bars agencies from submitting their budget requests directly to Congress. Moreover, OMB regulations provide for confidentiality in all budget requests and recommendations before the transmittal of the president's budget to Congress. However, it is not uncommon for budget recommendations for some programs to become public while the budget is still being formulated.

The format and content of the budget are partly determined by law, but the 1921 act authorizes the president to set forth the budget "in such form and detail" as he may determine. Over the years, there has been an increase in the types of information and explanatory material presented in the budget documents.

In most years, the budget is submitted as a multivolume set consisting of a main document set-

§7.42

Office of Management and Budget Publications for Agencies

The Office of Management and Budget (OMB) coordinates the preparation of the president's budget, and its submission to Congress, and oversees implementation of the spending laws passed by Congress. The following types of publications contain instructions and guidelines to federal agencies regarding budget-related activities:

- **Circulars**, expected to have a continuing effect of generally two years or more. OMB Circular A-11, updated annually, instructs agencies how to prepare their budget submissions.

- **Bulletins**, containing guidance of a more transitory nature that would normally expire after one or two years. Bulletins often address how apportionment is to occur under a continuing resolution.

- **Regulations** and **Paperwork**, daily reports that list regulations and paperwork under OMB review.

- **Financial Management** policies and **Grants Management** circulars and related documents.

- **Federal Register** submissions, including copies of proposed and final rules.

For information on OMB policies and publications, check the OMB web site (*<www.whitehouse.gov/omb>*) and the Federal Register, at GPO's Federal Digital System, at *<http://fdsys.gov>*.

ting forth the president's message to Congress and an analysis and justification of his major proposals (the *Budget*). Supplementary documents contain account and program-level details, historical information, and special budgetary analyses, among other things. (*See § 7.43, Volumes Containing and Explaining the President's Annual Budget.*)

During the congressional phase of the federal budget process, the *Appendix* volume in particular is a useful source of detailed financial information on individual programs and *appropriations accounts*. For each annually appropriated account, it provides: (1) the text of the current appropriation and proposed changes; (2) a program and financing schedule; (3) a narrative statement of programs and performance; (4) an object classification schedule; and (5) an employment summary. Among other financial information, the program and financing schedule shows obligations by programs (distinguishing between operating expenses and capital investments, where appropriate), budgetary resources available for obligation, and sources of new budget authority for each of the previous, current, and upcoming fiscal years. (*See § 7.44, Program and Financing Schedule in President's Budget Appendix.*) New budget authority available to an agency for obligation may come from several sources, not just discretionary appropriations. Other typical sources include *mandatory appropriations* and *offsetting collections*.

Much of the budget is an estimate of requirements under existing law rather than a request for congressional action. (More than half the budget authority in the budget becomes available without congressional action.)

The president is required to submit a budget update—reflecting changed economic conditions, congressional actions, and other factors—referred to as the *Mid-session Review*, by July 15 each year. The president may revise his recommendations anytime during the year.

§ 7.43

Volumes Containing and Explaining the President's Annual Budget

The principal volumes currently part of the president's annual budget submission include the following:

- **Budget** (officially the *Budget of the United States Government*)—includes the president's budget message, presentations on the president's major budgetary initiatives organized by department and major agencies (or, in some years, by budget function), discussions of management initiatives and performance data, and summary tables.

- **Appendix**—sets forth detailed information for accounts within each department and agency, including funding levels, program descriptions, proposed appropriations language, and object classification and employment data.

- **Analytical Perspectives**—contains analyses and information on specific aspects of the budget or budget-related areas, such as budget and performance integration, economic assumptions, and current services estimates; crosscutting programs, such as research and development, federal investment, and aid to state and local governments; and budget process reform proposals.

- **Historical Tables**—provides data, covering an extended time period, on receipts, budget authority, outlays, deficits and surpluses, federal debt, and other matters.

Within a few days of the submission of the budget, the president also transmits an annual ***Economic Report of the President*** to Congress, which includes the report of the Council of Economic Advisers.

The president is required by law to update his submissions, and he does this in a far briefer, more summary fashion in his ***Mid-session Review***, which is due by July 15.

Online access to the president's budget documents is available in several places, including the Office of Management and Budget web site, *<www.whitehouse.gov/omb>*, and GPO's Federal Digital System, at *<http://fdsys.gov>*, then under "Collections" select "Budget of the United States Government." Also see *<CDDocs.com>*.

Executive Interaction with Congress

OMB officials and other presidential advisors appear before congressional committees to discuss overall policy and economic issues, but they generally leave formal discussions of specific programs to the affected agencies. Agencies thus bear the principal responsibility for defending the president's program recommendations at congressional hearings and in other interactions and communications with Congress.

Agencies are supposed to justify the president's recommendations, not their own. OMB maintains an elaborate legislative clearance process to ensure that agency *budget justifications*, testimony, and other submissions are consistent with presidential policy. In recent years, agencies have been required to post their budget justifications on the agency web site shortly after the president's budget has been submitted. The materials typically run to hundreds or even thousands of pages and provide a wealth of details beyond what is provided in the Appendix to the president's budget.

One tool used by the president to signal his position on legislation in order to influence congressional action is a *Statement of Administration Policy* (SAP). These statements are issued at several

§7.44

Program and Financing Schedule in President's Budget Appendix

❶ Each account is identified by an 11-digit code. The first two digits indicate the agency; the next four digits are the account numbers; the seventh digit is the type of request (regular or supplemental); the eighth digit is the type of fund; and the last three digits specify the budget function. (*See § 7.54; the category 999 indicates that an account involves more than one function.*)

❷ The schedule covers three fiscal years: the past year (2016); the current year (2017); and the upcoming year, also referred to as the budget year (2018). The last column contains the president's most recent request request.

❸ Agency obligations are classified by program activity and if applicable, by operating and capital investment.

❹ New budget authority may be derived from several sources, including discretionary appropriations and (not shown here) mandatory appropriations and offsetting collections.

❺ Outlays may be derived from several sources as well. In this example, outlays for the Salaries and Expenses account of the Federal Bureau of Investigation result from new discretionary authority and balances from previous years.

Federal Bureau of Investigation
Salaries and Expenses
Program and Financing
(in millions of dollars)

	2016 actual	2017 est.	2018 est.
❶ Identification code 15-0200-0-1-999			
❸ Obligations by program activity:			
Intelligence	1,492	1,343	1,386
Counterterrorism/Counterintelligence	3,141	2,984	3,098
Criminal Enterprises and Federal Crimes	2,725	2,599	2,683
Criminal Justice Services	250	115	...
Direct program activities, subtotal	7,608	7,041	7,167
Intelligence	248	274	273
Counterterrorism/Counterintelligence	407	452	446
Criminal Enterprises and Federal Crimes	293	329	325
Criminal Justice Services	236	297	317
Subtotal	1,184	1,352	1,361
Total	8,792	8393	8,528
❹ Budget authority:			
Appropriations, discretionary:			
Appropriation	8,490	8,474	8,723
Appropriations transferred from other accounts	2	...	...
Unobligated balance of appropriations permanently reduced	−81	−81	195
Appropriation, discretionary (total)	8,411	8,393	8,528
❺ Outlays, gross:			
Outlays from new discretionary authority	7,295	7,582	8,033
Outlays from discretionary balances	2,167	2,087	1,824
Outlays, gross (total)	9,462	9,669	9,857

different stages of legislative activity and are maintained on the OMB web site. In a SAP, the president may indicate his concurrence with congressional action on a measure, identify provisions in the measure with which he disagrees, and even signal his intent to veto the measure if it is not adjusted according to his wishes. At the conclusion of the legislative process, presidents sometimes issue *signing statements* on legislation that is being signed into law, often using a statement to register objections to particular provisions in the law.

§ 7.50 Congressional Budget Process

The Congressional Budget and Impoundment Control Act of 1974 established the congressional budget process as the means by which Congress coordinates the various budget-related actions taken by it during the course of the year, such as the consideration of appropriations and revenue measures. The process is structured around an *annual concurrent resolution on the budget* (H. Con. Res. ___ or S. Con. Res. ___) that sets aggregate budget policies and functional spending priorities for at least the next five fiscal years. (The budget resolution and appropriations processes described in the following sections take place each year.)

Because a concurrent resolution is not a bill or joint resolution, it is not submitted to the president to be signed or vetoed. The budget resolution cannot have statutory effect; no money can be raised or spent pursuant to it. However, as a concurrent resolution, it requires House and Senate agreement to the same text to have maximum effect or utility to Congress. The budget resolution was designed to establish the framework within which Congress considers separate revenue, spending, and other budget-related legislation in a year. Revenue and spending amounts set in the budget resolution (and accompanying joint explanatory statement) establish the basis for the enforcement of congressional budget policies through points of order. The budget resolution also initiates the reconciliation process for conforming existing revenue and spending laws to congressional budget policies. (*For other explanations of the congressional budget process and other budget information, see the Senate Budget Committee's web site at <www.budget.senate.gov>, and the House Budget Committee's web site at <www.budget.house.gov>.*)

Formulation and Content of the Budget Resolution

The congressional budget process begins upon the presentation of the president's budget in January or February. (*See § 7.51, Congressional Budget Process Timetable; and § 7.53, Congressional Budget Process Flowchart.*) The timetable set forth in the 1974 Congressional Budget Act calls for the final adoption of the budget resolution by April 15, well before the beginning of the new fiscal year on October 1. Although the House and Senate often pass the budget resolution separately before April 15, they often do not reach final agreement on it until after the deadline—sometimes not at all. (*See § 7.52, Completion Dates of Budget Resolutions.*)

The 1974 Congressional Budget Act requires the budget resolution, for each fiscal year covered, to set forth budget aggregates and spending levels for each *functional category* of the budget. (*See § 7.54, Functional Categories in a Congressional Budget Resolution.*) The aggregates included in the budget resolution are as follows:
- total revenues (and the amount by which the total is to be changed by legislative action);
- total new budget authority and outlays;

§ 7.51

Congressional Budget Process Timetable[1]

Deadline	Action
First Monday in February	President submits budget to Congress[2]
February 15	Congressional Budget Office submits report on economic and budget outlook to Budget Committees
Six weeks after president's budget is submitted	House and Senate committees submit reports on views and estimates to respective Budget Committees
April 1	Senate Budget Committee reports budget resolution
April 15	Congress completes action on budget resolution
May 15	House usually begins action on annual appropriations bills
June 10	House Appropriations Committee reports last regular appropriations bill
June 30	House completes action on regular appropriations bills and any required reconciliation legislation
July 15	President submits mid-session review of his budget to Congress
October 1	Fiscal year begins[3]

1. While this timetable is set forth in statute, the deadlines generally are regarded as hortatory and Congress and the president sometimes do not meet them.

2. At any time after the president submits the budget for the upcoming fiscal year, he may submit revisions to the budget, referred to as budget amendments, as well as request supplemental appropriations for the current fiscal year.

3. One or more continuing resolutions may be needed until Congress and the president complete action on all pending appropriations bills.

- the deficit or surplus; and
- the debt limit.

For each of the functional categories, the budget resolution must indicate for each fiscal year the amounts of new budget authority and outlays. All figures in the budget resolution must be arithmetically consistent.

Amounts in the budget resolution do not reflect the revenues or spending of the off-budget Social Security trust funds, although these amounts are set forth separately in the budget resolution for purposes of Senate enforcement procedures. Amounts associated with the other off-budget entity, the Postal Service Fund, also are excluded from the budget resolutions. Data on off-budget revenue and spending levels are included, however, in the reports that accompany the budget resolution.

The budget resolution does not allocate funds among specific programs or accounts, but the major program assumptions underlying the functional amounts are often discussed in the reports accompanying each resolution and during floor debate. Some recent reports have contained detailed information on the program levels assumed in the resolution. While these assumptions are not binding on the affected committees, the vote on the budget resolution may sometimes be characterized as a vote on these program assumptions. Finally, the 1974 act allows certain additional matters to be

§ 7.52

Completion Dates of Budget Resolutions

The timetable in the 1974 Congressional Budget Act provides for the House and Senate to reach agreement on the budget resolution by April 15, but this deadline is not always met. During the more than 35 years that the congressional budget process has been in effect, the House and Senate did not reach final agreement six times (all shown here). Completion dates for the past 15 years are as follows:

Fiscal Year	Date
1998	June 5, 1997
1999	Not Completed
2000	April 15, 1999
2001	April 13, 2000
2002	May 10, 2001
2003	Not Completed
2004	April 11, 2003
2005	Not Completed
2006	April 28, 2005
2007	Not Completed
2008	May 17, 2007
2009	June 5, 2008
2010	April 29, 2009
2011	Not Completed
2012	Not Completed
2013	Not Completed
2014	Not Completed
2015	Not Completed
2016	May 5, 2015
2017	January 12, 2017
2018	October 26, 2017

included in the budget resolution. The most important optional feature of a budget resolution is *reconciliation* directives. (*See § 7.110, Reconciliation Legislation.*)

House and Senate Budget Committee Action. The House and Senate Budget Committees are responsible for marking up and reporting the budget resolution. (*See § 7.55, Membership on the House and Senate Budget Committees.*) In the course of developing the budget resolution, the Budget Committees hold hearings, receive *views and estimates* reports from other committees, and obtain analyses and information from the Congressional Budget Office (CBO). The views and estimates reports of House and Senate committees provide the budget committees with information on the preferences and legislative plans of congressional committees regarding budgetary matters within their jurisdiction. (Views and estimates are available from issuing committees and the Budget Committees; they can also often be found on committee web sites.)

CBO assists the budget committees in developing the budget resolution by issuing, early each year, a report on the budget and economic outlook, which includes *baseline budget projections*. The baseline projections presented in the report are supported by more detailed projections for accounts and programs; CBO usually revises the baseline projections once more (in March) before the budget committees mark up the budget resolution. In addition, CBO issues a report analyzing the president's budgetary proposals in light of CBO's own economic and technical assumptions.

The House and Senate Budget Committees include extensive information in their reports on the budget resolution, as required by the 1974 Congressional Budget Act. The Senate Budget Committee is directed to report a budget resolution by April 1 each year; there is no reporting deadline for the House Budget Committee.

The extent to which the budget committees (and the House and Senate) consider particular programs when they act on the budget resolution varies from year to year. Specific program decisions are supposed to be left to the Appropriations Committees and other committees of jurisdiction, but there is a strong likelihood that major issues are discussed in markup, in the budget committees' reports, and during floor consideration of the budget resolution. Although any programmatic assumptions generated in this process are not binding on the committees of jurisdiction, they often influence the final outcome.

Floor Consideration. A budget resolution is marked up and reported from a budget committee in the same fashion as most other measures are considered in other committees. Either the House or

Senate committee may report first, and either the House or Senate may consider a budget resolution first. Because of the need to adopt a budget resolution to allow orderly and timely consideration of budgetary legislation, action in the two committees and in the two chambers can occur simultaneously and within a short period of time.

Floor consideration of the budget resolution is expedited under procedures set forth in the 1974 Congressional Budget Act and is further guided by House and Senate rules and practices. In the House, the Rules Committee usually reports a *special rule* (a simple House resolution), which, once agreed to by the House, establishes the terms and conditions under which the budget resolution is considered by the House. This special rule typically sets aside a period for general debate, and specifies which amendments may be considered and the sequence in which they are to be offered and voted on. It has been the practice for many years to allow consideration of a limited number of amendments (as substitutes for the entire resolution) that present different major policy choices. In the Senate, the amendment process is less structured, relying on agreements reached by the leadership through a consultative process. The amendments offered in the Senate may entail major policy choices or may be focused on a single issue; unlike most other types of legislation, amendments attached to budget resolutions must be germane. Finally, the number of hours that a budget resolution can be debated in the Senate is subject to a limit of fifty hours. Subsequent consideration of a conference report is also limited.

The House and Senate normally pass budget resolutions with differences that are significant enough to warrant the convening of a conference. Conferees, typically drawn from the two budget committees, reconcile differences and prepare a conference report, which must be adopted in both houses.

Achievement of the policies set forth in the annual budget resolution depends on the legislative actions taken by Congress (and the president's approval or disapproval of those actions), the performance of the economy, and technical considerations. Many of the factors that determine whether budgetary goals will be met are beyond the direct control of Congress. If economic conditions—growth, employment levels, inflation, and so forth—vary significantly from projected levels, so too will actual levels of revenue and spending. Similarly, actual levels may differ substantially if the technical factors upon which estimates are based, such as the rate at which agencies spend their discretionary funds or participants become eligible for entitlement programs, prove faulty.

Budget Resolution Enforcement

Once a budget resolution is agreed to, Congress' regular tools for enforcing it are overall spending ceilings and revenue floors, and committee allocations and subdivisions of spending. (In addition, in some years the House and Senate have enforced discretionary-spending limits in the budget resolution, which parallel the discretionary-spending limits established in statute.) For enforcement procedures to work, Congress must have access to complete and up-to-date budgetary information so that it can relate individual measures to overall budget policies and determine whether adoption of a particular measure would be consistent with those policies, as explained below. Substantive and procedural *points of order* are designed to obtain congressional compliance with budget rules. A point of order may bar House or Senate consideration of legislation that violates the spending ceilings or revenue floors in the budget resolution, committee subdivisions of spending, or congressional budget procedures.

Continued on page 7-22

§ 7.53

Congressional Budget Process Flowchart

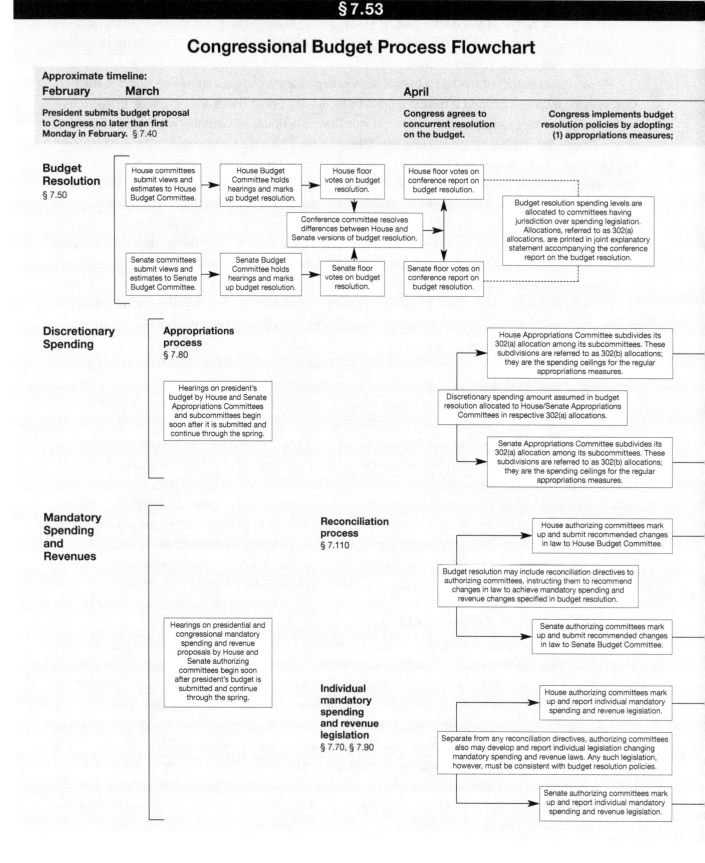

Approximate timeline:

February   March

President submits budget proposal to Congress no later than first Monday in February. § 7.40

April

Congress agrees to concurrent resolution on the budget.

Congress implements budget resolution policies by adopting: (1) appropriations measures;

Budget Resolution § 7.50

House committees submit views and estimates to House Budget Committee. → House Budget Committee holds hearings and marks up budget resolution. → House floor votes on budget resolution. → House floor votes on conference report on budget resolution.

Senate committees submit views and estimates to Senate Budget Committee. → Senate Budget Committee holds hearings and marks up budget resolution. → Senate floor votes on budget resolution. → Senate floor votes on conference report on budget resolution.

Conference committee resolves differences between House and Senate versions of budget resolution.

Budget resolution spending levels are allocated to committees having jurisdiction over spending legislation. Allocations, referred to as 302(a) allocations, are printed in joint explanatory statement accompanying the conference report on the budget resolution.

Discretionary Spending

Appropriations process § 7.80

Hearings on president's budget by House and Senate Appropriations Committees and subcommittees begin soon after it is submitted and continue through the spring.

House Appropriations Committee subdivides its 302(a) allocation among its subcommittees. These subdivisions are referred to as 302(b) allocations; they are the spending ceilings for the regular appropriations measures.

Discretionary spending amount assumed in budget resolution allocated to House/Senate Appropriations Committees in respective 302(a) allocations.

Senate Appropriations Committee subdivides its 302(a) allocation among its subcommittees. These subdivisions are referred to as 302(b) allocations; they are the spending ceilings for the regular appropriations measures.

Mandatory Spending and Revenues

Reconciliation process § 7.110

House authorizing committees mark up and submit recommended changes in law to House Budget Committee.

Budget resolution may include reconciliation directives to authorizing committees, instructing them to recommend changes in law to achieve mandatory spending and revenue changes specified in budget resolution.

Senate authorizing committees mark up and submit recommended changes in law to Senate Budget Committee.

Hearings on presidential and congressional mandatory spending and revenue proposals by House and Senate authorizing committees begin soon after president's budget is submitted and continue through the spring.

Individual mandatory spending and revenue legislation § 7.70, § 7.90

House authorizing committees mark up and report individual mandatory spending and revenue legislation.

Separate from any reconciliation directives, authorizing committees also may develop and report individual legislation changing mandatory spending and revenue laws. Any such legislation, however, must be consistent with budget resolution policies.

Senate authorizing committees mark up and report individual mandatory spending and revenue legislation.

§ 7.53 (continued)

May	June–September	Fiscal Year begins October 1
(2) individual mandatory spending and revenue legislation; and (3) reconciliation legislation (if required).		President signs (or vetoes) budget measures.

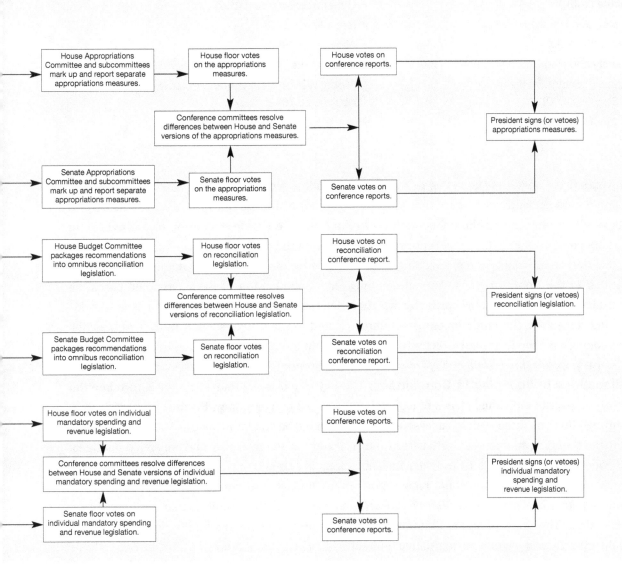

§ 7.54

Functional Categories in a
Congressional Budget Resolution

A budget resolution shows recommended spending both as aggregate levels and as allocations among the functional categories of the budget. The functional categories group programs by broad purposes without regard to the agencies that administer them; a function is further divided into subfunctions. The functional categories have been revised from time to time and their number (21 as of 2012) has changed over time.

- National Defense (050)
- International Affairs (150)
- General Science, Space, and Technology (250)
- Energy (270)
- Natural Resources and Environment (300)
- Agriculture (350)
- Commerce and Housing Credit (370)
- Transportation (400)
- Community and Regional Development (450)
- Education, Training, Employment, and Social Services (500)
- Health (550)

- Medicare (570)
- Income Security (600)
- Social Security (650)
- Veterans' Benefits and Services (700)
- Administration of Justice (750)
- General Government (800)
- Net Interest (900)
- Allowances (920)
- Undistributed Offsetting Receipts (950)
- Global War on Terrorism and Related Activities (970)

In years that Congress is late in agreeing to, or does not agree to, a budget resolution, the House and Senate independently may agree to a "deeming resolution" for the purpose of enforcing certain budget levels. A deeming resolution, sometimes in the form of a simple resolution or a provision in statute, specifies certain budget levels normally contained in the budget resolution, including aggregate spending and revenue levels, spending allocations to House and Senate committees, spending allocations to the Appropriations Committees only, or a combination of these. In some cases, an entire budget resolution, adopted earlier by one chamber, may be deemed to have been passed. Under a deeming resolution, the enforcement procedures related to the Congressional Budget Act, as discussed below, have the force and effect as if a budget resolution had been adopted by Congress. (*See § 6, Deeming Resolutions: Budget Enforcement in the Absence of a Budget Resolution.*)

Allocations of Spending to Committees. The key to enforcing budget policy is to relate the budgetary impact of individual pieces of legislation to overall budget policy. Because Congress operates through its committee system, an essential step in linking particular measures to the budget is to allocate the spending amounts set forth in the budget resolution among House and Senate committees.

Section 302(a) of the 1974 act provides for allocations to committees to be made in the statement of managers accompanying the conference report on the budget resolution (referred to as the joint explanatory statement). A *section 302(a) allocation* is made to each committee that has jurisdiction over spending. The Appropriations Committees receive allocations for the budget year (and sometimes the current year), while the legislative committees receive allocations both for the budget year and the full period covered by the budget resolution—at least five fiscal years.

The amounts of new budget authority and outlays allocated to committees in the House or Senate may not exceed the aggregate amounts of budget authority and outlays set forth in the budget resolution. Although these allocations are made by the budget committees, they are not the unilateral preferences of these committees. They are based on assumptions and understandings developed in the course of formulating the budget resolution.

After the allocations are made under section 302(a), the House and Senate Appropriations Committees subdivide the amounts they receive among their subcommittees, as required by section 302(b). The subcommittees' *section 302(b) allocations or subdivisions* may not exceed the total amount allocated to the committees. Each Appropriations Committee reports its subdivisions to its respective chamber.

Scorekeeping and Cost Estimates. *Scorekeeping* is the process of measuring the budgetary effects of pending and enacted legislation and assessing its impact on a budget plan—in this case, the budget resolution. In the congressional budget process, scorekeeping serves several broad purposes. First, it informs members of Congress and the public about the budgetary consequences of congressional actions. When a budgetary measure is under consideration, scorekeeping information lets members know whether adopting the amendment or passing the bill at hand would breach the budget. Further, such information enables members to judge what must be done in upcoming legislative action to achieve the year's budgetary goals. Finally, scorekeeping is designed to assist Congress in enforcing its budget plans. In this regard, scorekeeping is used largely to determine whether points of order under the 1974 Congressional Budget Act may be sustained against legislation violating budget resolution levels.

The principal scorekeepers for Congress are the House and Senate Budget Committees, which provide the presiding officers of the respective chambers with the estimates needed to determine if legislation violates the aggregate levels in the budget resolution, the committee subdivisions of spending, or other budgetary levels. The budget committees make summary scorekeeping reports available periodically, usually geared to the pace of legislative activity. CBO assists Congress in these activities by preparing *cost estimates* of legislation, which are included in committee reports, and reflected in the scorekeeping reports of the budget committees.

Cost estimates prepared by CBO show how a measure would affect spending or revenues over at least five fiscal years. While most cost estimates are provided in the committee report to accompany a measure, they may be provided at any stage of the legislative process, subject to available resources

§7.55

Membership on the House and Senate Budget Committees

The House Budget Committee, unlike other House standing committees (except the House Committee on Standards of Official Conduct), is composed of a rotating membership. House rules (with certain exceptions) limit a member's service on the committee to four Congresses in a period of six successive Congresses. In addition, House rules require five members from the Appropriations Committee, five members from the Ways and Means Committee, one member from the Rules Committee, one member designated by the elected majority party leadership, and one member designated by the elected minority party leadership to serve on the committee.

In contrast, membership on the Senate Budget Committee is permanent; Senate rules do not limit the duration of a senator's service on the committee.

of CBO. Estimates for revenue legislation are made by the Joint Committee on Taxation (JCT). (*See § 7.92, Revenue Estimates.*) CBO and JCT cost estimates are available on their respective web sites at *<www.cbo.gov>* and *<www.jct.gov>*.

Points of Order. The 1974 Congressional Budget Act provides points of order (parliamentary objections to the consideration of legislation, including amendments) to block substantive violations of budget resolution policies and violations of congressional budget procedures.

One element of substantive enforcement is based on section 311 of the act. The point of order provided for in this section bars Congress from considering legislation that would cause total revenues to fall below the level set in the budget resolution. It also forbids the consideration of legislation that would cause total new budget authority or total outlays to exceed the budgeted level.

Another point of order tied to substantive enforcement is found in Section 302(f) of the 1974 act, which bars the House and Senate from considering any spending measure that would cause the relevant committee's spending allocations to be exceeded. In the House, the point of order applies only to violations of allocations of new discretionary budget authority. Further, the point of order also applies (in both chambers) to suballocations of spending made by the Appropriations Committees.

In addition to points of order to enforce compliance with the budget resolution and the allocations and subdivisions made pursuant to it, the 1974 act contains points of order to ensure compliance with its procedures. Perhaps the most important of these is found in section 303, which bars consideration of any revenue, spending, entitlement, or debt-limit measure before adoption of the budget resolution. However, the rules of the House permit it to consider regular appropriations bills after May 15, even if the budget resolution has not yet been adopted.

When the House or Senate considers a revenue or spending measure, the chair of the respective budget committee sometimes makes a statement advising the chamber concerning whether the measure violates these or other budget-related points of order. If no point of order is raised, or if the point of order is waived, the House or Senate may consider a measure despite any potential violations of the 1974 act. When the House waives points of order, it usually does so by adopting a special rule. The Senate usually waives points of order by unanimous consent or by motion under section 904 of the act. The Senate requires a three-fifths vote of the membership (sixty senators, if no seats are vacant) to waive certain provisions of the act.

As mentioned previously, the House and Senate may include additional points of order for budget enforcement purposes as provisions in budget resolutions or as part of their standing rules. The Senate established a "pay-as-you-go" (PAYGO) point of order in 1993 as part of the FY1994 budget resolution and has amended it several times over the years. The Senate PAYGO rule generally requires direct spending and revenue legislation to be deficit-neutral over six-year and eleven-year periods. These two time periods encompass the current year, the budget year, and the ensuing nine out-years, and in this regard is generally compatible with the time periods used in the House CUTGO rule and the Statutory PAYGO Act of 2010. The Senate PAYGO rule also requires a three-fifths vote to waive.

In 2007, at the beginning of the 110th Congress, the House added a PAYGO requirement to its standing rules (as Clause 10 of Rule XXI) for the first time. The House PAYGO rule provided a point of order against the consideration of any direct spending or revenue measure that would increase the deficit or reduce the surplus during either the six-year period (covering the current year, the budget year, and the four following fiscal years) or the eleven-year period (the previously cited period and the ensuing five fiscal years). In 2009, after the Republicans regained a majority in the House, the House PAYGO rule was replaced by a "cut-as-you-go" (CUTGO) rule. The new rule bars the consideration of legislation that increases mandatory spending over the six-year and eleven-year periods; the revenue effects of legislation no longer are considered for purposes of the rule. (Consequently, the consideration of legislation reducing revenues during these time periods would not be prohibited by this rule.)

§ 7.60 Spending, Revenue, and Debt-Limit Legislation

Congress implements the policies of the budget resolution through the enactment of spending (§§ *7.70, 7.80*), revenue (*§ 7.90*), and debt-limit (*§ 7.100*) legislation. In many of the years since 1980, Congress has employed the reconciliation process (*§ 7.110*) to enact budget changes through legislation considered under expedited procedures. Reconciliation legislation can include revenue changes, changes in direct spending (but not usually changes in discretionary spending), and adjustments to the debt limit. Special procedures also apply to federal credit programs. (*See § 7.61, Budgeting for Direct and Guaranteed Loans.*)

§ 7.61

Budgeting for Direct and Guaranteed Loans

The Federal Credit Reform Act of 1990 made fundamental changes in the budgetary treatment of direct loans and guaranteed loans. Among its many provisions, the law required that budget authority and outlays be budgeted for the estimated subsidy cost of direct and guaranteed loans. This cost is defined in the 1990 law as the "estimated long-term cost to the Government of a direct loan or a loan guarantee, calculated on a net present value basis, excluding administrative costs. . . ." Under this law, Congress appropriates budget authority or provides indefinite authority equal to the subsidy cost. This budget authority is placed in a program account, from which funds are disbursed to a financing account.

§ 7.70 Spending Legislation

The spending policies of the budget resolution generally are implemented through two different types of spending legislation. Policies involving *discretionary spending* are implemented in the context of *annual appropriations acts*, whereas policies affecting *direct* or *mandatory spending* (which, for the most part, involves *entitlement* programs) are carried out in substantive legislation. (*See § 7.71, Differences between Discretionary and Direct Spending.*)

All discretionary spending is under the jurisdiction of the House and Senate Appropriations Committees. Direct spending is under the jurisdiction of the various legislative committees of the House and Senate; the House Ways and Means Committee and the Senate Finance Committee have the largest shares of direct-spending jurisdiction.

Congress considers major direct spending legislation in particular policy areas, such as highway spending and farm policy, on a multiyear cycle under regular legislative procedures. In some years, however, significant changes in direct-spending programs, from a budgetary standpoint, are made in the reconciliation process. (*See § 7.110, Reconciliation Legislation.*) The greatest focus usually falls on discretionary spending decisions because annual appropriations acts must be enacted each year.

§ 7.71

Differences between
Discretionary and Direct Spending

Feature	Discretionary Spending	Direct Spending
Budgetary impact of authorizing legislation	No direct impact; authorizes subsequent appropriations	Direct impact; provides budgetary resources
Committees that process budgetary legislation	Appropriations Committees	Authorizing committees; technically, Appropriations Committees for *appropriated entitlements* (like Medicaid)
Frequency of decision-making	Annual	Periodic
Means of enforcing budget resolution	Committee spending allocations and suballocations and points of order under Section 302	Committee spending allocations and points of order under Section 302 and the reconciliation process
Basis of computing budget impact	Current year's spending and president's request	Baseline budget projections
Impact of economic changes	Indirect	Direct, often automatic

§ 7.80 Authorizations and Appropriations Processes

To implement the constitutional "power of the purse," Congress has created the annual appropriations process. House Rule XXI and Senate Rule XVI require the prior enactment of authorizing measures before appropriations acts may be considered. Authorizing measures deal with substantive policy issues and appropriations measures deal with funding. In practice, the boundaries between the two types of legislation are not always clear.

Authorizing Measures

An *authorization act* is a law that (1) establishes a program or agency and the terms and conditions under which it operates, and (2) authorizes the enactment of *appropriations* for that program or agency. *Authorizing legislation*, which is used to make authorization law, is one type of legislation that Congress commonly considers. Authorizing legislation may originate in either the House or the Senate, and may be considered at any time during the year. It can prescribe what an agency must do—or proscribe what it may not do—in the performance of its assigned responsibilities. It can give the agency a broad grant of authority and discretion, or define parameters, decision-making, and decisions in great detail.

Unless an authorization measure contains direct spending, which itself enables an agency to enter into obligations, authorizing legislation does not have budgetary impact. It authorizes discretionary spending, for which funding is provided subsequently in annual appropriations acts.

House rules do not expressly require authorizations. Instead, they bar *unauthorized appropriations*. The House may waive the rule against unauthorized appropriations by adopting a special rule

§7.81

Limitations, Earmarks, and General Provisions

In addition to appropriating specific dollar amounts, appropriations and their accompanying reports contain numerous other provisions that affect how federal departments and agencies spend appropriations. The principal categories of these provisions include the following:

- **Limitation**—language in legislation or in legislative documents that restricts the availability of an appropriation by limiting its use or amount.

- **Earmark**—a set-aside within an appropriation for a specific purpose that might be included either in legislation or in legislative documents.

- **Directive**—an instruction, usually in a legislative document, to an agency concerning the manner in which an appropriation is to be administered or requiring a report to Congress on issues of concern.

- **General Provision**—policy guidance on spending included in an appropriations measure; it may affect some or all appropriation accounts in the measure or even have government-wide application; it may also be one-time or permanent.

Appropriations measures might also contain legislative provisions that are included in appropriations measures despite House and Senate rules discouraging the practice.

before taking up an appropriations bill. The House rule barring unauthorized appropriations applies only against *general appropriations measures*. Under House precedents, a *continuing appropriations measure* is not considered to be a general appropriations bill, and it may thus fund unauthorized programs.

Senate rules also bar unauthorized appropriations, although many exceptions are allowed. Accordingly, the House rule is stricter than the Senate rule.

House rules also prohibit the inclusion of appropriations in authorizing legislation. Senate rules do not contain this prohibition.

House rules bar *legislation in an appropriations bill*, but a special rule from the Rules Committee can waive this requirement. Legislation in appropriations is also prohibited by Senate rules.

Permanent versus Temporary Authorizations. An authorization is presumed to be permanent unless the authorizing law limits its duration. *Permanent authorizations* do not have any time limit and continue in effect until they are changed by Congress. An agency having a permanent authorization need only obtain appropriations to continue in operations. *Annual authorizations* (such as for the Department of Defense) are for a single year and, usually, for a fixed amount of money; specified authorization levels usually serve as a limit on what can be appropriated subsequently. These authorizations need to be renewed each year. *Multiyear authorizations* (such as for Federal Aviation Administration programs) are typically in effect for several years and must be renewed when they expire. New authorizations of programs or activities with annual or multiyear authority are often referred to as *reauthorizations*.

As a general matter, appropriations enacted into law when the authorizing measure has not been enacted may be spent by the agency. The agency also may spend appropriated amounts that exceed levels specified in the authorization legislation.

§ 7.82

Appropriations Subcommittee Organization

For several decades, Congress considered thirteen regular appropriations acts developed by thirteen parallel subcommittees; each regular appropriations act was developed by the relevant House and Senate Appropriations subcommittee. Realignment of the Appropriations subcommittees in the 109th Congress reduced the number to ten in the House and twelve in the Senate, resulting in subcommittees (and regular appropriations acts) that in some cases were no longer parallel. Further realignment in the 110th Congress resulted in twelve subcommittees in each committee and restored parallelism between them. In some cases, subcommittee jurisdictions were not the same in the 110th Congress as they had been before realignment occurred. The current Appropriations subcommittees are as follows:

- Agriculture, Rural Development, Food and Drug Administration, and Related Agencies
- Commerce, Justice, Science, and Related Agencies
- Defense
- Energy and Water Development
- Financial Services and General Government
- Homeland Security
- Interior, Environment, and Related Agencies
- Labor, Health and Human Services, Education, and Related Agencies
- Legislative Branch
- Military Construction, Veterans' Affairs, and Related Agencies
- State, Foreign Operations, and Related Programs
- Transportation, and Housing and Urban Development, and Related Agencies

Permanent authorizations rarely specify amounts of money. Temporary authorizations usually do. An authorization of appropriations in a specific amount is intended to serve as a guideline or limit for the Appropriations Committees in drafting appropriations measures and for Congress in approving them. However, one regularly finds large differences between enacted authorized and appropriated amounts. A member or group of members advocating "full funding" of a program is often in favor of an appropriation matching an authorization. Moreover, Congress does not need to make an appropriation for an authorization in law if it chooses not to fund an activity.

Annual Appropriations Measures

An appropriations act is a law passed by Congress that provides federal agencies with authority to incur *obligations* for the purposes specified for which payments are made out of the Treasury. As noted in § 7.00, the power to appropriate is a congressional power. Funds in the Treasury may not be withdrawn in the absence of an appropriation. Spending may occur only in accordance with the purposes and conditions Congress established in making an appropriation.

The Constitution does not require annual appropriations, but since the First Congress the practice has been to enact appropriations for a single fiscal year. Appropriations must be used (obligated) in the fiscal year for which they are provided, unless the law provides that they are available for a longer period of time. All provisions in an appropriations act, such as *limitations* on the use of funds, expire

§ 7.83

Sequence of Appropriations Measures through Congress

House	Senate
Subcommittee hearings	Subcommittee hearings
Subcommittee markup (no measure number is assigned yet)	Subcommittee markup (either a House-passed measure or an unnumbered Senate measure)
Full committee markup and report (measure is introduced and number is assigned)	Full committee markup and report (either a House-passed measure or a Senate measure is introduced and number is assigned)
House floor action	Senate floor action (if a Senate measure is considered, it is held at the stage of final passage so that the Senate can amend and pass the House measure, fulfilling the tradition that the House originates appropriations measures)

House-Senate Conference
(on a House-numbered measure)

House agrees to conference report (and any amendments in disagreement)	Senate agrees to conference report (and any amendments in disagreement)

Enrolled Measure Sent to President

at the end of the fiscal year, unless the language of the act extends their period of effectiveness. (*See § 7.81, Limitations, Earmarks, and General Provisions.*)

The president requests annual appropriations in his budget submitted each year. In support of the president's appropriations requests, agencies submit *justification* materials to the House and Senate Appropriations Committees. These materials provide considerably more detail than is contained in the president's budget and are used in support of agency testimony during appropriations subcommittee hearings on the president's budget.

Congress passes three main types of appropriations measures. *Regular appropriations acts* provide budget authority to agencies for the upcoming fiscal year. *Supplemental appropriations acts* provide additional budget authority during the current fiscal year when the regular appropriation is insufficient. Supplemental appropriations also finance activities not provided for in regular appropriations. *Continuing appropriations acts*, often referred to as *continuing resolutions* (after the form of legislation in which they are usually considered, the joint resolution [H.J. Res. ___]), provide stopgap funding for agencies that have not received regular appropriations. In some years, a series of continuing resolutions (CRs) provide funding for the entire fiscal year. For purposes of House and Senate rules, all regular and supplemental appropriations measures covering two or more agencies or purposes are considered *general appropriations measures*.

The number of regular appropriations acts was fixed for several decades at thirteen, but realignment of the Appropriations subcommittees in the 109th and 110th Congresses reduced that number; at present, there are twelve regular appropriations acts. (*See § 7.82, Appropriations Subcommittee*

Organization.) In some years, Congress merges two or more of the regular appropriations bills into an *omnibus measure.* In a typical session, Congress also acts on at least one supplemental appropriations measure. Because of recurring delays in the appropriations process, Congress also typically passes one or more continuing appropriations each year. The scope and duration of these measures depend on the status of the regular appropriations bills and the degree of budgetary conflict between Congress and the president. Funding levels for activities under a continuing appropriations act usually are restrictive and keyed to formulas, such as the lower of the current rate or the president's budget request, or the lower of the House-passed or Senate-passed amount.

In the House. By precedent, appropriations originate in the House of Representatives. In the House, appropriations measures are originated by the Appropriations Committee (when it marks up or reports the measures) rather than being introduced by an individual member.

Before the full Appropriations Committee acts on a measure, the measure is considered in the relevant subcommittee. The House subcommittees typically hold extensive hearings on appropriations requests shortly after the president's budget is submitted. In marking up their appropriations bills, the various subcommittees are guided by the spending suballocations made to them under the budget resolution, as required by section 302(b) of the 1974 Congressional Budget Act.

The subcommittees' recommendations generally are quite influential. It is common for the full Appropriations Committee to mark up and report an appropriations measure prepared for it by a subcommittee without making any substantive changes. The subcommittees also draft the committee reports that accompany appropriations measures to the floor. The Appropriations Committee usually begins reporting bills in early May.

Because general appropriations measures are privileged and thus have direct access to the House floor for consideration, they can be brought to the floor without first obtaining a special rule from the Rules Committee. Nonetheless, appropriations bills come to the floor under a rule waiving one or more standing rules, such as the rule against unauthorized appropriations. (*See § 7.83, Sequence of Appropriations Measures through Congress.*) Between April and the start of the fiscal year on October 1 (and sometimes until the end of the session), the House processes appropriations measures reported from the House Appropriations Committee or from the relevant conference committees.

In the Senate. Subcommittees of the Senate Appropriations Committee also begin their hearings on appropriations requests shortly after the president's budget is submitted. They are also guided by the section 302(b) spending suballocations. Hearings in Senate appropriations subcommittees may not be as extensive as those held by the counterpart subcommittees of the House Appropriations Committee. Subcommittee markup and reporting to the full Appropriations Committee is followed by full committee markup and reporting.

Up until the latter part of the 1990s, the Senate usually would consider appropriations measures after they had been passed by the House. When the Senate changed a House-passed appropriations measure, it did so by inserting amendments numbered consecutively through the measure.

Under current practice, the Senate sometimes first considers a Senate-numbered measure up to the stage of final passage, routinely using complex unanimous consent agreements to frame floor consideration. When the House-passed measure eventually is received in the Senate, it is amended with the text that the Senate has already agreed to (as a single amendment) and then passed by the Senate. This practice allows the Senate to consider appropriations measures without having to wait for the House to adopt its version, facilitating the timely consideration and completion of the regular appropriations measures.

Like the House, the Senate processes appropriations legislation reported from the Senate Appropriations Committee or from the relevant conference committees between spring and the start of the fiscal year (or sometimes until the end of the session).

Conference. As appropriations measures pass both the House and Senate, conference committees may be appointed to resolve differences. Conference reports must pass the House and Senate before an enrolled measure is transmitted to the president for signature or veto. Recently, the House and Senate sometimes have avoided using a conference to resolve differences over a bill, instead choosing to exchange amendments between the two chambers until differences are resolved. This approach may be used to expedite the process and minimize contentious votes.

Additional Congressional Controls in Appropriations Acts

The basic element of an appropriations act is an *account*. A single unnumbered paragraph in an appropriations act comprises one account. All provisions of that paragraph pertain to that account and to no other, unless the text expressly gives them broader scope. Any provision limiting the use of funds enacted in that paragraph is a restriction on that account alone.

Over the years, appropriations have been consolidated into a relatively small number of accounts with large "lump-sum" appropriations. It is typical for a federal agency to have a single account for all its expenses of operation and several additional accounts for other purposes, such as construction. Accordingly, most appropriations accounts encompass a number of activities or projects.

An appropriation sometimes *earmarks* specific amounts to particular activities within the account, but the more common practice is to provide detailed information on the amounts intended for each activity in other sources, principally the committee reports accompanying the measures. The House and Senate expanded the use of earmarks through 2010, but abuses led both chambers to adopt strict rules governing their use and to significantly curtail earmarks. Extensive information on earmarks, including identification of the requesting member of Congress, is provided in House and Senate Appropriations Committee reports accompanying the appropriations acts. (*See § 7.84, Examples of Appropriations Subcommittees' Requirements for Member Requests.*)

In addition to the substantive limitations and other provisions associated with each account, each appropriations act has *general provisions* that apply to all the accounts in a title or in the whole act. These general provisions appear as numbered sections, usually at the end of the title or act.

In a typical appropriations act, most funding is provided as *one-year appropriations* (the funds are available for obligation during the single fiscal year and lapse after the year has expired). The account language usually does not indicate the period that funds are available; instead, a general provision indicates that all funding provided in the act is available for one year unless otherwise indicated. Congress also makes *no-year appropriations* by specifying that the funds shall remain available until expended. No-year funds are carried over to future years, even if they have not been obligated. Congress sometimes makes *multiyear appropriations*, which provide for funds to be available for two or more fiscal years. *Permanent appropriations*, such as those to pay interest on the national debt or to pay the salaries of members of Congress, remain available without additional action by Congress. (Most, but not all, permanent appropriations are provided in substantive law, not annual appropriations acts.)

Continued on page 7-34

§ 7.84

Examples of Appropriations Subcommittees' Requirements for Member Requests

RODNEY P. FRELINGHUYSEN, NEW JERSEY, Chairman
HAROLD ROGERS, KENTUCKY
ROBERT B. ADERHOLT, ALABAMA
KAY GRANGER, TEXAS
MICHAEL K. SIMPSON, IDAHO
JOHN ABNEY CULBERSON, TEXAS
JOHN R. CARTER, TEXAS
KEN CALVERT, CALIFORNIA
TOM COLE, OKLAHOMA
MARIO DIAZ-BALART, FLORIDA
CHARLES W. DENT, PENNSYLVANIA
TOM GRAVES, GEORGIA
KEVIN YODER, KANSAS
STEVE WOMACK, ARKANSAS
JEFF FORTENBERRY, NEBRASKA
THOMAS J. ROONEY, FLORIDA
CHARLES J. FLEISCHMANN, TENNESSEE
JAIME HERRERA BEUTLER, WASHINGTON
DAVID P. JOYCE, OHIO
DAVID G. VALADAO, CALIFORNIA
ANDY HARRIS, MARYLAND
MARTHA ROBY, ALABAMA
MARK E. AMODEI, NEVADA
CHRIS STEWART, UTAH
DAVID YOUNG, IOWA
EVAN H. JENKINS, WEST VIRGINIA
STEVEN M. PALAZZO, MISSISSIPPI
DAN NEWHOUSE, WASHINGTON
JOHN R. MOOLENAAR, MICHIGAN
SCOTT TAYLOR, VIRGINIA

NITA M. LOWEY, NEW YORK
MARCY KAPTUR, OHIO
PETER J. VISCLOSKY, INDIANA
JOSÉ E. SERRANO, NEW YORK
ROSA L. DeLAURO, CONNECTICUT
DAVID E. PRICE, NORTH CAROLINA
LUCILLE ROYBAL-ALLARD, CALIFORNIA
SANFORD D. BISHOP, Jr., GEORGIA
BARBARA LEE, CALIFORNIA
BETTY McCOLLUM, MINNESOTA
TIM RYAN, OHIO
C. A. DUTCH RUPPERSBERGER, MARYLAND
DEBBIE WASSERMAN SCHULTZ, FLORIDA
HENRY CUELLAR, TEXAS
CHELLIE PINGREE, MAINE
MIKE QUIGLEY, ILLINOIS
DEREK KILMER, WASHINGTON
MATT CARTWRIGHT, PENNSYLVANIA
GRACE MENG, NEW YORK
MARK POCAN, WISCONSIN
KATHERINE M. CLARK, MASSACHUSETTS
PETE AGUILAR, CALIFORNIA

Congress of the United States
House of Representatives
Committee on Appropriations
Washington, DC 20515–6015

NANCY FOX
CLERK AND STAFF DIRECTOR

TELEPHONE:
(202) 225-2771

Dear Colleague,

As Chairman of the Appropriations Committee, I want to extend an opportunity for Members to respond to the President's fiscal year 2018 budget submission to the Congress. The Committee will be opening the member request database for further requests in response to the just-released budget from the President. The Committee will consider these submissions in addition to the submissions made to the Committee in March and April.

The procedures for receiving Members' programmatic and language submissions for consideration in the fiscal year 2018 appropriations bills will be the same as the previous procedures. Members must transmit submissions to the relevant subcommittee via electronic form, and in addition must upload a letter to the appropriations submissions system confirming those entries.

- The electronic submission system can be found at https://AppropriationsSubmissions.house.gov. The system will be available to accept submissions starting May 23, 2017.

- The deadline for submissions to the subcommittees on Commerce Justice Science, Defense, Energy and Water, Financial Services, Legislative Branch, and Military Construction and Veterans Affairs is close of business **May 30, 2017.**

- The deadline for submissions to the subcommittees on Agriculture, Homeland Security, Interior, Labor/Health and Human Services, State/Foreign Operations, and Transportation/HUD is close of business **June 6, 2017**.

THERE IS NO NEED TO RESUBMIT REQUESTS ALREADY SUBMITTED. This process is for NEW requests in response to the President's Budget.

I would like to emphasize that, at this time, under existing earmark policy, earmarks (as defined by clause 9(e) of Rule XXI of the Rules of the House) should not be included. Please also be aware that, should a Member request an earmark, such request invokes the Code of Official Conduct. Clause 17 of the Code prohibits Members from requesting a congressional earmark without disclosing certain information to the Chair of the Committee of jurisdiction. Members are advised to consider their submissions to the Committee carefully in light of this to avoid inadvertently triggering the earmark rules and requirements.

§ 7.84 (continued)

Examples of Appropriations Subcommittees' Requirements for Member Requests

As you prepare your submissions, please note the following guidelines:

- All submissions must be made electronically to the relevant subcommittee at the https://AppropriationsSubmissions.house.gov web site. Only submissions received electronically will be considered. Hard-copy submissions are not required and will not be accepted.

- Submissions must include an uploaded letter signed by the Member supporting the Member's requests. Letters should simply list and describe each submission briefly. Letters may be either an individual letter for each request or a consolidated letter for multiple requests made to this subcommittee. **Please note that the Member request website has been modified this year to allow consolidated letters to be uploaded only once, so that a letter with multiple requests does not need to be uploaded multiple times.**

- The electronic system will require Members to assign a priority rank order to all their submissions for each subcommittee. The relevant subcommittee will review your priority rankings based on what you enter into the database.

- For requests with multiple Member cosponsors, each cosponsor must enter the same request into the online database. In addition, each cosponsor should either scan and upload a copy of the group request letter, or include the group request in a consolidated letter of all the Member's requests for the subcommittee.

- The electronic system allows access to prior submissions, so you may review those submissions if that is helpful. Prior submissions are not subject to change.

Thank you for your interest in the programs and activities of the House Appropriations Committee. If you have any general questions or require further information, please contact the Committee staff at (202) 225-2771. Technical questions related specifically to the operation of the system should be directed to the Committee's IT office at (202) 225-2718.

I look forward to working with you throughout the fiscal year 2018 appropriations process.

Sincerely,

Appropriations measures also contain other types of provisions that serve specialized purposes, such as provisions that liquidate (pay off) obligations made pursuant to certain *contract authority* and that *reappropriate* funds provided in previous years. These provisions also *transfer* funds from one account to another; *rescind* funds (or release *deferred* funds); and set ceilings on the amount of obligations that can be made under permanent appropriations, on the amount of direct or guaranteed loans that can be made, or on the amount of administrative expenses that can be incurred during the fiscal year. In addition to providing funds, appropriations acts often contain substantive limitations on government agencies.

Detailed information on how funds are to be spent, along with other directives or guidance, is provided in the committee and conference reports accompanying the various appropriations measures. Although report language typically is not binding legally, agencies ordinarily abide by it in spending the funds appropriated by Congress.

The appropriations reports do not comment on every item of expenditure. Report language is most likely when the Appropriations Committee prefers to spend more or less on a particular item than the president has requested or when the committee wants to earmark funds for a particular project or activity. When a particular item is mentioned by the committee, there is a strong expectation that the agency will adhere to the instructions.

§ 7.90 Revenue Legislation

The Constitution requires that all revenue measures originate in the House of Representatives. The Senate, however, may amend a House-originated revenue measure. If the Senate adopts an original Senate measure carrying a revenue provision, the House usually enforces its constitutional prerogative over originating revenue measures by adopting a simple resolution stating that the Senate measure infringes upon the privileges of the House and returning the measure to the Senate, a process referred to as "blue-slipping." The term "blue-slipping" refers to the blue paper on which the resolution is printed.

In the House, revenue legislation is under the jurisdiction of the Ways and Means Committee; in the Senate, jurisdiction is held by the Finance Committee. House rules bar other committees from reporting revenue legislation. Sometimes, however, another committee will report legislation levying user fees on a class that benefits from a particular service or program or that is being regulated by a federal agency. In many of these cases, the user-fee legislation in the House is referred subsequently to the Ways and Means Committee.

Most revenues derive from existing provisions of the tax code or Social Security law, which generally continues in effect from year to year unless changed by Congress. Congress usually makes some changes in the tax laws each year, either to raise or lower revenues or to redistribute the tax burden. (*See § 7.91, Tax Expenditures.*)

Congress typically acts on revenue legislation pursuant to proposals in the president's budget. An early step in congressional work on revenue legislation is publication by the Congressional Budget Office (CBO) of its own estimates of the revenue impact of the president's budget proposals, developed with assistance from the Joint Committee on Taxation. The congressional estimates often differ significantly from those presented in the president's budget.

The revenue totals in the budget resolution establish the framework for subsequent action on

§7.91

Tax Expenditures

In enacting revenue legislation, Congress often establishes or alters tax expenditures. As defined in the 1974 Congressional Budget Act, "tax expenditures" include revenue losses due to deductions, exemptions, credits, and other exceptions to the basic tax structure. Tax expenditures are a means by which Congress pursues public policy objectives and, frequently, can be regarded as alternatives to other policy instruments such as grants and loans. The Joint Committee on Taxation estimates the revenue effects of legislation changing tax expenditures, and also publishes five-year projections of these provisions as an annual committee print. Every two years, the Senate Budget Committee issues a compendium of tax expenditures (prepared by the Congressional Research Service). An example of a well-known tax expenditure is the mortgage-interest deduction available to homeowners.

§7.92

Revenue Estimates

The Joint Committee on Taxation (JCT) *<http://jct.gov>* prepares estimates of proposed revenue legislation for Congress. Generally, the estimates measure the effects of revenue proposals on the revenue projections under existing law. In recent years, some members of Congress have questioned whether or not the estimates of revenue proposals currently provided by the JCT (referred to as "static" by some) adequately take into account macroeconomic effects and incorporate such effects into revenue estimates (referred to as "dynamic estimates").

House standing rules require a "macroeconomic impact analysis" of most revenue measures reported by the Committee on Ways and Means, unless the JCT determines that such an analysis is "not calculable."

The House rule defines a "macroeconomic impact analysis" as:

(i) an estimate prepared by the Joint Committee on Internal Revenue [sic] Taxation of the changes in economic output, employment, capital stock, and tax revenues expected to result from enactment of the proposal; and

(ii) a statement from the Joint Committee on Internal Revenue [sic] Taxation identifying the critical assumptions and the source data underlying that estimate.

Neither the House rule nor the 1974 Congressional Budget Act requires that such estimates be used for budget enforcement purposes.

revenue measures. The budget resolution contains only revenue totals and the amounts by which total revenues should be changed by legislative action. It does not allocate these totals among revenue sources or specify which provisions of the tax code are to be changed.

The House and Senate periodically consider major revenue measures under their regular legislative procedures. (*See § 7.92, Revenue Estimates.*) However, as has been the case with direct-spending programs, many of the most significant changes in revenue policy in recent years have been made in the context of the reconciliation process. (*See § 7.110, Reconciliation Legislation.*) Although revenue changes sometimes are incorporated along with spending changes (and sometimes debt-limit increases) into a single, omnibus budget reconciliation measure, at other times revenue reconciliation legislation is considered on a separate track (for example, the Tax Increase Prevention and Reconciliation Act of 2005 (*P.L. 109-222; 120 Stat. 345*)).

§ 7.100 Debt-Limit Legislation

When the revenues collected by the federal government are not sufficient to cover its expenditures, it must finance the shortfall through borrowing. In addition, the federal government is compelled to incur debt because of requirements that trust fund surpluses be invested in federal securities. Federal borrowing is subject to a public-debt limit established by statute. As long as the federal government incurs annual deficits and trust funds incur annual surpluses, the public-debt limit must be increased periodically. The frequency of congressional action to raise the debt limit has ranged in the past from several times in one year to once in several years.

Legislation to raise the public-debt limit falls under the jurisdiction of the House Ways and Means Committee and the Senate Finance Committee. Congress has developed debt-limit legislation over the years in three ways: (1) under regular legislative procedures; (2) as part of reconciliation legislation; or (3) in the House, under the former Rule XXVII (referred to as the "Gephardt rule" after its author, former Representative Richard Gephardt, D-MO). House Rule XXVII required that the House Clerk automatically engross and transmit to the Senate, upon the adoption of the budget resolution, a joint resolution changing the public debt limit to the level specified in the budget resolution. This automatic engrossing process was added to the House rules in 1979, remained in the House rules until it was removed at the beginning of the 107th Congress, was restored at the beginning of the 108th Congress, and was removed again at the beginning of the 112th Congress in 2011. The Senate has had no procedure comparable to the Gephardt rule.

§ 7.110 Reconciliation Legislation

Beginning in 1980, Congress has used *reconciliation legislation* to implement many of its most significant budget policies. Section 310 of the 1974 Congressional Budget Act sets forth procedures for the development and consideration of reconciliation legislation. Reconciliation legislation is used by Congress to bring existing revenue, spending, and debt-limit law into conformity with the policies in a budget resolution. Reconciliation is an optional process, but Congress has used it more years than not since 1980.

The reconciliation process has two stages—the adoption of *reconciliation directives* in the budget resolution and the enactment of reconciliation legislation that implements changes in revenue or spending laws. Although reconciliation has been used for some time, specific procedures tend to vary from year to year.

Reconciliation is used to change the amount of revenues, budget authority, or outlays generated by existing law. In a few instances, reconciliation has been used to adjust the public-debt limit. On the spending side, the process focuses on entitlement laws; it may not be used, however, to impel changes in Social Security law. Reconciliation sometimes has been applied to discretionary authorizations, which are funded in annual appropriations acts, but this is not the usual practice.

Reconciliation Directives

Reconciliation begins with a directive in a budget resolution instructing one or more designated committees to recommend legislation changing existing law. These directives have three components: (1) they name the committee or committees directed to recommend legislation; (2) they specify the amounts of changes in revenues or outlays that are to be achieved by changes in existing law, but do not usually indicate how these changes are to be made, which laws are to be altered, or the programs to be affected; and (3) they usually set a deadline by which the designated committee or committees must recommend the changes in law. The directives cover the same fiscal years covered by the budget resolution. The dollar amounts are computed with reference to the Congressional Budget Office *baseline* that underlies the budget resolution. Thus, a change represents the amount by which revenues or spending would decrease or increase from baseline levels as a result of changes made in existing law.

Although the instructions generally do not mention the programs to be changed, they are based on assumptions concerning the savings or deficit reduction (or, in some cases, increases) that would result from particular changes in revenue provisions or spending programs. These program assumptions are sometimes printed in the reports on the budget resolution. Even when the assumptions are not published, committees and members usually have a good idea of the specific program changes contemplated by the reconciliation directives.

A committee has discretion to decide the legislative changes to be recommended. It is not bound by the program changes recommended or assumed by the budget committees in the reports accompanying the budget resolution. However, a committee is expected to recommend legislation estimated to produce the dollar changes delineated in its reconciliation directives.

When a budget resolution containing a reconciliation directive has been approved by Congress, the instruction has the status of an order by the House and Senate to designated committees to recommend legislation, usually by a date certain.

Development and Consideration of Reconciliation Measures

When more than one committee in the House and Senate is subject to reconciliation directives, the proposed legislative changes are consolidated by the budget committees into an omnibus bill. The 1974 Congressional Budget Act does not permit the budget committees to revise substantively the legislation recommended by the committees of jurisdiction. This restriction pertains even when the budget committees estimate that the proposed legislation will fall short of the dollar changes called for in the instructions. Sometimes, the budget committees—working with the leadership—develop alternatives to the committee recommendations. These alternatives may be offered as floor amendments to achieve greater compliance with the reconciliation directives.

The 1974 act requires that amendments offered to reconciliation legislation in either the House or the Senate be deficit-neutral. To meet this requirement, an amendment reducing revenues or increasing spending must offset these deficit increases by equivalent revenue increases or spending cuts. In addition, nongermane amendments may not be offered in either chamber.

During the first several years of experience with reconciliation, the legislation contained many provisions that were extraneous to the purpose of the reconciliation measures, such as reducing the deficit. The reconciliation submissions of committees included such things as provisions that had no budgetary effect, that had a budgetary effect merely incidental to a significant policy change, or that violated another committee's jurisdiction. In 1985, the Senate adopted a rule (commonly referred to as the *Byrd rule*, after Senator Robert C. Byrd, D-WV) on a temporary basis as a means of curbing these practices. The Byrd rule has been extended and modified several times over the years. In 1990, the Byrd rule was incorporated into the 1974 Congressional Budget Act as section 313 and made permanent. The Senate, nonetheless, may waive the Byrd rule by unanimous consent or by a waiver motion requiring a three-fifths vote of the membership. Although the House has no rule comparable to the Senate's Byrd rule, it may use other devices to control the inclusion of extraneous matter in reconciliation legislation. In particular, the House has used *special rules* to make in order amendments to strike extraneous matter.

Senate debate on reconciliation legislation is limited to twenty hours. The Senate may continue to consider amendments, motions, and appeals after that time, but no additional debate is allowed. The House is not restricted by the 1974 act in debate on reconciliation legislation, but it typically adopts a special rule limiting general debate, amendments, and other floor procedures.

§ 7.120 Implementation of the Budget by Executive Agencies

Federal agencies implement the various spending and revenue measures enacted into law through thousands of discrete actions. While the submission of the president's budget proposals and the subsequent consideration of them by Congress in the legislative process usually garner considerable attention in the media, less scrutiny often is paid to what actually happens to funds after congressional action is finished. Three categories of executive agency actions are of particular interest to Congress: apportionment (*§ 7.130*), transfer and reprogramming (*§ 7.140*), and impoundment (*§ 7.150*).

§ 7.130 Apportionment

After legislation providing budget authority is enacted into law, one of the first steps in making the funds available for spending by agencies is *apportionment*. Apportionment procedures are set forth in the Antideficiency Act (*31 U.S.C. §§ 1341–1342, 1512–1519*), which evolved from legislation first enacted in the 1870s. Under these procedures, the Office of Management and Budget (OMB) determines how increments of budget authority will be advanced to each agency on an account-by-account basis. For a typical account, OMB apportions one-fourth of the available budget authority at the beginning of each fiscal quarter. A violation of the Antideficiency Act may occur when an agency obligates more funds than were apportioned to it; the comptroller general is tasked by Congress with monitoring such violations.

In the absence of an appropriations act, such as when a continuing resolution (CR) is not enacted in a timely manner, the Antideficiency Act requires the affected agencies to shut down.

§ 7.140 Transfer and Reprogramming

After spending measures have been enacted into law, agencies sometimes shift funds from one purpose to another. A *transfer* involves the shifting of funds from one account to another, while a *reprogramming* involves shifting funds from one program to another within the same account. In either case, Congress is involved in these adjustments, although in varying degrees.

Permanent law, in Title 31 (Money and Finance) of the U.S. Code, requires that agencies spend funds only according to the purposes specified in law. For this reason, the transfer of funds from one account to another requires the enactment of a law. In some cases, Congress anticipates the need to transfer funds and may grant a department or agency head transfer authority in advance, subject to limitations. In other instances, Congress might enact legislation providing for specified transfers after the need has been identified.

Unlike transfers, reprogrammings do not shift funds from one account to another and therefore do not require the enactment of a law. The Appropriations Committees exert control over reprogrammings by establishing specific rules that agencies must follow when pursuing such actions. In recent years, these rules have been included as provisions in annual appropriations acts. The rules set forth restrictions such as requiring prior committee notification and approval for reprogrammings beyond a certain dollar threshold and barring reprogrammings from terminating any existing program or creating a new one.

§ 7.150 Impoundment: Deferrals and Rescissions

Although an appropriation limits the amounts that can be spent, it also establishes the expectation that the available funds will be used in full. Hence, when an agency fails to use all or part of an appropriation, it deviates from the intentions of Congress. The Impoundment Control Act of 1974 (*P.L. 93-344, title X; 88 Stat. 332–339*), enacted as part of the Congressional Budget and Impoundment Control Act of 1974, prescribes rules and procedures for instances in which available funds are *impounded. (See § 7.10, Key Budget Process Laws.*)

An impoundment is an action or inaction by the president or a federal agency that delays or withholds the obligation or expenditure of budget authority provided in law. The 1974 Impoundment Control Act divides impoundments into two categories and establishes distinct procedures for each. A *deferral* delays the use of funds; a *rescission* is a presidential request that Congress rescind (cancel) an appropriation or other form of budget authority. Deferral and rescission are exclusive and comprehensive categories. An impoundment is either a rescission or a deferral—it cannot be both or something else.

To propose a rescission, the president must submit a message to Congress specifying the amount to be rescinded, the accounts and programs involved, the estimated fiscal and program effects, and the reasons for the rescission. Multiple rescissions can be grouped in a single message. After the message has been submitted to it, Congress has forty-five days of "continuous session" (usually a larger number of calendar days) during which it can pass a rescission bill. Congress may rescind all, part, or none of the amount proposed by the president.

If Congress does not approve a rescission in legislation by the expiration of this period, the president must make the funds available for obligation and expenditure. If the president fails to release funds at the expiration of the forty-five-day period for proposed rescissions, the comptroller general may bring suit to compel their release. This has been a rare occurrence, however.

To defer funds, the president submits a message to Congress setting forth the amount, the affected account and program, the reasons for the deferral, the estimated fiscal and program effects, and the period of time during which the funds are to be deferred. The president may not propose a deferral for a period of time beyond the end of the fiscal year, and he may not propose a deferral that would cause the funds to lapse or otherwise prevent an agency from spending appropriated funds prudently. In accounts where unobligated funds remain available beyond the fiscal year, the president may defer the funds again in the next fiscal year.

At present, the president may defer only for the reasons set forth in the Antideficiency Act, including to provide for contingencies, to achieve savings made possible by or through changes in requirements or greater efficiency of operations, and as specifically provided by law. He may not defer funds for policy reasons (for example, to curtail overall federal spending or because he is opposed to a particular program).

The comptroller general, head of the Government Accountability Office (GAO), reviews all proposed rescissions and deferrals and advises Congress of their legality and possible budgetary and program effects. The comptroller general also notifies Congress of any rescission or deferral not reported by the president. The comptroller general may also reclassify an improperly classified impoundment. In all cases, a notification to Congress by the comptroller general has the same legal effect as an impoundment message of the president. The president's impoundment messages, as well as the comptroller general's reports, are printed as House documents (H. Doc. ___). The GAO also issues its reports separately.

The 1974 Impoundment Control Act provided for special types of legislation—rescission bills and deferral resolutions—for Congress to use in exercising its impoundment control powers. However, pursuant to court decisions that held the *legislative veto* to be unconstitutional, Congress may not use deferral resolutions to disapprove a deferral. Further, Congress has been reluctant to use rescission bills regularly. Congress, instead, usually acts on impoundment matters within the framework of the annual appropriations measures.

Line-Item Veto

During the 104th Congress, the Line Item Veto Act (*P.L. 104-130; 110 Stat. 1200*) was enacted as an amendment to the 1974 Impoundment Control Act. President Clinton applied the line-item veto to several measures in 1997, but the Supreme Court ruled the Line Item Veto Act unconstitutional in June 1998 and the earlier line-item vetoes were nullified. (*Clinton v. City of New York*, 524 U.S. 417 (1998).) The authority granted to the president under the Line Item Veto Act, which differed markedly from the veto authority available to most chief executives at the state level, was intended to reverse the presumption underlying the process for the consideration of rescissions under the 1974 Impoundment Control Act. Under the Line Item Veto Act, presidential proposals would take effect unless overturned by legislative action. The act authorized the president to identify at enactment individual items in legislation that he proposed should not go into effect. The identification was based not just upon the statutory language, but on the entire legislative history and documentation. The president had to notify Congress promptly of his proposals and provide supporting information. Congress had to respond within a limited period of time by enacting a law if it wanted to disapprove the president's proposals. Otherwise, the president's proposals would take effect.

In the wake of the Line Item Veto Act's nullification, there have been proposals that the president be given enhanced rescission authority, under which he could propose rescissions that Congress would be forced to act on (but not required to pass) under expedited procedures.

§7.160

Budget Process Glossary

Account: Control and reporting unit for budgeting and accounting.

Appropriated Entitlement: An entitlement for which budget authority is provided in annual appropriations acts.

Appropriation: Provision of law providing budget authority that permits federal agencies to incur obligations and make payments out of the Treasury.

Authorization: Provision in law that establishes or continues a program or agency and authorizes appropriations for it.

Baseline: Projection of future revenues, budget authority, outlays, and other budget amounts under assumed economic conditions and participation rates without a change in current policy.

Borrowing Authority: Spending authority that permits a federal agency to incur obligations and to make payments for specified purposes out of funds borrowed from the Treasury or the public.

Budget Authority: Authority in law to enter into obligations that normally result in outlays.

Budget Resolution: Concurrent resolution incorporating an agreement by the House and Senate on an overall budget plan; may contain reconciliation instructions.

Byrd Rule: A Congressional Budget Act rule (Section 313), named after its author, Senator Robert C. Byrd (D-WV), that prohibits extraneous matter in a reconciliation measure considered in the Senate. Under the rule, extraneous matter includes, among other things specified in the act, any provision that has no direct budgetary effect or that increases the deficit (or reduces the surplus) in a fiscal year beyond those covered in the reconciliation measure.

Continuing Appropriations Act: An appropriations act that provides stop-gap funding for agencies that have not received regular appropriations. (Also referred to as a continuing resolution.)

Cost Estimate: An estimate of the impact of legislation on revenues, spending, or both, generally as reported by a House or Senate committee or a conference committee; the 1974 Congressional Budget Act requires the Congressional Budget Office to prepare cost estimates on all committee-reported bills.

Credit Authority: Authority to incur direct loan obligations or make loan guarantee commitments.

Deferral: Action or inaction that temporarily withholds, delays, or effectively precludes the obligation or expenditure of budget authority.

Direct Spending: Spending controlled outside of annual appropriations acts, and specifically including the Food Stamp program (now the Supplemental Nutrition Assistance Program (SNAP)); also referred to as mandatory spending.

Discretionary Spending: Spending provided in, and controlled by, annual appropriations acts.

Earmark: For expenditures, an amount set aside within an appropriation account for a specified purpose.

Entitlement Authority: Law that obligates the federal government to make payments to eligible persons, businesses, or governments.

Fiscal Year: The period from October 1 through September 30; fiscal year 2018 began October 1, 2017, and ended September 30, 2018.

Impoundment: Action or inaction by an executive official that delays or precludes the obligation or expenditure of budget authority.

Mandatory Spending: *See Direct Spending.*

Continued on page 7-42

§ 7.160 (continued)

Budget Process Glossary

Obligation: A binding agreement that requires payment.

Outlays: Payments to liquidate obligations.

PAYGO (Pay-As-You-Go): Process by which direct spending increases or revenue decreases must be offset so that the deficit is not increased or the surplus reduced. A statutory PAYGO requirement is in effect and the Senate has a PAYGO rule.

Reconciliation: Process by which Congress changes existing laws to conform revenue and spending levels to the levels set in a budget resolution.

Regular Appropriations Act: An appropriations act that provides budget authority for the next fiscal year.

Reprogramming: Shifting funds from one program to another in the same appropriations account.

Rescission: Cancellation of budget authority previously provided by Congress.

Revenues: Income from individual and corporate income taxes, social insurance taxes, excise taxes, fees, tariffs, and other sources collected under the sovereign powers of the federal government.

Scorekeeping: Process for tracking and reporting on the status of congressional budgetary actions affecting budget authority, outlays, revenues, and the surplus or deficit.

Supplemental Appropriations Act: An appropriations act that provides additional budget authority during the current year when the regular appropriation is insufficient.

Tax Expenditure: Loss of revenue attributable to an exemption, deduction, preference, or other exclusion under federal tax law.

Transfer: Shift of budgetary resources from one appropriation account to another, as authorized by law.

Views and Estimates: Annual report of each House and Senate committee on budgetary matters within its jurisdiction.

A large legislative glossary is located at the back the book and online: <*TCNLG.com*>.

§ 7.170 Chapter Summary and Discussion Questions
Summary

- The Constitution vests governmental power to tax and spend in Congress, which it exercises by passing legislation that the president may then sign or veto.
- Through lawmaking, Congress has given the president many responsibilities for the federal budget, in addition to his constitutional duty to carry out tax and spending laws. For example, the president is required to propose a budget annually to Congress.
- Congress has also exercised its constitutional authority under the Necessary and Proper Clause (*see Chapter Eight, Legislating in Congress: Special Procedures and Considerations*) to direct how the president implements tax and spending laws. For example, the Antideficiency Act prevents an agency from spending more money than Congress has made available to it.
- Congress also in 1974 passed a law, the Congressional Budget Act, to give structure to its own consideration of budgetary legislation. By passing a concurrent resolution on the budget after reviewing the president's annual budget, Congress makes a comprehensive decision on total

revenues, total spending, and the deficit for a fiscal year. This comprehensive decision is then enforced against individual pieces of budgetary legislation as they are considered by the House and Senate.

- The Congressional Budget Act added a new process to existing authorizations and appropriations processes, whereby Congress sought to consider two kinds of legislation: policymaking authorization bills, on the one hand, and spending bills, called appropriations bills, that make budget authority available for programs and agencies, on the other. Spending in appropriations bills is called discretionary spending since Congress must pass an appropriation annually for budget authority to be available to a program or agency.

- Another kind of spending is called direct or mandatory spending, where a law requires money to be spent for a program. Only a change in the law can affect coverage or cost of the program; the appropriations process cannot be used to increase or decrease spending. Major social programs such as Social Security, Medicare, and Medicaid are examples of direct spending programs.

- In the Congressional Budget Act, Congress also established the reconciliation process, which provides a mechanism for Congress to enforce a decision made in a budget resolution by directing committees to report certain budgetary legislation and by expediting the consideration of such legislation on the floor, particularly in the Senate.

Discussion Questions

- Think about the nature of the legislative and executive branches, for example, 535 representatives and senators compared to one president, or decision-making in a bicameral legislature compared to executive authority constitutionally residing in president. Why might Congress have shared its budgetary powers with the president and executive branch, and what might it have hoped to achieve?

- Under the Constitution, what taxing and spending power would Congress be unable to share with the president?

- What political purposes might the budget development process in the executive branch serve? Think about presidential priorities related to taxes, spending programs, and the deficit and debt, and gathering support in Congress and among the public for those priorities.

- Notice that in some of the years that Congress has not completed action on a congressional budget resolution, the House, Senate, and presidency were all under the same party's control. Single-party control does not mean ready agreement. It suggests that budget decision-making is not just a policy decision but a political decision, as is the case with nearly all decision-making in Congress. Think about the budget debate occurring this year. What does this debate tell you about trying to find a budget policy that a majority in each house of Congress could support?

- What national or international occurrences in recent years have affected levels of revenue and spending? How have these occurrences limited Congress and the president's ability to control spending and the deficit?

- Considering budget enforcement mechanisms Congress uses now or has used in the past, how efficacious might they be in addressing today's federal deficit and debt concerns? What process changes, if any, might assist Congress in controlling the deficit and debt? Are these changes politically feasible—how could a majority in each house be obtained to support the changes?

Congressional Research Service
Informing the legislative debate since 1914

The Budget Reconciliation Process: Stages of Consideration

Megan S. Lynch
Specialist on Congress and the Legislative Process

James V. Saturno
Specialist on Congress and the Legislative Process

January 4, 2017

Congressional Research Service
7-5700
www.crs.gov
R44058

Summary

The purpose of the reconciliation process is to enhance Congress's ability to bring existing spending, revenue, and debt limit laws into compliance with current fiscal priorities and goals established in the annual budget resolution. In adopting a budget resolution, Congress is agreeing upon its budgetary goals for the upcoming fiscal year. Because it is in the form of a concurrent resolution, however, it is not presented to the President or enacted into law. As a consequence, any statutory changes concerning spending or revenues that are necessary to implement these policies must be enacted in separate legislation.

Budget reconciliation is an optional congressional process that operates as an adjunct to the budget resolution process and occurs only if reconciliation instructions are included in the budget resolution. Reconciliation instructions are the means by which Congress can establish the roles that specific committees will play in achieving these budgetary goals. Reconciliation consists of several different stages, which are described in this report. For more information on budget reconciliation bills enacted into law, please see CRS Report R40480, *Budget Reconciliation Measures Enacted Into Law: 1980-2010*, by Megan S. Lynch.

Contents

Figures

Contacts

The Reconciliation Process

The purpose of the reconciliation process is to allow Congress to use an expedited procedure when considering legislation that would bring existing spending, revenue, and debt limit laws into compliance with current fiscal priorities established in the annual budget resolution.[1] In adopting a budget resolution, Congress is agreeing upon budgetary goals for the upcoming fiscal year (as well as for a period of at least four additional outyears). In some cases, for these goals to be achieved, Congress must enact legislation that alters current revenue, direct spending,[2] or debt limit laws. In this situation, Congress seeks to *reconcile* existing law with its current priorities. Since its first use in 1980, these expedited procedures have been used to pass 24 reconciliation bills.[3]

Budget reconciliation is an optional, expedited legislative process that consists of several different stages (as described below) beginning with the adoption of the budget resolution. If Congress intends to use the reconciliation process, reconciliation directives (also referred to as reconciliation instructions) must be included in the annual budget resolution. These directives trigger the second stage of the process by instructing individual committees to develop and report legislation that would change laws within their respective jurisdictions related to direct spending, revenue, or the debt limit.

Once a specified committee develops legislation, the reconciliation directive may further direct it to report the legislation for consideration in their respective chamber or submit it to the Budget Committee to be included in an omnibus reconciliation measure. Reported reconciliation legislation is eligible to be considered under expedited procedures in both the House and Senate. As with all legislation, any differences in the reconciliation legislation passed by the two chambers must be resolved before the bill can be sent to the President for approval or veto.

---

[1] As provided in Section 310 of the Congressional Budget Act of 1974 as amended (P.L. 93-344) (the Budget Act).

[2] Direct spending consists of entitlement authority (including appropriated entitlements), the food stamp program, and any other budget authority (and resulting outlays) provided in laws other than appropriation acts. The term *direct spending* is often used interchangeably with the terms *entitlement* and *mandatory spending*. Such federal programs are those under which individuals, businesses, or units of government that meet the requirements or qualifications established by law are entitled to receive certain payments if they seek such payments. Major examples include Social Security, Medicare, Medicaid, unemployment insurance, and military and federal civilian pensions. In current practice, reconciliation directives concerning spending are made only with respect to direct spending in the jurisdiction of House and Senate legislative committees and not to discretionary spending in the jurisdiction of the Appropriations Committees.

[3] For a list of all reconciliation bills, see CRS Report R40480, *Budget Reconciliation Measures Enacted Into Law: 1980-2010*, by Megan S. Lynch. Although the House and Senate first used the reconciliation process in 1980 (for FY1981), this report focuses on the period covering 1989 (for FY1990) through 2009 (for FY2010).

Figure 1. Major Stages of the Reconciliation Process

1. Budget resolution adopted that includes reconciliation directives to individual committees

2B. When applicable, Budget Committee packages committee responses together and reports bill to full chamber

4. Differences resolved between chambers (conference committee or amendment exchange)

2A. Specific committees report legislation in response to reconciliation directives

3. Reconciliation bill considered on chamber floor

5. Reconciliation bill enacted into law or vetoed

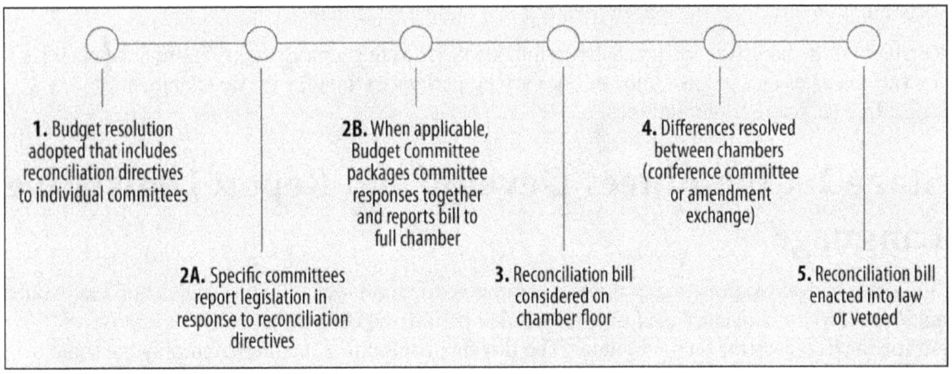

Source: Congressional Research Service.

Stage 1: Budget Resolution Adopted That Includes Reconciliation Directives

Congress has the option of including reconciliation directives in its annual budget resolution. These directives are necessary to trigger the reconciliation process, and without their inclusion in a budget resolution, no measure would qualify to be considered under the expedited reconciliation procedures.

When reconciliation directives are included in an annual budget resolution, their purpose is to require committees to develop and report legislation and allow Congress to consider legislation to achieve the budgetary goals set forth in the annual budget resolution under special expedited procedures. These directives detail which committee(s) should report reconciliation legislation, the date by which the committee(s) should report, the dollar amount of budgetary change that should be in the resulting reconciliation legislation, and the time period over which the impact of this budgetary change should be measured. They might also include language regarding the type of budgetary change that should be reported as well as other procedural provisions, contingencies, and non-binding language concerning policy or programmatic direction.[4]

Section 310(a) of the Budget Act provides for three types of budgetary changes that committees may be directed to report: direct spending, revenue, and debt limit. The Budget Act also provides that committees may be directed to report any of these types of budgetary changes. Instructions have been in the form of directing a committee specifically to reduce or increase one (or more) of these types of changes, as well as to achieve deficit reduction.

Any legislative committee with jurisdiction over spending, revenue, or the debt limit may be directed to report reconciliation legislation, and numerous committees have been instructed to report reconciliation legislation at some point. Because the Senate Finance Committee and the House Committee on Ways and Means have jurisdiction within their respective chambers over not only major direct spending programs but also all revenue and debt limit legislation, these

---

[4] For more information on reconciliation directives, see CRS Report R41151, *Budget Reconciliation Process: Timing of Committee Responses to Reconciliation Directives*, by Megan S. Lynch.

8-5

committees have often been directed to report some type of reconciliation legislation when reconciliation directives have been included in a budget resolution.[5]

Reconciliation directives include submission deadlines to the committee(s). These have been set for various dates and so have allowed for varying periods of time for the development of legislative language by committees.

Stage 2: Committees Develop and Report Legislative Language

While the budget resolution may direct a committee to report reconciliation legislation that would achieve a certain budgetary goal over a specified period, the Budget Act does not impose any additional requirements on committees. The directed committees, therefore, employ the same rules and practices used otherwise in their legislative work.

In addition, the programmatic details of the legislation—including how the specified budgetary goals should be met—are left to the discretion of the specified committee. In general, a committee may report any matter within their jurisdiction, regardless of any assumptions concerning policy or programmatic direction indicated in the budget resolution.[6]

If a committee is given more than one directive—for instance, both to increase revenues and to decrease spending—then the committee may respond with separate recommendations. Under current Senate practice, the language in Section 310(a) is interpreted to mean that no more than one measure of each type would be eligible to be considered under expedited procedures as a reconciliation bill. Under current practice, therefore, as many as three measures could qualify for consideration under expedited reconciliation procedures in the Senate—but no more than one each for spending, revenue, and the debt limit.

Compliance with the dollar amount set forth in a reconciliation directive is measured on a net basis. This means that legislation responding to a directive to reduce spending, for instance, could be in order even if it includes a provision that would increase spending for a certain program so long as the legislation, taken as a whole, would satisfy the overall spending decreases set forth in the reconciliation directive.

Although a reconciliation directive may instruct a committee to report legislation that would affect spending levels, a committee may respond to the directive by recommending either changes to direct spending programs or changes in offsetting collections within its jurisdiction. Offsetting collections or receipts, such as user fees or royalties for water or mineral rights on federal land, are treated as negative amounts of spending rather than as revenues.

Reconciliation directives pertaining to direct spending generally refer to changes in outlay levels. The outlay level is the projected level of disbursed federal funds. Outlays differ from budget authority (which gives agencies the authority to incur obligations) and are used to assess the impact of the legislative changes on the federal deficit.

---

[5] Since the 101st Congress, of the 14 budget resolutions that have included reconciliation directives to Senate and House committees, 13 have directed the Senate Finance Committee and House Ways and Means Committee to report reconciliation legislation.

[6] However, Section 310(g) of the Budget Act specifically prohibits inclusion of changes to the old age, survivors, and disability insurance program established under Title II of the Social Security Act, and Section 313 (the Byrd rule, which is discussed below) prohibits the inclusion of extraneous provisions in the Senate.

Reconciliation directives may instruct a committee to recommend legislation that would increase or decrease revenues. Reconciliation directives to alter current revenue laws fall under the jurisdiction of the Senate Finance Committee and House Ways and Means Committee.

If a reconciliation directive instructs a committee to report legislation increasing revenues by a specific amount, that amount would be considered the minimum by which the legislation should increase revenues. Conversely, if a reconciliation directive includes instructions to decrease revenue, that amount would be considered the maximum by which revenue should be decreased.

There is a statutory limit on the total amount of debt that the federal government may incur at any time. In the event that Congress determines the debt limit to be too high or too low, legislation can be enacted to alter it. The reconciliation process is one of three methods Congress has utilized used to consider debt limit legislation over the last four decades, although it is the least frequently used, being employed only four times.[7]

Once a committee has developed legislative language in response to its reconciliation instructions, the committee will then meet to mark up and vote whether to report that language. The committee may vote to report the language favorably or unfavorably, the latter meaning that although it satisfied its directive, the committee did not support the language.[8]

Although committees have often responded to their directives early and on time, there is no procedural mechanism to compel committee action prior to the date specified in the budget resolution or even at all.[9] Committees have responded to their directive after the date specified, with no impact on whether the submitted language could be included in a reconciliation bill, if it had not yet been reported by the Budget Committee. A late response has also not had an impact on whether the resultant legislation could be considered as a reconciliation bill. In other words, late or incomplete responses to a reconciliation directive have not caused a measure to lose its privileged status as a reconciliation bill.[10]

Committee Compliance with Reconciliation Directives

If a reconciliation directive instructs a committee to report legislation reducing spending by a specific amount, that amount is considered a minimum, meaning a committee may report greater net spending reductions but not less. Conversely, if a reconciliation instruction directs a committee to report language increasing direct spending by a certain amount, that amount would be considered the maximum by which spending should be increased.

When either the House Ways and Means Committee or the Senate Finance Committee receives instructions concerning both spending and revenues, the Budget Act provides some flexibility

[7] For more information on consideration of debt limit legislation in the House and Senate, see CRS Report 98-453, Debt-Limit Legislation in the Congressional Budget Process, by Bill Heniff Jr.

[8] For example, on October 15, 1990, the House Post Office and Civil Service Committee voted unanimously to report unfavorably reconciliation language to satisfy its reconciliation directive.

[9] In some years, committees have not formally responded to the reconciliation directive instructing them to report legislation. There may be several reasons for the lack of a formal committee submission. For instance, there may have been a shift in policy priorities and Congress no longer desired to pass reconciliation legislation. It could also be that a committee fails to approve reconciliation language, or it may be that although committees did not respond formally to the directive, they reported freestanding legislation that was not considered under reconciliation procedures but which may have satisfied the goal of the reconciliation directive.

[10] For more information on timing of committee responses to reconciliation directives, see CRS Report R41151, *Budget Reconciliation Process: Timing of Committee Responses to Reconciliation Directives*, by Megan S. Lynch.

8-7

concerning how they may respond with a combination of spending and revenue changes. An example of such a directive is as follows:

> [T]he Committee on Ways and Means of the House of Representatives shall report to the House of Representatives a reconciliation bill not later than May 18, 2001, that consists of changes in laws within its jurisdiction sufficient to reduce revenues by not more than $1,250,000,000,000 for the period of fiscal years 2001 through 2011 and the total level of outlays may be increased by not more than $100,000,000,000 for the period of fiscal years 2001 through 2011.[11]

Section 310(c)(1) of the Budget Act, referred to as the "fungibility rule," allows a committee with both spending and revenue directives to substitute changes in one for the other, up to 20% of each directive, as long as the total amount of changes reported is equal to the total amount of changes instructed.

There is no procedural mechanism to ensure that legislation submitted by a committee in response to reconciliation directives will be in compliance with the instructed levels. If a committee does not report legislation, or such legislation is not in compliance with their instructions, however, there are methods that each chamber may employ in order to move forward with reconciliation legislation. In either situation, legislative language that falls within the non-compliant committee's jurisdiction can be added to a reconciliation bill during floor consideration that would bring it into compliance with its reconciliation instructions. These methods vary by chamber.

In the House, if a committee has failed to recommend changes in compliance with a reconciliation directive, the Budget Act provides that the House Rules Committee may make in order amendments to a reconciliation bill that would achieve the necessary changes.[12]

In the Senate, if a committee has not responded to a reconciliation directive, it still may be possible to take action on the Senate floor that would satisfy the committee's directive. In such a circumstance, it would be in order to offer a motion to recommit the reconciliation bill to that committee with instructions that it report the measure back to the Senate forthwith with an amendment that would bring the committee into compliance. Unlike amendments to the reconciliation bill, the motion to recommit would not be subject to the germaneness requirement in Section 305(b)(2). Such a motion to recommit would allow any Senator to craft legislative language within the directed committee's jurisdiction.

Omnibus Legislation Prepared by the Budget Committee

Reconciliation instructions in a budget resolution may direct either a single committee in each chamber or multiple committees to report. The Budget Act provides that in cases when only one committee has been directed to report, that committee may report its reconciliation legislation directly to the full chamber. If the budget resolution instructs more than one committee to report reconciliation legislation, however, those committees must submit their legislative recommendations to their respective Budget Committee.[13] The Budget Act states that the Budget Committee must then package the committee responses into an omnibus budget reconciliation bill and report the measure to its respective chamber without "any substantive revision." In fulfilling

---

[11] H.Con.Res. 83 (107th Congress).

[12] Section 310(d)(5) of the Budget Act. For more information on special rules and the amending process, see CRS Report 98-612, *Special Rules and Options for Regulating the Amending Process*, by Megan S. Lynch.

[13] Section 310(b)(2) of the Budget Act.

this requirement, the Budget Committee will typically hold a business meeting before voting to report to the chamber, and while amendments are not in order during the markup, members of the Budget Committee may still communicate support or concern related to the underlying legislation.

In addition, as the official scorekeeper for budgetary legislation generally, the committee may secure cost estimates necessary to ensure compliance with reconciliation directives and general consistency with the parameters established in the budget resolution.

At this stage, the Senate Budget Committee will also examine the recommendations submitted to determine whether any of the provisions might be in violation of the Byrd rule.[14] The Byrd rule was first adopted in 1985 in response to concerns that committees were including recommendations in their reconciliation submissions that were extraneous to achieving the budgetary goals established in the budget resolution. The Byrd rule generally prohibits the inclusion of material considered extraneous to the purpose of a reconciliation bill.[15]

Because the Budget Committee is required to include the language submitted by instructed committees without substantive revisions, however, the Budget Committee may not delete such language prior to it being reported. Instead, any Senator may raise a point of order against such provisions once the measure has been brought to the Senate floor for consideration. The Senate Budget Committee is required to submit for the record a list of provisions considered to be extraneous, although the inclusion or exclusion of a provision on such a list does not constitute a determination of extraneousness by the presiding officer of the Senate.[16]

Stage 3: Floor Consideration

Once a reconciliation measure has been reported, it is placed on the appropriate calendar of the House or Senate and becomes available for consideration by the full chamber.

House

Consideration of reconciliation measures in the House has historically been governed by the provisions of special rules reported from the House Rules Committee. These special rules have established the duration of a period for general debate and specified a limited number of amendments that will be in order. In most cases, the period for general debate has been specified as one or three hours, equally divided and controlled by the majority and minority floor managers.[17] The number of amendments made in order under these special rules has always been

---

[14] Section 313 of the Budget Act.

[15] *Extraneous*, as defined in the Budget Act, comprises provisions that (1) do not produce a change in outlays or revenues; (2) produce an outlay increase or revenue decrease when the instructed committee is not in compliance with its instructions; (3) are outside of the jurisdiction of the committee that submitted the title or provision for inclusion in the reconciliation measure; (4) produce a change in outlays or revenues that is merely incidental to the non-budgetary components of the provision; (5) would increase the deficit for a fiscal year beyond the period covered by the reconciliation measure; or (6) recommend changes in Social Security. For more information on the Byrd rule, see CRS Report RL30862, *The Budget Reconciliation Process: The Senate's "Byrd Rule"*, by Bill Heniff Jr.

[16] Further, under Section 313(c) of the Budget Act, the list is required only to include provisions considered extraneous under three of the six categories of extraneous (those that don't produce a change in outlays or revenues, those that produce an outlay increase or revenue decrease when the instructed committee is not in compliance with its instructions, and those that would produce an increase in the deficit for a fiscal year beyond the period covered by the reconciliation measure) and so may not be a complete list of all potentially extraneous provisions.

[17] Generally, this has been the chair and ranking minority member of the Budget Committee, except in cases where a (continued...)

limited, and, in most recent cases, there have been one or zero amendments in order to be offered during consideration of the bill.[18] In addition to these amending opportunities, however, House rules also allow for a motion to recommit the bill before the House votes on final passage. A Member from the minority party would have preference to make this motion, which may include amendatory instructions.[19] In effect, therefore, a motion to recommit with amendatory instructions provides one last opportunity for the minority party to offer an amendment to the bill. Amendatory instructions are subject to the same requirements or limits as any other amendment.

There are provisions in House rules and the Congressional Budget Act that could limit the subject and budgetary impact of amendments to reconciliation measures. For example, House Rule XVI, clause 7, prohibits nongermane amendments generally, and Section 310(d)(1) of the Budget Act prohibits amendments to the reconciliation bill that would increase spending above or reduce revenues below the amounts provided in the bill. However, in most circumstances, because special rules have limited the amendments to be offered (if any) to those specified in the special rule or the accompanying report, these limits have not been manifest during consideration.

Senate

Although the rules, precedents, and practices of the Senate do not place general limits on either the content of amendments that may be offered to legislation or the duration of their consideration, a distinguishing characteristic of the reconciliation process is that specific limits are placed on both. Consideration of reconciliation legislation in the Senate has been governed generally under the terms of Section 310(e) of the Congressional Budget Act. This section provides, in turn, that the provisions of Section 305 of the act concerning the consideration of a budget resolution also apply to the consideration of a reconciliation measure, except as specifically provided otherwise. As a consequence, reconciliation measures, like budget resolutions, are privileged, so motions to proceed to their consideration are not debatable.[20]

Once a motion to proceed is agreed to, the provisions of the Budget Act place specific time limits on debate of a reconciliation bill. Section 310(e)(2) limits total debate time on the measure—including all amendments, motions, or appeals—to 20 hours. This time must be equally divided and controlled by the majority and minority,[21] with debate on any amendment to the measure limited to two hours, equally divided and controlled, and debate on any amendment to an amendment, debatable motion, or appeal limited to one hour, equally divided and controlled.[22]

(...continued)

single committee received a reconciliation directive and was instructed to report the measure as a separate measure. For example, during consideration of H.R. 4297 (109th Cong.), which became the Tax Increase Prevention and Reconciliation Act of 2005 (P.L. 109-222), the time was equally divided and controlled by the chair and ranking minority member from the Committee on Ways and Means.

[18] In addition to amendments made in order to be offered during consideration of the bill, these special rules have sometimes included self-executing provisions that would consider specified amendments as adopted and incorporated in the bill upon the adoption of the special rule.

[19] See CRS Report 98-383, *Motions to Recommit in the House*, by Megan S. Lynch.

[20] Although the Budget Act does not explicitly state that reconciliation legislation is privileged, it does state that Senate procedure for considering reconciliation shall be the same as those for the budget resolution, which is privileged. See, for example, U.S. Congress, Senate, *Riddick's Senate Procedure, Precedents and Practices*, by Floyd M. Riddick and Alan S. Frumin, 101st Cong., 2nd sess., S.Doc. 101-28 (Washington: GPO 1992), p. 600; and Senate debate, *Congressional Record*, vol. 127 (May 12, 1981), p. 9455.

[21] Section 305(b)(1).

[22] Section 305(b)(2).

Even after time has expired, Senators may continue to offer amendments and make other motions or appeals, but without further debate. This period is often referred to as a "vote-a-rama." Although no further debate time is available, the Senate has typically agreed by unanimous consent to consider amendments under accelerated voting procedures, allowing a nominal amount of time to identify and explain an amendment and a 10-minute limit for vote time.[23] Although the Budget Act imposes no procedural limit on the duration of a vote-a-rama, the limit on debate time has meant, historically, that it has been unnecessary to invoke cloture in order to reach a final vote on a reconciliation bill in the Senate.

In addition to limits on debate time, the Budget Act places several limits on the subject matter and budgetary impact in both the measure and any amendments, which may be enforced by points of order.[24] Points of order are not self-enforcing, however. A point of order may be raised on the floor against legislation that is alleged to violate these rules at the time it is being considered. In general, the presiding officer may rule on whether the point of order is well taken and, thus, whether the measure, provision, or amendment is in order. In practice, however, it is possible in the Senate to preempt a ruling by the presiding officer by offering a motion to waive the application of points of order related to enforcing the limits associated with the Budget Act. In most cases, the motion to waive requires a vote of at least three-fifths of all Senators duly chosen and sworn (60 votes if there are no vacancies) to be successful. If a waiver motion fails, the presiding officer will then rule the provision or amendment out of order.

Under the terms of Section 313, as discussed above, extraneous provisions are not allowed to be included in the measure or offered as amendments to it. Instructed committees may not include extraneous provisions in the legislative language submitted to the Budget Committee for inclusion in an omnibus reconciliation measure. If a point of order is sustained under this section against a provision in the reconciliation measure as reported, the provision in question is stricken, but further consideration of the bill may proceed. If the point of order is sustained against an amendment or motion, further consideration of that amendment or motion would not be in order.

There are also rules intended to limit the content of amendments to reconciliation bills that are in order. Section 305(b)(2) requires that all amendments be germane to the provisions in the bill, meaning that amendments cannot be used to introduce new subjects or expand the scope of the bill. In addition, the Budget Act, and related requirements, place limits on the budgetary impact of amendments. Section 310(d)(1) prohibits the consideration of amendments to reconciliation legislation that would increase the level of outlays (or decrease the level of revenues) provided in the bill, and Section 310(d)(2) prohibits the consideration of amendments that would increase the level of outlays (or decrease the level of revenues) as measured in relation to the level of a committee's reconciliation instructions.

In addition, all other budget rules would apply to reconciliation bills the same way they would to any other budgetary measure. One notable example is Section 311(a)(2) of the Budget Act, which prohibits consideration of legislation that would cause new budget authority or outlays to exceed or revenues to fall below the levels set forth in the budget resolution.[25] Another is Section 404(a) of S.Con.Res. 13 (111th Congress), which prohibits consideration of direct spending or revenue

---

[23] For a discussion of this practice, see U.S. Senate Budget Committee, *Senate Procedures for Consideration of the Budget Resolution/Reconciliation*, 111th Cong., 1st sess., S.Hrg. 111-106, February 12, 2009.

[24] See CRS Report R43885, *Points of Order Limiting the Contents of Reconciliation Legislation: In Brief*, by James V. Saturno.

[25] For budget authority or outlays, this point of order would apply for the first fiscal year in the budget resolution, while for revenues it would apply for the first fiscal year and the total of all fiscal years.

legislation that would cause a net increase in the deficit in excess of $10 billion in any fiscal year provided for in the most recently adopted budget resolution unless it is fully offset over the period in the most recent budget resolution.

Finally, in order to ensure that changes to Social Security are considered under the regular procedures of the Senate, Section 310(g) explicitly prohibits consideration of changes to the old-age, survivors, and disability insurance program established under Title II of the Social Security Act, and the prohibition in Section 313 against extraneous provisions would also apply to these same changes.

Stage 4: Resolving Differences

As with all legislation, any differences in reconciliation legislation as passed by the two chambers must be resolved before the bill can be sent to the President for the final stage of the process.[26]

For reconciliation bills, the most common avenue for resolving differences between the House and Senate has been through creating a conference committee and appointing conferees from both chambers to negotiate. For a conference to reach agreement, a majority of the House conferees and a majority of the Senate conferees must sign the conference report. Once reported, the conference report must be approved by both chambers. Conference reports are privileged and debatable in both the House and Senate, but they may not be amended.

The House and Senate may also negotiate an agreement through an exchange of amendments between the houses. Although such an approach may be taken as an alternative to conference, historically it has not been used in the case of reconciliation legislation.[27]

In general, Budget Act points of order that would apply to the consideration of a reconciliation bill also apply to the consideration of a conference report or amendments between the chambers. In the Senate, this includes the Byrd rule, so that a conference report or an amendment between the chambers might be vulnerable to a point of order if it were to include an extraneous provision.

In the Senate, the Budget Act provides that debate on a conference report or a message between houses and all amendments or debatable motions is limited to 10 hours, equally divided and controlled by the majority and minority leaders.

Stage 5: Final Action by the President

Only after the House and Senate have reached agreement on the same text in the same bill can it be enrolled for presentation to the President, as provided in Article I, Section 7, of the Constitution. The President has a 10-day period (excluding Sundays) after the bill is presented in which he may sign the bill into law. Alternately, the President may veto the measure and return it to Congress. If both chambers vote by a two-thirds supermajority to override the veto, the measure would become law.

---

[26] For more on resolving differences generally, see CRS Report 98-696, *Resolving Legislative Differences in Congress: Conference Committees and Amendments Between the Houses*, by Elizabeth Rybicki.

[27] In the case of the Restoring Americans' Healthcare Freedom Reconciliation Act of 2015 (H.R. 3762, 114th Cong., vetoed), the House agreed to the amendment of the Senate. In addition, for Consolidated Omnibus Budget Reconciliation Act of 1985 (P.L. 99-272), the two chambers used an exchange of amendments to resolve outstanding differences after they had failed to agree to a conference report that had been negotiated by House and Senate conferees.

If the President chooses not to sign the bill and Congress remains in session, it would become law without his signature. However, if Congress has adjourned within the 10-day period after presentation, thereby preventing the return of the bill to Congress, by withholding his signature the President would prevent the bill from becoming law—a practice called a "pocket" veto.[28]

In four instances the President has vetoed reconciliation legislation.[29] In none of these cases has Congress successfully voted to override the President's veto.

Author Contact Information

Megan S. Lynch
Specialist on Congress and the Legislative Process
mlynch@crs.loc.gov, 7-7853

James V. Saturno
Specialist on Congress and the Legislative Process
jsaturno@crs.loc.gov, 7-2381

---

[28] See CRS Report RS22188, *Regular Vetoes and Pocket Vetoes: In Brief*, by Meghan M. Stuessy.

[29] In three of these cases, the measure was vetoed by President Clinton. The Balanced Budget Act of 1995 (H.R. 2491, 104th Cong.), vetoed December 6, 1995; the Taxpayer Refund and Relief Act of 1999 (H.R. 2488, 106th Cong.), vetoed September 23, 1999; and the Marriage Tax Relief Reconciliation Act of 2000 (H.R. 4810. 106th Cong.), vetoed August 5, 2000. In one case, the measure was vetoed by President Obama: the Restoring Americans' Healthcare Freedom Reconciliation Act of 2015 (H.R. 3762, 114th Cong.), vetoed January 8, 2016. In all four cases the measures were referred to committee. In two cases the House subsequently voted but failed to achieve the two-thirds supermajority necessary to override the President's veto. For H.R. 4810 (106th Cong.), the vote was 270-158. See *Congressional Record* (daily edition), vol. 146 (September 13, 2000), p. H7520. For H.R. 3762 (114th Cong.), the vote was 241-186. See *Congressional Record* (daily edition), vol. 162 (February 2, 2016), p. H482.

Congressional
Research Service
Informing the legislative debate since 1914

The Budget Reconciliation Process: The Senate's "Byrd Rule"

Bill Heniff Jr.
Analyst on Congress and the Legislative Process

November 22, 2016

Congressional Research Service
7-5700
www.crs.gov
RL30862

Summary

Reconciliation is a procedure under the Congressional Budget Act of 1974 by which Congress implements budget resolution policies affecting mainly permanent spending and revenue programs. The principal focus in the reconciliation process has been deficit reduction, but in some years reconciliation has involved revenue reduction generally and spending increases in selected areas. Although reconciliation is an optional procedure, it has been used most years since its first use by the House and Senate in 1980 (20 reconciliation bills have been enacted into law and four have been vetoed).

During the first several years' experience with reconciliation, the legislation contained many provisions that were extraneous to the purpose of implementing budget resolution policies. The reconciliation submissions of committees included such things as provisions that had no budgetary effect, that increased spending or reduced revenues when the reconciliation instructions called for reduced spending or increased revenues, or that violated another committee's jurisdiction.

In 1985 and 1986, the Senate adopted the Byrd rule (named after its principal sponsor, Senator Robert C. Byrd) on a temporary basis as a means of curbing these practices. The Byrd rule was extended and modified several times over the years. In 1990, the Byrd rule was incorporated into the Congressional Budget Act of 1974 as Section 313 and made permanent (2 U.S.C. 644).

A Senator opposed to the inclusion of extraneous matter in reconciliation legislation may offer an amendment (or a motion to recommit the measure with instructions) that strikes such provisions from the legislation, or, under the Byrd rule, a Senator may raise a point of order against such matter. In general, a point of order authorized under the Byrd rule may be raised in order to strike extraneous matter already in the bill as reported or discharged (or in the conference report), or to prevent the incorporation of extraneous matter through the adoption of amendments or motions. A motion to waive the Byrd rule, or to sustain an appeal of the ruling of the chair on a point of order raised under the Byrd rule, requires the affirmative vote of three-fifths of the membership (60 Senators if no seats are vacant).

The Byrd rule provides six definitions of what constitutes extraneous matter for purposes of the rule (and several exceptions thereto), but the term is generally described as covering provisions unrelated to achieving the goals of the reconciliation instructions.

The Byrd rule has been in effect during Senate consideration of 19 reconciliation measures from late 1985 through the present. Actions were taken under the Byrd rule in the case of 15 of the 19 measures. In total, 70 points of order and 57 waiver motions were considered and disposed of under the rule, largely in a manner that favored those who opposed the inclusion of extraneous matter in reconciliation legislation (60 points of order were sustained, in whole or in part, and 48 waiver motions were rejected).

This report has been updated to include the consideration of the Restoring Americans' Healthcare Freedom Reconciliation Act of 2015 (H.R. 3762, 114th Congress).

Contents

Tables

Appendixes

Contacts

Introduction

Reconciliation is a process established under Section 310 of the Congressional Budget Act of 1974 (P.L. 93-344, as amended).[1] The purpose of reconciliation is to change substantive law so that revenue and mandatory spending levels are brought into line with budget resolution policies. Reconciliation generally has been used to reduce the deficit through spending reductions or revenue increases, or a combination of the two. In some years, however, the reconciliation process also encompassed revenue reduction generally and spending increases in selected program areas.

Reconciliation is a two-step process. Under the first step, reconciliation instructions are included in the budget resolution, directing one or more committees in each House to develop legislation that changes spending or revenues (or both) by the amounts specified in the budget resolution. If more than one committee in each House is given instructions, each instructed committee submits reconciliation legislation to its respective Budget Committee, which incorporates all submissions, without any substantive revision, into a single, omnibus budget reconciliation measure. Reconciliation procedures during a session usually have applied to multiple committees and involved omnibus legislation.

Under the second step, the omnibus budget reconciliation measure is considered in the House and Senate under expedited procedures (for example, debate time in the Senate on a reconciliation measure is limited to 20 hours and amendments must be germane). The process culminates with enactment of the measure, thus putting the policies of the budget resolution into effect.

Reconciliation, which was first used by the House and Senate in 1980, is an optional procedure, but it has been used in most years. Over the period covering from 1980 to the present, 20 reconciliation bills have been enacted into law and four have been vetoed.[2]

During the first several years' experience with reconciliation, the legislation contained many provisions that were extraneous to the purpose of reducing the deficit. The reconciliation submissions of committees included such things as provisions that had no budgetary effect, that increased spending or reduced revenues, or that violated another committee's jurisdiction.

In 1985 and 1986, the Senate adopted the Byrd rule (named after its principal sponsor, Senator Robert C. Byrd) as a means of curbing these practices. Initially, the rule consisted of two components, involving a provision in a reconciliation act and a Senate resolution. The Byrd rule has been modified several times over the years.

The purpose of this report is to briefly recount the legislative history of the Byrd rule, summarize its current features, and describe its implementation from its inception through the present.

Legislative History of the Byrd Rule

During the first five years that the Byrd rule was in effect, from late 1985 until late 1990, it consisted of two separate components—(1) a provision in statute applying to initial Senate consideration of reconciliation measures, and (2) a Senate resolution extending application of portions of the statutory provision to conference reports and amendments between the two

---

[1] For further information on the reconciliation process, see CRS Report R44058, *The Budget Reconciliation Process: Stages of Consideration*, by Megan S. Lynch and James V. Saturno.

[2] For additional information on reconciliation measures that became law, see CRS Report R40480, *Budget Reconciliation Measures Enacted Into Law: 1980-2010*, by Megan S. Lynch.

houses. Several modifications were made to the Byrd rule in 1986 and 1987, including extending its expiration date from January 2, 1987, to January 2, 1988, and then to September 30, 1992, but the two separate components of the rule were preserved. In 1990, these components were merged together and made permanent when they were incorporated into the Congressional Budget Act (CBA) of 1974 as Section 313. There have been no further changes in the Byrd rule since 1990.

The Byrd rule originated on October 24, 1985, when Senator Robert C. Byrd, on behalf of himself and others, offered Amendment No. 878 (as modified) to S. 1730, the Consolidated Omnibus Budget Reconciliation Act (COBRA) of 1985.[3] The Senate adopted the amendment by a vote of 96-0.[4] In this form, the Byrd rule applied to initial Senate consideration of reconciliation measures.

Senator Byrd explained that the basic purposes of the amendment were to protect the effectiveness of the reconciliation process (by excluding extraneous matter that often provoked controversy without aiding deficit reduction efforts) and to preserve the deliberative character of the Senate (by excluding from consideration under expedited procedures legislative matters not central to deficit reduction that should be debated under regular procedures). He opened his remarks by stating

> we are in the process now of seeing ... the Pandora's box which has been opened to the abuse of the reconciliation process. That process was never meant to be used as it is being used. There are 122 items in the reconciliation bill that are extraneous. Henceforth, if the majority on a committee should wish to include in reconciliation recommendations to the Budget Committee any measure, no matter how controversial, it can be brought to the Senate under an ironclad built-in time agreement that limits debate, plus time on amendments and motions, to no more than 20 hours.
>
> It was never foreseen that the Budget Reform Act would be used in that way. So if the budget reform process is going to be preserved, and more importantly if we are going to preserve the deliberative process in this U.S. Senate—which is the outstanding, unique element with respect to the U.S. Senate, action must be taken now to stop this abuse of the budget process.[5]

The Byrd amendment was included in modified form in COBRA of 1985 (P.L. 99-272), which was not enacted into law until April 7, 1986, as Section 20001 (100 Stat. 390-391). The Byrd rule, in this form, thus became effective on April 7. As originally framed, the Byrd rule was set to expire on January 2, 1987.

---

[3] For a detailed legislative history of the Byrd rule, see the following print of the Senate Budget Committee: *Budget Process Law Annotated—1993 Edition*, by William G. Dauster, 103rd Cong., 1st sess., S. Prt. 103-49, October 1993, notes on pp. 229-246.

[4] See the Senate's consideration of and vote on the amendment in the *Congressional Record*, daily edition (October 24, 1985), pp. S14032-S14038.

[5] See the remarks of Senator Robert C. Byrd in the *Congressional Record*, daily edition (October 24, 1985), p. S14032.

Table 1. Laws and Resolutions Establishing the Byrd Rule

P.L. 99-272, Consolidated Omnibus Budget Reconciliation Act of 1985, Section 2001 (100 Stat. 390-391), April 7, 1986.

S.Res. 286 (99th Congress, 1st Session), December 19, 1985.

S.Res. 509 (99th Congress, 2nd Session), October 16, 1986.

P.L. 99-509, Omnibus Budget Reconciliation Act of 1986, Section 7006 (100 Stat. 1949-1950), October 21, 1986.

P.L. 100-119, Increasing the Statutory Limit on the Public Debt, Section 205 (101 Stat. 784-785), September 29, 1987.

P.L. 101-508, Omnibus Budget Reconciliation Act of 1990, Section 13214 (104 Stat. 1388-621 through 1388-623), November 5, 1990.

P.L. 105-33, Balanced Budget Act of 1997, Section 10113(b)(1) (111 Stat. 688), August 5, 1997.

Over the years, the Senate has expanded and revised the Byrd rule through the adoption of two resolutions and the inclusion of provisions in four laws. **Table 1** lists the laws and resolutions that have established and revised the Byrd rule.

On December 19, 1985, the Senate adopted by voice vote a resolution (S.Res. 286), sponsored by Senator Alan Simpson and others, that extended the application of portions of the statutory provision to conference reports and amendments between the two houses. Because the enactment of COBRA of 1985 was delayed until early 1986, the portion of the Byrd rule dealing with conference reports became effective first. The provisions of S.Res. 286 were set to expire on the same date as the provision in COBRA of 1985 (January 2, 1987).

In the following year, the Senate was involved in two actions affecting the Byrd rule. First, the Senate adopted S.Res. 509 by voice vote on October 16, 1986. The measure, offered by Senator Alan Simpson and others, modified S.Res. 286 in a technical fashion. Second, the Omnibus Budget Reconciliation Act of 1986 was enacted into law, as P.L. 99-509, on October 21, 1986. Section 7006 of the law made several minor changes in the Byrd rule and extended its expiration date by one year—until January 2, 1988.

Further changes in the Byrd rule were made in 1987. These changes were included in a measure increasing the statutory limit on the public debt, modifying procedures under the Balanced Budget and Emergency Deficit Control Act of 1985, and making other budget process changes (P.L. 100-119, signed into law on September 29; see Title II (Budget Process Reform)). Section 205 of the law added an item to the list of definitions of extraneous matter in the Byrd rule and extended its expiration until September 30, 1992.

In 1990, Congress and the President agreed to further modifications of the budget process by enacting the Budget Enforcement Act (BEA) of 1990 (Title XIII of the Omnibus Budget Reconciliation Act of 1990). Section 13214 of the law made significant revisions to the Byrd rule and incorporated it (as permanent law) into the CBA of 1974 as Section 313 (2 U.S.C. 644).

Finally, the Budget Enforcement Act of 1997 (Title X of the Balanced Budget Act of 1997) made minor technical changes in Section 313 of the CBA of 1974 to correct drafting problems with the BEA of 1990.

Current Features of the Byrd Rule

A Senator opposed to the inclusion of extraneous matter in reconciliation legislation has two principal options for dealing with the problem. First, a Senator may offer an amendment (or a motion to recommit the measure with instructions) that strikes such provisions from the legislation. Second, under the Byrd rule, a Senator may raise a point of order against extraneous matter.

The Byrd rule is a relatively complex rule[6] that applies to two types of reconciliation measures considered pursuant to Section 310 of the CBA of 1974—reconciliation bills and reconciliation resolutions.[7] (A reconciliation resolution could be used to make changes in legislation that had passed the House and Senate but had not yet been enrolled and sent to the President. The practice of the House and Senate has been to consider only reconciliation bills.)

In general, a point of order authorized under the Byrd rule may be raised in order to strike extraneous matter already in the bill as reported or discharged (or in the conference report), or to prevent the incorporation of extraneous matter through the adoption of amendments or motions. A point of order may be raised against a single provision or two or more provisions (as designated by title or section number, or by page and line number), and may be raised against a single amendment or two or more amendments. The chair may sustain a point of order as to all of the provisions (or amendments) or only some of them. Once material has been struck from reconciliation legislation under the Byrd rule, it may not be offered again as an amendment.

A motion to waive the Byrd rule, or to sustain an appeal of the ruling of the chair on a point of order raised under the Byrd rule, requires the affirmative vote of three-fifths of the membership (60 Senators if no seats are vacant).[8] A single waiver motion can (1) apply to the Byrd rule as well as other provisions of the Congressional Budget Act; (2) involve multiple as well as single provisions or amendments; (3) extend (for specified language) through consideration of the conference report as well as initial consideration of the measure or amendment; and (4) be made prior to the raising of a point of order, thus making the point of order moot.

When a reconciliation measure, or a conference report thereon, is considered, the Senate Budget Committee must submit for the record a list of potentially extraneous matter included therein.[9] This list is advisory, however, and does not bind the chair in ruling on points of order. In practice, the list has been inserted into the *Congressional Record* in some years but not in others. Further, in some years, the chairman and the ranking minority member of the committee each have submitted their own lists.[10] Finally, in some cases the list merely has stated that no extraneous matter was included in the measure.

---

[6] Some of the complexities of the Byrd rule are examined in: (1) *Riddick's Senate Procedure* (S.Doc. 101-28, 101st Cong., 2nd sess., 1992), by Floyd M. Riddick and Alan S. Frumin, pp. 624-626; and (2) *Budget Process Law Annotated—1993 Edition*, by William G. Dauster, op. cit., beginning on p. 198.

[7] Part of the Byrd rule, Section 313(a), also applies to reconciliation measures considered pursuant to Section 258C of the Balanced Budget and Emergency Deficit Control Act of 1985. This section, which never was invoked, provided for the consideration of reconciliation legislation in the fall in order to achieve deficit reductions that would obviate the need for an expected sequester under the original statutory pay-as-you-go (PAYGO) requirement (or, previously, the deficit targets). The PAYGO requirement effectively expired at the end of the 107th Congress (see CRS Report RS21378, *Termination of the "Pay-As-You-Go" (PAYGO) Requirement for FY2003 and Later Years*, by Robert Keith; out of print; available upon request). A new statutory PAYGO requirement was enacted in P.L. 111-139, but it does not involve Section 258C of the 1985 act. All of the reconciliation measures considered by the Senate thus far have originated pursuant to Section 310 of the CBA of 1974.

[8] In the Senate, many points of order under the CBA of 1974 require a three-fifths vote of the membership to waive (or to sustain an appeal of the ruling of the chair). Most of these three-fifths waiver requirements are temporary but are extended from time to time; in the case of the Byrd rule, the three-fifths waiver requirement is permanent.

[9] For an example of such a list, see the remarks of Senator Pete Domenici regarding the conference report on the Balanced Budget Act of 1997 in the *Congressional Record*, daily edition (July 31, 1997), pp. S8406-S8408.

[10] For example, see the lists provided by: (1) Chairman Pete Domenici and Ranking Minority Member James Exon regarding the Balanced Budget Act of 1995, inserted into the *Congressional Record*, daily edition (October 26, 1995), pp. S15832-S15834 and pp. S15834-S15840, respectively; and (2) Chairman Judd Gregg regarding the Deficit Reduction Act of 2005, inserted into the *Congressional Record*, daily edition (November 8, 2005), pp. S12522-S12523, and Ranking Minority Member Kent Conrad, inserted into the *Congressional Record*, daily edition (November 2, (continued...)

Determinations of budgetary levels for purposes of enforcing the Byrd rule are made by the Senate Budget Committee.

Definitions of Extraneous Matter

Subsection (b)(1) of the Byrd rule provides definitions of what constitutes extraneous matter for purposes of the rule. The Senate Budget Committee, in its report on the budget resolution for FY1994, noted "'Extraneous' is a term of art. Broadly speaking, the rule prohibits inclusion in reconciliation of matter unrelated to the deficit reduction goals of the reconciliation process."[11]

A provision is considered to be extraneous if it falls under one or more of the following six definitions:

- it does not produce a change in outlays or revenues or a change in the terms and conditions under which outlays are made or revenues are collected;
- it produces an outlay increase or revenue decrease when the instructed committee is not in compliance with its instructions;
- it is outside of the jurisdiction of the committee that submitted the title or provision for inclusion in the reconciliation measure;
- it produces a change in outlays or revenues which is merely incidental to the non-budgetary components of the provision;
- it would increase the deficit for a fiscal year beyond the "budget window" covered by the reconciliation measure;[12] and
- it recommends changes in Social Security.

The last definition complements a ban in Section 310(g) of the CBA of 1974 against considering any reconciliation legislation that contains recommendations pertaining to the Social Security. For purposes of these provisions, Social Security is considered to include the Old-Age, Survivors, and Disability Insurance (OASDI) program established under Title II of the Social Security Act; it does not include Medicare or other programs established as part of that act.

Exceptions to the Definition of Extraneous Matter

Subsection (b)(2) of the Byrd rule provides that a Senate-originated provision that does not produce a change in outlays or revenues shall not be considered extraneous if the chairman and ranking minority members of the Budget Committee and the committee reporting the provision certify that—

(...continued)

2005), pp. S12213-S12214. In some cases the lists have been fairly similar, but in other instances they have differed significantly.

[11] See the report of the Senate Budget Committee to accompany S.Con.Res. 18, Concurrent Resolution on the Budget, FY1994 (S.Rept. 103-19, March 12, 1993), p. 49.

[12] The "budget window" refers to the period covered by the budget resolution, and to any reconciliation directives included therein and the resultant reconciliation legislation. Beginning in the late 1980s, the budget resolution is required to cover at a minimum the "budget year" (the fiscal year beginning on October 1 in the session that the budget resolution is adopted) and the four following fiscal years (the "outyears"). In addition, budget resolutions sometimes cover the "current year" (the fiscal year preceding the budget year) and up to five additional outyears. Accordingly, the longest budget window that has applied to a budget resolution and associated reconciliation legislation covered 11 years, including the current year.

- the provision mitigates direct effects clearly attributable to a provision changing outlays or revenues and both provisions together produce a net reduction in the deficit; or

- the provision will (or is likely to) reduce outlays or increase revenues: (1) in one or more fiscal years beyond those covered by the reconciliation measure; (2) on the basis of new regulations, court rulings on pending legislation, or relationships between economic indices and stipulated statutory triggers pertaining to the provision; or (3) but reliable estimates cannot be made due to insufficient data.

Additionally, under subsection (b)(1)(A), a provision that does not change outlays or revenues in the net, but which includes outlay decreases or revenue increases that exactly offset outlay increases or revenue decreases, is not considered to be extraneous.

The full text of the Byrd rule in its current form is provided in the **Appendix**.

Implementation of the Byrd Rule

Congress and the President considered 24 omnibus reconciliation measures (as shown in **Table 2**) between calendar year 1980, when the reconciliation process was first used, and the present.[13] As stated previously, 20 of these measures were enacted into law and four were vetoed.

The Byrd rule has been in effect during the consideration of the last 19 of these 24 measures, covering from the end of calendar year 1985 through 2015. The Byrd rule had not been established when the first five reconciliation bills were considered. As discussed in more detail below, actions were taken under the Byrd rule during the consideration of 15 of the 19 reconciliation measures.

The Byrd rule was only partially in effect during the consideration of the first of these 19 reconciliation bills. During consideration of that bill, the Consolidated Omnibus Budget Reconciliation Act (COBRA) of 1985, the Byrd rule applied to the consideration of an exchange of amendments between the two chambers, but not to initial consideration of the bill.

The 19 reconciliation bills considered and passed by the House and Senate during this period stemmed from reconciliation directives in 17 different budget resolutions. Two budget resolutions, in 1997 (for FY1998) and 2005 (for FY2006), led to the enactment of two reconciliation measures in each year.

---

[13] The Senate also considered two measures linked to the reconciliation process. On December 15, 1975, the Senate considered, amended, and passed H.R. 5559, the Revenue Adjustment Act of 1975, which reduced revenues by about $6.4 billion pursuant to a budget resolution instruction. The measure was not regarded as a reconciliation bill when it was considered by the House, but it was considered under reconciliation procedures in the Senate. The President vetoed the measure later in the year and the House sustained his veto. See the remarks of Senator Russell Long and the presiding officer on p. 40540 and the remarks of Senator Edmund Muskie and others on pp. 40544-40550 in the *Congressional Record* of December 15, 1975, regarding the status of H.R. 5559 as a reconciliation bill.

The Deficit Reduction Act of 1984 (P.L. 98-369) was regarded as a reconciliation bill when it was considered in the House, but was stripped of that classification when it was considered in the Senate (in April and May of 1984). The House also has considered reconciliation measures that were not considered in the Senate.

For more information on the consideration of reconciliation measures, see CRS Report RL30458, *The Budget Reconciliation Process: Timing of Legislative Action*, by Megan S. Lynch.

Table 2. Budget Reconciliation Measures Enacted Into Law or Vetoed: 1980-2016

	Reconciliation Act	Public Law Number	Statutes-at-Large Citation	Date Enacted (or Vetoed)
Byrd Rule Not in Effect				
1	Omnibus Reconciliation Act of 1980	P.L. 96-499	94 Stat. 2599-2695	12-05-1980
2	Omnibus Budget Reconciliation Act of 1981	P.L. 97-35	95 Stat. 357-933	08-13-1981
3	Tax Equity and Fiscal Responsibility Act of 1982	P.L. 97-248	96 Stat. 324-707	09-03-1982
4	Omnibus Budget Reconciliation Act of 1982	P.L. 97-253	96 Stat. 763-807	09-08-1982
5	Omnibus Budget Reconciliation Act of 1983	P.L. 98-270	98 Stat. 157-162	04-18-1984
Byrd Rule in Effect (Partially for COBRA of 1985)				
6	Consolidated Omnibus Budget Reconciliation Act of 1985	P.L. 99-272	100 Stat. 82-391	04-07-1986
7	Omnibus Budget Reconciliation Act of 1986	P.L. 99-509	100 Stat. 1874-2078	10-21-1986
8	Omnibus Budget Reconciliation Act of 1987	P.L. 100-203	101 Stat. 1330, 1-472	12-22-1987
9	Omnibus Budget Reconciliation Act of 1989	P.L. 101-239	103 Stat. 2106-2491	12-19-1989
10	Omnibus Budget Reconciliation Act of 1990	P.L. 101-508	104 Stat. 1388, 1-630	11-05-1990
11	Omnibus Budget Reconciliation Act of 1993	P.L. 103-66	107 Stat. 312-685	08-10-1993
12	Balanced Budget Act of 1995	—	(H.R. 2491, vetoed)	12-06-1995
13	Personal Responsibility and Budget Reconciliation Act of 1996	P.L. 104-193	110 Stat. 2105-2355	08-22-1996
14	Balanced Budget Act of 1997	P.L. 105-33	111 Stat. 251-787	08-05-1997
15	Taxpayer Relief Act of 1997	P.L. 105-34	111 Stat. 788-1103	08-05-1997
16	Taxpayer Refund and Relief Act of 1999	—	(H.R. 2488, vetoed)	09-23-1999
17	Marriage Tax Relief Reconciliation Act of 2000	—	(H.R. 4810, vetoed)	08-05-2000
18	Economic Growth and Tax Relief Reconciliation Act of 2001	P.L. 107-16	115 Stat. 38-150	06-07-2001
19	Jobs and Growth Tax Relief Reconciliation Act of 2003	P.L. 108-27	117 Stat. 752-768	05-28-2003
20	Deficit Reduction Act of 2005	P.L. 109-171	120 Stat. 4-184	02-08-2006
21	Tax Increase Prevention and Reconciliation Act of 2005	P.L. 109-222	120 Stat. 345-373	05-17-2006
22	College Cost Reduction and Access Act of 2007	P.L. 110-84	121 Stat. 784-822	09-27-2007
23	Health Care and Education Reconciliation Act of 2010	P.L. 111-152	124 Stat. 1029-1083	03-30-2010
24	Restoring Americans' Healthcare Freedom Reconciliation Act of 2015	—	(H.R. 3762, vetoed)	01-08-2016

Source: Prepared by the Congressional Research Service.

As **Table 3** shows, there have been 70 points of order and 57 waiver motions, for a total of 127 actions, considered and disposed of under the Byrd rule. The 127 actions involve only those instances in which the Byrd rule was cited specifically; due to the manner in which budget enforcement provisions operate in the Senate, the Byrd rule potentially could have been involved in other instances which cannot be identified.[14]

There is not a one-to-one correspondence between points of order and waiver motions. A point of order can be raised under the Byrd rule without a waiver motion being offered; conversely, a waiver motion can be offered without a point of order having been raised.

On the whole, the points of order and waiver motions were disposed of in a manner that favored by a large margin those who opposed the inclusion of extraneous matter in reconciliation legislation, as discussed in more detail below.[15]

---

[14] The Byrd rule is only one of many point-of-order provisions in Titles III and IV of the CBA of 1974, as amended (2 U.S.C. 644). In some instances, points of order or waiver motions are made under the act by general reference only (such as a Senator raising a point of order "under Title III of the Act") rather than by specific reference to the provision(s) involved. When only general references are made, it often is impossible to determine (principally by reference to debate in the *Congressional Record*) which provisions of the act are involved. In addition, a provision or amendment may violate the Byrd rule and one or more other enforcement provisions; a Senator raising a point of order may cite one of the other enforcement provisions as the basis for the action. Consequently, this report reflects only those instances when specific reference was made to Section 313 of the act or to the Byrd rule and may undercount the number of actions potentially involving the rule.

[15] It is difficult, if not impossible, to accurately determine the deterrent effect of the Byrd rule, so this aspect is not addressed in this report.

Table 3. Budget Reconciliation Acts: Summary of Points of Order and Waiver Motions Under the Byrd Rule

Public Law (or Vetoed Bill) Number	Calendar Year(s) of Senate Action	Points of Order — To Strike Provision(s) From Amendment, Bill, or Conference Report: Sustained	Fell	Total	To Bar Consideration of Amendment: Sustained	Fell	Total	Total	Waiver Motions: Approved	Rejected	Total	Total Points of Order and Waiver Motions
P.L. 99-272	1985	—	—	—	—	—	—	—	—	—	—	—
P.L. 99-509	1986	1	1	2	—	—	—	2	1	1	2	4
P.L. 100-203	1987	—	—	—	—	—	—	—	1	—	1	1
P.L. 101-239	1989	—	—	—	—	—	—	—	—	—	—	—
P.L. 101-508	1990	3	1	4	2	—	2	6	1	2	3	9
P.L. 103-66	1993	2	2	4	3	—	3	7	—	4	4	11
H.R. 2491	1995	4	—	4	4	—	4	8	—	7	7	15
P.L. 104-193	1996	4	1	5	1	—	1	6	1	3	4	10
P.L. 105-33	1997	2	2	4	3	—	3	7	2	3	5	12
P.L. 105-34	1997	1	2	3	6	—	6	9	2	6	8	17
H.R. 2488	1999	1	—	1	2	—	2	3	1	3	4	7
H.R. 4810	2000	—	1	1	2	—	2	3	—	2	2	5
P.L. 107-16	2001	—	—	—	—	—	—	—	—	—	—	—
P.L. 108-27	2003	—	—	—	1	—	1	1	—	1	1	2
P.L. 109-171	2005	1	—	1	—	—	—	1	—	1	1	2
P.L. 109-222	2005-2006	—	—	—	1	—	1	1	—	1	1	2
P.L. 110-84	2007	—	—	—	—	—	—	—	—	—	—	—
P.L. 111-152	2010	2	—	2	9	—	9	11	—	9	9	20
H.R. 3762	2015	1	—	1	4	—	4	5	—	5	5	10
Total		**22**	**10**	**32**	**38**	**—**	**38**	**70**	**9**	**48**	**57**	**127**

Source: Prepared by the Congressional Research Service from data provided in the Legislative Information System.

CRS-9

Five of the six definitions of extraneousness (the exception being recommending changes in Social Security) have been cited as bases for points of order under the Byrd rule. The most common basis, that the provision or amendment did not change outlays or revenues, was cited as the sole basis in 34 instances and as one of two bases in three other instances. None of the other bases were cited as often; the second-most cited basis, that the provision or amendment was outside an instructed committee's jurisdiction, was cited in 15 instances. In some instances, the basis for the point of order was not cited.

The Byrd rule has been used primarily during initial consideration of a reconciliation measure. It has been invoked only five times during consideration of a conference report—twice in 1993, once in 1995, once in 1997, and once in 2005:

- in 1993, two points of order against matter characterized as extraneous in a conference report were rejected by the chair. In both instances, the chair's ruling was upheld upon appeal. The two motions to appeal the chair's rulings were defeated by identical votes, 43-57;

- in 1995, two sections were struck from a conference report and the two chambers had to resolve the final differences with a further amendment between them;

- in 1997, a section in the conference report was retained following a successful vote (78-22) to waive a point of order; and

- finally, in 2005, three provisions were struck from a conference report (another provision was retained), necessitating action on a further amendment between the two chambers.

As shown in **Table 3**, points of order and waiver motions under the Byrd rule have occurred more frequently in the 1990s (81) compared to the 1980s (5) or the 2000s (41 so far). The middle years of the decade of the 1990s, covering calendar years 1993 through 1997, were especially active in this regard, accounting for 65 of the total 81 points of order and waiver motions during that decade. The most active single year was 2010, which involved 20 points of order and waiver motions.

Points of Order

In total, 70 points of order were raised and disposed of under the Byrd rule. Points of order generally were raised successfully; 60 were sustained (in whole or in part), enabling Senators to strike extraneous matter from the legislation in 22 cases and to bar the consideration of extraneous amendments in 38 cases.

Ten of the points of order fell, either upon the adoption of a waiver motion or upon the ruling of the chair. Two points of order were withdrawn and are not counted in **Table 3**.

In two instances, a point of order was not raised because a waiver motion previously had been offered and approved, thus making the point of order moot.

In many instances, a point of order was raised against multiple provisions, sections, or titles of the bill, sometimes covering a variety of different topics. In a few cases, the chair ruled that most, but not all, of the provisions violated the Byrd rule.

Waiver Motions

A total of 57 motions to waive the Byrd rule, to permit the inclusion of extraneous matter, were offered and disposed of by the Senate. Waiver motions generally were not offered successfully; nine were approved and 48 were rejected.

Two other waiver motions were withdrawn and a third waiver motion was changed to a unanimous consent request; they are not counted in **Table 3**.

Eight of the nine successful motions were used to protect committee-reported language in the bill or language in the conference report; only one motion to protect a floor amendment was successful.

Eight of the successful waiver motions exceeded the required 60-vote threshold by between two votes and 21 votes; on average, they exceeded the threshold by nearly 12 votes. The remaining successful waiver motion was approved by voice vote.

With regard to the 48 unsuccessful waiver motions, 47 of them fell short of the threshold by between one vote and 43 votes; on average, they fell short of the threshold by about 13 votes. The remaining unsuccessful waiver motion was rejected by voice vote. Nineteen of the unsuccessful waiver motions garnered at least 51 votes.

In one instance, the Senate set aside the Byrd rule without employing a waiver motion. The FY1988 budget resolution, in Section 4, set forth reconciliation instructions to various House and Senate committees, including the House Ways and Means and Senate Finance Committees. Section 6(a) of the budget resolution stated the assumption that in complying with their instructions, the two committees would establish a "deficit reduction account." Section 6(b) waived the Byrd rule for the consideration of any legislation reported under the assumed procedure:

> (b) Legislation reported pursuant to subsection (a) shall not be considered to be extraneous for purposes of section 20001 of the Consolidated Omnibus Reconciliation Act of 1985 (as amended by section 7006 of the Omnibus Budget Reconciliation Act of 1986) or Senate Resolution 509 (99th Congress, 2d Session).[16]

The references in Section 6(b) were to the legislation that initially established the Byrd rule and extended it temporarily, before it was incorporated into the CBA of 1974 act on a permanent basis as Section 313.

Table 4, at the end of this section, provides more detailed information on points of order and waiver motions made under the Byrd rule from 1985 through 2015.

Instances in Which the Byrd Rule Was Not Invoked

The Senate considered four different reconciliation measures without taking any actions under the Byrd rule. First, no points of order were raised, or waiver motions offered, under the Byrd rule during final consideration of the Consolidated Omnibus Budget Reconciliation Act (COBRA) of 1985 in late 1985 and early 1986; as previously mentioned, this was the first instance in which the Byrd rule applied.[17]

---

[16] See the conference report to accompany the FY1988 budget resolution, H.Con.Res. 93 (H.Rept. 100-175, June 22, 1987, pp. 17 and 36).

[17] The Senate agreed to the conference report accompanying COBRA of 1985 (H.R. 3128) on December 19, 1985; see the *Congressional Record* of that date at pp. 38503-38543. Later that day, the Senate adopted S.Res. 286, a measure (continued...)

In 1989, no actions involving the Byrd rule occurred, in large part because the Senate leadership chose to use an amendment rather than the Byrd rule to deal with extraneous matter in the bill. On October 13, 1989, during consideration of the Omnibus Budget Reconciliation of 1989, the Senate adopted Mitchell Amendment No. 1004 by voice vote. The amendment struck extraneous matter from the bill; its stated purpose was "to strike all matter from the bill that does not reduce the deficit."[18]

In 2001, no actions under the Byrd rule were taken during consideration of a significant revenue-reduction measure, the Economic Growth and Tax Relief Reconciliation Act of 2001. The potential application of the Byrd rule to the measures was averted by the inclusion of "sunset" provisions that limited the duration of the tax cuts, thereby preventing deficit increases beyond the applicable budget window.

Finally, the Byrd rule was not invoked during consideration of the College Cost Reduction and Access Act of 2007.

In another instance, the Senate considered two reconciliation bills in 2005 (the Deficit Reduction Act of 2005 and the Tax Increase Prevention and Reconciliation Act of 2005); final Senate action on the tax measure carried over into 2006. While points of order were raised successfully under the Byrd rule with regard to both measures in 2005, no actions under the rule occurred in 2006 as the Senate completed action on the tax measure.[19]

Byrd Rule Controversies

Although the Byrd rule has advocates in the House and Senate, its use sometimes has engendered much controversy, especially between the two houses. Several of the major controversies are discussed below.

Impact on House-Senate Relations in 1993 and 1994

In 1993 and 1994, during the 103rd Congress, the stringent application of the Byrd rule by the Senate significantly influenced the final shape of the reconciliation act and later affected the deliberations of the Joint Committee on the Organization of Congress.

The House considered its version of the Omnibus Budget Reconciliation Act of 1993, H.R. 2264, on May 27. The Senate considered its version, S. 1134, on June 23 and June 24 (after completing consideration of S. 1134, the Senate amended and passed H.R. 2264 for purposes of conference with the House). Senator Pete Domenici, ranking minority member of the Senate Budget

---

(...continued)

making the Byrd rule applicable to the consideration of conference reports and amendments between the two chambers (pp. 38559-38560). Also that day, the House disagreed to the conference report on COBRA. Subsequently, the House and Senate engaged in an exchange of amendments in order to resolve their differences regarding the measure. The Senate considered the measure further on December 20, 1985 and several days in mid-March 1986 (despite the enactment of COBRA into law on April 7, 1986, the designation "1985" was retained in the act's title). Thus, the portion of the Byrd rule contained in S.Res. 286 was not in effect when the Senate considered and agreed to the conference report on COBRA, but it was in effect during Senate action on the subsequent amendment exchange with the House.

[18] See the *Congressional Record* (daily ed.) of October 13, 1989, p. S13349. The Senate leadership used an amendment for similar purposes during consideration of the Omnibus Budget Reconciliation Act of 1981.

[19] Senate actions on the two measures is discussed in CRS Report RL33132, *Budget Reconciliation Legislation in 2005-2006 Under the FY2006 Budget Resolution*, by Robert Keith (out of print; available upon request).

Committee, inserted a list of potentially extraneous matters included in S. 1134 in the *Congressional Record* of June 24 (at p. S7984).[20] The list identified more than a dozen sections in five titles of the bill as possibly being in violation of the Byrd rule, specifically Section 313(b)(1)(A) (i.e., producing no change in outlays or revenues).

At the House-Senate conference stage, the Senate leadership directed the parliamentarian and Senate Budget Committee staff to thoroughly review the legislation to identify any provisions originating in the House or Senate that might violate the Byrd rule.[21] As a result of this review, many provisions were deleted from the legislation in conference.

During Senate consideration of the conference report, Senator James Sasser, Chairman of the Senate Budget Committee, discussed this process:

> with regard to the Byrd rule, we worked very hard and very faithfully over a period of well over a week in going over this bill to try to clarify and remove items that might be subject to the Byrd rule.

> As the distinguished ranking member indicated, I think over 150 items were removed from the reconciliation instrument here, because it was felt that they would be subject to the Byrd rule....

> I might say some of our House colleagues could not understand, and I do not blame them because there were a number of things that were pulled out of this budget reconciliation that had been voted on and passed by large majorities in both houses. But simply because they violated the Byrd rule, we had to go to the chairmen of the appropriate House committees and tell them they had to come out. They simply did not understand it. I think it made them perhaps have a little less high esteem for some of us here in the Senate.... In the final analysis, their leadership had to demand that some of these provisions subject to the Byrd rule come out.[22]

During House consideration of the conference report, several Democratic Members criticized the Byrd rule and discussed its impact on the legislation. For example, Representative Dan Rostenkowski, chairman of the House Ways and Means Committee, stated

> I also have to express my grave concerns regarding the other body's so-called Byrd rule. As a result of this procedural rule, policies that would have significantly improved the Medicare Program could not even be considered. Over 80 pages of statutory language were stripped out of the Medicare title. Staff wasted countless hours, scrutinizing every line to ensure that there is nothing that would upset our friends at the other end of the Capitol. Even more absurd is the fact that most of the items stripped were minor and technical provisions that received bipartisan support when they passed both the House and the Senate last year.

> I hope that Members on both sides of the aisle share my grave concerns about how this rule has been used, and its impact on reconciliation. I sincerely hope that this rule will be reconsidered before we ever return to the reconciliation process again.[23]

---

[20] This requirement was added by Section 13214 of the Omnibus Budget Reconciliation Act of 1990. Consequently, its first application was to consideration of the Omnibus Budget Reconciliation Act of 1993.

[21] See the discussion of "Preemptive Editing of the Conference Report" in *Budget Process Law Annotated—1993 Edition*, by William G. Dauster, op. cit., pp. 245-246. Also, see (1) Richard E. Cohen, "Running Up Against the 'Byrd Rule'," *National Journal*, September 4, 1993, p. 2151; (2) George Hager, "The Byrd Rule: Not an Easy Call," *Congressional Quarterly Weekly Report*, July 31, 1993, p. 2027; and (3) Mary Jacoby, "Senate Parliamentarian Purges Budget Bill of Measures That Could Violate Byrd Rule," *Roll Call*, August 5, 1993, p. 9.

[22] See the remarks of Senator Sasser in the *Congressional Record*, daily edition (August 6, 1993), p. S10662.

[23] See the remarks of Representative Rostenkowski in the *Congressional Record*, daily edition, (August 5, 1993), p. H (continued...)

Controversy over the Byrd rule persisted during late 1993 and into 1994. The Joint Committee on the Organization of Congress, co-chaired by Representative Lee Hamilton and Senator David Boren, was slated to make recommendations on congressional reform, including changes in the budget process, in December of 1993. Representative Martin Olav Sabo, chairman of the House Budget Committee, wrote to Co-Chair Hamilton in October, telling him that "widespread use [of the Byrd rule] this year was extremely destructive and bodes ill for the reconciliation process in the future." Further, he stated that "the use of mechanisms like the Byrd rule greatly distorts the balance of power between the two bodies" and that strict enforcement of the Byrd rule "requires that too much power be delegated to unelected employees of the Congress."[24]

Chairman Sabo attached two Budget Committee staff documents to his letter: (1) a 29-page listing of reconciliation provisions "dropped or modified" in conference in order to comply with the Byrd rule, and (2) a three-page statement identifying specific problems caused by the rule (including a bar against including authorizations savings in reconciliation, the forcing of piecemeal legislation, incentives to use counterproductive drafting techniques to mitigate effects, and a bar against provisions achieving savings or promoting efficiency when the Congressional Budget Office was unable to assign particular savings to them).

The Senate Members of the Joint Committee on the Organization of Congress recommended in their final report that a provision clarifying "that the 'Byrd rule' is permanent, applies to conference reports, requires sixty votes to waive, and applies to extraneous matters" be included in a broad reform bill.[25] Legislation embodying the Senate recommendations (S. 1824) was introduced on February 3, 1994 (the recommendation pertaining to the Byrd rule was set forth in Section 312 of the bill). The House Members of the Joint Committee did not include any recommendations regarding the Byrd rule in their report or legislation (H.R. 3801, also introduced on February 3, 1994).

The day after the two reform bills were introduced, the chairmen of 15 House committees wrote to Speaker Tom Foley. They urged him to meet with Senate Majority Leader George Mitchell in order to get Section 312 of S. 1824, dealing with the Byrd rule, removed from the reform package.[26]

On July 19, 1994, Chairman Sabo introduced H.R. 4780. The bill would have amended the CBA of 1974 to make the Byrd rule "applicable to the Senate only," chiefly by removing references to conference reports in Section 313 of the act.[27]

None of the three bills cited above were acted upon before the 103rd Congress adjourned.

(...continued)

6126. He discusses specific programs dropped from the conference report because of the Byrd rule p. H6124. Also, see the remarks that same day of Representatives de la Garza (p. H6143), Vento (p. H6235), and Stenholm (p. H6257).

[24] Letter from Representative Martin Olav Sabo to Representative Lee H. Hamilton, October 26, 1993, 2 pp.

[25] See Organization of the Congress, *Final Report of the Senate Members of the Joint Committee on the Organization of Congress*, S.Rept. 103-215, vol. I, December 1993, pp. 14 and 15.

[26] The letter is discussed in: Karen Foerstel, "Byrd Rule War Erupts Once Again," *Roll Call*, February 24, 1994, pp. 1 and 13.

[27] See the following article for a discussion of the Sabo bill: Mary Jacoby, "Sabo Bill Would Kill Byrd Rule For Good," *Roll Call*, July 25, 1994, p. 12.

Effects on Tax-Cut Legislation

During the 106th Congress, the budget resolutions for FY2000 and FY2001 included reconciliation instructions directing the House Ways and Means and Senate Finance Committees to develop legislation implementing substantial reductions in revenue.[28] The reconciliation instructions in the two budget resolutions called for total revenue reduction over five years of $142 billion and $150 billion, respectively.[29] Neither budget resolution included any instructions regarding spending. This marked the first time that the House and Senate had recommended substantial reductions in revenue through the reconciliation process without offsetting savings to be achieved in spending programs. Any resultant reconciliation legislation was expected under these budget resolutions to reduce large surpluses, not to incur or worsen deficits.

In each of these two years, there was controversy in the Senate regarding the appropriateness of using reconciliation procedures under circumstances that worsened the federal government's fiscal posture. Some Senators argued that the use of reconciliation, with its procedural restrictions that sharply curtail debate time and limit the offering of amendments in comparison to the usual Senate procedures, could be justified only when it was necessary to reduce or eliminate a deficit (or to preserve or increase a surplus). Other Senators maintained that reconciliation is neutral in its orientation—the language in Section 310 of the CBA of 1974 refers to "changes" in spending and revenue amounts, not increases or decreases—and is intended to expedite the consideration of important and potentially complex budgetary legislation.

Against the backdrop of the larger issue of the appropriate use of reconciliation under these circumstances, Senators also debated in particular the impact of the Byrd rule on the scope of the resultant tax-cut legislation. One of the determinants of extraneousness under the Byrd rule is whether the legislation reduces revenues or increases spending in the net beyond the budget window (i.e., the period to which the reconciliation instructions apply). Changes in tax law, however, often are made on a permanent basis. As a consequence, reconciliation legislation recommending permanent tax cuts may run afoul of the Byrd rule.

During consideration of the Taxpayer Refund and Relief Act of 1999 and the Marriage Tax Relief Reconciliation Act of 2000, the Byrd rule was used successfully to ensure the inclusion of sunset provisions in the bills, limiting the effectiveness of the tax cuts to the period covered by the reconciliation instructions.[30]

During the first session of the 107th Congress, the Senate again addressed these issues as it considered H.R. 1836, largely embodying President Bush's proposal for a $1.6 trillion tax cut.[31] In addition to debating the appropriateness of using the reconciliation process to expedite tax-cut

---

[28] See Sections 104 and 105 of H.Con.Res. 68, the FY2000 budget resolution (the conference report was H.Rept. 106-91, April 14, 1999), and Sections 103 and 104 of H.Con.Res. 290, the FY2001 budget resolution (the conference report was H.Rept. 106-577, April 12, 2000). The FY2001 budget resolution also included reconciliation instructions directing the House Ways and Means Committee to develop legislation reducing the debt held by the public.

[29] The instructions in the FY2000 budget resolution covered 10 fiscal years, while the instructions in the FY2001 budget resolution covered five fiscal years. The reconciliation instructions in the FY2000 budget resolution also provided for total revenue reductions of $778 billion over 10 years.

[30] Proceedings under this aspect of the Byrd rule, in the case of the Taxpayer Refund and Relief Act of 1999, occurred on July 28, 1999; see the remarks of Senators Roth, Moynihan, Conrad, Gramm, and others in the *Congressional Record*, daily edition (July 28, 1999), pp. S9478-S9484. With regard to the Marriage Tax Relief Reconciliation Act of 2000, see the remarks of Senator Roth in the *Congressional Record* (July 14, 2000), pp. S6782-S6784.

[31] See, for example, the remarks of Senator Robert C. Byrd, "Reconciliation Process Reform," in the *Congressional Record*, daily edition (February 15, 2001), pp. S1532-S1536, and opening remarks of Senator Byrd and others during Senate consideration of H.R. 1836 in the *Congressional Record*, daily edition (May 17, 2001), p. S5028.

---

legislation, Senators argued for and against the inclusion of the 10-year "sunset" provision necessary to achieve compliance with the Byrd rule. Some Senators maintained that permanent changes in tax law should be allowed under reconciliation procedures, just as they often are customarily made in freestanding tax legislation. Other Senators praised the value of being able to reexamine such significant modifications in budgetary policy in future years when economic circumstances may have changed materially.

The sunset provision was retained in the final version of the legislation, as Section 901 (115 Stat. 150) of P.L. 107-16, the Economic Growth and Tax Relief Reconciliation Act of 2001.

In 2003, during the first session of the 108th Congress, the Byrd rule influenced the form of revenue reconciliation directives in the FY2004 budget resolution (H.Con.Res. 95).[32] Initially, House and Senate leaders indicated that they would settle on a conference agreement instructing the House Ways and Means Committee to reduce revenues through reconciliation by $550 billion or more for the period covering FY2003-FY2013 and the Senate Finance Committee to reduce revenues by $350 billion for the same period. A majority of Senators had indicated their opposition to revenue reductions greater than $350 billion.

The use of dual reconciliation instructions in the budget resolution would enable the leadership to secure passage of the budget resolution while leaving open the possibility that a subsequent conference on the differing versions of the revenue reconciliation measure passed by the two houses might reach an acceptable compromise between these two amounts.

However, it soon became apparent that, if the Senate initially passed a revenue reconciliation measure consistent with the directive in the budget resolution (i.e., reducing revenues by $350 billion), the later consideration of a conference agreement reflecting a compromise level of revenue reductions greater than $350 billion could violate the Byrd rule. In particular, Section 313(b)(1)(B) defines as extraneous any provision reported by a committee that reduces revenues (or increases outlays) if the net effect of all of the committee's provisions is that it fails to achieve its reconciliation instructions. Proposing revenue reductions greater than the level of reductions set in the reconciliation instructions would be considered a failure to achieve the instructions.

In order to resolve the problem, the conference agreement on the FY2004 budget resolution instructed both the House Ways and Means Committee and the Senate Finance Committee to reduce revenues by $550 billion over FY2003-FY2013, but a point of order barred the initial consideration in the Senate of a reconciliation measure (as distinct from a conference report) containing revenue reductions in excess of $350 billion for this period.[33] The FY2004 budget resolution further provided that the Senate point of order could be waived only by the affirmative vote of three-fifths of the Members duly chosen and sworn (i.e., 60 Senators, if no seats are vacant). This procedural formulation strengthened the position of those who favored initial Senate passage of a reconciliation measure limited to $350 billion in revenue reductions, but removed the potential Byrd rule hurdle should a majority of Senators later choose to support a conference agreement providing as much as $550 billion in revenue reductions.[34]

---

[32] See H.Rept. 108-71 (April 10, 2003).

[33] The reconciliation directives are set forth in Section 201 of H.Con.Res. 95; the Senate point of order is set forth in Section 202. A portion of the reconciled amounts is set forth as outlay increases in order to accommodate changes in tax programs (e.g., refundable tax credits) that are scored as outlays. Consequently, the aggregate instruction of $550 billion is actually $535 billion in revenue reductions and $15 billion in outlay increases in the House, and $522.524 billion in revenue reductions and $27.476 billion in outlay increases in the Senate.

[34] For further discussion of this matter, see CRS Report RL31902, *Revenue Reconciliation Directives in the FY2004 Budget Resolution*, by Robert Keith (out of print; available upon request). Also, see (1) "Concessions to Moderates (continued...)

Government Series: The Federal Budget Process

The Budget Reconciliation Process: The Senate's "Byrd Rule"

Senator Max Baucus, the ranking minority member of the Senate Finance Committee, questioned whether the directive to the committee should be regarded as $350 billion or $550 billion.[35] Ultimately, Senator Charles Grassley, chairman of the Senate Finance Committee, indicated that he had reached agreement with other Senators to adhere to the $350 billion level in the conference on the reconciliation measure, notwithstanding the fact that the limitation in Section 202 of the budget resolution only applied to initial consideration of the measure.[36] The resultant reconciliation measure (H.R. 2), according to final estimates of the Congressional Budget Office and Joint Tax Committee, contained $349.7 billion in revenue reductions and related outlay changes.[37] The bill, which became P.L. 108-27, the Jobs and Growth Tax Relief Reconciliation Act of 2003, on May 28, 2003, included sunset provisions in Section 107 (117 Stat. 755-756) and Section 303 (117 Stat. 764).

During the 109th Congress, the House and Senate considered separate revenue and spending reconciliation bills pursuant to the FY2006 budget resolution. The budget resolution provided for a revenue reconciliation bill that reduced revenues by up to $70 billion over the five-year budget window (FY2006-FY2010) used in the budget resolution. The conference agreement on the revenue reconciliation bill, H.R. 4297, recommended significant revenue reduction beyond the budget window, principally with respect to extensions of current capital gains and dividends provisions through December 31, 2010.[38] Instead of incorporating sunset provisions in order to comply with the Byrd rule, as had been done in the past, the conferees included offsets of the revenue losses. The JCT estimated the total revenue loss over 10 years (FY2006-FY2015) at $69.084 billion, an amount nearly $900 million smaller than the five-year revenue loss. The measure became P.L. 109-222, the Tax Increase Prevention and Reconciliation Act of 2005, on May 17, 2006.

Comprehensive Policy Changes: Health Care and Education Reform

At the beginning of the 111th Congress, in 2009, President Barack Obama proposed a legislative agenda focusing on health care reform, as well as broad initiatives in education and other policy areas. An immediate point of contention was whether the proposals regarding health care reform should be pursued through the regular legislative process or the expedited procedures available under the reconciliation process. The Democratic leadership in the Senate was concerned, in particular, that passage of the proposals in the Senate could be stymied by a filibuster conducted by Republican opponents. Use of the reconciliation process, with its debate limitations and other expedited features, would ensure that a filibuster could not be employed against the legislation. On the other hand, in such a comprehensive reform proposal, many important provisions might be

---

(...continued)

Imperil Early GOP Tax Cutting Accord," by Andrew Taylor, *CQ Weekly*, April 12, 2003; and (2) "Grassley Promises GOP Moderates Final Tax Cut Will Not Top $350 Billion," by Bud Newman, BNA's *Daily Report for Executives*, Monday, April 14, 2003, p. G-7.

[35] See the remarks of Senator Max Baucus in the *Congressional Record*, daily edition (April 11, 2003), pp. S5296-S 5298, in which he inserts a letter from Senate Parliamentarian Alan Frumin to Senate Democratic Leader Thomas Daschle regarding the potential application of the Byrd rule to the consideration of reconciliation legislation.

[36] See the remarks of Senator Grassley in the *Congressional Record*, daily edition (April 11, 2003), pp. S5295-S5296.

[37] See the CBO cost estimate on H.R. 2 (108th Cong.) of May 23, 2003, available at http://www.cbo.gov.

[38] Although the capital gains and dividends provisions would sunset on December 31, 2010, they would incur revenue losses in succeeding years (e.g., in FY2012, a $12.698 billion revenue loss for the capital gains provision and a $6.326 billion revenue loss for the dividends provision).

Congressional Research Service

17

vulnerable to challenge under the Byrd rule and other enforcement procedures; the resulting legislation might become like "Swiss cheese" if many parliamentary challenges were successful.

Congressional leaders decided to consider health care reform (and education reform) proposals under the regular legislative process, but to include reconciliation directives in the FY2010 budget resolution so that reconciliation procedures could be used as a fallback if regular legislative procedures failed. One of the factors influencing the decision was that, at the time, the Democrats held a 60-seat majority in the Senate, exactly the minimum number of votes needed to invoke cloture (i.e., to terminate a filibuster). Title II of the FY2010 budget resolution, S.Con.Res. 13, included reconciliation directives for FY2009-FY2014 to three House and two Senate committees that would accommodate health care and education reform initiatives.[39]

The House and Senate passed separate versions of health care reform legislation in late 2009 but did not resolve their differences before the session ended. The House passed H.R. 3962 on November 7 by a vote of 220-215. The Senate chose another House-passed bill dealing with unrelated subject matter, H.R. 3590, and transformed it into a health care reform measure; the Senate passed the bill on December 24 by a vote of 60-39. (In addition, the House passed an education reform measure in 2009, H.R. 3221, but the Senate did not.)

In early 2010, the Democratic leadership in the Senate found an altered political situation; a special election held in Massachusetts in January to fill a vacant seat (due to the death of Senator Ted Kennedy) resulted in a changeover to Republican control of the seat, thereby reducing the Democratic majority in the Senate to 59 seats. In assessing how to resolve the House-Senate differences in the health care reform legislation, the Democratic leadership faced a dilemma: the Democrats no longer held the 60-seat majority necessary to thwart a filibuster (and Republican opposition to the measure was unified), and the House could not pass the Senate version without change, thereby sending it to the President, because that version was not acceptable to a majority of House Members.

The solution to the dilemma settled on by the Democratic leadership was for the House to pass the Senate version of health care reform legislation, H.R. 3590, while simultaneously passing a reconciliation measure (referred to colloquially as a "sidecar") that would amend H.R. 3590 in a manner acceptable to majorities in both chambers. In this manner, comprehensive health care reform legislation could be enacted without concern about challenges under the Byrd rule that could strip away many of its provisions, while the revisions to the measure necessary to accommodate the political agreement could be achieved through an expedited reconciliation process that relied upon a simple majority vote in the Senate rather than a 60-vote supermajority. Education reform provisions also would be included in the reconciliation measure. Compared with the comprehensive health care reform measure, the reconciliation bill was much more narrow in scope and focused on budgetary matters.[40]

To execute this strategy, the House on March 21, 2010, adopted a special rule reported by the House Rules Committee, H.Res. 1203, by a vote of 224-206. Under the terms of the special rule, the House then concurred in the Senate amendments to H.R. 3590 (thus clearing the bill for the President) by a vote of 219-212. Finally, the House passed H.R. 4872, the reconciliation measure, by a vote of 220-211.

---

[39] The instructions included the House Education and Labor, House Energy and Commerce, and House Ways and Means Committees and the Senate Finance and Senate Health, Education, Labor, and Pensions Committees.

[40] One measure of the different scope of the two bills is that, in enrolled form, the health care and education reform bill was 906 pages in length and the reconciliation bill was 55 pages in length.

Following the House's actions on March 21, the Senate considered H.R. 4872 on March 23, 24, and 25, passing the measure on March 25 by a vote of 56-43. Republican opponents of the measure offered a series of amendments and motions to recommit to the bill, all of which were defeated by motions to table or points of order. Nine of the amendments fell when points of order raised under the Byrd rule were sustained (in each instance, after a waiver motion had been rejected). All but one of the points of order were raised on the ground that the amendment included provisions outside the jurisdiction of the instructed committees.[41]

Toward the end of Senate consideration of the reconciliation measure on March 25, Senator Judd Gregg successfully raised two points of order under the Byrd rule, striking two brief provisions in the education reform portion of the measure dealing with the Pell grant program.[42] The provisions were judged to be in violation of the Byrd rule on the ground that they produced no changes in outlays or revenues.

As required under the Byrd rule, the Senate then returned the reconciliation measure (with the two provisions pertaining to the Pell grant program removed) to the House for further action. On March 25, the House agreed to a special rule, H.Res. 1225, providing for the consideration of a motion for the House to concur in the Senate amendment to H.R. 4872. The House agreed to the motion by a vote of 220-207, thus clearing the measure for the President.

President Obama signed H.R. 3590, the Patient Protection and Affordable Care Act, into law on March 23 as P.L. 111-148, and H.R. 4872, the Health Care and Education Reconciliation Act of 2010, into law on March 30 as P.L. 111-152.

[41] For example, two of the amendments included tax-related provisions with offsets in the form of rescissions of appropriations provided in the American Recovery and Reinvestment Act of 2009 under the jurisdiction of the Senate Appropriations Committee.

[42] See the *Congressional Record* (daily ed.), March 25, 2010, p. S2086. In addition, Senator Chuck Grassley submitted for the record a list of five points of order, four of them involving the Byrd rule; the chair indicated that, had the points of order been raised, they would not have been sustained (see pp. S2084-S2085).

Table 4. Listing of Actions Under the Senate's Byrd Rule, by Act: 1985-2015

Object of Point of Order[a]	Basis of Point of Order[b]	Subject Matter	Waiver Motion[c]	Disposition of Point of Order
1. Consolidated Omnibus Budget Reconciliation Act of 1985 (P.L. 99-272; 4/7/1986)[d]				
a. To Strike Provision(s) from Bill or Conference Report				
[none]				
b. To Bar Consideration of Amendment(s)				
[not applicable]				
2. Omnibus Budget Reconciliation Act of 1986 (P.L. 99-509; 10/21/1986)				
a. To Strike Provision(s) from Bill or Conference Report				
Section 403	Outlay increase when committee not in compliance	Conservation programs	Rejected, 32-61	Sustained; section struck (September 19, 1986)
p. 139, line 1-p. 161, line 17; and p. 162, lines 1-24	Outside committee's jurisdiction	Program fraud civil remedies	Approved, 79-15	Fell (September 19, 1986)
b. To Bar Consideration of Amendment(s)				
[none]				
3. Omnibus Budget Reconciliation Act of 1987 (P.L. 100-203; 12/22/1987)				
a. To Strike Provision(s) from Bill or Conference Report				
[none]				
b. To Bar Consideration of Amendment(s)				
Byrd-Dole Amendment No. 1254; Kassebaum Amendment No. 1259; and Gramm Amendment No. 1260	[specific basis not cited]	[various topics]	Approved, 81-13	[none raised]
4. Omnibus Budget Reconciliation Act of 1989 (P.L. 101-239; 12/19/1989)[e]				
a. To Strike Provision(s) from Bill or Conference Report				
[none]				
b. To Bar Consideration of Amendment(s)				
[none]				
5. Omnibus Budget Reconciliation Act of 1990 (P.L. 101-508; 11/5/1990)				
a. To Strike Provision(s) from Bill or Conference Report				

CRS-20

Object of Point of Order[a]	Basis of Point of Order[b]	Subject Matter	Waiver Motion[c]	Disposition of Point of Order
Section 7405(i)	Outside committee's jurisdiction	Apportionment of highway funds between states	None	Sustained; subsection struck (October 17, 1990)
p. 1017, line 5-p. 1018, line 19; and p. 1018, line 22-p. 1019, line 18	Budgetary changes merely incidental to non-budgetary components	Occupational Safety and Health Administration (OSHA) penalties	None	Sustained; provisions struck (October 18, 1990)
Sections 4003-4016	No change in outlays or revenues	Harvesting of timber in the Tongass National Forest in Alaska	None	Sustained; sections struck (October 18, 1990)
Title III, Subtitle B (as modified)	No change in outlays or revenues	National aviation noise policy, limitations on airport improvement program revenues, high density traffic airport rules, and related matters	Approved, 69-31	Fell (October 18, 1990)
b. To Bar Consideration of Amendment(s)				
Graham Amendment No. 3025	No change in outlays or revenues	Authorize Federal Deposit Insurance Corporation (FDIC) to develop risk-based insurance system	Rejected, voice vote	Sustained; amendment fell (October 18, 1990)
Symms Amendment No. 3039	No change in outlays or revenues	Deposit of all increased motor fuel taxes (other than taxes on railroads) into Highway Trust Fund	Rejected, 48-52	Sustained, amendment fell (October 18, 1990)

CRS-21

Object of Point of Order[a]	Basis of Point of Order[b]	Subject Matter	Waiver Motion[c]	Disposition of Point of Order
6. Omnibus Budget Reconciliation Act of 1993 (P.L. 103-66; 8/10/1993)				
a. To Strike Provision(s) from Bill or Conference Report				
Section 1105(c)	No change in outlays or revenues	Commercial use of bovine growth hormone in other countries	Rejected, 38-60	Sustained; subsection struck (June 24, 1993)
Section 7801; Section 7803(a) (proposing in part new Sections 2106 and 2108(b)(2) of the Social Security Act); and Section 8252(a)(2), (b), and (c)	No change in outlays or revenues	Childhood immunizations and tax return preparer standards	None	Sustained; most provisions struck[f] (June 24, 1993)
Section 13631(b) (proposing in part a new Section 1928 of the Social Security Act)	No change in outlays or revenues; budgetary changes merely incidental to non-budgetary components	Childhood immunizations	None	Fell. Motion to appeal Chair's ruling rejected, 43-57 (August 6, 1993)
Section 1106(a)	Budgetary changes merely incidental to non-budgetary components	Imposition of domestic content requirements on U.S. cigarette manufacturers	None	Fell. Motion to appeal Chair's ruling rejected, 43-57 (August 6, 1993)
b. To Bar Consideration of Amendment(s)				
Domenici/Nunn Amendment No. 544	No change in outlays or revenues	Extend discretionary caps on defense, international, and domestic spending through FY1995	Rejected, 53-45	Sustained; amendment fell (June 24, 1993)
Bradley Amendment No. 542	No change in outlays or revenues	Separate enrollment requirement for appropriations and tax expenditures	Rejected, 53-45	Sustained; amendment fell (June 24, 1993)
Gramm Amendment No. 557	No change in outlays or revenues	Restoration of maximum deficit amounts	Rejected, 43-55	Sustained; amendment fell (June 24, 1993)
7. Balanced Budget Act of 1995 (H.R. 2491; vetoed 12/6/1995)				
a. To Strike Provision(s) from Bill or Conference Report				
Section 7171	No change in outlays or revenues	Raising the age of Medicare eligibility	None	Sustained; section struck (October 27, 1995)
Section 7191(a)	No change in outlays or revenues	Bar against the use of federal funding of abortions under Medicaid	Rejected, 55-45	Sustained; subsection struck (October 27, 1995)

CRS-22

Object of Point of Order[a]	Basis of Point of Order[b]	Subject Matter	Waiver Motion[c]	Disposition of Point of Order
49 provisions in various titles of the bill	[various bases cited]	[various topics, dealing primarily with welfare reform]	Rejected, 53-46	Sustained against 46 provisions, which were struck; not sustained against 3 provisions, which remained in bill (October 27, 1995)
Section 8001 (proposing in part a new Section 1853(f) to the Social Security Act) and Section 13301	No change in outlays or revenues; budgetary changes merely incidental to non-budgetary components	Application of antitrust rule to provider-sponsored organizations (MedicarePlus) and exemption of physician office laboratories.	Rejected, 54-45	Sustained; provisions struck from conference report (November 17, 1995)

b. To Bar Consideration of Amendment(s)

Dorgan Amendment No. 2977	[specific basis not cited]	Ending deferral for U.S. shareholders on income of controlled foreign corporations attributable to imported property	Rejected, 47-52	Sustained; amendment fell (October 26, 1995)
Specter Modified Amendment No. 2986	No change in outlays or revenues	Expressing sense of the Senate regarding a flat tax	Rejected, 17-82	Sustained; amendment fell (October 27, 1995)
Bumpers Amendment No. 3028	No change in outlays or revenues	Prohibition against the scoring of assets sales as budget savings	Rejected, 49-50	Sustained; amendment fell (October 27, 1995)
Byrd/Dorgan Amendment No. 2942	No change in outlays or revenues	Increase time limit on debate in Senate on reconciliation legislation	Rejected, 47-52	Sustained; amendment fell (October 27, 1995)

8. Personal Responsibility and Work Opportunity Reconciliation Act of 1996 (P.L. 104-193; 8/22/1996)

a. To Strike Provision(s) from Bill or Conference Report

Section 2923 (proposing a new Section 1511 of the Social Security Act), p. 772, line 13-p. 785, line 22	Outlay increase when committee not in compliance	Medicaid supplemental umbrella fund	None	Sustained; provision struck (July 18, 1996)
Section 408(a)(2)	No change in outlays or revenues	Family cap (no additional cash assistance for children born to families receiving assistance)	Rejected, 42-57	Sustained; provision struck (July 23, 1996)
Section 2104	No change in outlays or revenues	Social services provided by charitable or private organizations	Approved, 67-32	Fell (July 23, 1996)

Object of Point of Order[a]	Basis of Point of Order[b]	Subject Matter	Waiver Motion[c]	Disposition of Point of Order
Section 2909	No change in outlays or revenues	Abstinence education programs	Rejected, 52-46	Sustained; provision struck (July 23, 1996)
22 provisions in various titles of the bill	[various bases cited]	Various topics involving the Food Stamp, School Lunch, and Child Nutrition programs and welfare reform	None	Sustained against 21 provisions, which were struck from the bill; not sustained against 1 provision, which remained in the bill (July 23, 1996)
b. To Bar Consideration of Amendment(s)				
First Modified Amendment No. 4914	No change in outlays or revenues	Expressing the sense of Congress that the President should ensure approval of state welfare reform waiver requests	Rejected, 55-43	Sustained; amendment fell (July 19, 1996)
9. Balanced Budget Act of 1997 (P.L. 105-33; 8/5/1997)				
a. To Strike Provision(s) from Bill or Conference Report				
Section 5611	No change in outlays or revenues	Raising the age of Medicare eligibility	Approved, 62-38	Fell (June 24, 1997)
Section 5822	Budgetary changes merely incidental to non-budgetary components	Enrollment eligibility (Welfare-to-Work Grant Program)	[waiver motion withdrawn]	Sustained; provision struck (June 25, 1997)
Section 1949(a)(2)	No change in outlays or revenues	Bar against the use of federal funding of abortions under Medicaid	None	[point of order withdrawn]
Sections 5713, 5833, and 5987	Outside committee's jurisdiction	[various topics]	None	Sustained; sections struck (June 25, 1997)
Section 5001	No change in outlays or revenues	Establishment of a Medicare Choice program (balanced billing protection)	Approved, 62-37	Fell (June 25, 1997)
b. To Bar Consideration of Amendment(s)				
Levin Amendment No. 482	No change in outlays or revenues	Allowing vocational educational training to be counted as a work activity under the Temporary Assistance for Needy Families program	Rejected, 55-45	Sustained; amendment fell (June 25, 1997)

Object of Point of Order[a]	Basis of Point of Order[b]	Subject Matter	Waiver Motion[c]	Disposition of Point of Order
Kennedy Amendment No. 490	Increase in deficit or reduction of surplus in fiscal year beyond those covered by instructions	Student loan programs	Rejected, 43-57	Sustained; amendment fell (June 25, 1997)
Kennedy Amendment No. 504	[no basis cited]	Immediate transfer to Medicare Part B of certain home health benefits	Rejected, 38-62	Sustained; amendment fell (June 25, 1997)

10. Taxpayer Relief Act of 1997 (P.L. 105-34; 8/5/1997)

a. To Strike Provision(s) from Bill or Conference Report

Object of Point of Order[a]	Basis of Point of Order[b]	Subject Matter	Waiver Motion[c]	Disposition of Point of Order
Section 602	No change in outlays or revenues	District of Columbia Government reform	[waiver motion withdrawn]	Sustained; section struck (June 26, 1997)
Section 702(d)	No change in outlays or revenues	Intercity passenger rail funding	Approved, 77-21	Fell (June 27, 1997)
Section 1604(f)(3)	No change in outlays or revenues	Crediting of new cigarette tax against "global settlement"	Approved, 78-22	Fell (July 31, 1997)

b. To Bar Consideration of Amendment(s)

Object of Point of Order[a]	Basis of Point of Order[b]	Subject Matter	Waiver Motion[c]	Disposition of Point of Order
Gramm Amendment No. 566	No change in outlays or revenues	Balanced budget enforcement procedures	Rejected, 37-63	Sustained; amendment fell (June 27, 1997)
Bumpers Amendment No. 568	[no basis cited]	Prohibition against scoring, for budget purposes, revenues from sale of certain federal lands	Rejected, 48-52	Sustained; amendment fell (June 27, 1997)
Craig Amendment No. 569	No change in outlays or revenues	Prohibition in PAYGO budget process against using tax increases to pay for mandatory spending increases	Rejected, 42-58	Sustained; amendment fell (June 27, 1997)
Brownback/Kohl Amendment No. 570	No change in outlays or revenues	Balanced budget enforcement procedures	Rejected, 57-43	Sustained; amendment fell (June 27, 1997)
First Amendment No. 571	No change in outlays or revenues	Balanced budget enforcement procedures	Rejected, 59-41	Sustained; amendment fell (June 27, 1997)
Abraham Amendment No. 538	No change in outlays or revenues	Reservation of future revenue windfalls for tax or deficit reduction	Rejected, 53-47	Sustained; amendment fell (June 27, 1997)

CRS-25

Object of Point of Order[a]	Basis of Point of Order[b]	Subject Matter	Waiver Motion[c]	Disposition of Point of Order
11. Taxpayer Refund and Relief Act of 1999 (H.R. 2488; vetoed 9/23/1999)				
a. To Strike Provision(s) from Bill or Conference Report				
Section 1502	Increase in deficit or reduction of surplus in fiscal year beyond those covered by instructions	General extension of revenue-reduction provisions	Rejected, 51-48	Sustained; section struck (July 28, 1999)
Section 202	Increase in outlays	Enhancement of the Earned Income Tax Credit for married couples	Approved, voice vote	[none raised]
b. To Bar Consideration of Amendment(s)				
Bingaman Amendment No. 1462	No change in outlays or revenues	Expressing the sense of the Senate regarding investment in education	Rejected, 48-52	Sustained; amendment fell (July 30, 1999)
First Amendment No. 1467	No change in outlays or revenues	Expressing the sense of the Senate regarding the Medicare Reserve Fund	Rejected, 54-46	Sustained; amendment fell (July 30, 1999)
12. Marriage Tax Relief Reconciliation Act of 2000 (H.R. 4810; vetoed 8/5/2000)				
a. To Strike Provision(s) from Bill or Conference Report				
Section 4	Increase in outlays	Enhancement of the Earned Income Tax Credit for married couples	On July 17, the waiver motion (made on July 14) was changed to a unanimous consent request and agreed to	Fell (July 17, 2000)
b. To Bar Consideration of Amendment(s)				
Roth Amendment No. 3864	Increase in deficit or reduction of surplus in fiscal year beyond those covered by instructions	Striking the sunset provision in the legislation	Rejected, 48-47 (waiver motion also applied to amendment listed below)	Sustained; amendment fell (July 17, 2000)
Roth Amendment No. 3865	Increase in deficit or reduction of surplus in fiscal year beyond those covered by instructions	Striking the sunset provision in the legislation	Rejected, 48-47 (waiver motion also applied to amendment listed above)	Sustained; amendment fell (July 17, 2000)
13. Economic Growth and Tax Relief Reconciliation Act of 2001 (P.L. 107-16; 6/7/2001)				
a. To Strike Provision(s) from Bill or Conference Report				

CRS-26

Object of Point of Order[a]	Basis of Point of Order[b]	Subject Matter	Waiver Motion[c]	Disposition of Point of Order
[none]				
b. To Bar Consideration of Amendment(s)				
[none]				
14. Jobs and Growth Tax Relief Reconciliation Act of 2003 (P.L. 108-27; 5/28/2003)				
a. To Strike Provision(s) from Bill or Conference Report				
[none]				
b. To Bar Consideration of Amendment(s)				
Sessions Amendment No. 639	Increase in deficit or reduction of surplus in fiscal year beyond those covered by instructions	Applying the sunset provision to the revenue increase provisions	Rejected, 51-49	Sustained; amendment fell (May 15, 2003)

CRS-27

Object of Point of Order[a]	Basis of Point of Order[b]	Subject Matter	Waiver Motion[c]	Disposition of Point of Order
15. Deficit Reduction Act of 2005 (P.L. 109-171; 2/8/2006)				
a. To Strike Provision(s) from Bill or Conference Report				
Section 5001(b)(3) and (b)(4), a portion of Section 6043(a), and Section 7404	No change in outlays or revenues (Section 5001(b)(3) and (b)(4)), and budgetary changes merely incidental to non-budgetary components (a portion of Section 6043(a) and Section 7404)	Requiring the Secretary of Health and Human Services to submit to Congress by August 1, 2007, a report on the plan for the hospital value based purchasing program under Medicare (Section 5001(b)(3); requiring the Medicare Payment Advisory Commission to submit to Congress by June 1, 2007, a report that includes detailed recommendations on a structure of value based payment adjustments for hospital services under Medicare (Section 5001(b)(4); the negligent standard for hospitals and physicians who treat Medicaid patients (a portion of Section 6043(a); and eligibility for foster care maintenance payments and adoption assistance (Section 7404)	Rejected, 52-48 (waiver motion applied to first three provisions, but did not apply to Section 7404)	Sustained against first three provisions, which were struck from the bill; not sustained against Section 7404, which remained in the bill (December 21, 2005)
b. To Bar Consideration of Amendment(s)				
[none]				
16. Tax Increase Prevention and Reconciliation Act of 2005 (P.L. 109-222; 5/17/2006)				
a. To Strike Provision(s) from Bill or Conference Report				
[none]				
b. To Bar Consideration of Amendment(s)				
Grassley Amendment No. 2654	No change in outlays or revenues	Sense of the Senate statement on extension of tax policy and health care reform	Rejected, 53-45	Sustained; amendment fell (November 17, 2005)

CRS-28

Object of Point of Order[a]	Basis of Point of Order[b]	Subject Matter	Waiver Motion[c]	Disposition of Point of Order
17. College Cost Reduction and Access Act of 2007 (P.L. 110-84; 9/27/2007)				
a. To Strike Provision(s) from Bill or Conference Report				
[none]				
b. To Bar Consideration of Amendment(s)				
[none]				
18. Health Care and Education Reconciliation Act of 2010 (P.L. 111-152; 3/30/2010)				
a. To Strike Provision(s) from Bill or Conference Report				
Section 2101(a)(2)(C) (page 118, lines 15-25), in part proposed a new Section 401(b)(8)(C)(iv) to the Higher Education Act of 1965	No change in outlays or revenues	Limitation on decreases under the formula setting the maximum Pell grant amount annually	None	Sustained; provision struck (March 25, 2010)
Section 2101(a)(2)(D) and (E) (page 120, lines 3-5), proposed striking Section 401(b)(8)(E) of the Higher Education Act of 1965 (and the redesignating subparagraph (F) as (E))	No change in outlays or revenues	Repeal and redesignation of subparagraphs pertaining to technical aspects of Pell grant funding	None	Sustained; provision struck (March 25, 2010)
b. To Bar Consideration of Amendment(s)				
Grassley/Roberts Amendment No. 3564	Outside committee's jurisdiction	To make sure the President, Cabinet Members, all White House Senior staff and Congressional Committee and Leadership Staff are purchasing health insurance through the health insurance exchanges established by the Patient Protection and Affordable Care Act	Rejected, 43-56	Sustained; amendment fell (March 24, 2010)
LeMieux Amendment No. 3586	Outside committee's jurisdiction	To enroll Members of Congress in the Medicaid program	Rejected, 40-59	Sustained; amendment fell (March 24, 2010)

CRS-29

Object of Point of Order[a]	Basis of Point of Order[b]	Subject Matter	Waiver Motion[c]	Disposition of Point of Order
Roberts Amendment No. 3577	Budgetary changes merely incidental to non-budgetary components	To protect Medicare beneficiary access to hospital care in rural areas from recommendations by the Independent Payment Advisory Board	Rejected, 42-54	Sustained; amendment fell (March 24, 2010)
Grassley Amendment No. 3699	Outside committee's jurisdiction	To provide a temporary extension of certain programs	Rejected, 40-56	Sustained; amendment fell (March 24, 2010)
Hutchison Amendment No. 3635	Outside committee's jurisdiction	To repeal the sunset on marriage penalty relief and to make the election to deduct State and local sales taxes permanent (with an offset from the rescission of certain unobligated balances under the American Recovery and Reinvestment Act of 2009)	Rejected, 40-55	Sustained; amendment fell (March 24, 2010)
Ensign Amendment No. 3593	Outside committee's jurisdiction	To improve access to pro bono care for medically underserved or indigent individuals by providing limited medical liability protections	Rejected, 40-55	Sustained; amendment fell (March 25, 2010)
Coburn Amendment No. 3700	Outside committee's jurisdiction	To help protect Second Amendment rights of law-abiding Americans	Rejected, 45-53	Sustained; amendment fell (March 25, 2010)
Vitter Amendment No. 3665	Outside committee's jurisdiction	To prevent the new government entitlement program from further increasing an unsustainable deficit	Rejected, 39-56	Sustained; amendment fell (March 25, 2010)

Object of Point of Order[a]	Basis of Point of Order[b]	Subject Matter	Waiver Motion[c]	Disposition of Point of Order
Murkowski Amendment No. 3711	Outside committee's jurisdiction	To provide an inflation adjustment for the additional hospital insurance tax on high-income taxpayers (with an offset from the rescission of certain unobligated balances under the American Recovery and Reinvestment Act of 2009)	Rejected, 42-57	Sustained; amendment fell (March 25, 2010)

19. Restoring Americans' Healthcare Freedom Reconciliation Act of 2015 (H.R. 3762; vetoed 1/8/2016)

a. To Strike Provision(s) from Amendment, Bill, or Conference Report

Section 105(b) in Enzi (for McConnell) Amendment No. 2916 (to Amendment No. 2874)	Budgetary changes merely incidental to non-budgetary components	Sunset risk corridors for plans in individual and small group markets program established by Section 1342 of the Patient Protection and Affordable Care Act	Rejected, 52-47	Sustained; provision struck (December 3, 2015)

b. To Bar Consideration of Amendment(s)

Cornyn Amendment No. 2912 (to Amendment No. 2874)	Outside committee's jurisdiction	Relating to the Protect America Act	Rejected, 55-44	Sustained; amendment fell (December 3, 2015)
Feinstein Amendment No. 2910 (to Amendment No. 2874)	Outside committee's jurisdiction	To increase public safety by permitting the Attorney General to deny the transfer of firearms or the issuance of firearms and explosives licenses to known or suspected dangerous terrorists	Rejected, 45-54	Sustained; amendment fell (December 3, 2015)
Grassley Amendment No. 2914 (to Amendment No. 2874)	Outside committee's jurisdiction	To address gun violence, improve the availability of records to the National Instant Criminal Background Check System, address mental illness in the criminal justice system, and end straw purchases and trafficking of illegal firearms	Rejected, 53-46	Sustained; amendment fell (December 3, 2015)

CRS-31

Object of Point of Order[a]	Basis of Point of Order[b]	Subject Matter	Waiver Motion[c]	Disposition of Point of Order
Manchin/Toomey Amendment No. 2908 (to Amendment No. 2874)	Outside committee's jurisdiction	To protect Second Amendment rights, ensure that all individuals who should be prohibited from buying a firearm are listed in the National Instant Criminal Background Check System, and provide a responsible and consistent background check process	Rejected, 48-50	Sustained; amendment fell (December 3, 2015)

a. The Byrd rule is Section 313 of the Congressional Budget Act of 1974, as amended (2 U.S.C. 644). There are many point-of-order provisions in Titles III and IV of the act. In some instances, points of order or waiver motions are made under the act by general reference only (such as a Senator raising a point of order "under Title III of the Act") rather than by specific reference to the provision(s) involved. When only general references are made, it usually is impossible to determine (by reference to debate in the *Congressional Record* alone) which provision of the act is involved. Consequently, this table reflects only those instances when specific reference was made to Section 313 of the act or to the Byrd rule. The object of a point of order under the Byrd rule may be to strike one or more provisions (as designated by title or section number, or by page and line number) in a reconciliation measure or a conference report thereon, or to bar consideration of one or more amendments thereto.

b. A provision is regarded as extraneous under the Byrd rule if it:
(1) does not produce a change in outlays or revenues;
(2) produces an outlay increase or revenue decrease when the instructed committee is not in compliance with its instructions;
(3) is outside of the jurisdiction of the committee that submitted the title or provision for inclusion in the reconciliation measure;
(4) produces a change in outlays or revenues which is merely incidental to the non-budgetary components of the provision;
(5) would increase the deficit for a fiscal year beyond those covered by the reconciliation measure; or
(6) recommends changes in Social Security.
The Byrd rule sets forth specific exceptions to the criteria to determine extraneousness.

c. Under the Byrd rule, a successful waiver motion requires the affirmative vote of three-fifths of the membership (60 Senators, if no seats are vacant). A single waiver motion can: (1) apply to the Byrd rule as well as other provisions of the CBA of 1974; (2) involve multiple as well as single provisions or amendments; (3) extend (for specified language) through consideration of the conference report as well as initial consideration of the measure or amendment; and (4) be made prior to the raising of a point of order, thus making the point of order moot.

d. On October 24, 1985, Senator Robert C. Byrd offered an amendment containing the Byrd rule to the Consolidated Omnibus Budget Reconciliation Act (COBRA) of 1985, which the Senate adopted. In this form, the Byrd rule applied to initial Senate consideration of reconciliation measures. On December 19, 1985, the Senate adopted S.Res. 286, which extended the application of portions of the provision in COBRA of 1985 to conference reports and amendments between the two houses. Because the enactment of COBRA of 1985 was delayed until early 1986, the portion of the Byrd rule dealing with conference reports became effective first. Senate consideration of the conference report on COBRA of 1985, and amendments between the two houses thereon, occurred beginning on December 19, 1985. Therefore, only the portion of the Byrd rule dealing with conference reports and amendments between the two houses applied during the consideration of COBRA of 1985. No actions were taken under the rule.

e. On October 13, 1989, during consideration of the Omnibus Budget Reconciliation Act of 1989, the Senate adopted Mitchell Amendment No. 1004 by voice vote. The amendment struck extraneous matter from the bill; its stated purpose was "to strike all matter from the bill that does not reduce the deficit"; (see the *Congressional Record*, daily edition (October 13, 1989), p S13349).

f. The point of order was not sustained against that part of Section 7803(a) proposing a new Section 2106 of the Social Security Act.

CRS-33

Appendix. Text of the Byrd Rule

(Section 313 of the Congressional Budget Act of 1974)

EXTRANEOUS MATTER IN RECONCILIATION LEGISLATION

Sec. 313. (a) **In General.**—When the Senate is considering a reconciliation bill or a reconciliation resolution pursuant to Section 310, (whether that bill or resolution originated in the Senate or the House) or Section 258C of the Balanced Budget and Emergency Deficit Control Act of 1985 upon a point of order being made by any Senator against material extraneous to the instructions to a committee which is contained in any title or provision of the bill or resolution or offered as an amendment to the bill or resolution, and the point of order is sustained by the Chair, any part of said title or provision that contains material extraneous to the instructions to said Committee as defined in subsection (b) shall be deemed struck from the bill and may not be offered as an amendment from the floor.

(b) **Extraneous Provisions.**—(1)(A) Except as provided in paragraph (2), a provision of a reconciliation bill or reconciliation resolution considered pursuant to Section 310 shall be considered extraneous if such provision does not produce a change in outlays or revenues, including changes in outlays and revenues brought about by changes in the terms and conditions under which outlays are made or revenues are required to be collected (but a provision in which outlay decreases or revenue increases exactly offset outlay increases or revenue decreases shall not be considered extraneous by virtue of this subparagraph);

> (B) any provision producing an increase in outlays or decrease in revenues shall be considered extraneous if the net effect of provisions reported by the Committee reporting the title containing the provision is that the Committee fails to achieve its reconciliation instructions;

> (C) a provision that is not in the jurisdiction of the Committee with jurisdiction over said title or provision shall be considered extraneous;

> (D) a provision shall be considered extraneous if it produces changes in outlays or revenues which are merely incidental to the non-budgetary components of the provision;

> (E) a provision shall be considered to be extraneous if it increases, or would increase, net outlays, or if it decreases, or would decrease, revenues during a fiscal year after the fiscal years covered by such reconciliation bill or reconciliation resolution, and such increases or decreases are greater than outlay reductions or revenue increases resulting from other provisions in such title in such year; and

> (F) a provision shall be considered extraneous if it violates Section 310(g).

(2) A Senate-originated provision shall not be considered extraneous under paragraph (1)(A) if the Chairman and Ranking Minority Member of the Committee on the Budget and the Chairman and Ranking Minority Member of the Committee which reported the provision certify that

> (A) the provision mitigates direct effects clearly attributable to a provision changing outlays or revenues and both provisions together produce a net reduction in the deficit;

> (B) the provision will result in a substantial reduction in outlays or a substantial increase in revenues during fiscal years after the fiscal years covered by the reconciliation bill or reconciliation resolution;

(C) a reduction of outlays or an increase in revenues is likely to occur as a result of the provision, in the event of new regulations authorized by the provision or likely to be proposed, court rulings on pending litigation, or relationships between economic indices and stipulated statutory triggers pertaining to the provision, other than the regulations, court rulings or relationships currently projected by the Congressional Budget Office for scorekeeping purposes; or

(D) such provisions will be likely to produce a significant reduction in outlays or increases in revenues but, due to insufficient data, such reduction or increase cannot be reliably estimated.

(3) A provision reported by a committee shall not be considered extraneous under paragraph (1)(C) if

(A) the provision is an integral part of a provision or title, which if introduced as a bill or resolution would be referred to such committee, and the provision sets forth the procedure to carry out or implement the substantive provisions that were reported and which fall within the jurisdiction of such committee; or

(B) the provision states an exception to, or a special application of, the general provision or title of which it is a part and such general provision or title if introduced as a bill or resolution would be referred to such committee.

(c) **Extraneous Materials**.—Upon the reporting or discharge of a reconciliation bill or resolution pursuant to Section 310 in the Senate, and again upon the submission of a conference report on such reconciliation bill or resolution, the Committee on the Budget of the Senate shall submit for the record a list of material considered to be extraneous under subsections (b)(1)(A), (b)(1)(B), and (b)(1)(E) of this section to the instructions of a committee as provided in this section. The inclusion or exclusion of a provision shall not constitute a determination of extraneousness by the Presiding Officer of the Senate.

(d) **Conference Reports**.—When the Senate is considering a conference report on, or an amendment between the Houses in relation to, a reconciliation bill or reconciliation resolution pursuant to Section 310, upon—

(1) a point of order being made by an Senator against extraneous material meeting the definition of subsections (b)(1)(A), (b)(1)(B), (b)(1)(D), (b)(1)(E), or (b)(1)(F), and

(2) such point of order being sustained, such material contained in such conference report or amendment shall be deemed struck, and the Senate shall proceed, without intervening action or motion, to consider the question of whether the Senate shall recede from its amendment and concur with a further amendment, or concur in the House amendment with a further amendment, as the case may be, which further amendment shall consist of only that portion of the conference report or House amendment, as the case may be, not so struck. Any such motion in the Senate shall be debatable for 2 hours. In any case in which such point of order is sustained against a conference report (or Senate amendment derived from such conference report by operation of this subsection), no further amendment shall be in order.

(e) **General Point of Order**.—Notwithstanding any other law or rule of the Senate, it shall be in order for a Senator to raise a single point of order that several provisions of a bill, resolution, amendment, motion, or conference report violate this section. The Presiding Officer may sustain the point of order as to some or all of the provisions against which the Senator raised the point of order. If the Presiding Officer so sustains the point of order as to some of the provisions (including provisions of an amendment, motion, or conference report) against which the Senator raised the point of order, then only those provisions (including provisions of an amendment, motion, or conference report) against which the Presiding Officer sustains the point or order shall be deemed struck pursuant to this section. Before the Presiding Officer rules on such a point of order, any Senator may move to waive such a point of order as it applies to some or all of the provisions against which the point of order was raised. Such a motion to waive is amendable in accordance with the rules and precedents of the Senate. After the Presiding Officer rules on such a point of order, any Senator may appeal the ruling of the Presiding Officer on such a point of order as it applies to some or all of the provisions on which the Presiding Officer ruled.

Author Contact Information

Bill Heniff Jr.
Analyst on Congress and the Legislative Process
wheniff@crs.loc.gov, 7-8646

Acknowledgments

This report was written by Robert Keith, formerly a Specialist in American National Government at CRS. The analyst listed on the cover of this report, and under the "author contact information," is available to answer questions concerning the Senate's "Byrd Rule" and the content of this report.

Congressional Research Service
Informing the legislative debate since 1914

The Congressional Appropriations Process: An Introduction

James V. Saturno, Coordinator
Specialist on Congress and the Legislative Process

Bill Heniff Jr.
Analyst on Congress and the Legislative Process

Megan S. Lynch
Specialist on Congress and the Legislative Process

November 30, 2016

Congressional Research Service
7-5700
www.crs.gov
R42388

Summary

Congress annually considers several appropriations measures, which provide discretionary funding for numerous activities—for example, national defense, education, and homeland security—as well as general government operations. Congress has developed certain rules and practices for the consideration of appropriations measures, referred to as the *congressional appropriations process*. The purpose of this report is to provide an overview of this process.

Appropriations measures are under the jurisdiction of the House and Senate Appropriations Committees. In recent years these measures have provided approximately 35% to 39% of total federal spending. The remainder of federal spending comprises direct (or mandatory) spending, controlled by House and Senate legislative committees, and net interest on the public debt.

The annual appropriations cycle is initiated with the President's budget submission, which is due on the first Monday in February. This is followed by congressional consideration of a budget resolution that, in part, sets spending ceilings for the upcoming fiscal year. The target date for completion of the budget resolution is April 15. Committee and floor consideration of the annual appropriations bills occurs during the spring and summer months and may continue through the fall and winter until annual appropriations are enacted. Floor consideration of appropriations measures is subject to procedural rules that may limit the content of those measures and any amendments thereto.

Congress has established a process that provides for two separate types of measures associated with discretionary spending: authorization bills and appropriation bills. These measures perform different functions. Authorization bills establish, continue, or modify agencies or programs. Appropriations measures subsequently provide funding for the agencies and programs authorized.

There are three types of appropriations measures. *Regular appropriations bills* provide most of the funding that is provided in all appropriations measures for a fiscal year and must be enacted by October 1, the beginning of the fiscal year. If regular bills are not enacted by the beginning of the new fiscal year, Congress adopts *continuing resolutions* to continue funding, generally until regular bills are enacted. *Supplemental appropriations bills* provide additional appropriations to become available during a fiscal year.

Budget enforcement for appropriations measures under the congressional budget process has both statutory and procedural elements. The statutory elements are derived from the Budget Control Act of 2011, which imposes limits on discretionary spending for each of the fiscal years between FY2012 and FY2021. The procedural elements generally stem from requirements under the Congressional Budget Act that are normally associated with the budget resolution. Through this Budget Act process, the Appropriations Committee in each chamber, as well as each of their subcommittees, receives procedural limits on the total amount of budget authority for the upcoming fiscal year (referred to as 302(a) and 302(b) allocations). Enforcement of the statutory limits occurs primarily through sequestration, while enforcement of the procedural limits occurs through points of order. Discretionary appropriations may be designated or otherwise provided so that they are effectively exempt from statutory and procedural budget enforcement. Such designations include "emergency requirements," "overseas contingency operations/global war on terrorism," and for "disaster relief."

Rescissions are provisions of law that cancel previously enacted budget authority. As budget authority providing the funding must be enacted into law, so too a rescission cancelling the budget authority must be enacted into law. Rescissions can be included either in separate rescission measures or any of the three types of appropriations measures.

The Congressional Appropriations Process: An Introduction

Contents

Contacts

Introduction

Congress annually considers several appropriations measures, which provide discretionary funding for numerous activities—such as national defense, education, and homeland security—as well as general government operations. Appropriations acts are characteristically annual and generally provide funding authority that expires at the end of the federal fiscal year, September 30.[1]

These measures are considered by Congress under certain rules and practices, referred to as the *congressional appropriations process*. This report discusses the following aspects of this process:

- The annual appropriations cycle,
- The relationship between authorization and appropriation measures,
- Types of appropriations measures,
- Budget enforcement for appropriations measures, and
- Rescissions.

When considering appropriations measures, Congress is exercising the power granted to it under the Constitution, which states, "No money shall be drawn from the Treasury, but in Consequence of Appropriations made by Law."[2] The power to appropriate is a legislative power. Congress has enforced its prerogatives through certain laws. The so-called Antideficiency Act, for example, strengthened the application of this section by, in part, explicitly prohibiting federal government employees and officers from making contracts or other obligations in advance of or in excess of an appropriation, unless authorized by law, and providing administrative and criminal sanctions for those who violate the act.[3] Furthermore, under law, public funds may be used only for the purpose(s) for which Congress appropriated the funds.[4]

The President has an important role in the appropriations process by virtue of the constitutional power to approve or veto entire measures, which Congress can override only by two-thirds vote of both chambers. The President also has influence, in part, because of various duties imposed by statute, such as submitting an annual budget to Congress.

The House and Senate Committees on Appropriations have jurisdiction over the annual appropriations measures. Each committee is organized into subcommittees, with each subcommittee having responsibility for developing one regular annual appropriations bill to provide funding for departments and activities within its jurisdiction.[5] Each House appropriations subcommittee is paired with a Senate appropriations subcommittee and the two subcommittees' jurisdictions are generally identical. The current appropriations subcommittee structure includes the following 12 subcommittees[6]:

---

[1] The federal fiscal year begins on October 1 and ends the following September 30.

[2] U.S. Constitution, Article I, Section 9.

[3] 31 U.S.C. §§1341(a)-1342 and 1349-1350.

[4] 31 U.S.C. §1301(a).

[5] For more information on the jurisdiction of the House and Senate appropriations subcommittees by agency, see CRS Report R40858, *Locate an Agency or Program Within Appropriations Bills*, by Justin Murray.

[6] For additional information, see CRS Report RL31572, *Appropriations Subcommittee Structure: History of Changes from 1920 to 2015*, by James V. Saturno.

1. Agriculture, Rural Development, Food and Drug Administration, and Related Agencies;
2. Commerce, Justice, Science, and Related Agencies;
3. Defense;
4. Energy and Water Development, and Related Agencies;
5. Financial Services and General Government;
6. Homeland Security;
7. Interior, Environment, and Related Agencies;
8. Labor, Health and Human Services, Education, and Related Agencies;
9. Legislative Branch;
10. Military Construction, Veterans Affairs, and Related Agencies;
11. State, Foreign Operations, and Related Programs; and
12. Transportation, Housing and Urban Development, and Related Agencies.

Annual Appropriations Cycle

President Submits Budget

The President initiates the annual budget cycle with the submission of an annual budget proposal for the upcoming fiscal year to Congress. The President is required to submit the annual budget on or before the first Monday in February.[7] Congress has, however, provided deadline extensions both statutorily and, sometimes, informally.[8]

The President recommends spending levels for various programs and agencies of the federal government in the form of *budget authority* (or BA). Such authority does not represent cash provided to or reserved for agencies. Instead, the term refers to authority provided by federal law to enter into contracts or other financial *obligations* that will result in immediate or future expenditures (or *outlays*) involving federal government funds. Most appropriations are a form of budget authority that also provides the legal authority to make the subsequent payments from the Treasury.

A FY2016 appropriations act, for example, provided $77,349,000 in new budget authority for FY2016 to the National Institute of Environmental Health Sciences for agency operations.[9] That is, the act gave the institute legal authority to sign contracts to purchase supplies and pay salaries. The agency could not commit the government to pay more than the $77 million provided for these covered activities. The outlays occur when government payments are made.

Budget authority must be obligated in the fiscal year(s) in which the funds are made available, but outlays may occur over time. In the case of the institute's activities, it may not pay for all the supplies until the following fiscal year.

The amount of outlays in a fiscal year may vary among activities funded because the length of time to complete the activities differs. For example, outlays to pay salaries may occur in the year

---

[7] 31 U.S.C. §1105(a).

[8] For information on past deadline extensions in presidential transition years, see CRS Report RS20752, *Submission of the President's Budget in Transition Years*, by Michelle D. Christensen.

[9] P.L. 114-113, Division G, 129 Stat. 2568.

the budget authority is made available, while outlays for a construction project may occur over several years as various stages of the project are completed.

As Congress considers appropriations measures providing new budget authority for a particular fiscal year, discussions on the resulting outlays involve estimates based on historical trends. Data on the actual outlays for a fiscal year are not available until the fiscal year has ended.

After the President submits the budget proposal to Congress, each agency generally provides additional detailed *justification* materials to the House and Senate appropriations subcommittees with jurisdiction over its funding.[10]

Congress Adopts Budget Resolution

The Congressional Budget and Impoundment Control Act of 1974 (CBA)[11] provides for the annual consideration of a concurrent resolution on the budget.[12] The budget resolution is Congress's response to the President's budget. It is a concurrent resolution because it is an agreement between the House and Senate that establishes overall budgetary and fiscal policy to be carried out through subsequent legislation. The budget resolution must cover at least five fiscal years: the upcoming fiscal year (referred to as the "budget year") plus the four subsequent fiscal years.[13]

The budget resolution, in part, sets total new budget authority and outlay levels for each fiscal year covered by the resolution. It also allocates federal spending among 20 functional categories (such as national defense, agriculture, and transportation), setting budget authority and outlay levels for each function.

Within each chamber, the total new budget authority and outlays for each fiscal year are also allocated among committees with jurisdiction over spending, thereby setting spending ceilings for each committee.[14] The House and Senate Committees on Appropriations receive allocations only for the upcoming fiscal year, because appropriations measures are annual. Once the appropriations committees receive their spending ceilings, they separately subdivide the amount among their respective subcommittees, providing spending ceilings for each subcommittee.

The budget resolution is not sent to the President and does not become law. It does not provide budget authority or raise or lower revenues; instead, it is a guide for the House and Senate as they consider various budget-related bills, including appropriations and tax measures. Both the House and Senate have established parliamentary rules to enforce some of these spending ceilings when legislation is considered on the House or Senate floor, respectively.

These spending ceilings for the upcoming fiscal year may be enforced through points of order during House consideration of each appropriation measure. During Senate consideration of each appropriations bill, the total new budget authority and outlay levels for the upcoming fiscal year

---

[10] For further information on budget justifications, see CRS Report RS20268, *Agency Justification of the President's Budget*, by Michelle D. Christensen.

[11] P.L. 93-344, as amended.

[12] Budget resolutions are under the jurisdiction of the House and Senate Committees on the Budget.

[13] In general, the CBA requirements that apply to the content of the budget resolution do not also apply to the President's budget submission. Requirements for the President's budget submission are in 31 U.S.C. §1105.

[14] The committee allocations are usually provided in the joint explanatory statement included in the conference report to the budget resolution. For more details, see "Budget Enforcement for Appropriations Measures" below.

as well as the subcommittee spending ceilings—but not the committee ceilings—may be enforced.

The CBA establishes April 15 as the target date for congressional adoption of the budget resolution. Since FY1977, Congress has frequently not met this target date. In many instances in recent years (FY1999, FY2003, FY2005, FY2007, FY2011-FY2015, and FY2017), Congress did not adopt a budget resolution.[15]

There is no penalty if the budget resolution is not completed before April 15 or not at all. Under the CBA, however, certain enforceable spending ceilings associated with the budget resolution are not established until the budget resolution is completed. The act also prohibits both House and Senate floor consideration of appropriations measures for the upcoming fiscal year before Congress completes the budget resolution and, in the Senate, before the Senate Appropriations Committee receives its spending ceilings.[16] The CBA allows the House, however, to consider most appropriations measures after May 15, even if the budget resolution has not been adopted by Congress.[17] The Senate may adopt a motion to waive this CBA requirement for spending ceilings by a majority vote.

If Congress delays completion of the annual budget resolution (or does not adopt one), each chamber may adopt a deeming resolution to address these procedural difficulties.[18]

Timetable for Consideration of Appropriations Measures

The timing of the various stages of the appropriations process tends to vary from year to year. Although timing patterns for each stage tend to be discernible over time, certain anomalies from these general patterns occur in many years.

Traditionally, the House of Representatives initiated consideration of regular appropriations measures, and the Senate subsequently considered and amended the House-passed bills. More recently, the Senate appropriations subcommittees and committee have sometimes not waited for the House bills; instead they have reported original Senate bills. Under this more recent approach, the House and Senate appropriations committees and their subcommittees have often considered the regular bills simultaneously.

The House Appropriations Committee reports the 12 regular appropriations bills separately to the full House. The committee generally reports the bills in May and June.[19] Generally, the full House starts floor consideration of the regular appropriations bills in May or June as well.

---

[15] For more information on budget resolutions, see CRS Report RL30297, *Congressional Budget Resolutions: Historical Information*, by Bill Heniff Jr.

[16] Section 303.

[17] This exception applies to *general appropriations bills*, which the House defines as regular appropriations bills and supplemental appropriations measures that provide funding for more than one agency. (For more information, see "Types of Appropriations Measures" below.)

[18] For information on deeming resolutions, see "Allocations and Other Limits on Appropriations Associated with the Budget Resolution" below and CRS Report R44296, *Deeming Resolutions: Budget Enforcement in the Absence of a Budget Resolution*, by Megan S. Lynch.

[19] Although historically there has been significant variance in this general pattern, in recent years the House Appropriations Committee has reported most of the regular bills before July. For example, of the 12 regular bills, the committee reported 10 of the FY2015 bills before July 1 and one after. In both FY2016 and FY2017, the committee reported 10 before July 1 and two after.

The Senate Appropriations Committee typically begins reporting the bills in June and generally completes committee consideration prior to the August recess.[20] The Senate typically begins floor consideration of the bills beginning in June or July.

Consideration by the full House and Senate may continue through the fall. While Congress has traditionally considered and approved each regular appropriations bill separately, delays in their consideration may mean that one or more appropriations measures may not receive separate initial consideration in one or both chambers and that several appropriations bills may subsequently get combined into a single legislative vehicle prior to enactment, referred to as omnibus appropriations measures.

If this process is not completed prior to the start of the fiscal year (October 1), Congress may need to enact one or more measures to provide temporary funding authority pending the final disposition of the regular appropriations bills, either separately or as part of an omnibus measure. Because budget authority is typically provided for a single fiscal year, temporary funding measures are necessary if action on a regular appropriations measure has not been completed prior to the beginning of a fiscal year in order to prevent a funding gap that could require an agency to cease non-excepted activities. Traditionally, temporary funding has been provided in the form of a joint resolution to allow agencies or programs to continue to obligate funds at a particular rate (such as the rate of operations for the previous fiscal year) for a specific period of time, which may range from a single day to an entire fiscal year. These measures are known as continuing resolutions (or CRs).[21]

Work of the Appropriations Committees

After the President submits the budget, the House and Senate appropriations subcommittees hold hearings on the segments of the budget under their jurisdiction. They focus on the details of the agencies' justifications, which provide supporting materials to the budget submission. The hearings, at which primarily agency officials testify, may also be supplemented by meetings and communications between the subcommittee staff and agency officials. At the same time, the subcommittees may solicit requests from Members of Congress for programmatic levels and language to be included in the appropriations bills and committee reports.

After conducting these hearings, the House and Senate Appropriations Committees make their suballocations, and the subcommittees begin to draft, mark up, and report the regular bills under their jurisdiction to their respective full committees.[22] Both Appropriations Committees consider each subcommittee's recommendations separately. The committees may adopt amendments to a subcommittee's recommendations prior to reporting the bills and making them available for further consideration by their respective chambers.

---

[20] For FY2017, the Senate Appropriations Committee reported all 12 regular bills prior to July 1.

[21] For information on continuing resolutions, see "Continuing Resolutions" below.

[22] The chair usually proposes a draft bill (the *chair's mark*). The chair and other subcommittee members discuss amendments to the draft and may agree to include some during a markup of the bill). Regular appropriations bills are not introduced prior to full committee markup. Because House rules allow the Appropriations Committee to report an original bill, the bill is not introduced and assigned a bill number until the House Appropriations Committee reports it. In the Senate there have been occasions in previous years in which some subcommittees did not formally report a regular bill to the full committee. Instead, in these instances, formal committee action on the regular bill began at full-committee markup.

House Floor Consideration

Prior to floor consideration of an appropriations bill, the House almost always considers a special rule reported by the House Rules Committee setting parameters for floor consideration of the bill.[23] If the House adopts the special rule, it usually considers the appropriations bill soon thereafter.

The House considers the bill in the Committee of the Whole House on the State of the Union (or Committee of the Whole), of which all Representatives are members.[24] A special rule on an appropriations bill usually provides for one hour of general debate on the bill. The debate includes opening statements by the chair and ranking minority member of the appropriations subcommittee with jurisdiction over the regular bill, as well as other interested Representatives.

After the Committee of the Whole debates the bill, it considers amendments. The appropriations bill is generally read for amendment, by paragraph.[25] Amendments to general appropriations bills are governed by a variety of requirements:

- House standing rules and precedents that establish several requirements applicable to all types of measures, such as requiring amendments to be germane to the bill;

- House standing rules and precedents that establish a separation between appropriations and other legislation;[26]

- Separate orders establishing certain requirements, such as those requiring a "spending reduction account" section in each regular appropriations bill and limiting permissible amendments to that section[27];

- Spending limits imposed by the congressional budget process (see "Allocations and Other Limits on Appropriations Associated with the Budget Resolution" below); and

---

[23] Because the regular appropriations bills must be completed in a timely fashion, House Rule XIII, clause 5, provides that these appropriations bills are privileged. This allows the House Appropriations Committee to make a motion to bring a regular appropriations bill directly to the floor without the Rules Committee reporting a special rule providing for the measure's consideration, as is necessary for most major bills. However, in recent years, the House Appropriations Committee has usually used the special rule procedure.

These special rules typically include waivers of certain parliamentary rules regarding the consideration of appropriations bills and certain provisions within them. Special rules may also be used for other purposes, such as structuring or restricting floor amendments. For further information, see CRS Report R42933, *Regular Appropriations Bills: Terms of Initial Consideration and Amendment in the House, FY1996-FY2015*, by Jessica Tollestrup.

[24] House Rule XVIII, clause 3, requires that appropriations measures be considered in the Committee of the Whole before the House votes on final passage of the measures. (For more on Committee of the Whole, see CRS Report 95-563, *The Legislative Process on the House Floor: An Introduction*, by Christopher M. Davis; and CRS Report RL32200, *Debate, Motions, and Other Actions in the Committee of the Whole*, by Bill Heniff Jr. and Elizabeth Rybicki

[25] For more information, see CRS Report 98-995, *The Amending Process in the House of Representatives*, by Christopher M. Davis.

[26] See "Relationship Between Authorization and Appropriations Measures" below. Also, for further information, see CRS Report R41634, *Limitations in Appropriations Measures: An Overview of Procedural Issues*, by James V. Saturno.

[27] Section 3(d) of H.Res. 5 (114th Cong.) allows amendments that would transfer appropriations in a pending general appropriations bill to a spending reduction account, which is required in each such bill. Only amendments transferring funds into the account are allowed; therefore, the House may not consider an amendment withdrawing funds from the account.

- Provisions of a special rule or unanimous consent agreement providing for consideration of a particular appropriations bill.[28]

If an amendment violates any of these requirements, any Representative may raise a point of order to that effect. These points of order are not self-enforcing. A Member must raise a point of order that an amendment violates a specific rule. If the presiding officer rules the amendment out of order, it cannot be considered by the House. A special rule or unanimous consent agreement, however, may waive requirements imposed by House rules or the budget process, thereby allowing the House to consider the amendment.

During consideration of individual appropriations bills, the House sometimes sets additional parameters, either by adopting a special rule or by unanimous consent. For example, the House has sometimes agreed to limit consideration to a specific list of amendments or to limit debate on individual amendments by unanimous consent.

After the Committee of the Whole completes consideration of the measure, it rises and reports the bill and any amendments that have been adopted to the full House. The House then votes on the amendments and final passage. After House passage, the bill is sent to the Senate.

Senate Floor Consideration

The recent practice has been for the full Senate to consider the text of a bill as reported by its Appropriations Committee in the form of a substitute to the House-passed appropriations bill.[29] The Senate does not have a device like a special rule to set parameters for consideration of bills by majority vote. Before taking up the bill, however, or during its consideration, the Senate sometimes sets parameters by unanimous consent.

When the bill is brought up on the floor, the chair and ranking minority member of the appropriations subcommittee make opening statements on the contents of the bill as reported.

Committee and floor amendments to the reported bills must meet requirements established under the Senate standing rules and precedents and congressional budget process as well as any requirements agreed to by unanimous consent. The specifics of the Senate and House rules for general appropriations bills differ, including the waiver procedures, but include the following common themes[30]:

- Separate consideration of legislation and appropriations[31]; and
- Enforcement of the spending limits imposed by the congressional budget process.

---

[28] For further information on how special rules and unanimous consent agreements have previously been used to govern consideration of regular appropriations bills on the House floor, see CRS Report R42933, *Regular Appropriations Bills: Terms of Initial Consideration and Amendment in the House, FY1996-FY2015*, by Jessica Tollestrup.

[29] Recently, the Senate Appropriations Committee has generally either (1) reported the House-passed bill with a committee substitute, or (2) reported an original Senate bill, waited until the House-passed bill was received in the Senate, and then offered a committee substitute (comprising the text of the Senate bill) to the House-passed bill. In either case, the Senate considers the committee's recommendations in the form of a committee amendment to the House-passed bill.

[30] The Senate may waive these rules either by unanimous consent or, in some cases, by motion.

[31] Senate Rule XVI also prohibits amendments that are not germane to the subject matter in the bill, but the Senate standard for germaneness and procedures for determining whether an amendment is germane are different than the House. For information about germaneness and Senate Rule XVI, paragraph 4, see Riddick and Frumin, *Riddick's Senate Procedure*, pp. 161-171. See also the report section "Relationship Between Authorization and Appropriations Measures."

The Senate generally does not require that amendments be considered in the order of the bill. Senators may propose amendments to any portion of the bill at any time it is pending unless the Senate agrees to set limits.

House and Senate Conference Action

The Constitution requires that the House and Senate approve the same measure in precisely the same form before it may be presented to the President for his signature or veto. Consequently, once the House and Senate have both completed initial consideration of an appropriations measure, the Appropriations Committees in each chamber will endeavor to negotiate a resolution of the differences between their respective versions. The practice has generally been for the House and Senate to convene a conference committee to resolve differences between the chambers on appropriations bills.[32] Alternatively, agreement may be reached through an exchange of amendments between the houses.[33]

In current practice, the Senate typically passes the House bill with the Senate version attached as a single substitute amendment. As a result, the House and Senate resolve their differences based on disagreement on the measure as a whole. Members of the House and Senate appropriations subcommittees having jurisdiction over a particular regular appropriations bill, as well as the chair and ranking minority members of the full committees, are designated as conferees or managers and tasked with meeting to negotiate over differences between the House- and Senate-passed versions.[34]

The purpose of the negotiations is to resolve differences between the two chambers, and therefore House and Senate rules generally require conferees to negotiate within the scope of the differences on those matters in disagreement.[35] Additionally, they may not include in the conference report new *directed spending provisions*, defined as

> any item that consists of a specific provision containing a specific level of funding for any specific account, specific program, specific project, or specific activity, when no specific funding was provided for such specific account, specific program, specific project, or specific activity in the measure originally committed to the conferees by either House.[36]

Completion of the conference report is not on a specified timeline, so negotiations are concluded only when a majority of the conferees from each chamber sign the conference report. Once conferees reach agreement on all points of difference, they report the conference report, which proposes a new conference substitute for the bill as a whole. In addition, the conference report

---

[32] For more on resolving differences, see CRS Report 96-708, *Conference Committee and Related Procedures: An Introduction*, by Elizabeth Rybicki; and CRS Report 98-696, *Resolving Legislative Differences in Congress: Conference Committees and Amendments Between the Houses*, by Elizabeth Rybicki.

[33] Although this method has been used on occasion, it remains rare for appropriations measures. For information on amendment exchanges, see CRS Report 98-812, *Amendments Between the Houses: A Brief Overview*, by Elizabeth Rybicki and James V. Saturno; and CRS Report R41003, *Amendments Between the Houses: Procedural Options and Effects*, by Elizabeth Rybicki.

[34] In practice, if the Senate and/or House does not pass an individual appropriations bill, informal negotiations may still take place on the basis of the reported version of that chamber(s) (such has been the case, for example, for some provisions included in omnibus appropriations measures in recent years; see "Regular Appropriations Bills" section below).

[35] House Rule XXII, clause 9, and Senate Rule XXVIII.

[36] Senate Rule XLIV, paragraph 8.

includes a joint explanatory statement (or managers' statement) explaining the new substitute. A conference report may not be amended in either chamber.

Usually, the House considers conference reports on appropriations measures first. The first chamber to consider the conference report may vote to adopt it, reject it, or recommit it to the conference for further consideration. After the first house adopts the conference report, the conference is automatically disbanded; therefore, the second house has two options—to adopt or reject the conference report. In cases in which the conference report is either rejected or recommitted to the conference committee, the two chambers may negotiate further over the matters in dispute.[37] The measure cannot be sent to the President until both houses have agreed to the entire text of the bill.

The rules governing the content of the conference report may be enforced or waived during House and Senate consideration of it. Prior to consideration of the conference report, the House typically adopts a special rule waiving all points of order against the conference report or its consideration. In the Senate, such points of order may be waived through unanimous consent or (in some cases) motions to waive. If a point of order is sustained, the conference report falls.

A mechanism is available, however, through which new matter or new directed spending provisions included in a conference report can be stricken while the remaining provisions are effectively retained for further Senate consideration. If the presiding officer sustains a point of order against new matter or one or more new directed spending provisions, the offending language is stricken from the conference report. After all points of order under both requirements have been disposed of, the Senate considers a motion to send the remaining provisions to the House as an amendment between the houses since the changed legislative text can no longer be considered as a conference report. The House would then consider the amendment. The House may choose to further amend the Senate amendment and return it to the Senate for further consideration. If the House, however, agrees to the amendment, the measure is cleared for presidential action.[38] Alternatively, the Senate may choose to retain such provisions by voting to waive these points of order. To succeed, the motion must be adopted by a three-fifths vote of all Senators duly chosen and sworn (60 Senators if there are no vacancies). An appeal of a ruling by the presiding officer on one of these points of order would also require a vote of three-fifths of all Senators.

Presidential Action

Under the Constitution,[39] after a measure is presented to the President, he has 10 days to sign or veto the measure. If he takes no action, the bill automatically becomes law at the end of the 10-day period if Congress is in session. Conversely, if he takes no action when Congress has adjourned, he may pocket veto the bill.

If the President vetoes the bill, he sends it back to Congress. Congress may override the veto by a two-thirds vote in both houses. If Congress successfully overrides the veto, the bill becomes law. If Congress is unsuccessful, the bill dies.

---

[37] If either house rejects the conference report, the two houses normally agree to further conference, usually appointing the same conferees.

[38] For more detailed information on these Senate rules, see CRS Report RS22733, *Senate Rules Restricting the Content of Conference Reports*, by Elizabeth Rybicki.

[39] U.S. Constitution, Article I, Section 7, known as the Presentment Clause.

Relationship Between Authorization and Appropriations Measures

Congress has established a process that provides for two separate types of measures—authorization measures and appropriation measures. These measures perform different functions. Authorization acts establish, continue, or modify agencies or programs. For example, an authorization act may establish or modify programs within the Department of Defense. An authorization act may also explicitly authorize subsequent appropriations for specific agencies and programs, frequently setting spending ceilings for them. These authorizations of appropriations provisions may be permanent, annual, or multiyear authorizations. Annual and multiyear provisions require reauthorizations when they expire. Congressional rules generally restrict appropriations measures to provide new budget authority only for programs, activities, or agencies previously authorized by law. Congress, however, is not required to provide appropriations for an authorized discretionary spending program.

House and Senate rules enforce the separation of these functions into different measures by separating committee jurisdiction over appropriations and other types of legislation and rules prohibiting measures from including both appropriations and other legislation.[40] Authorization measures are under the jurisdiction of legislative committees, such as the House Committees on Agriculture and Homeland Security or the Senate Committees on Armed Services and the Judiciary. Appropriations measures are under the jurisdiction of the House and Senate Appropriations Committees.

The House and Senate prohibit, in various ways, language in appropriations bills providing appropriations for purposes not authorized by law or legislation on an appropriations bill. An appropriation for purposes not authorized by law, commonly called an *unauthorized appropriation*, is new budget authority in an appropriations measure (including an amendment or conference report) for agencies or programs with no current authorization or for which budget authority exceeds the ceiling authorized.[41] *Legislation* refers to language in appropriations measures that changes existing law, such as establishing new law or amending or repealing current law. Legislation is under the jurisdiction of the legislative committees.

Although House rules prohibit both unauthorized appropriations and legislation in regular appropriations bills and supplemental appropriations measures that provide funds for two or more agencies, the House may choose to waive their application.[42] However, House rules do not prohibit such provisions in continuing resolutions. The House prohibition applies to bills reported by the House Appropriations Committee, amendments, and conference reports. The point of order applies to the text of the bill as well as any amendments or conference reports.

Senate rules regarding legislation on appropriations bills restrict the content of amendments to regular bills, supplementals that provide funds for more than one purpose or agency, and continuing resolutions. Such amendments include those that are:

---

[40] House Rule XXI, clause 2; House Rule XXII, clause 5; and Senate Rule XVI prohibit the inclusion of legislative provisions in appropriations measures. House Rule XXI, clause 4; and House Rule XXII, clause 5 also prohibit appropriations in legislation in other types of measures or conference reports.

[41] For further information on the relationship between authorizations and appropriations, see CRS Report R42098, *Authorization of Appropriations: Procedural and Legal Issues*, by James V. Saturno and Brian T. Yeh.

[42] This is typically done through special rules providing for their consideration, described in "House Floor Consideration" above.

- offered on the Senate floor,
- reported by the Senate Appropriations Committee to the House-passed measure, or
- proposed as a substitute for the House-passed text.[43]

In other words, Senate rules prohibit legislation in both Senate Appropriations Committee amendments and non-committee amendments.[44] They also prohibit non-germane amendments.[45]

These Senate rules do not apply to provisions in Senate bills or conference reports.[46] Recently, the practice of the Senate Appropriations Committee has been either to (1) report the House-passed bill with a committee substitute, or (2) report an original Senate bill, wait until the Senate receives the House-passed bill, and then offer a committee substitute (comprising the text of the Senate bill) to the House-passed bill. In either case, the Senate considers the committee's recommendations in the form of a committee amendment.

Senate rules are generally considered to be less restrictive than the House regarding what may be interpreted as unauthorized appropriations, and they prohibit such appropriations in comparatively fewer situations. For example, the Senate Appropriations Committee may report committee amendments containing appropriations not previously authorized by law. Similarly, an amendment moved by direction of the committee with legislative jurisdiction or in pursuance of an estimate submitted in accordance with law would not be prohibited under Rule XVI. An appropriation is also considered authorized if the Senate has previously passed the authorization during the same session of Congress, even if the bill has not been enacted into law. As a result, while the Senate rule generally prohibits unauthorized appropriations, Senators rarely raise this point of order.

The division between an authorization and an appropriation is a construct of House and Senate rules created to apply to congressional consideration so that the term "unauthorized appropriations" does not convey a legal meaning with regard to funding. If unauthorized appropriations or legislation remain in an appropriations measure as enacted, either because no one raised a point of order or the House or Senate waived the rules, the provision will still have the force of law. Unauthorized appropriations, if enacted, are therefore generally available for obligation or expenditure. Legislative provisions enacted in an annual appropriations act also generally have the force of law for the duration of that act unless otherwise specified.

Types of Appropriations Measures

There are generally three types of appropriations measures: regular appropriations bills, continuing resolutions, and supplemental appropriations measures.

---

[43] The Senate rule also applies to amendments between the houses.

[44] Senate Rule XVI, paragraph 2. Under Senate precedents, an amendment containing legislation may be considered if it is germane to language in the House-passed appropriations bill. That is, if the House opens the door by including a legislative provision in an appropriations bill, the Senate has an "inherent right" to amend it. However, if the Senate considers an original Senate bill rather than the House-passed bill with amendments, there is no House language to which the legislative provision could be germane. Therefore, the *defense of germaneness* is not available.

[45] For information about germaneness and Senate Rule XVI, paragraph 4, see Riddick and Frumin, *Riddick's Senate Procedure*, pp. 161-171.

[46] The Senate rule reflects Senate practices at the time the rule was established. The Senate Appropriations Committee traditionally reported amendments to the House-passed appropriations bill, instead of reporting an original Senate bill. Therefore, the rule's prohibition only applies to amendments, both committee and floor amendments.

In general, during a calendar year, Congress may consider:

- 12 regular appropriations bills for the fiscal year that begins on October 1 (often referred to as the budget year) to provide the annual funding for the agencies, projects, and activities funded therein;
- one or more continuing resolutions for that same fiscal year; and
- one or more supplemental appropriations measures for the current fiscal year.

Regular Appropriations Bills

The appropriations process assumes the consideration of 12 regular appropriations measures annually. The House and Senate Appropriations Committees are both organized into 12 subcommittees, with each subcommittee having responsibility for developing one regular annual appropriations bill.

Regular appropriations bills contain a series of unnumbered paragraphs with headings, generally reflecting a unique budget account. The basic unit of regular and supplemental appropriations bills is the account. Under these measures, funding for each department and large independent agency is organized in one or several accounts. Each account generally includes similar programs, projects, or items, such as a research and development account or a salaries and expenses account, although a few accounts include only a single program, project, or item. For small agencies, a single account may fund all of the agency's activities. These acts typically provide a lump-sum amount for each account as well as any conditions, provisos, or specific requirements that apply to that account.

In report language,[47] the House and Senate Committees on Appropriations may provide more detailed expectations or directions to the departments and agencies on the distribution of funding among various activities funded within an account.

Appropriations measures may also provide transfer authority.[48] Transfers shift budget authority from one account or fund to another or allow agencies to make such shifts. For example, an agency moving new budget authority from a salaries and expenses account to a research and development account would be a transfer. Agencies are prohibited from making such transfers without statutory authority.

Agencies may, however, generally shift budget authority from one activity to another within an account without additional statutory authority. This is referred to as reprogramming.[49] The appropriations subcommittees have established notification and other oversight procedures for various agencies to follow regarding reprogramming actions. Generally, these procedures differ with each subcommittee.

---

[47] The term *report language* refers to information provided in reports accompanying committee-reported legislation as well as joint explanatory statements included in conference reports. Although the entire document is generally referred to as a conference report, it comprises two separate parts. The conference report contains a conference committee's proposal for legislative language resolving the House and Senate differences on a measure, while the joint explanatory statement explains the conference report.

[48] Authorization measures may also provide transfer authority. For more information on transfers, see CRS Report R43098, *Transfer and Reprogramming of Appropriations: An Overview of Authorities, Limitations, and Procedures*, by Michelle D. Christensen.

[49] Transfer authority may be required, however, in cases in which the appropriations act includes a set-aside for a specified activity within an account.

Omnibus Appropriations

Congress has traditionally considered and approved each regular appropriations bill separately, but Congress has also combined several bills together into a single legislative vehicle prior to enactment. These packages are referred to as omnibus appropriation measures.[50]

In these cases, Congress typically begins consideration of each regular bill separately but has generally combined some of the bills together at a later stage in the legislative process, particularly while one or more is in conference. During conference on one of the regular appropriations bills, the conferees have typically added to the conference report the final agreements on other outstanding regular appropriations bills, thereby creating an omnibus appropriations measure.[51]

Omnibus acts may provide the full text of each regular appropriations bill included in the act or may incorporate the full text by reference. Omnibus acts may also be in the form of full-year continuing resolutions.[52] Those that provide funding either by including the text of the regular bills or by incorporating them by reference may be considered omnibus bills, but those resolutions providing spending rates—such as is typically included in continuing resolutions—would not.

Packaging regular appropriations bills can be an efficient means for resolving outstanding differences within Congress or between Congress and the President. The negotiators may be able to make more convenient trade-offs between issues among several bills and complete consideration of appropriations using fewer measures. Omnibus measures may also be used to achieve a timely end to the annual appropriations process.

Continuing Resolutions

In general, budget authority provided in regular appropriations expires at the end of the fiscal year—September 30—unless otherwise specified. If action on one or more regular appropriations measures has not been completed by the start of the fiscal year, on October 1, the agencies funded by these bills must cease non-excepted activities due to lack of budget authority.[53]

Traditionally, temporary funding has been provided in the form of a joint resolution to allow agencies or programs to continue to obligate funds at a particular rate (such as the rate of operations for the previous fiscal year) for a specific period of time, which may range from a single day to an entire fiscal year. These measures are known as continuing resolutions (or CRs).

In only four instances since FY1977 (FY1977, FY1989, FY1995, and FY1997) were all regular appropriations enacted by the start of the fiscal year. In all other instances, at least one CR was necessary to fund governmental activities until action on the remaining regular appropriations bills was completed.[54]

---

[50] There is no agreed upon definition of omnibus appropriations measure, but the term *minibus appropriations measure* has sometimes been used to refer to a measure including only a few regular appropriations bills, while *omnibus appropriations measure* refers to a measure containing several regular bills. See CRS Report RL32473, *Omnibus Appropriations Acts: Overview of Recent Practices*, by James V. Saturno and Jessica Tollestrup.

[51] In a few cases, a similar combination has been achieved through an exchange of amendments.

[52] See "Continuing Resolutions" below.

[53] For more information, see CRS Report RL34680, *Shutdown of the Federal Government: Causes, Processes, and Effects*, coordinated by Clinton T. Brass.

[54] For further information, see CRS Report R42647, *Continuing Resolutions: Overview of Components and Recent* (continued...)

On or before the start of the fiscal year, Congress and the President generally complete action on an initial CR that temporarily funds the outstanding regular appropriations bills. In contrast to funding practices in regular bills (i.e., providing separate appropriations levels for each account), temporary CRs generally provide funding at a rate or formula, with certain exceptions. Recently, the CRs have generally provided a rate at the levels provided in the previous fiscal year for all accounts in each regular bill covered, with some account-specific adjustments, termed anomalies. The initial CR typically provides temporary funding until a specific date or until the enactment of the applicable regular appropriations acts, if earlier. Once the initial CR becomes law, additional interim CRs may be used to sequentially extend the expiration date. These subsequent CRs sometimes change the funding methods.

Less frequently, a full-year CR may be enacted that continues funding—at a specific rate or formula for accounts in outstanding regular bills, typically with numerous account-specific exceptions—through the end of the fiscal year. For example, the FY2007 full-year CR (P.L. 110-5) covered nine regular bills, the FY2011 full-year CR (P.L. 112-10) covered 11 regular bills, and the FY2013 full-year CR (P.L. 113-6) covered seven regular bills.

Supplemental Appropriations Measures

In addition to the amounts provided in a regular appropriations measure, the President may request, and Congress may enact, additional funding for selected activities in the form of one or more supplemental appropriations measures (or supplementals). In general, supplemental funding may be enacted to address cases where resources provided through the annual appropriations process are determined to be inadequate or not timely. Supplementals have been used to provide funding for unforeseen needs, such as response and recovery costs due to a disaster. One recent example is the supplemental appropriations bill that was enacted in the wake of Hurricane Sandy in 2013. These measures, like regular appropriations bills, provide specific amounts of funding for individual accounts rather than funding based on a rate for operations (like a CR). Sometimes Congress includes supplemental appropriations in regular bills and CRs rather than in a separate supplemental bill.[55]

Budget Enforcement for Appropriations Measures

Budget enforcement for appropriations measures under the congressional budget process has both statutory and procedural elements. The statutory elements are derived from the Budget Control Act of 2011 (BCA), which imposes limits on discretionary spending each fiscal year through FY2021. The procedural elements of budget enforcement generally stem from requirements under the Congressional Budget Act of 1974 (CBA) that are normally associated with the budget resolution. Through this CBA process, the Appropriations Committee in each chamber, as well as each of their subcommittees, receives a procedural limit on the total amount of budget authority for the upcoming fiscal year.

(...continued)

Practices, by James V. Saturno and Jessica Tollestrup.

[55] In recent years, supplemental appropriations have often been designated or otherwise provided so that they are effectively exempt from the budget enforcement limits. For further information, see the report section "Emergency Spending."

Statutory Discretionary Spending Limits

The BCA places separate limits on two categories of discretionary spending: "defense" and "nondefense." The defense category includes all discretionary spending under budget function 050 (defense).[56] The nondefense category includes discretionary spending in all the other budget functions. The BCA limits were first implemented in FY2012 and are applicable for each of the fiscal years through FY2021.

Pursuant to procedures under the BCA, the limits initially established for FY2014 through FY2021 were further lowered each fiscal year to achieve certain additional budgetary savings.[57] The amount of the revised limits for the upcoming fiscal year is calculated by the Office of Management and Budget (OMB) and reported with the President's budget submission each year.[58] The timing of this calculation, which is to occur many months prior to the beginning of the fiscal year, is intended to allow time for congressional consideration of appropriations measures that comply with the revised limits.

Enforcement

If discretionary spending is enacted in excess of the statutory limits, enforcement primarily occurs through "sequestration," which is the automatic cancelation of budget authority through largely across-the-board reductions of non-exempt programs and activities.[59] Any such across-the-board reductions affect only non-exempt spending subject to the breached limit and are in the amount necessary to reduce spending so that it complies with the limit. The evaluation of the spending limits and any necessary sequestration occurs at specified times after appropriations measures are enacted. The first such evaluation occurs 15 days after Congress adjourns a session *sine die*. If appropriations measures are enacted after that time, subsequent evaluations of the budgetary effects of these measures and any necessary sequestration occurs 15 days after enactment.[60]

The discretionary spending limits are also enforceable procedurally through points of order raised under Section 314(f) of the CBA. Section 314(f) prohibits the House or Senate from considering any measure, amendment thereto, or conference report that would cause one or both of the limits to be exceeded. The House can waive Section 314(f) through a special rule and the Senate by a three-fifths vote of Members.[61]

---

[56] For information on the budget functions, see CRS Report 98-280, *Functional Categories of the Federal Budget*, by Bill Heniff Jr.

[57] The lowering of the limits was triggered when the BCA "joint committee" process did not result in the enactment of legislation to achieve a targeted level of spending reductions. For information on this process, see CRS Report R41965, *The Budget Control Act of 2011*, by Bill Heniff Jr., Elizabeth Rybicki, and Shannon M. Mahan.

[58] The procedures through which these limits are reduced are in Section 251A of the Balanced Budget and Emergency Deficit Control Act of 1985 (BBEDCA). For a description of these procedures and how they were initially carried out for the FY2014 reductions, see OMB Report to Congress on the Joint Committee Reductions for Fiscal Year 2014, pp. 11-16, available at http://www.whitehouse.gov/sites/default/files/omb/assets/legislative_reports/fy14_preview_and_joint_committee_reductions_reports_05202013.pdf.

[59] Procedures for discretionary spending sequestration are established in Sections 251 and 256 of the BBEDCA. Exempt programs and activities are listed in Section 255 of the BBEDCA.

[60] BBEDCA, Section 251(a). In addition, after June 30, if appropriations were enacted for the fiscal year that exceed one or both of the limits, the affected limit(s) for the following fiscal year would be reduced by the amount or amounts of the breach.

[61] CBA, Section 904(c)(2).

Allocations and Other Limits on Appropriations Associated with the Budget Resolution

As mentioned previously, within each chamber, the total budget authority and outlays included in the annual budget resolution are allocated among the House and Senate committees with jurisdiction over spending, including the House and Senate Committees on Appropriations. Through this allocation process, the budget resolution sets total spending ceilings for each House and Senate committee (referred to as the *302(a) allocations*).[62]

The 302(a) allocation of the Appropriations Committee includes both discretionary spending and direct spending (including net interest).[63] Discretionary spending is controlled by appropriations acts, which are under the jurisdiction of the House and Senate Committees on Appropriations. In addition to budget authority for all programs funded by discretionary spending, appropriations measures also include budget authority to finance the obligations of some direct spending programs controlled by legislation under the jurisdiction of the legislative (or authorizing) committees.[64]

The budget authority for direct spending provided in appropriations measures is predominantly for entitlement programs, referred to as *appropriated entitlements*. These entitlements are funded through a two-step process.[65] First, legislation becomes law that sets program parameters (through eligibility requirements and benefit levels, for example); then the appropriations committees *must* provide the budget authority needed to finance the commitment. The Appropriations Committees have limited control over the amount of budget authority provided, since the amount needed is the result of previously enacted commitments in law.[66]

After the House and Senate Appropriations Committees receive their 302(a) allocations, they separately subdivide this amount among their subcommittees, providing each subcommittee with a ceiling. These subdivisions are referred to as the *302(b) suballocations*.[67] The authority for making 302(b) suballocations belongs to the House and Senate Appropriations Committees, and they may later be revised by the committees to reflect further action on appropriations. Such allocations become effective (and enforceable) once they have been reported by the committee.

---

[62] This refers to Section 302(a) of the CBA. Typically, these are provided in the joint explanatory statement that accompanies the conference report on the budget resolution.

[63] "In the federal budget, net interest comprises the government's interest payments on debt held by the public, offset by interest income that the government receives on loans and cash balances and by earnings of the National Railroad Retirement Investment Trust." U.S. Congressional Budget Office, *Glossary of Budgetary and Economic Terms*, available at http://www.cbo.gov.

[64] For example, Social Security and Medicare Part A are under the jurisdiction of the House Ways and Means Committee and Senate Finance Committee. Most of the other standing committees are also legislative committees, such as the House and Senate Armed Services Committees, the House Oversight and Governmental Committee, and the Senate Homeland Security and Government Affairs Committee.

[65] Alternatively, direct spending authority may also be provided through a one-step process in which the legislative act sets the program parameters and provides the budget authority, such as Social Security.

[66] Sometimes appropriations measures include amendments to the authorization laws that control the formula for mandatory appropriations, thereby changing the amount of appropriations subsequently needed. Because such amendments are legislative in nature, they violate the parliamentary rules separating authorizations and appropriations (see "Relationship Between Authorization and Appropriations Measures").

[67] This refers to Section 302(b) of the CBA.

The spending ceilings associated with the annual budget resolution that apply to appropriations measures are generally for a single fiscal year (the upcoming fiscal year), because appropriations measures are annual.

If the budget resolution is significantly delayed (or is never completed), there may not be 302(a) allocations or 302(b) suballocations to enforce until the budget resolution is in place. In such instances, the House and Senate have often adopted alternative mechanisms to provide at least temporary 302(a) allocations for their respective Appropriations Committees, thereby establishing some enforceable spending ceilings. Such mechanisms have been referred to as a "deeming resolutions."[68] The method of adopting such alternative mechanisms for one or both chambers may take a variety of forms. For example, when Congress did not complete a FY2007 budget resolution, both the House and Senate adopted separate deeming resolutions in 2006. The House adopted a special rule[69] that, in part, deemed the House-adopted FY2007 budget resolution[70] and accompanying committee report in effect for enforcement purposes. As a result, the FY2007 total spending ceilings and 302(a) allocations (and therefore, subsequent 302(b) suballocations) were in effect. The Senate included in a FY2006 supplemental appropriations act a deeming provision that, in part, set FY2007 302(a) allocations for the Senate Appropriations Committee.[71] For FY2014 and FY2015, an alternative mechanism for budget enforcement, which included a means to establish 302(a) allocations for appropriations, was enacted in the Bipartisan Budget Act of 2013.[72] In the absence of a budget resolution, this mechanism allowed the chairs of the House and Senate Appropriations Committees to enter statements into the *Congressional Record* of budgetary levels for their respective chambers. Those statements, which included a 302(a) allocation for the chambers' Appropriations Committees, formed the basis for the subsequent 302(b) suballocations for the subcommittees.

Enforcement

The restrictions on appropriations associated with the budget resolution are enforced procedurally through points of order that can be raised on the House and Senate floors when the appropriations measures are considered.

House

Two CBA points of order, under Sections 302(f) and 311(a), are available to enforce the 302(a) allocation to the Appropriations Committees and the 302(b) suballocations to their subcommittees. These CBA points of order apply to committee-reported appropriations bills,[73] certain non-reported appropriations bills,[74] amendments, and conference reports to these measures

---

[68] For information on deeming resolutions, see CRS Report R44296, *Deeming Resolutions: Budget Enforcement in the Absence of a Budget Resolution*, by Megan S. Lynch

[69] H.Res. 818, Section 2 (109th Cong.).

[70] H.Con.Res. 376 (109th Cong.).

[71] P.L. 109-234, Section 7035(a); 120 Stat. 418.

[72] P.L. 113-67, Sections 111, 115, and 116.

[73] The House Appropriations Committee typically reports regular and major supplemental appropriations bills. However, it does not generally report CRs.

[74] If a special rule expedites consideration of a measure by ordering the previous question directly to passage, the form of the measure considered is subject to the points of order. Some continuing resolutions have been considered by this procedure.

during their consideration. If such an appropriation violates these rules, the legislation or amendment cannot be considered.

The 302(f) point of order prohibits floor consideration of a measure, amendment, or conference report providing new budget authority for the upcoming fiscal year that would cause the applicable committee 302(a) or subcommittee 302(b) allocations of new budget authority for that fiscal year to be exceeded. The application of this point of order on appropriations measures is generally limited to discretionary spending (and any changes in direct spending initiated in the appropriations measures).[75] For example, if a committee-reported regular appropriations bill had provided total new discretionary budget authority equal to the subcommittee's 302(b) allocation, any amendment proposing additional new discretionary budget authority would violate the 302(f) point of order.

The 311(a) point of order prohibits floor consideration of a measure, amendment thereto, or conference report that would cause the applicable total budget authority and outlay ceilings in the budget resolution for that fiscal year to be exceeded.[76] As the amounts of all the spending measures considered in the House accumulate, they could potentially reach or exceed these ceilings. This point of order would typically affect the last spending bills to be considered, such as supplemental appropriations measures or the last regular appropriations bills. In the House, the so-called *Fazio Exception*, however, exempts legislation if it would not cause the applicable committee 302(a) allocations to be exceeded.[77]

Separate orders adopted at the beginning of the 112th through 114th Congresses, established new requirements applicable to House consideration of amendments to appropriations bills. Section 3(d)(3) of H.Res. 5 (114th Congress) provides a point of order against an amendment (or amendments offered en bloc) that proposes a net increase in budget authority, even if the level of budget authority in the bill is below the ceiling established under the appropriate 302(b) subdivision. This establishes a secondary enforcement mechanism intended to preserve any savings below the 302(b) subdivision achieved by the Appropriations Committee or through floor amendments. This new point of order applies only to general appropriations bills.

In addition, the FY2015 budget resolution established points of order in both the House and Senate that prohibit language in appropriations measures that would produce a net increase in the cost of direct spending programs above levels specified in the resolution (for FY201-FY2019).[78]

---

[75] The point of order does not apply to increases in the level of direct spending required to finance current law.

[76] Since 2005, the House has adopted a separate order for each Congress that extends enforcement of 302(b) allocations to appropriations bills as amended in the Committee of the Whole, most recently in H.Res. 5 Section 3(e)(2) (114th Cong.). The order establishes a point of order in the Committee of the Whole against a motion to rise and report to the House an appropriations bill that, as amended, exceeds the applicable 302(b) allocation in new budget authority. If the presiding officer sustains a point of order against such a motion, the Committee of the Whole must decide, by a vote, whether to adopt the motion even though the amended measure exceeds the allocation. If the committee votes against "rising," it may consider one proper amendment, such as an amendment reducing funds in the bill to bring it into compliance with the allocation. The separate order also provides an up-or-down vote on the amendment. Only one such point of order may be raised against a single measure. For more detailed information on motions to rise, see CRS Report RL32200, *Debate, Motions, and Other Actions in the Committee of the Whole*, by Bill Heniff Jr. and Elizabeth Rybicki.

[77] Section 311(c) of the CBA. The title of the exception refers to former Representative Victor Herbert Fazio Jr.

[78] See S.Con.Res. 11 (114th Cong.), Section 3103.

Senate

Three points of order typically enforce spending ceilings associated with the budget resolution. Two are CBA points of order, as provided in Sections 302(f) and 311(a). The Senate application of these rules, however, varies from the House versions. The Senate 302(f) point of order prohibits floor consideration of such legislation providing new budget authority for the upcoming fiscal year that would cause the applicable 302(b) suballocations in new budget authority and outlays for that fiscal year to be exceeded. In contrast to the House, it (1) does not apply to 302(a) allocations, but (2) does enforce the outlay level associated with the 302(b) subdivisions. The 311(a) point of order in the Senate is similar to the House version. The Senate, however, does not provide for an exception similar to the Fazio Exception in the House.

In addition, the FY2015 budget resolution established points of order in both the House and Senate that prohibit language in appropriations measures that would produce a net increase in the cost of direct spending programs above levels specified in the resolution (for FY201-FY2019).[79]

Senators may make motions to waive these points of order at the time the issue is raised. Currently, a vote of three-fifths of all Senators (60 Senators if there are no vacancies) is required to approve a waiver motion for any of these points of order. A vote to appeal the presiding officer's ruling also requires a three-fifths vote of all Senators.

Emergency Spending

In the House and Senate, discretionary appropriations may be designated or otherwise provided so that they are effectively exempt from the budget enforcement limits.[80] Such designations or allowances for additional budget authority are provided pursuant to Section 251(b)(2)(A)-(D) of the Balanced Budget and Emergency Deficit Control Act (BBEDCA) and include the following:

- Appropriations designated as emergency requirements;
- Appropriations designated as Overseas Contingency Operations/Global War on Terrorism (OCO/GWOT);
- Certain appropriations for continuing disability reviews and redeterminations;
- Certain appropriations for the health care fraud and abuse control (HCFAC); and
- Appropriations designated as for disaster relief.

The BBEDCA does not limit the amount of budget authority that can be designated as emergency requirements or for OCO/GWOT each fiscal year, nor does it specify the types of activities that are eligible for such designations. In practice, the emergency requirements designation has generally been used to provide additional budget authority for unanticipated needs.[81] The OCO/GWOT designation has generally been used for expenses associated with overseas operations, such as in Iraq and Afghanistan, as well as other purposes.[82]

---

[79] See S.Con.Res. 11 (114th Cong.), Section 3103.

[80] These include points of order under Titles III and IV of the CBA, such as 302(f) and 311(a) points of order, as well as the statutory discretionary spending limits.

[81] For example, almost all of the budget authority in the supplemental appropriations act to assist with the Hurricane Sandy recovery (P.L. 113-2) was designated as emergency requirements. More recently, budget authority in the supplemental appropriations act for Department of Defense activities associated with the Iron Dome program (P.L. 113-145) were also designated in this manner.

[82] For further information on OCO/GWOT spending in recent years, see CRS Report R44519, *Overseas Contingency* (continued...)

The allowable purposes for the continuing disability reviews and redeterminations budget authority are such activities under Titles II and XVI of the Social Security Act and for the costs associated with conducting redeterminations of eligibility under Title XVI. The purposes for the HCFAC funds are any for that program at the Department of Health and Human Services. The BBEDCA specifies the maximum amounts for these programs that would be effectively exempt from the spending limits, if appropriated, for each of the fiscal years between FY2012 and FY2021.

Budget authority eligible for the disaster relief designation is for the cost of activities carried out pursuant to a declaration of a major disaster under the Stafford Act (42 U.S.C. 5122(2)).[83] The amount for this disaster designation is capped each fiscal year to the 10-year rolling average for such budget authority minus the high and low fiscal years during that period. If the entire allowable amount that can be designated for a fiscal year is not appropriated, the unused amount of the designation may be carried over to the following fiscal year.

Section 314(d) of the CBA allows House amendments to strike amounts that are designated as an emergency in appropriations measures or amendments thereto, notwithstanding their budgetary effects. In the Senate, amounts that are designated as an emergency are subject to a point of order under Section 314(e). That point of order may be waived by a three-fifths vote of the Senate. If the point of order is not waived and the presiding officer sustains the point of order, the designation is stricken, and the measure or amendment may be vulnerable to the various enforceable spending limits.[84]

The House also considers the emergency, OCO/GWOT, and disaster relief designations to be legislative and prohibits their inclusion in general appropriations bills, amendments thereto, or conference reports.[85] The Senate, however, does not consider such designations to be legislative.

Rescissions

Rescissions are provisions of law that cancel previously enacted budget authority. For example, if Congress provided $50 million to an agency, it could enact subsequent legislation cancelling some or all of the budget authority prior to its obligation. Rescissions are an expression of changed or differing priorities. They may also be used to offset increases in budget authority for other activities.

The President may recommend rescissions to Congress, but they must be enacted into law in order to take effect. Under Title X of the CBA,[86] if Congress does not enact a bill approving the President's rescissions within 45 days of continuous session of Congress, the budget authority must be made available for obligation.

(...continued)

Operations Funding: Background and Status, coordinated by Lynn M. Williams and Susan B. Epstein.

[83] For further information on appropriations to the disaster relief designation, see CRS Report R42352, *An Examination of Federal Disaster Relief Under the Budget Control Act*, by Bruce R. Lindsay, William L. Painter, and Francis X. McCarthy

[84] These designations may be subject to other points of order under the CBA. For general information on Budget Act points of order, see CRS Report 97-865, *Points of Order in the Congressional Budget Process*, by James V. Saturno.

[85] House Rule XXI, clause 2(b) and (c), and Rule XXII, clause 5(b). This interpretation effectively requires a waiver of these provisions in order to consider appropriations with these designations. See "Relationship Between Authorization and Appropriations Measures."

[86] Title X is referred to as the Impoundment Control Act.

In response to the President's recommendation, Congress may decide not to approve the amount specified by the President, approve the total amount, or approve a different amount. For example, in 2005, the President requested a rescission of $106 million from the Department of Defense (DOD), Operations and Maintenance, Defense-Wide account and $48.6 million from DOD, Research, Development, Test, and Evaluation, Army account. Congress provided a rescission of $80 million from the first account in the DOD, Emergency Supplemental Appropriations to Address Hurricanes in the Gulf of Mexico, and Pandemic Influenza Act, 2006, but it did not provide a rescission from the second account.[87]

Congress may also initiate rescissions. For example, in the above act, Congress also included a rescission of $10 million from the Department of State, Diplomatic and Consular Programs account.

As budget authority providing the funding must be enacted into law, so too a rescission cancelling the budget authority must be enacted into law. Rescissions can be included either in separate rescission measures or any of the three types of appropriations measures.

Author Contact Information

James V. Saturno, Coordinator
Specialist on Congress and the Legislative Process
jsaturno@crs.loc.gov, 7-2381

Megan S. Lynch
Specialist on Congress and the Legislative Process
mlynch@crs.loc.gov, 7-7853

Bill Heniff Jr.
Analyst on Congress and the Legislative Process
wheniff@crs.loc.gov, 7-8646

Acknowledgments

This report was originally authored and updated by Sandy Streeter and Jessica Tollestrup, former Analysts on Congress and the Legislative Process. The listed authors have produced the most recent update of the report and are available to respond to inquiries on the subject.

---

[87] P.L. 109-148, 119 Stat. 2680.

Congressional
Research
Service

Allocations and Subdivisions in the Congressional Budget Process

Bill Heniff Jr.
Analyst on Congress and the Legislative Process

November 29, 2010

Congressional Research Service

7-5700

www.crs.gov

RS20144

CRS Report for Congress ——————————————
Prepared for Members and Committees of Congress

The annual budget resolution sets forth total spending and revenue levels for at least five fiscal years. The spending amounts are allocated, or "crosswalked," to the House and Senate committees having jurisdiction over discretionary spending (the Appropriations Committees) and direct spending (the legislative committees). The committee allocations provide Congress with one means of enforcing the spending levels of a budget resolution after it has been adopted.

While the budget resolution allocates spending among the 20 major functional categories of the federal budget for the purpose of providing a broad statement of budget priorities, the functional categories do not correspond to the committee system by which Congress operates. The committee allocations reformulate the functional category amounts in a budget resolution to correspond to committee jurisdictions. By allocating the spending among committees responsible for spending legislation, the committee allocations allow Congress to hold its committees accountable for staying within the spending limits established in the budget resolution.

Section 302(a) of the Congressional Budget Act of 1974 (Titles I-IX of P.L. 93-344, 88 Stat. 297-332), as amended, requires that the total budget authority and outlays set forth in the budget resolution be allocated to each House and Senate committee that has jurisdiction over specific spending legislation. These committee allocations usually are included in the joint explanatory statement accompanying the conference report on a budget resolution. Section 302(b) of the Budget Act requires the Appropriations Committee of each chamber to subdivide its committee allocation among its subcommittees as soon as practicable after a budget resolution has been adopted. The Appropriations Committees are then required to report these subdivisions to their respective chamber and may revise the subdivisions any time during the appropriations process to reflect actions taken on spending legislation. Section 302(c) of the Budget Act provides a point of order against the consideration of any appropriations measures before the Appropriations Committees report their subdivisions.

The spending allocations may be revised after a budget resolution has been adopted if provided for in the resolution. For instance, Congress usually includes reserve fund provisions in the annual budget resolution, which provide the chairs of the House and Senate Budget Committees the authority to revise the committee spending allocations if certain legislation is reported by the appropriate committee or other conditions are met.

The House and Senate Appropriations Committees have jurisdiction over the regular appropriations acts and other appropriations acts. The Appropriations Committees of each chamber have parallel subcommittees, each of which is responsible for one of the regular appropriations acts. After extensive hearings, each of the subcommittees reports one of the regular appropriations bills to its respective full committee. Then, the full Appropriations Committees report the bills to their respective chamber. A cost estimate of each bill is prepared and compared to the amount allocated or subdivided to the relevant subcommittee.

Section 302(f) of the Budget Act prohibits any measure or amendment that would cause the 302(a) or 302(b) allocations to be exceeded. In the House, these committee allocations and suballocations are the primary focus of enforcement since Section 311(c) of the Budget Act, known as the "Fazio exception," allows the overall limit of spending to be breached so long as a committee's 302(a) allocation is not exceeded.

The allocation limits are not self-enforcing; a Member must raise a point of order for an allocation to be enforced. The points of order may also be waived. In the House, a special rule may be adopted, or unanimous consent may be granted, waiving any budgetary points of order. In the Senate, the point of order against violations of the spending allocations may be waived by a motion under Section 904 of the Budget Act or by unanimous consent. A motion to waive the point of order requires a three-fifths vote of all Senators duly sworn and chosen (60 votes if there is no more than one vacancy).

Author Contact Information

Bill Heniff Jr.
Analyst on Congress and the Legislative Process
wheniff@crs.loc.gov, 7-8646

Congressional
Research Service
Informing the legislative debate since 1914

Omnibus Appropriations Acts: Overview of Recent Practices

James V. Saturno
Specialist on Congress and the Legislative Process

Jessica Tollestrup
Specialist on Congress and the Legislative Process

January 14, 2016

Congressional Research Service

7-5700

www.crs.gov

RL32473

Summary

Omnibus appropriations acts have become a significant feature of the legislative process in recent years as Congress and the President have used them more frequently to bring action on the regular appropriations cycle to a close. Following a discussion of pertinent background information, this report reviews the recent enactment of such measures and briefly addresses several issues raised by their use.

For nearly two centuries, regular appropriations acts were considered by the House and Senate as individual measures and enacted as standalone laws. In 1950, the House and Senate undertook a one-time experiment in improving legislative efficiency by considering all of the regular appropriations acts for FY1951 in a single bill, the Omnibus Appropriations Act of 1950. The following year, the House and Senate returned to the practice of considering the regular appropriations acts individually.

During the 31-fiscal year period covering FY1986-FY2016, a total of 390 regular appropriations acts were enacted or covered by full-year continuing appropriations. Of these, 191 (48.9%) were enacted as standalone measures, 170 (43.6%) were enacted in omnibus measures, and 29 (6.9%) were enacted in other forms (largely full-year continuing appropriations acts). Each year, a median of six regular appropriations acts were enacted as standalone measures, and 5.5 were enacted in omnibus measures.

During this period, 22 different omnibus measures were enacted for 19 different fiscal years. (Two separate omnibus appropriations acts were enacted for FY2001, FY2009, and FY2012.) Each of the omnibus acts funded between two and 13 regular appropriations acts (7.5 median).

Eighteen of the omnibus measures were bills or joint resolutions carrying the designation "omnibus," "consolidated," or "omnibus consolidated" appropriations in the title; seven were titled as continuing appropriations acts (FY1986, FY1987, FY1988, FY2009, the first for FY2012, FY2013; and FY2015); and one was the VA-HUD Appropriations Act for FY2001, which also included the Energy and Water Development Appropriations Act for FY2001.

In addition to the customary concern—of sacrificing the opportunity for debate and amendment for greater legislative efficiency—that arises whenever complex legislation is considered under time constraints, the use of omnibus appropriations acts has generated controversy for other reasons. These include whether adequate consideration was given to regular appropriations acts prior to their incorporation into omnibus appropriations legislation, the use of across-the-board rescissions, and the inclusion of significant legislative (rather than funding) provisions.

This report will be updated at the conclusion of the annual appropriations process.

Contents

Tables

Contacts

Introduction

Omnibus appropriations acts have become a significant feature of the legislative process in recent years as Congress and the President have resorted more frequently to their use to bring action on the regular appropriations cycle to a close. Following a discussion of pertinent background information, this report reviews the recent use of such measures and briefly addresses several issues that their use raises.

Background

Each year, Congress and the President may enact discretionary spending[1] in the form of regular appropriations acts, as well as continuing and supplemental appropriations acts.[2] The number of regular appropriations bills had been fixed at 13 for several decades,[3] but a realignment of the House and Senate Appropriations subcommittees at the beginning of the 109th Congress reduced the number of regular appropriations bills normally considered each year to 11 (starting with the FY2006 cycle).[4] The number of regular appropriations bills was increased to 12 at the beginning of the 110th Congress (starting with the FY2008 cycle) due to further subcommittee realignment and has remained at that level through the date of this report.

If action is not completed on all of the regular appropriations acts toward the end of a congressional session, Congress will sometimes combine the unfinished regular appropriations into an omnibus measure. In some instances, action on the unfinished acts carries over into the following session. An omnibus act may set forth the full text of each of the regular appropriations acts included therein, or it may enact them individually by cross-reference.

The House and Senate consider annual appropriations acts (and other budgetary legislation) within constraints established in a yearly budget resolution required by the Congressional Budget Act of 1974, as amended. Budget resolution policies are enforced by points of order that may be raised during House and Senate consideration of spending, revenue, and debt limit legislation.[5] On occasion, budget policies may be modified by agreements reached between congressional leaders and the President; such modifications may be accommodated during legislative action through the use of waivers of points of order, emergency spending designations, and other budgetary or procedural devices.

Discretionary spending has also been subject to statutory limits. These were first implemented between FY1991 and FY2002 by the Budget Enforcement Act (BEA) of 1990, as amended.

---

[1] *Discretionary spending*, which accounts for roughly one-third of total federal spending, is spending that is under the jurisdiction of the House and Senate Appropriations Committees. For the most part, discretionary spending funds the routine operations of the federal government. It is distinguished from *direct spending*, which is controlled by the legislative committees in substantive law and funds such mandatory programs as Social Security and Medicare. Discretionary spending and direct spending together make up total federal spending.

[2] For background on the appropriations process, see CRS Report R42388, *The Congressional Appropriations Process: An Introduction*, by Jessica Tollestrup.

[3] For information on changes in the number of regular appropriations acts over the years, see CRS Report RL31572, *Appropriations Subcommittee Structure: History of Changes from 1920 to 2015*, by James V. Saturno and Jessica Tollestrup.

[4] The Senate Appropriations Committee reported a twelfth regular appropriations act, for the District of Columbia, but in final legislative action it was incorporated into another bill.

[5] For a general discussion of budget enforcement procedures, see CRS Report 98-721, *Introduction to the Federal Budget Process*, coordinated by James V. Saturno.

Under this statutory mechanism, separate discretionary spending limits were applied to two different measurements of spending: budget authority and outlays. The discretionary spending limits were enforced by the sequestration process, which involved automatic, largely across-the-board reductions in discretionary spending in order to eliminate any breach of the limits.[6] Pursuant to the Budget Control Act of 2011 (P.L. 112-25), discretionary budget authority for FY2012-FY2021, with some exceptions, is again subject to statutory spending limits on defense and non-defense spending.[7]

For nearly two centuries, regular appropriations bills were considered by the House and Senate as individual measures and enacted by the President as standalone laws. In 1950, the House and Senate undertook a one-time experiment in improving legislative efficiency by considering all of the regular appropriations acts for FY1951 in a single bill, the Omnibus Appropriations Act of 1950 (81st Congress, P.L. 759, September 6, 1950).[8] The following year, the House and Senate returned to the practice of considering the regular appropriations acts individually.

Over the past few decades, however, the House and Senate on several occasions have combined multiple regular appropriations acts into "consolidated" appropriations measures, sometimes enacting individual bills by cross-reference. Beginning in the late 1970s, certain omnibus acts have also sometimes been titled by Congress as "continuing appropriations acts," despite the fact that these acts generally incorporate the texts of multiple regular appropriations acts for full-year funding or enact such texts by reference. This is in contrast to the usual form of continuing appropriations, which provides funding at a rate with anomalies.[9] This report includes only the former type of "continuing appropriations act" in its account of omnibus appropriations acts.

Omnibus Appropriations Acts: FY1986-FY2016

During the 31-year period covering FY1986-FY2016, 22 different omnibus measures were enacted for 19 different fiscal years. (Two separate omnibus appropriations acts were enacted for FY2001, FY2009, and FY2012.[10]) The 22 omnibus appropriations acts covered a total of 170 regular appropriations acts. Each of the omnibus acts funded between two and 13 regular appropriations acts, on average funding almost eight (7.7) of them.

---

[6] The sequestration process is discussed in detail in CRS Report RL31137, *Sequestration Procedures Under the 1985 Balanced Budget Act*, by Robert Keith.

[7] The spending caps and enforcement procedures contained in the Budget Control Act are discussed in detail in CRS Report R41965, *The Budget Control Act of 2011*, by Bill Heniff Jr., Elizabeth Rybicki, and Shannon M. Mahan.

[8] See Dalmus H. Nelson, "The Omnibus Appropriations Act of 1950," *Journal of Politics*, vol. 15, no. 2 (May 1953).

[9] For more information on practices relating to the use of continuing appropriations acts, see CRS Report R42647, *Continuing Resolutions: Overview of Components and Recent Practices*, by Jessica Tollestrup.

[10] P.L. 106-553 was enacted as an omnibus measure and enacted the Commerce-Justice-State-Judiciary Appropriations Act for FY2001 and the District of Columbia Appropriations Act for FY2001 by cross-reference. However, the District of Columbia appropriations provision was repealed; therefore, P.L. 106-553 is not counted in this report as an omnibus measure.

Table 1. Omnibus Appropriations Acts: FY1986-FY2016

1. Further Continuing Appropriations Act, 1986
(P.L. 99-190; December 19, 1985)

2. Continuing Appropriations Act, 1987
(P.L. 99-591; October 18, 1986)

3. Further Continuing Appropriations Act, 1988
(P.L. 100-202; December 22, 1987)

4. Omnibus Consolidated Rescissions and Appropriations Act of 1996
(P.L. 104-134; April 26, 1996)

5. Omnibus Consolidated Appropriations Act, 1997
(P.L. 104-208; September 30, 1996)

6. Omnibus Consolidated and Emergency Supplemental Appropriations Act, 1999
(P.L. 105-277; October 21, 1998)

7. Consolidated Appropriations Act, 2000
(P.L. 106-113; November 29, 1999)

8. Consolidated Appropriations Act, 2001
(P.L. 106-554; December 21, 2000)

9. VA-HUD Appropriations Act, 2001
(P.L. 106-377; October 27, 2000)

10. Consolidated Appropriations Resolution, 2003
(P.L. 108-7; February 20, 2003)

11. Consolidated Appropriations Act, 2004
(P.L. 108-199; January 23, 2004)

12. Consolidated Appropriations Act, 2005
(P.L. 108-447; December 8, 2004)

13. Consolidated Appropriations Act, 2008
(P.L. 110-161; December 26, 2007)

14. Consolidated Security, Disaster Assistance, and Continuing Appropriations Act, 2009
(P.L. 110-329; September 30, 2008)

15. Omnibus Appropriations Act, 2009
(P.L. 111-8; March 11, 2009)

16. Consolidated Appropriations Act, 2010
(P.L. 111-117; December 16, 2009)

17. Consolidated and Further Continuing Appropriations Act, 2012
(P.L. 112-55; November 18, 2011)

18. Consolidated Appropriations Act, 2012
(P.L. 112-74; December 23, 2011)

19. Consolidated and Further Continuing Appropriations Act, 2013
(P.L. 113-6; March 26, 2013)

20. Consolidated Appropriations Act, 2014
(P.L. 113-76; January 17, 2014)

21. Consolidated and Further Continuing Appropriations Act, 2015
(P.L. 113-235; December 16, 2014)

22. Consolidated Appropriations Act, 2016
(P.L. 114-113; December 18, 2015)

Source: Prepared by the Congressional Research Service (CRS) using data from the Legislative Information System (LIS).

Eighteen of the omnibus measures were bills or joint resolutions carrying the designation "omnibus," "consolidated," or "omnibus consolidated" appropriations in the title; seven were titled as continuing appropriations acts (FY1986, FY1987, FY1988, the first ones for FY2009 and FY2012, FY2013; and FY2015); and one was the VA-HUD Appropriations Act for FY2001, which also included the Energy and Water Development Appropriations Act for FY2001 (see **Table 1**, and, at the end of the report, **Table 3**).

During this period, a total of 390 regular appropriations acts were enacted or covered by full-year continuing appropriations. Of these, 191 (48.9%) were enacted as standalone measures, 158 (43.6%) were enacted in omnibus measures, and 29 (6.9%) were enacted in other forms (largely full-year continuing appropriations acts).[11] Each year, a median of six regular appropriations acts were enacted as standalone measures, and 5.5 were enacted in omnibus measures.

Sixty-five (16.7%) of the 390 regular appropriations acts were enacted on or before October 1, the start of the fiscal year. Nine of these bills were included in omnibus measures (six in FY1997 and three in FY2009), and the rest were enacted as standalone measures. On average, about two (2.1) regular appropriations bills per year were enacted before the start of the fiscal year during this period.

Ten of the 18 omnibus appropriations acts bearing the designation "omnibus," "consolidated," or "omnibus consolidated" in their title originated in the House as a regular appropriations bill and were expanded in coverage (and their titles redesignated) at the stage of resolving House-Senate differences. These included the appropriations acts for

- Defense (H.R. 3610) in FY1997;
- Transportation (H.R. 4328) in FY1999;
- District of Columbia (H.R. 3194) in FY2000;
- Labor-HHS-Education (H.R. 4577) in FY2001;
- Agriculture (H.R. 2673) in FY2004;
- Foreign Operations (H.R. 4818) in FY2005;
- State-Foreign Operations (H.R. 2764) in FY2008;
- Transportation, Housing and Urban Development (H.R. 3288) in FY2010;
- Agriculture (H.R. 2112) and Military Construction-VA (H.R. 2055) in FY2012 and
- Military Construction-VA (H.R. 2029) in FY2016.

In the case of the FY1997, FY1999, FY2000, FY2001, FY2004, FY2005, FY2010, and the second FY2012 omnibus appropriations acts, the transformation from a regular appropriations bill into a consolidated appropriations measure occurred as part of the conference proceedings

---

[11] In FY1992, funding for activities covered by the Foreign Operations Appropriations bill for that year was provided by a full-year CR in P.L. 102-266, enacted on April 1, 1992. In FY2007, funding for activities covered by nine of the appropriations bills for that year was provided by a full-year CR in P.L. 110-5, enacted on February 15, 2007. Funding for the activities covered by 11 of the FY2011 appropriations bills was provided by a full-year CR in Division B of P.L. 112-10, enacted on April 15, 2011. In addition, the full text of the Department of Defense Appropriations Act for FY2011 was included in Division A of that act. Funding for the activities covered by seven of the FY2013 appropriations bills was provided by a full-year CR in P.L. 113-6, enacted on March 26, 2013. (That law also contained omnibus appropriations for the five remaining regular appropriations acts for that fiscal year.) For further information on full-year continuing resolutions, see CRS Report R42647, *Continuing Resolutions: Overview of Components and Recent Practices*, by Jessica Tollestrup.

between the House and Senate. For the first FY2012 omnibus, the additional appropriations acts were added as a Senate floor amendment to a House-passed regular appropriations bill before conference occurred. For FY2008, conference procedures were not used and the transformation occurred in connection with an exchange of amendments between the two chambers.

The acts for FY2000 and FY2001 enacted regular appropriations measures by cross-reference instead of including their full text (except for FY2000 appropriations for the District of Columbia).

None of the other seven omnibus appropriations acts bearing such designations involved the transformation of a regular appropriations act. Four of the acts (one for FY1996, two for FY2009, and one for FY2013) originated as omnibus measures and retained this status throughout consideration. In FY2003, the omnibus measure originated in the House as a simple continuing resolution (H.J.Res. 2) but was expanded in coverage and redesignated during Senate floor action. Most recently, the vehicles for the FY2014 and FY2015 omnibus acts were originally non-appropriations measures (H.R. 3547 and H.R. 83, respectively) that were amended to include omnibus appropriations.

Selected Issues in the Use of Omnibus Appropriations Acts

Several issues pertaining to the use of omnibus appropriations have been the focus of debate in recent years. These issues include the extent to which regular appropriations that are enacted in omnibus measures have been passed by the House and Senate prior to final congressional action, the use of across-the-board rescissions, and the inclusion of legislative provisions.

Prior Passage of Regular Appropriations Bills

One of the chief concerns regarding the use of omnibus appropriations acts is that it reduces the opportunities for Members to debate and amend the regular appropriations acts that are incorporated therein. This concern may be lessened if the regular appropriations acts incorporated into omnibus measures have been previously passed by the House and Senate before action on a final version.

During the FY1986-FY2016 period, the House was more likely than the Senate to have passed the regular appropriations on initial consideration that were eventually incorporated into omnibus acts, with the House passing 116 out of the 170 regular appropriations bills, while the Senate passed 72 (see **Table 2**). For both the House and the Senate, between FY1986 and FY2001, the majority of appropriations acts that were ultimately included in omnibus measures were previously passed by the House and Senate each fiscal year. However, during certain fiscal years between FY2003 and FY2016, one or both chambers passed fewer than half of the regular appropriations bills that were ultimately enacted in omnibus form. For the House, this occurred in five different instances over four fiscal years: FY2003, FY2009, FY2012, and FY2014. For the Senate, this occurred in eight different instances over six fiscal years: FY2005, FY2009, and FY2012-FY2016.

Table 2. Prior Passage of Regular Appropriations Bills That Were Eventually Enacted in Omnibus Acts: FY1986-FY2016

| Fiscal Year | Omnibus Appropriations Act | | | |
	Title	Number of Regular Appropriations Acts Enacted Therein	House Prior Passage	Senate Prior Passage
1986	Further Continuing Appropriations Act, 1986	7	6	4
1987	Continuing Appropriations Act, 1987	13	11	7
1988	Further Continuing Appropriations Act, 1988	13	10	10
1996	Omnibus Consolidated Rescissions and Appropriations Act of 1996	5	5	4
1997	Omnibus Consolidated Appropriations Act, 1997	6	5	1
1999	Omnibus Consolidated and Emergency Supplemental Appropriations Act, 1999	8	7	5
2000	Consolidated Appropriations Act, 2000	5	4	4
2001	Consolidated Appropriations Act, 2001	3	3	2
	VA-HUD Appropriations Act, 2001	2	2	2
2003	Consolidated Appropriations Resolution, 2003	11	3	11[a]
2004	Consolidated Appropriations Act, 2004	7	7	6
2005	Consolidated Appropriations Act, 2005	9	8	2
2008	Consolidated Appropriations Act, 2008	11	11	6
2009	Consolidated Security, Disaster Assistance, and Continuing Appropriations Act, 2009	3	1	0
	Omnibus Appropriations Act, 2009	9	0	0
2010	Consolidated Appropriations Act, 2010	6	6	3
2012	Consolidated and Further Continuing Appropriations Act, 2012	3	1	3[b]
	Consolidated Appropriations Act, 2012	9	5	1
2013	Consolidated and Further Continuing Appropriations Act, 2013	5	4	0
2014	Consolidated Appropriations Act, 2014	12	4	0
2015	Consolidated and Further Continuing Appropriations Act, 2015	11	7	0
2016	Consolidated Appropriations Act, 2016	12	6	1
Total:	—	170	116	72

Source: Prepared by the CRS using data from the appropriations status tables for FY1999-FY2016 (available at http://www.crs.gov/pages/AppropriationsStatusTable.aspx) and House calendars for the 99th-105th Congresses.

a. For FY2003, during the Senate's prior consideration of H.J.Res. 2, a continuing resolution, the Senate amended it to be an omnibus appropriations measure that contained the texts of 11 regular appropriations bills, thereby allowing consideration of such regular appropriations to occur simultaneously. Differences were subsequently resolved through conference proceedings, and final passage of H.J.Res. 2 occurred through House and Senate adoption of the conference report. Each of these 11 bills is counted as having been previously passed by the Senate for the purposes of this report.

b. For FY2012, during the Senate's prior consideration of H.R. 2112 (the FY2012 Agriculture Appropriations bill), the texts of two additional appropriations bills were added as an amendment to H.R. 2112, thereby allowing consideration of such regular appropriations to occur simultaneously. Differences were subsequently resolved through conference proceedings, and final passage of H.R. 2112 occurred through House and Senate adoption of the conference report. Each of these three bills is counted as having been previously passed by the Senate for the purposes of this report.

Across-the-Board Rescissions

To adhere to restraints imposed by congressional budget resolutions, the discretionary spending limits, and ad hoc budget agreements between congressional leaders and the President (or to meet other purposes), Congress and the President from time to time incorporate across-the-board rescissions in discretionary budget authority into annual appropriations acts.[12] During the 15 fiscal years covering FY2000-FY2016, six government-wide, across-the-board rescissions were included in omnibus appropriations acts.[13]

The government-wide across-the-board rescissions included in omnibus appropriations acts ranged in size from 0.032% to 0.80% of covered appropriations:

- 0.38% rescission for FY2000 in P.L. 106-113;
- 0.22% rescission for FY2001 in P.L. 106-554;
- 0.65% rescission for FY2003 in P.L. 108-7;
- 0.59% rescission for FY2004 in P.L. 108-199;[14]
- 0.80% rescission for FY2005 in P.L. 108-447; and
- 0.032% rescission for security budget authority[15] and 0.2% rescission for nonsecurity budget authority for FY2013[16] in P.L. 113-6.[17]

---

[12] This topic is discussed in more detail in CRS Report RL32153, *Across-the-Board Spending Cuts in End-of-Session Appropriations Acts*, by Robert Keith (available from the authors of this report), and CRS Report R43234, *Across-the-Board Rescissions in Appropriations Acts: Overview and Recent Practices*, by Jessica Tollestrup.

[13] Across-the-board rescissions may also be included in appropriations measures that are enacted in separate vehicles. For example, an across-the-board rescission was included in the Defense Appropriations Act for FY2006, a year in which all of the regular appropriations acts were enacted separately. The act, which became P.L. 109-148 on December 30, 2005, included in Division B, §3801(a), a government-wide spending cut of 1% (118 Stat. 2791-2792). Emergency requirements and spending for the Department of Veterans Affairs were exempted from the cut, which was expected to reduce total budget authority by about $8.5 billion. For additional information, see OMB Bulletin 06-02, *Guidance on Implementing the Government-wide Across-the-Board Reduction in the Department of Defense Appropriations Act, FY2006 (H.R. 2863)*, January 5, 2006, http://www.whitehouse.gov/sites/default/files/omb/assets/omb/bulletins/fy2006/b06-02.pdf.

[14] The 0.59% across-the-board cut in nondefense programs for FY2004 in P.L. 108-199 was accompanied by a requirement that defense appropriations, which were exempt from the 0.59% cut, be reduced by a fixed amount ($1.8 billion). This requirement was repealed by §9003(c) of the Defense Appropriations Act for FY2005, which President Bush signed into law on August 5, 2004, as P.L. 108-287 (118 Stat. 951 et. seq.).

[15] As defined by §250(c)(4)(A) of the Balanced Budget and Emergency Deficit Control Act (BBEDCA), security budget authority includes discretionary appropriations associated with agency budgets for the Department of Defense, the Department of Homeland Security, the Department of Veterans Affairs, the National Nuclear Security Administration, intelligence community management, and budget function 150.

[16] As defined by §250(c)(4)(B) of the BBEDCA, nonsecurity budget authority includes all discretionary appropriations that are not security budget authority.

[17] The across-the-board rescissions in §3004 of P.L. 113-6 were intended to prevent the possibility that the new budget authority provided in the act would exceed the FY2013 discretionary spending limits in §251(c)(2) of the BBEDCA (continued...)

Omnibus appropriations acts sometimes include other across-the-board rescissions that apply to individual appropriations acts as set forth in separate divisions of the measure. P.L. 108-199, for example, included two requirements for uniform spending cuts in nondefense programs: (1) a 0.465% rescission of budget authority in the Commerce-Justice-State Appropriations division; and (2) a rescission of $50 million in administrative expenses for the Departments of Labor, Health and Human Services, and Education. Further, P.L. 108-447 included three other provisions requiring across-the-board rescissions focused on particular divisions of the act: (1) a 0.54% rescission in the Commerce-Justice-State Appropriations division, (2) a 0.594% rescission in the Interior Appropriations division, and (3) a rescission of $18 million in the Labor-HHS-Education Appropriations division, applicable to administrative and related expenses for departmental management (except for the Food and Drug Administration and the Indian Health Service).

More recently, Section 3001 of P.L. 113-6 provided across-the-board rescissions that were applicable to various projects and activities in certain divisions of the act. For security discretionary budget authority in Divisions A through E, 0.1% was rescinded. For nonsecurity discretionary budget authority, 2.513% was rescinded in Divisions A and E, and 1.877% was rescinded in Division B.

The significance of these across-the-board rescissions has differed with regard to budget enforcement. The FY2000 and FY2013 rescissions were an integral component of the plan that successfully avoided a sequester at the end of the session. The FY2001 rescission contributed to overall discretionary spending being below the statutory limits, but the across-the-board rescission proved to be unnecessary in avoiding a sequester. With regard to the FY2003 rescission, the House and Senate did not reach agreement on a budget resolution and the statutory discretionary limits had expired the fiscal year before; nonetheless, the across-the-board rescission was used to adhere to an informal limit reached between congressional leaders and President Bush and to avoid a veto of the omnibus appropriations act. Similarly, the FY2004, FY2005, and FY2008 rescissions were used to keep the costs of the measures under overall limits acceptable to the President.

Inclusion of Legislative Provisions

Although House and Senate rules and practices over the decades have promoted the separate consideration of legislation and appropriations, this separation was created to serve congressional purposes and has not always been ironclad. In many instances, during the routine operation of the annual appropriations process, minor provisions are included in appropriations acts that technically might be regarded under the precedents as legislative in nature but arguably do not significantly undermine the distinction between legislation and appropriations. At other times, however, the legislative provisions included in annual appropriations acts—especially omnibus appropriations acts—have been much more substantial and have represented a deliberate suspension of the usual procedural boundaries.

(...continued)

due to estimating differences between the Congressional Budget Office and the Office of Management and Budget (OMB). As enacted, §3004 provided two separate across-the-board rescissions—one for nonsecurity budget authority and one for security budget authority—of 0%. The section required that the percentages be increased if OMB estimated that additional rescissions would be needed to avoid exceeding the discretionary spending limits for FY2013. Subsequent to the enactment of P.L. 113-6, OMB announced that it had calculated that these limits would be exceeded. Consequently, the across-the-board rescissions in §3004 were increased by OMB to 0.032% for security budget authority and 0.2% for nonsecurity budget authority.

Both House and Senate rules prohibit the inclusion of legislation in appropriations bills in specified circumstances. Clauses 2(b) and 2(c) of House Rule XXI prohibit the inclusion of legislative provisions on regular appropriations bills reported by the committee or added during the floor process. However, continuing resolutions are not considered by House rules to be regular appropriations bills and thus do not fall under the purview of these restrictions. In the Senate, Rule XVI prohibits the inclusion of legislative provisions in general appropriations legislation but allows exceptions in specified circumstances. The rules in the House and Senate barring the inclusion of legislation in appropriations are not self-enforcing, can be waived, and allow some exceptions. Thus, omnibus appropriations acts have sometimes been used as vehicles to address substantive legislative concerns.

Over the past two decades, there are some instances of the incorporation of significant legislative provisions within omnibus appropriations acts. For example, the Consolidated Appropriations Resolution for FY2003 (P.L. 108-7) included the Agricultural Assistance Act of 2003, amendments to the Price-Anderson Act and the Homeland Security Act, and provisions dealing with the U.S.-China Economic and Security Review Commission, among other legislative matters. The Consolidated Appropriations Act for FY2008 (P.L. 110-161) included such items as the Emergency Steel Loan Guarantee Act of 1999 Amendments, the Harmful Algal Bloom and Hypoxia Research and Control Act of 1998 Amendments, the ED 1.0 Act, and the Kids in Disasters Well-being, Safety, and Health Act of 2007. Most recently, Divisions M through P of the Consolidated Appropriations Act, 2016 (P.L. 114-113) contained the texts of a number of significant legislative provisions, reauthorizations, and new laws, including:

- the Intelligence Authorization Act for Fiscal Year 2016;
- the Cybersecurity Act of 2015; and
- the James Zadroga 9/11 Victim Compensation Reauthorization.

Table 3. Detail on Omnibus Appropriations Acts: FY1986-FY2016

Fiscal Year	Regular Appropriations Acts for the Fiscal Year	Regular Appropriations Enacted by Start of Fiscal Year[a]	Form of Enactment of Regular Appropriations			Omnibus Appropriations Act
			Enacted as Standalone Measures	Enacted in Omnibus Measures	Other	
1986	13	0	6	7	0	Further Continuing Appropriations Act, FY1986 (P.L. 99-190; December 19, 1985)
1987	13	0	0	13	0	Continuing Appropriations Act, FY1987 (P.L. 99-591; October 18, 1986)
1988	13	0	0	13	0	Further Continuing Appropriations Act, FY1988 (P.L. 100-202; December 22, 1987)
1989	13	13	13	0	0	[none]
1990	13	1	13	0	0	[none]
1991	13	0	13	0	0	[none]
1992	13	3	12	0	1[b]	[none]
1993	13	1	13	0	0	[none]
1994	13	2	13	0	0	[none]
1995	13	13	13	0	0	[none]
1996	13	0	8	5	0	Omnibus Consolidated Rescissions and Appropriations Act of 1996 (P.L. 104-134; April 26, 1996)
1997	13	13	7	6	0	Omnibus Consolidated Appropriations Act, 1997 (P.L. 104-208; September 30, 1996)
1998	13	1	13	0	0	[none]
1999	13	1	5	8	0	Omnibus Consolidated and Emergency Supplemental Appropriations Act, 1999 (P.L. 105-277; October 21, 1998)
2000	13	4	8	5	0	Consolidated Appropriations Act, 2000 (P.L. 106-113; November 29, 1999)

CRS-10

Fiscal Year	Regular Appropriations Acts for the Fiscal Year	Regular Appropriations Enacted by Start of Fiscal Year[a]	Form of Enactment of Regular Appropriations			Omnibus Appropriations Act
			Enacted as Standalone Measures	Enacted in Omnibus Measures	Other	
2001	13	2	8	5	0	Consolidated Appropriations Act, 2001 [3 acts] (P.L. 106-554; December 21, 2000), and VA-HUD Appropriations Act, 2001 [2 acts] (P.L. 106-377; October 27, 2000)
2002	13	0	13	0	0	[none]
2003	13	0	2	11	0	Consolidated Appropriations Resolution, 2003 (P.L. 108-7; February 20, 2003)
2004	13	3	6	7	0	Consolidated Appropriations Act, 2004 (P.L. 108-199; January 23, 2004)
2005	13	1	4	9	0	Consolidated Appropriations Act, 2005 (P.L. 108-447; December 8, 2004)
2006	11	2	11	0	0	[none]
2007	11	1	2	0	9c	[none]
2008	12	0	1	11	0	Consolidated Appropriations Act, 2008 (P.L. 110-161; December 26, 2007)
2009	12	3	0	12	0	Consolidated Security, Disaster Assistance, and Continuing Appropriations Act, 2009 (P.L. 110-329; September 30, 2008), and Omnibus Appropriations Act, 2009 (P.L. 111-8; March 11, 2009)
2010	12	1	6	6	0	Consolidated Appropriations Act, 2010 (P.L. 111-117; December 16, 2009)
2011	12	0	0	0	12d	[none]
2012	12	0	0	12	0	Consolidated and Further Continuing Appropriations Act, 2012 (P.L. 112-55; November 18, 2011), and Consolidated Appropriations Act, 2012 (P.L. 112-74; December 23, 2011)
2013	12	0	0	5e	7e	Consolidated and Further Continuing Appropriations Act, 2013 (P.L. 113-6; March 26, 2013)

CRS-11

Fiscal Year	Regular Appropriations Acts for the Fiscal Year	Regular Appropriations Enacted by Start of Fiscal Year[a]	Form of Enactment of Regular Appropriations			Omnibus Appropriations Act
			Enacted as Standalone Measures	Enacted in Omnibus Measures	Other	
2014	12	0	0	12	0	Consolidated Appropriations Act, 2014 (P.L. 113-76; *January 17, 2014*)
2015	12	0	1	11	0	Consolidated and Further Continuing Appropriations Act, 2015 (P.L. 113-235; *December 16, 2014*)
2016	12	0	0	12	0	Consolidated Appropriations Act, 2016 (P.L. 114-113; *December 18, 2015*)
Total		65	191	170	29	—
Median		1	6	5.5	0	—

Source: Prepared by CRS using calendars of the U.S. House of Representatives, 99th-112th Congresses, and the Legislative Information System.

a.   Includes appropriations acts enacted on or before October 1 of the budget year.

b.   Funding for activities covered by the FY1992 Foreign Operations Appropriations bill was provided by a full-year CR in P.L. 102-266, enacted on April 1, 1992.

c.   Funding for activities covered by nine of the FY2007 appropriations bills was provided by a full-year CR in P.L. 110-5, enacted on February 15, 2007.

d.   Funding for the activities covered by 11 of the FY2011 appropriations bills was provided by a full-year CR in Division B of P.L. 112-10, enacted on April 15, 2011. In addition, the full text of the Department of Defense Appropriations Act for FY2011 was included in Division A of that act.

e.   Funding for the activities covered by seven of the FY2013 appropriations bills was provided by a full-year CR in P.L. 113-6, enacted on March 26, 2013. That law also contained omnibus appropriations for the five remaining regular appropriations acts for that fiscal year.

Author Contact Information

James V. Saturno
Specialist on Congress and the Legislative Process
jsaturno@crs.loc.gov, 7-2381

Jessica Tollestrup
Specialist on Congress and the Legislative Process
jtollestrup@crs.loc.gov, 7-0941

Acknowledgments

The original version of this report was written by Robert Keith, formerly a specialist in American National Government at CRS. The listed authors have revised and updated this report and are available to respond to inquiries on the subject.

Congressional
Research Service
Informing the legislative debate since 1914 _____

Appropriations Report Language: Overview of Development, Components, and Issues for Congress

Jessica Tollestrup
Analyst on Congress and the Legislative Process

July 28, 2015

Congressional Research Service

7-5700

www.crs.gov

R44124

Summary

In general, congressional reports may accompany appropriations measures as part of either the committee stage or the resolving differences stage of the legislative process. Although this language is not considered binding in the same manner as language in the statute, the congressional understanding of an appropriations measure is closely related to its development. There are appropriations-specific components and practices related to report language that have been developed by the House and Senate Appropriations Committees to better enable their oversight of the agencies. There are also components that have come about as a result of chamber rules to provide greater information on appropriations measures in order to facilitate their congressional consideration. The purpose of this report is to provide an overview of appropriations report language.

Although appropriations report language is primarily developed by the House and Senate Appropriations Committees, those committees have formal and informal practices that enable input on the language from a variety of sources, including programmatic requests that are submitted to the committees from Members of Congress. When appropriators meet to mark up an appropriations measure, amendments to the draft report may also be offered and considered in committee. While report language cannot be directly amended on the floor, it is sometimes possible to propose amendments to an appropriations bill that have the effect of overriding language in the report. During the resolving differences stage of the legislative process, congressional negotiators also seek to address differences between the relevant House and Senate appropriations report language in the joint explanatory statement or other explanatory text produced as a result of those negotiations. In current practice, report language does not accompany formulaic continuing resolutions (CRs), even if funds are provided in this manner for the remainder of the fiscal year.

In current practice, appropriations report language has a number of typical components. The bulk of appropriations report language is devoted to a "section-by-section" analysis of each account and a lengthy table that provides a "comparative statement of new budget authority" in the bill. The report language may also provide general directives to the agencies funded in the bill related to budget preparation and execution, including the form of budget justifications, other reporting guidelines and committee initiatives, "program, project, or activity" (PPA) definitions, and reprogramming. The Congressional Budget Act requires that the House and Senate Appropriations Committee reports for regular and supplemental appropriations measures include a statement comparing levels in the measure to the applicable 302(b) suballocations. House and Senate rules also mandate that committee reports for general appropriations measures provide lists of appropriations not authorized by law. Finally, the House has additional requirements that rescissions and transfers, as well as language changing existing law, be listed in committee reports accompanying general appropriations measures.

Appropriations report language raises certain issues for Congress. Each fiscal year, as the Appropriations Committees choose the directives that will be made to agencies, they must decide which of these directives to include in the bill itself and which to include in report language. Over time, as the House and Senate develop rules that govern the content of appropriations report language, each chamber must assess its informational needs as it engages in appropriations decisionmaking. The House and Senate may choose to take similar or differing approaches to its rules relating to appropriations report language, and such rules may be altered as the institutional needs of each chamber evolve.

Appropriations Report Language: Overview of Components and Issues for Congress

Contents

Introduction

Since the first Congress, the congressional appropriations process has involved the annual consideration of appropriations measures to fund the activities of most federal government agencies.[1] Over the years, this process has evolved so that it currently assumes the consideration of 12 *regular appropriations* bills to provide discretionary spending for the upcoming fiscal year.[2] If some or all of the regular appropriations measures are not enacted prior to the beginning of the fiscal year (October 1), one or more *continuing resolutions* (CRs) might be enacted to provide temporary appropriations until either regular appropriations are enacted or the fiscal year ends. *Supplemental appropriations* might also be enacted during the fiscal year to provide funds in addition to those in regular appropriations acts or CRs.[3]

The congressional process for considering these various types of appropriations measures has developed in the context of institutional considerations that are both internal and external. Internal considerations include long-standing congressional rules that encourage the separation of money and policy decisions ("appropriations" and "authorizations," respectively), as well as the constraints of previously agreed upon fiscal policies and goals, such as those associated with the budget resolution. Additional external considerations, which largely derive from the relationship between Congress and the agencies funded through the annual appropriations process, include issues such as the level of flexibility that Congress grants to agencies in budget execution. One way that the congressional appropriations process has evolved to address these internal and external considerations has been in the form and content of report language that accompanies appropriations measures.

In general, report language is used by House and Senate committees for two broad purposes. First, report language explains the provisions of a measure to the chamber or chambers that will subsequently consider it. Second, report language may also communicate legislative intent to the agencies that will carry out the measure once it becomes law. Although report language itself is not law and therefore not binding in the same manner as language in the statute, agencies usually seek to comply with any directives contained therein. As one congressional scholar has observed, "the criticisms and suggestions carried in the reports accompanying each bill are expected to influence the subsequent behavior of the agency. Committee reports are not the law, but it is expected that they be regarded almost as seriously."[4] For this reason, congressional interest in the

---

[1] An appropriation is a type of budget authority. Budget authority is authority provided by federal law to enter into contracts or other financial obligations that will result in immediate or future expenditures (or outlays) involving federal government funds. For a further explanation of these terms, see U.S. Government Accountability Office (GAO), *A Glossary of Terms Used in the Federal Budget Process*, GAO-05-734SP, September 2005, http://www.gao.gov/new.items/d05734sp.pdf, pp. 20-21.

[2] The congressional budget process distinguishes between *discretionary* spending, which is controlled through appropriations acts, and *direct* (or mandatory) spending, which is controlled through permanent law. For further information on this distinction, see CRS Report 98-721, *Introduction to the Federal Budget Process*, coordinated by Bill Heniff Jr. The annual appropriations process is also used to provide appropriations necessary to finance certain direct spending programs that lack a funding source in the authorizing statute. Such "appropriated mandatory" or "appropriated entitlement" spending is discussed in CRS Report RS20129, *Entitlements and Appropriated Entitlements in the Federal Budget Process*, by Bill Heniff Jr.

[3] For a general overview of the annual appropriations process, see CRS Report R42388, *The Congressional Appropriations Process: An Introduction*, by Jessica Tollestrup.

[4] Richard Fenno, *The Power of the Purse: Appropriations Politics in Congress* (Boston: Little, Brown and Company, (continued...)

mechanics of the appropriations process is not limited to the procedures and practices for considering measures but also encompasses the report language that accompanies those measures.

Typically, report language may be used to supplement the legislative text of a measure at either of two different stages of the legislative process. First, written reports may accompany the version of the bill that is reported by a committee to its parent chamber. The House has required that written reports accompany bills reported from committee since 1880.[5] While Senate rules do not require written reports, measures reported from committee are usually accompanied by or otherwise associated with them. Second, when resolving differences between the House and Senate, a joint explanatory statement (JES), which accompanies a conference report prior to final action by each chamber, is also a form of report language. The JES may be used to reconcile areas of disagreement between the House and Senate committee reports from earlier stages of the legislative process or to provide additional information about the agreement. For measures not reported from committee that receive congressional consideration, including when differences are resolved through an amendment exchange, explanatory text from the committee of jurisdiction is sometimes entered into the *Congressional Record* and may be regarded similarly to report language for certain purposes.[6] In addition, in some cases, report language in the JES may be enacted by reference in the appropriations law that it accompanies, giving it statutory effect.

This CRS report provides an overview of appropriations report language. It generally does not explain those report language components and related practices that are more broadly applicable to all types of legislation.[7] The first section of this CRS report explains how appropriations report language is developed. The second section discusses the origins, purposes, and forms of the major report language components that are particular to appropriations measures, with illustrative examples. The third section summarizes appropriations report language issues related to congressional influence over agency budgetary decisionmaking, as well as the institutional dynamics within Congress itself.

Appropriations Report Language Development

Agency, Public, and Member Input

In general, the report language accompanying an appropriations measure is developed by the appropriations committees in each chamber. While it is a committee product, it has significant importance for the congressional consideration of that appropriations measure, as well as agency budget execution once the measure becomes law. When determining the language to be included

---

(...continued)

1966), p. 18.

[5] W[illia]m Holmes Brown, Charles W. Johnson, and John V. Sullivan, *House Practice: A Guide to the Rules, Precedents and Procedures of the House*, 112th Cong., 1st sess. (Washington: GPO, 2011) [hereinafter, *House Practice*], ch. 11, §28. This requirement is currently codified in House Rule XIII, clause 2.

[6] For further information about resolving differences using a conference report or amendment exchange, see CRS Report 98-696, *Resolving Legislative Differences in Congress: Conference Committees and Amendments Between the Houses*, by Elizabeth Rybicki.

[7] For general information on the required components of House and Senate committee reports, see CRS Report 98-169, *House Committee Reports: Required Contents*, by Judy Schneider, and CRS Report 98-305, *Senate Committee Reports: Required Contents*, by Elizabeth Rybicki.

in the report, the Appropriations Committees engage in certain formal and informal practices through which they may receive input on the language. For example, a review of the agency budget justifications that are submitted after the President's budget request may inform prospective funding allocations and congressional directives contained in the report.[8] Other committee communications with the agency, both before and after the budget submission, may also help inform the language that is ultimately included. In addition, stakeholders and other interested groups outside of Congress may also choose to communicate their report language and other appropriations preferences to the Appropriations Committees through letters or other modes of communication.[9]

Members of the House and Senate may also communicate to the Appropriations Committees their preferences with regard to each of the 12 annual appropriations bills and accompanying report language. While such communications might occur throughout the budget cycle, the committees encourage Members to express their preferences for the upcoming fiscal year through the submission of so-called "programmatic and language requests." These are requests for specific funding levels or other language to be included in a particular appropriations bill or the accompanying committee report. These requests are usually due to the committees in March or April after the President's budget request has been presented to Congress.[10]

The parameters for these requests for each of the appropriations bills may be specified through Dear Colleague letters or other communications from the committee.[11] In general, both the House and Senate Appropriations Committees have discouraged programmatic requests for congressionally directed spending items (also referred to as "earmarks").[12] Once programmatic and language requests for a bill are submitted, the committee must decide whether to include the requested language in the bill or accompanying report, include a modified version of it, or not include it at all. In some instances, if language is requested for inclusion in the bill, the committee might decide to include a version of that language in the committee report instead.

Committee and Initial Floor Consideration

Each appropriations bill that is reported from committee—which, in current practice, includes regular and some supplemental appropriations bills—is usually accompanied by a written

---

[8] An early discussion of the role of agency budget justifications in the formulation of report language is in Jeffrey L. Pressman, *House vs. Senate: Conflict in the Appropriations Process* (New Haven: Yale University Press, 1966), p. 18.

[9] See, for example, Kate Ackley, "Appropriations Lobbying Thrives Despite Earmarks Ban," *CQ News*, May 11, 2015.

[10] Because supplemental appropriations measures are considered on an as-needed basis, there is usually not a formal process for making programmatic requests to the appropriations committees.

[11] See, for example, House of Representatives, Dear Colleague, "Members' Programmatic and Language Requests for FY 2015 Defense Appropriations Bill," February 24, 2014; House of Representatives, Dear Colleague, "Member Submissions for FY 2015 Energy and Water Development Appropriations," February 24, 2014; House of Representatives, Dear Colleague, "Member Submissions for FY2014 Transportation, Housing and Urban Development, and Related Agencies Appropriations," February 21, 2014; House of Representatives, Dear Colleague, "Member Submissions FY2015 State, Foreign Operations, and Related Programs Appropriations," February 20, 2014. Available from the author.

[12] See, for example, ibid; U.S. Senate Committee on Appropriations, "Cochran Statement on Earmark Moratorium," press release, November 16, 2010; and U.S. Senate Committee on Appropriations, "Senate Appropriations Committee Announces Extension of Earmark Moratorium," press release, February 2, 2012. For further information about the definitions of *earmark* under House and Senate rules, see CRS Report RL34462, *House and Senate Procedural Rules Concerning Earmark Disclosure*, by Sandy Streeter.

committee report. Committee preparation of an appropriations bill for a markup also includes compiling a draft of the committee report that will accompany it. When the Appropriations Committee meets to mark up each appropriations bill, amendments to the draft report may also be offered and considered. In the House, the final version of the committee's written report is filed when the bill is reported to the chamber. In the Senate, it is typically filed at the same time the bill is reported or soon thereafter. While appropriations measures that are reported from committee typically receive formal committee reports, those regular appropriations measures that are not reported from committee are often associated with draft committee report text that is released in the context of negotiations to resolve differences.[13]

Because the written committee report is a product of that committee's deliberations rather than a legislative measure itself, it is not directly amendable during the subsequent floor consideration of the appropriations measure. However, floor amendments have previously been offered that would have the effect of directly or indirectly overriding the directives or funding allocations in the committee report language. For example, during the 109th Congress, the House Appropriations Committee report for the FY2007 Agriculture appropriations bill contained a provision that allocated "$229,000 for dairy education in Iowa" (H.Rept. 109-463, p. 56). Subsequently, an amendment was offered on the House floor that proposed to insert the provision, "None of the funds made available by this Act may be used to fund dairy education in Iowa."[14] Had that amendment become law as part of the appropriations act, it would have prevented the $229,000 in funds set aside in the committee report from being spent on that particular activity.

Resolving Differences

When congressional negotiators resolve differences between the House and Senate versions of an appropriations measure, such negotiators are usually drawn from the House and Senate Appropriations Committees. In addition to producing a final version of the measure, these negotiators also agree to further report language in the form of a JES or other explanatory text. In instances where explanatory text is entered into the *Congressional Record*, a provision of the measure usually indicates that it is to be treated by the agencies in the same way as a joint explanatory statement.[15] This explanatory text is usually considered to be the most authoritative

---

[13] For example, four FY2015 regular appropriations bills were not reported by the Senate Appropriations Committee during the 113th Congress. Once it was determined that these bills would not be reported from committee around the time of the August recess, three of the relevant subcommittees—the Labor, Health and Human Services, Education, and Related Agencies Subcommittee; the Energy and Water Development Subcommittee; and the Financial Services and General Government Subcommittee—released the draft bill and report language that was reported from the subcommittees but not acted on by the full committee. The fourth subcommittee, which had not held a subcommittee markup—the Interior, Environment, and Related Agencies Subcommittee—released the chairman's recommended bill text and draft report. For further information, see CRS Report R43776, *Congressional Action on FY2015 Appropriations Measures*, by Jessica Tollestrup, pp. 9-10.

[14] H.Amdt. 904 to H.R. 5384 (109th Cong.); House debate, *Congressional Record*, vol. 152, part 7 (May 23, 2006), p. H3104.

[15] For example, during the 113th Congress, differences between the chambers with regard to H.R. 83 were resolved using an amendment exchange and not a conference report. On December 11, 2014, explanatory text related to that omnibus measure was entered into the *Congressional Record* (vol. 160, no. 151, book II, December 11, 2014, pp. H9307-10003). Section 4 of H.R. 83 provided, "The explanatory statement regarding this Act, printed in the House of Representatives section of the Congressional Record on or about December 11, 2014 by the Chairman of the Committee on Appropriations of the House, shall have the same effect with respect to the allocation of funds and implementation of divisions A through K of this Act as if it were a joint explanatory statement of a committee of conference."

source of congressional legislative intent with regard to that measure.[16] Once the final version of the legislative text has been agreed to by the House and Senate, there are no further formal opportunities to make changes to the accompanying report language.

The explanatory text may be used to reconcile any differences between the House and Senate Appropriations Committee reports. For example, the House and Senate committee report language may address certain issues in ways that are difficult to reconcile harmoniously. In these types of instances, the explanatory text normally seeks to clarify how the affected agency is to proceed. In other cases, one committee might have included language in its report that addresses an issue to which the other committee's report is silent. If disagreement exists between the committees with regard to this report language, the explanatory statement might clarify what action the agency should take. On the other hand, if the original committee language is ultimately acceptable to both committees, the explanatory statement might be silent due to an expectation that the agency will follow the original directive.[17] As a consequence, in addition to the explanatory text, the committee reports might also provide an important indication of congressional intent even after an appropriations measure has been enacted.[18]

Continuing Resolutions

In recent years, appropriations measures that provide continuing appropriations based on a formula have typically not been accompanied by report language, even when such appropriations are for an entire fiscal year.[19] For example, for the FY2013 Consolidated and Further Continuing Appropriations Act (P.L. 113-6), which contained both regular and full-year continuing appropriations, detailed explanatory text was provided only for the accounts that received regular appropriations.[20] For full-year CRs, the committee report language from the current fiscal year that accompanies the regular appropriations covered by that CR may provide some indication of congressional intent.[21] However, the extent to which the funding provided via the CR's formula is

---

[16] See GAO, Office of the General Counsel, *Principles of Federal Appropriations Law* (3d ed., 2004), vol. 1 [hereinafter "Red Book"], at 2-98 and 2-99.

[17] In current practice, the explanatory statement accompanying the final version of an appropriations measure usually states this explicitly. For example, the explanatory statement accompanying the FY2015 Agriculture Appropriations Act contained the following instruction:

> The explanatory statement is silent on provisions that were in both the House Report (H.Rept. 113-468) and Senate Report (S.Rept. 113-164) that remain unchanged by this agreement, except as noted in this explanatory statement.... The House and Senate report language that is not changed by the explanatory statement is approved and indicates congressional intentions. The explanatory statement, while repeating some report language for emphasis, does not intend to negate the language referred to above unless expressly provided herein." (*Congressional Record*, vol. 160, no. 151, book II, December 11, 2014, p. H9308)

[18] Red Book, at 2-99 and 2-100.

[19] Although it is not currently the practice to consider CRs in committee and provide them with report language, committees commonly considered and reported these types of measures as recently as the 102nd Congress. (See, for example, H.Rept. 102-216 and H.Rept. 102-266.) Because the form of appropriations in CRs usually differs from regular and supplemental appropriations measures, many of the report language components for the committee reports accompanying those CRs also differ from those that are discussed is this report.

[20] See Consolidated and Further Continuing Appropriations Act, *Congressional Record*, daily edition, vol. 159, no. 34 (March 11, 2013), pp. S1287-S1588.

[21] A CR typically funds activities that are usually identified with reference to unenacted appropriations measures for the current fiscal year or the appropriations enacted for a previous fiscal year. These referenced measures or laws are the CR's "coverage." For further information, see CRS Report R42647, *Continuing Resolutions: Overview of Components* (continued...)

difficult to reconcile with the allocations and directives in the relevant committee reports—and the extent to which those committee allocations and directives conflict with one another because there is no relevant explanatory text to resolve such conflicts—may limit the report's applicability.

Appropriations Report Language Components

As previously stated, the components of report language that are specific to appropriations measures have evolved in the context of both internal and external congressional needs. In many cases, the components and related practices were developed by the House and Senate Appropriations Committees to better enable their oversight of the agencies. In other cases, the components came about as a result of chamber rules to require information to facilitate congressional consideration of appropriations measures. This has led to the development of certain categories of report language that are used in many or all of the appropriations committee reports each fiscal year and, in some cases, the JES that resolves differences between those reports. This section describes the origin, purposes, and current forms of these report language components.

Overview of Accounts and Other Directives

The bulk of the House and Senate reports on appropriations bills are devoted to an overview of each account in the bill. This derives from the general practice that reports accompanying legislation summarize each section or title of the measure, which is often referred to as a "section-by-section" (or "title-by-title") summary. Because appropriations bills are organized by unnumbered headings, with each heading generally corresponding to an account, section-by-section summaries of the appropriations bills are organized by account and also include a short description of other provisions included in the bill that are not part of the appropriations accounts.[22] Such provisions include "administrative provisions" that are specific to particular accounts or agencies, as well as "general provisions" that are more broadly applicable to all funds in the bill (or a specified title of the bill).

The account-by-account summary is intended primarily to explain the purpose of the account and what it funds. It is typically framed as a justification of the funding levels proposed for that account compared to those provided the previous fiscal year, as well as those proposed in the President's budget request. Senate Appropriations Committee reports also compare proposed levels to those that were proposed by the House Appropriations Committee, if applicable. These committee justifications of recommended funding levels can provide helpful context for Members as they evaluate the measure and potential floor amendments.

The account summaries in the reports also give the appropriations committees the opportunity to provide additional directives to the agencies funded therein and guidance concerning

---

(...continued)

and Recent Practices, by Jessica Tollestrup.

[22] Some reports also include policy or program highlights that address multiple accounts prior to the account-by-account summary. See, for example, H.Rept. 113-417, pp. 2-3; H.Rept. 113-551, pp. 4-8; S.Rept. 113-71, pp. 8-15; and S.Rept. 113-195, pp. 11-16.

13-9

congressional intent for their use of funds. This guidance varies in intensity—from encouragement or support for a specified action to concerns and requirements for an agency to engage in or refrain from particular actions. Three examples, from the House Appropriations Committee report accompanying the FY2015 Agriculture appropriations bill (H.Rept. 113-468), are illustrative. In the first example, which applies to the Agricultural Programs—Office of Inspector General (OIG) account, the committee indicates support of action that is currently being undertaken:

> The Committee appreciates OIG's continued efforts to raise public awareness of successful Federal investigations of fraud. Such efforts are intended to deter participants from engaging in the misuse of taxpayer dollars and to maintain a high level of integrity in all of USDA's programs. The Committee encourages OIG to continue its efforts to work with all of USDA's agencies to deter fraud, waste, and abuse in the Department's programs. (p. 9)

In the second example, which applies to the Agricultural Programs—Office of the Under Secretary for Farm and Foreign Agricultural Services account, the committee requires that a specific action be taken:

> The Committee is concerned about waste, fraud, and abuse in programs administered by the Farm Service Agency (FSA) and the Risk Management Agency (RMA). Therefore, the Secretary is directed to certify that any newly approved payment, loan, grant, subsidy, or insurance claim from a program administered by FSA or RMA does not include individuals or entities that have been permanently debarred from participating in USDA programs. (p. 28)

In the third example, which applies to the Agricultural Programs—Office of the Under Secretary for Research, Education, and Economics, the committee directs the agency to refrain from taking an action until certain conditions are met:

> The Committee is concerned about the Foundation for Food and Agriculture Research created by the 2014 farm bill and reports that the Department intends to obligate $200,000,000 in mandatory funds to the Foundation by the end of the fiscal year but before the Foundation has been established and any matching funds have been received as required by law. The Committee directs USDA not to expend any funds except those related to the appointment of members of the board and the preparation of by-laws, conflict of interest policies, and standards of conduct until the Committee receives and approves these documents. The Committee directs USDA to report to it no later than January 1, 2015. (p. 11)

In many instances, additional directives to agencies in report language also include more detail on the allocation of funds than what is provided in the bill itself. For example, the FY2015 Department of Homeland Security appropriations bill included an account for Departmental Management and Operations—Office of the Secretary and Executive Management. In the Senate Appropriations Committee–reported version of the measure (S. 2534), a lump sum of $124,571,000 was provided for the entire account with no further allocation of the funds in the statute (except for a limitation on official reception and representation expenses). However, the accompanying committee report divided the amount in that account into specific allocations for certain purposes:

Figure 1: Detailed Funds Allocation

OFFICE OF THE SECRETARY AND EXECUTIVE MANAGEMENT
[In thousands of dollars]

	Fiscal year 2014 enacted	Fiscal year 2015 budget request	Committee recommendations
Immediate Office of the Secretary	4,050	3,950	3,939
Immediate Office of the Deputy Secretary	1,750	1,751	1,740
Office of the Chief of Staff	2,050	2,112	2,062
Executive Secretary	7,400	7,719	7,477
Office of Policy	36,500	38,470	37,559
Office of Public Affairs	8,550	8,741	8,591
Office of Legislative Affairs	5,350	5,583	5,403
Office of Intergovernmental Affairs	2,250	2,429	2,273
Office of General Counsel	19,750	21,310	19,950
Office for Civil Rights and Civil Liberties	21,500	22,003	21,719
Citizenship and Immigration Services Ombudsman	5,250	6,428	5,825
Privacy Officer	7,950	8,273	8,033
Total, Office of the Secretary and Executive Management	122,350	128,769	124,571

Source: S.Rept. 113-198, p. 12.

Even though funding and other directives (such as these additional allocations illustrated above) that are only in report language are not legally binding, the Appropriations Committees expect that the agencies will adhere to them.[23]

Comparative Statement of New Budget Authority

Tables in appropriations reports that summarize the appropriations in the bill, the budgetary effects of other provisions, and certain additional allocations in the report have been in use for at least the past century.[24] These tables assist with the congressional evaluation of the amounts in the bill, as well as some of the additional allocations of those amounts in the report.[25] In current practice, the specific categories of information displayed and compared in the summary table depend on the chamber and stage of action but may include amounts for:

- the prior fiscal year,
- the President's budget request (or "budget estimate"),
- the other chamber ("allowance"), and
- the committee recommendation.

---

[23] In the event that an agency wishes to deviate from the directives in report language as to the allocation of funds, it might seek to alter that allocation through a "reprogramming." This topic is discussed further in the section of this report, "Reprogramming Guidelines."

[24] For some early examples of these tables, see H.Rept. 59-1106, pp. 1-3; H.Rept. 59-927, pp. 3-4; H.Rept. 59-2171, pp. 11-26; and S.Rept. 59-1782, pp. 2-3. In current practice, these tables are variously titled "Comparative Statement of New Budget Authority," "Comparative Statement of Budget Authority," or "Comparative Statement of New (Obligational) Budget Authority."

[25] In some cases, the table might also list budgetary resources that are made available to the agency outside the annual appropriations process to provide additional context for appropriations decisionmaking. See, for example, the amounts for "fee accounts" listed for the U.S. Customs and Border Protection in S.Rept. 113-198, p. 178.

The JES will list the final funding levels for the relevant accounts and other activities that were agreed to when differences were resolved on the measure.

The example below is from the Senate Appropriations Committee report accompanying the FY2015 Military Construction-Veterans Affairs appropriations bill (S.Rept. 113-174, p. 109). It includes all of the categories of information listed above.

Figure 2: Comparative Statement of New Budget Authority

COMPARATIVE STATEMENT OF NEW BUDGET (OBLIGATIONAL) AUTHORITY FOR FISCAL YEAR 2014 AND BUDGET ESTIMATES AND AMOUNTS RECOMMENDED IN THE BILL FOR FISCAL YEAR 2015

Item	2014 appropriation	Budget estimate	House allowance	Committee recommendation	Senate Committee recommendation compared with (+ or −) 2014 appropriation	Budget estimate	House allowance
TITLE I—DEPARTMENT OF DEFENSE							
Military construction, Army	1,104,875	539,427	526,427	539,427	− 565,448		+ 13,000
Military construction, Navy and Marine Corps	1,629,690	1,018,772	998,772	1,018,772	− 610,918		+ 20,000
Military construction, Air Force	1,052,756	811,774	719,551	811,774	− 241,022		+ 92,223
Military construction, Defense-Wide	3,445,423	2,061,890	2,021,690	1,961,890	− 1,483,533	− 100,000	− 59,800
Total, Active components	7,232,784	4,431,863	4,266,440	4,331,863	− 2,900,921	− 100,000	+ 65,423

General Directives Related to Budget Preparation and Budget Execution

In addition to the instructions that are included in the account summaries, general directives that apply to budget preparation and budget execution are often also included in appropriations report language. Such directives, which typically relate to many or all of the accounts in the bill, are usually in the first pages of the report and may specify the form of budget justifications for future fiscal years, other reporting guidelines and committee initiatives, "program, project, or activity" (PPA) definitions, and reprogramming guidelines.

Form of Budget Justifications

Congressional budget justifications supplement the President's budget request with additional information for the appropriations committees. Agencies provide this information to the committees soon after the President's budget request has been submitted.[26] The description of budgetary accounts in these budget justifications, such as the types of agency activities conducted with funds in the account, is much more detailed than the budget submission.[27] This additional information helps the appropriations committees better evaluate the budgetary resources that have been requested for the upcoming fiscal year.

The form of the budget justifications and the information contained therein is generally the result of consultations between the agency and appropriations committees.[28] Instructions from the

---

[26] Agency budget justifications are also typically made available on agency websites. For information on recent budget justifications, see CRS Report R43470, *Selected Agency Budget Justifications for FY2016*, by Justin Murray.

[27] For further information on budget justifications generally, see CRS Report RS20268, *Agency Justification of the President's Budget*, by Michelle D. Christensen.

[28] The Office of Management and Budget (OMB) has generally instructed agencies to consult with the committees (continued...)

appropriations committees as to the content of budget justifications for future fiscal years, however, are also often included in report language. These instructions may include the level of detail that should be provided for each account, as well as specific directions for certain programs or activities.[29] In some instances, the agencies funded in the bill may be told how to address certain informational deficiencies in the future, such as by providing more detail about grants or staffing changes.[30] An agency might also be more generally directed to coordinate the content of certain analytical materials with the committee in advance of the submission.[31] For example, the Senate committee report that accompanied the FY2015 State-Foreign Operations appropriations bill included the following directives (S.Rept. 113-195):

> Timely budget information in the congressional budget justification [CBJ] that is clearly, concisely, and accurately presented must be a priority of the administration. The Committee expects the Department of State, USAID, and other agencies funded by this act to submit CBJs within 4 weeks of the release of the President's fiscal year 2016 budget request. The Committee also directs the Department of State, USAID, and other agencies to include detailed information on all reimbursable agreements....

> The Committee directs that CBJs include estimated savings from any proposed office or mission closing and actual prior year representation expenses for each department and agency that is authorized such expenses. (p. 9)

Other Reporting Guidelines and Committee Initiatives

Although reporting requirements that are for specific accounts are primarily located in the relevant account summaries, language elsewhere in committee reports may provide general guidance about the timing or form of agency reports to be provided. For example, the Senate Appropriations Committee report that accompanied the FY2015 Agriculture appropriations bill included the following instructions related to agency reports (S.Rept. 113-164):[32]

> The Committee has, throughout this report, requested agencies to provide studies and reports on various issues. The Committee utilizes these reports to evaluate program performance and make decisions on future appropriations. The Committee directs that all studies and reports be provided to the Committee as electronic documents in an agreed upon format within 120 days after the date of enactment, unless an alternative submission schedule is specifically stated in the report request. (p. 6)

"Program, Project, or Activity" Definitions

A PPA is an element in a budget account.[33] As was previously mentioned, budget accounts generally correspond to the paragraph headings in appropriations acts. Such accounts generally

---

(...continued)

ahead of modifications to the form of the budget justifications. See OMB Circular A-11, *Preparation, Submission, and Execution of the Budget*, July 2014, revised November 2014, §§22.6 and 240.4.

[29] See, for example, S.Rept. 113-181, pp. 7-8.

[30] See, for example, H.Rept. 113-464, pp. 3-4; and S.Rept. 113-80, p. 7.

[31] See, for example, S.Rept. 113-182, pp. 5-6.

[32] See also S.Rept. 113-80, pp. 6-7; S.Rept. 113-195, p. 10-11; and H.Rept. 113-486, p. 12.

[33] GAO, *Glossary of Terms*, p. 80.

provide a lump sum for the purposes of the account and may also "set aside" specific amounts within that lump sum for certain purposes. In addition to those statutory set-asides, it has been the practice for a number of decades that specific elements in these budget accounts, including PPAs, have been identified in report language (and also in the congressional budget justifications that correspond to that act).[34] For example, the House Appropriations Committee report accompanying the FY2015 Department of Homeland Security appropriations bill identified four PPAs in the Customs and Border Protection (CBP) Automation Modernization account, which funds information technology support for CBP personnel (H.Rept. 113-481, p. 43):[35]

1. information technology,

2. automated targeting systems,

3. the Automated Commercial Environment/International Trade Data System, and

4. current operations protection and processing support.

As with other funding allocations in report language, the PPAs that are identified for each account allow Congress to provide direction as to the amounts to be expended for particular activities in which the agency is engaged. The PPAs are also significant for "reprogramming," which is discussed further in the report section entitled "Reprogramming Guidelines."

The PPAs that are identified for each account are also significant for the sequestration budget enforcement mechanism under the Balanced Budget and Emergency Deficit Control Act of 1985 (BBEDCA; P.L. 99-177). If such a sequestration is required for a fiscal year, budgetary resources for affected accounts must be reduced on a largely across-the-board basis. The BBEDCA further requires that these reductions must be proportionately implemented by the agencies, within each affected account, at the PPA level.[36]

Starting in FY1987, the first full fiscal year after the sequestration mechanism was in effect for discretionary spending, some House Appropriations Committee reports included PPA definitions for the purposes of the BBEDCA.[37] PPA definitions have continued to be included in appropriations reports during the periods since FY1987, during which sequestration could potentially affect discretionary spending.[38] Such report language might be used to clarify what a PPA is for the purposes of the BBEDCA or impose a different definition of PPA than would otherwise be in effect. For example, the Senate Appropriations Committee report accompanying the FY2014 Financial Services and General Government appropriations bill provided the following instructions (S.Rept. 113-80):

> During fiscal year 2014, for the purposes of the Balanced Budget and Emergency Deficit Control Act of 1985 (P.L. 99-177), as amended, with respect to appropriations contained in the accompanying bill, the terms 'program, project, and activity' [PPA] shall mean any item

---

[34] OMB Circular A-11, *Preparation, Submission, and Execution of the Budget*, July 2014, revised November 2014, §22.6.

[35] These PPAs had also been identified in the Department of Homeland Security FY2015 Budget Justification, p. 458, available at http://www.dhs.gov/sites/default/files/publications/DHS-Congressional-Budget-Justification-FY2015.pdf.

[36] BBEDCA, §256(k).

[37] For early examples of this report language, see H.Rept. 99-669, p. 8; H.Rept. 99-686, p. 127; and H.Rept. 99-675, p. 71.

[38] Most recently, this is due to the enactment of the statutory discretionary spending limits in the Budget Control Act of 2011 (P.L. 112-25).

for which a dollar amount is contained in appropriations acts (including joint resolutions providing continuing appropriations) or accompanying reports of the House and Senate Committees on Appropriations, or accompanying conference reports and joint explanatory statements of the committee of conference. (p. 5)

This language directed that only the items identified in the listed sources, which do not include additional items identified in the FY2014 budget justification (if any), should be considered to be a PPA for the purposes of any BBEDCA sequestration of discretionary spending in FY2014.[39]

Reprogramming Guidelines

Agencies are generally required to carry out the terms of appropriations laws as enacted, including the statutory allocation of funds therein. As previously discussed, both report language and the congressional budget justifications further allocate funds below the account level into PPAs. In general, when funds are moved between PPAs in the same account, this is referred to as "reprogramming."[40] Agencies are generally permitted to reprogram funds, subject to restrictions in law. This is in contrast to a "transfer"—moving funds between accounts—which requires a statutory authorization in order to occur.[41]

The level of detail regarding the purposes and amounts for funds in annual appropriations acts has changed considerably over two centuries.[42] Prior to the early 20th century, the statutory language for appropriations accounts tended to include numerous line items specifying particular purposes and amounts therein. Over the next few decades, the appropriations committees determined that the activities in which the government was engaged, such as World War II, required that certain agencies be given more budgetary flexibility.[43] In addition, as authorization acts began to contain more detailed statutory instructions to agencies, appropriations acts began to provide more general lump sums for those authorized purposes, with detailed allocations generally being provided through nonstatutory means such as report language.[44] As agencies were transitioned to accounts with lump-sum appropriations, an understanding was reached that the Appropriations Committee would be consulted when agencies reprogrammed the amounts for items in those accounts that had not been specified in law.[45]

In current practice, statutory restrictions on reprogramming are usually carried in the general or administrative provisions of appropriations acts. These restrictions often prohibit reprogramming that meets certain criteria or that is above a certain spending threshold unless certain requirements

---

[39] For other recent examples PPA definitions in Appropriations Committee reports, see S.Rept. 113-182, p. 4; S.Rept. 113-198, p. 150; S.Rept. 113-211, p. 6; and H.Rept. 113-464, pp. 1-2.

[40] For further information with regard to reprogramming, see CRS Report R43098, *Transfer and Reprogramming of Appropriations: An Overview of Authorities, Limitations, and Procedures*, by Michelle D. Christensen.

[41] Red Book, at 2-24 and 2-30.

[42] For a detailed discussion of this evolution, see CRS Report R43862, *Changes in the Purposes and Frequency of Authorizations of Appropriations*, by Jessica Tollestrup.

[43] Stephen Horn, *Unused Power: The Work of the Senate Committee on Appropriations* (Washington, D.C.: Brookings Institution, 1970), pp. 192-198.

[44] Alan Schick, *Legislation, Appropriations, and Budgets: The Development of Spending Decision-Making in Congress*, Congressional Research Service, May 1984, p. 31.

[45] Louis Fisher, *Presidential Spending Power* (Princeton, N.J.: Princeton University Press, 1975), pp. 76-77, 81-84.

related to congressional notification have been met. For example, the FY2015 State-Foreign Operations Appropriations Act prohibits reprogramming that:

- creates new programs;

- eliminates a program, project, or activity;

- increases funds or personnel by any means for any project or activity for which funds have been denied or restricted;

- relocates an office or employees;

- closes or opens a mission or post;

- creates, closes, reorganizes, or renames bureaus, centers, or offices;

- reorganizes programs or activities; or

- contracts out or privatizes any functions or activities presently performed by federal employees.[46]

Section 7015 further provides that such reprogramming would be allowable if the appropriations committees are notified 15 days in advance. Once appropriations are enacted for a fiscal year, agencies typically submit a "spending" or "operating" plan to the appropriations committees to establish a baseline for the application of reprogramming and transfer authorities for that fiscal year.[47]

In addition to the requirements in appropriations acts, guidance on the specific reprogramming procedures that are to be followed is often provided in report language. Such guidance could include the level of detail that triggers notification requirements or special procedures for certain accounts.[48] The form of notification and approval, the information that the committee requires from the agency in order to evaluate the reprogramming request, and a final deadline for all such requests during the fiscal year might also be addressed.[49] For example, the Senate Appropriations Committee report that accompanied the FY2015 State-Foreign Operations bill included the following instructions that supplemented the statutory guidance discussed above (S.Rept. 113-195):

> The Committee directs the Department of State and other agencies funded by this act to notify the Committee of reprogrammings of funds as required by section 7015 and 7019 of this act at the most detailed level of either the CBJ, the act, or the report accompanying this act, and the Committee expects to be notified of any significant departure from the CBJ or of any commitment that will require significant funding in future years. The Committee directs that staffing levels and future year impacts of reprogrammings be included with such notifications. (p. 10)

---

[46] P.L. 113-235, Division J, Title VII, §7015.

[47] See, for example, H.R. 5016 (113th Cong.), §608, for a statutory requirement for an operation plan and additional specifications as to the contents. Such requirements and specifications may also be provided by report language. See, for example, S.Rept. 113-182, p. 4; S.Rept. 113-182, p. 4; S.Rept. 113-195, p. 10; and H.Rept. 113-508, pp. 5-6.

[48] See, for example, S.Rept. 113-182, p. 4; S.Rept. 113-181, pp. 6-7; and H.Rept. 113-551, pp. 8-10.

[49] See H.Rept. 113-448, p. 6; H.Rept. 113-464, pp. 2-3; and H.Rept. 113-508, pp. 5-6.

Additional guidance in report language, such as the example above, could be provided annually or on a standing basis.[50]

Comparison with the Budget Resolution

The level of budget authority provided in appropriations measures is procedurally limited by the budget resolution, which is subject to enforcement in the House and Senate.[51] Through the budget resolution, the Appropriations Committee in each chamber receives a procedural limit on the total amount of discretionary budget authority for the upcoming fiscal year, which is referred to as a 302(a) allocation.[52] The Appropriations Committees subsequently divide this allocation among their 12 subcommittees. These are referred to as 302(b) suballocations.[53] The 302(b) suballocation for a subcommittee restricts the amount of budget authority available for the agencies, projects, and activities under its jurisdiction, effectively acting as a procedural cap on the amount of spending in each of the 12 regular appropriations bills. Enforcement of the 302(a) allocation and 302(b) suballocations occurs through Budget Act points of order.[54]

The Budget Act was intended to provide a framework for Congress to evaluate the future effects of budgetary decisions that had already been made, as well as those that were currently under consideration. To support this end, the Budget Act also required the inclusion of certain information in reports accompanying any legislation "providing new budget authority or tax expenditures" that would be relevant to such budgetary decisionmaking.[55] In addition to these general requirements, for regular and supplemental appropriations measures (but not CRs), the Budget Act mandates that committee reports include a statement comparing levels in the measure to the applicable 302(b) suballocations.[56] This statement must also be included in a conference report, if available in a timely manner, and is to be provided after consultation with the Congressional Budget Office.[57]

The information required by the Budget Act is usually provided in a separate section of House and Senate appropriations reports, as illustrated by the excerpt below from the House report accompanying the FY2015 Military Construction-Veterans Affairs appropriations bill:

---

[50] See, for example, S.Rept. 113-211, p. 7, which notes that the standing guidance with regard to reprogramming that was previously provided in H.Rept. 110-279 continues to be in effect.

[51] As provided under the Congressional Budget Act of 1974 (P.L. 93-344; 88 Stat. 297; 2 U.S.C. §§601-688).

[52] Congressional Budget Act, §302(a).

[53] Ibid., §302(b).

[54] Primarily, these allocations are enforced through points of order under the Congressional Budget Act, §302(f) and §311. Enforcement of the statutory spending caps may occur through points of order that are raised during House or Senate floor consideration under the Congressional Budget Act, §314(f). For further information with regard to points of order in the congressional budget process, see CRS Report 97-865, *Points of Order in the Congressional Budget Process*, by James V. Saturno.

[55] For example, whenever a committee reports such a measure, the committee must include in the accompanying report certain budgetary information, including an estimate by the CBO of the five-year outlay projections associated with the budget authority in the bill, if timely submitted before such report is filed (Congressional Budget Act, §308(a)(1)(B)). If the committee reports a committee amendment, that information must be provided in a statement. This information must also be included in a conference report if available in a timely manner. These requirements do not apply to continuing appropriations.

[56] Congressional Budget Act, §308(a)(1)(A).

[57] The House reiterated this Budget Act requirement in Rule XIII, clause 3(c)(2).

Figure 3: Comparison with the Budget Resolution

COMPARISON WITH THE BUDGET RESOLUTION

Pursuant to clause 3(c)(2) of rule XIII of the Rules of the House of Representatives and section 308(a)(1)(A) of the Congressional Budget Act of 1974, the following table compares the levels of new budget authority provided in the bill with the appropriate allocation under section 302(b) of the Budget Act.

[In millions of dollars]

	302(b) allocation		This bill	
	Budget authority	Outlays	Budget Authority	Outlays
Mandatory	85,315	85,070	85,315	¹ 85,070
Discretionary	71,499	77,455	71,499	76,101

¹ Includes outlays from prior-year authority.

Source: H.Rept. 113-416, p. 71.

Language Changing Existing Law

Both the House and the Senate have internal rules that promote the separation of money and policy decisions. These rules are derived from the principle that the debates and decisions about the activities of government should be distinct from the debates and decisions about the level at which those activities are funded. As a result of those rules and long-standing practices, Congress differentiates between the authorization process—where government entities, activities, or programs are established—and the appropriations process—where those entities, activities, and programs are to be funded.

The rules of the House and Senate typically prohibit legislative provisions from being included in appropriations measures. These rules were formally established in both chambers in the mid-19th century to address concern that the inclusion of extraneous legislative matters was leading to delays in the appropriations process.[58] As currently provided in House Rule XXI, clause 2, the House prohibits legislative provisions in general appropriations bills and amendments thereto.[59] Senate Rule XVI prohibits amendments to general appropriations measures that propose legislative language not contained in existing law, except under certain circumstances.[60] Proper "limitations," however, which restrict or prohibit the use of funds for certain purposes without being legislative, are allowable under House and Senate Rules.[61]

---

[58] Asher C. Hinds, *Hinds' Precedents of the House of Representatives of the United States* (Washington: GPO, 1907-1908), vol. 4, §3578; Schick, *Legislation, Appropriations, and Budgets*, pp. 14-19.

[59] In the House, general appropriations bills are the annual appropriations acts (or any combination thereof) and any supplemental appropriations acts that cover more than one agency. CRs are not considered to be general appropriations bills. *House Practice*, ch. 4, §3.

[60] In the Senate, general appropriations bills are the annual appropriations acts (or any combination thereof) and any supplemental or continuing appropriations acts that cover more than one agency or purpose. See Floyd M. Riddick and Alan S. Frumin, *Riddick's Senate Procedure: Precedents and Practices*, 101st Cong., 2nd sess., S. Doc. 101-28 (Washington: GPO, 1992) [hereafter *Riddick's Senate Procedure*], pp. 159.

[61] For further information about these general principles, including what constitutes legislative provisions in appropriations laws, see CRS Report R41634, *Limitations in Appropriations Measures: An Overview of Procedural Issues*, by Jessica Tollestrup.

Beginning in the 1930s, a number of the House Appropriations subcommittees began to include either lists of legislation and limitations in appropriations measures (or statements to the effect that the measure contains no new legislative provisions or limitations) in their accompanying committee reports.[62] However, the form and level of detail in those lists was highly variable. In order to provide the House with more consistent information about the legislation that the committee was including in general appropriations measures, the House added a requirement in 1974 that the Appropriations Committee reports include "a concise statement describing the effect of any provision of the accompanying bill that directly or indirectly changes the application of existing law."[63] This requirement, which encompasses legislative language, is currently codified in House Rule XIII, clause 3(f)(1)(A).[64] An example of this list is provided by the report accompanying the FY2015 Agriculture appropriations bill excerpted below:

Figure 4: Changes in the Application of Existing Law

CHANGES IN THE APPLICATION OF EXISTING LAW

Pursuant to clause 3(f)(1)(A) of rule XIII of the Rules of the House of Representatives, the following statements are submitted describing the effect of provisions in the accompanying bill that directly or indirectly change the application of existing law.

The bill includes a number of provisions which place limitations on the use of funds in the bill or change existing limitations and which might, under some circumstances, be construed as changing the application of existing law:

1. *Office of the Secretary.*—Language is included to limit the amount of funds for official reception and representation expenses, as determined by the Secretary.

2. *Departmental Administration.*—Language is included to reimburse the agency for travel expenses incident to the holding of hearings

Source: H.Rept. 113-468, pp. 68.

In the Senate, there is no similar rule that requires the Senate Appropriations Committee to include in committee reports a list or description of legislative provisions in the appropriations measures or committee amendments thereto reported from the committee. However, Senate Rule XXVI, paragraph 12, sometimes referred to as the "Cordon Rule," requires that the committee report include a comparative print of language "repealing or amending any statute." Any legislative language that would directly repeal or amend existing law would be included in that comparative display.

Appropriations Not Authorized by Law

As previously mentioned, the rules of the House and Senate distinguish between authorizations and appropriations. These rules also require that an agency, program, or activity be authorized by law prior to when appropriations are provided. The authorization for subsequent appropriations

---

[62] For early examples of these lists, see H.Rept. 73-1195, pp. 17-21; H.Rept. 73-335, p. 15; H.Rept. 73-449, pp. 27-28.

[63] H.Res. 988, 93rd Cong. For further information on the purpose of this requirement, see House debate, *Congressional Record*, vol. 120, part 26 (October 8, 1974), pp. 34416-34419.

[64] In addition to the requirement for a summary of changes in existing law, House Rule XIII, clause 3(e)(1)—sometimes referred to as the "Ramseyer Rule"—requires that all committee reports include a comparative print of language in the bill "proposing to repeal or amend a statute or part thereof." Any legislative language that would repeal or amend existing law would also be included in that comparative display.

may be explicit (i.e., "there is hereby authorized to be appropriated") or implied by the statutory authority that creates and governs the entity.[65] An appropriation is said to be "unauthorized" when such an authorization (explicit or implicit) has never been enacted or, if previously enacted, has terminated or expired.

Congressional concern related to the advisability of providing appropriations not authorized by law is long-standing.[66] Like the prohibitions on legislative language discussed above, formal rules in the House and Senate that restrict appropriations not authorized by law have been in effect for more than a century—dating back to 1837 in the House and 1850 in the Senate.[67] House Rule XXI, clause 2, prohibits appropriations not authorized by law in general appropriations measures and amendments thereto. In contrast, the prohibition on unauthorized appropriations in Senate Rule XVI, paragraph 2, applies in a comparatively more narrow set of circumstances and most significantly to amendments offered by individual Senators during consideration of general appropriations measures.[68]

Notwithstanding these congressional rules, appropriations not authorized by law have been provided for certain purposes for more than a century, although with increasing frequency over the past several decades. In response to concerns that insufficient information about such appropriations was available during their congressional consideration, both the House and Senate adopted rules requiring that committee reports for general appropriations measures identify the unauthorized appropriations contained therein.[69] In the Senate, these requirements were initially adopted in 1970 and are currently in Senate Rule XVI, paragraph 7.[70] This rule provides that the Senate Appropriations Committee report must "identify each recommended amendment which proposes an item of appropriation which is not made to carry out the provisions of an existing law, a treaty stipulation, or an act or resolution previously passed by the Senate during that session." Even when the committee reports an original Senate bill and not an amendment to a House bill, it usually includes the list of unauthorized appropriations that the committee has included in the bill. An example of this Senate list is provided by the report accompanying the FY2015 Transportation-Housing and Urban Development appropriations bill excerpted below:

---

[65] In the absence of an explicit authorization of appropriations, it is generally understood that statutory authority to administer a program or engage in an activity, sometimes referred to as organic or enabling legislation, also provides implicit authorization to appropriate for such program or activity (Red Book, at 2-41).

[66] For a summary of congressional practices related to the form of authorizations and their effect on the occurrence and frequency of unauthorized appropriations, see CRS Report R43862, *Changes in the Purposes and Frequency of Authorizations of Appropriations*, by Jessica Tollestrup.

[67] Schick, *Legislation, Appropriations, and Budgets*, pp. 16-17.

[68] For further information on congressional rules that restrict appropriations not authorized by law, see CRS Report R42098, *Authorization of Appropriations: Procedural and Legal Issues*, by Jessica Tollestrup and Brian T. Yeh.

[69] See footnotes 57 and 58 for an explanation of what constitutes a general appropriations bill under the rules of the House and Senate.

[70] S.Res. 413, 91st Cong. For an explanation of the specific context that led to the adoption of this rule, see *Congressional Record*, vol. 116, part 25 (September 25, 1970), p. 33785.

Figure 5: Senate List of Appropriations Not Authorized by Law

COMPLIANCE WITH PARAGRAPH 7, RULE XVI, OF THE
STANDING RULES OF THE SENATE

Paragraph 7 of rule XVI requires that Committee reports on general appropriations bills identify each Committee amendment to the House bill "which proposes an item of appropriation which is not made to carry out the provisions of an existing law, a treaty stipulation, or an act or resolution previously passed by the Senate during that session."

The Committee is filing an original bill, which is not covered under this rule, but reports this information in the spirit of full disclosure.

The Committee recommends funding for the following programs or activities which currently lack authorization for fiscal year 2015:

TITLE I—DEPARTMENT OF TRANSPORTATION

National Infrastructure Investments
Federal Highway Administration
Federal Motor Carrier Safety Administration
National Highway Traffic Safety Administration

Source: S.Rept. 113-182, p. 159.

In the House, prior to the adoption of a formal rule, the lists of legislation and limitations in committee reports that were discussed in the section above occasionally included unauthorized appropriations.[71] In 1995, at the beginning of the 104th Congress, the House amended its rules to explicitly require that Appropriations Committee reports accompanying regular appropriations bills include a list of appropriations not currently authorized by law.[72] Six years later, at the beginning of the 107th Congress, this rule was expanded to require more detailed information, including:[73]

- the last year for which such appropriations were authorized,

- the level of appropriations authorized for that year,

- the actual level of appropriations for that year, and

- the level of appropriations in the bill.

This requirement is currently codified in House Rule XIII, clause 3(f)(1)(B).

The House's rationale for this list also relates to issues that can arise between the authorizing and appropriations committees with regard to unauthorized appropriations and legislative provisions when such provisions are included in appropriations bills by the House Appropriations Committee. For the past few decades, special rules have been used to waive points of order against unauthorized appropriations and legislative provisions that are in the committee version of the bill.[74] However, if the authorizing committee of jurisdiction objects to any of those provisions, the Rules Committee will often choose to leave them unprotected by the waiver in the special

---

[71] See, for example, H.Rept. 93-1132, pp. 41-42; H.Rept. 99-747, pp. 100-115; H.Rept. 103-190, pp. 168-171.

[72] H.Res. 6, 104th Cong. The requirements in this rule do not apply to classified intelligence or national security programs, projects, or activities.

[73] H.Res. 5, 107th Cong.

[74] For further information, see CRS Report R42933, *Regular Appropriations Bills: Terms of Initial Consideration and Amendment in the House, FY1996-FY2015*, by Jessica Tollestrup.

rule. The House has recognized this practice as the "Armey Protocol"[75] since the 104th Congress. The requirement for this list that was also adopted at that time may serve a purpose related to that protocol: providing relevant information to the authorization committees—and also the Rules Committee—as to the unauthorized appropriations or legislative provisions in the measure.

A recent example of the House list of Appropriations Not Authorized by Law is provided by the report accompanying the FY2015 Transportation-Housing and Urban Development appropriations bill (H.Rept. 113-464, pp. 127-129), which is excerpted below:

Figure 6: House List of Appropriations Not Authorized by Law

Appropriations Not Authorized by Law and Expiring Authorizations [Dollars in Thousands]				
Program	Last year of authorization	Authorization Level	Appropriations in last year of authorization	Appropriations in this bill
Title I - Department of Transportation				
Federal Highway Administration				
Federal-aid Highways	2014	$40,995,000	$40,995,000	$40,995,000
Federal Motor Carrier Safety Administration 2/				
Motor Carrier Safety Operations & Programs	2014	$259,000	$259,000	$259,000
Motor Carrier Safety Grants	2014	$313,000	$313,000	$313,000
National Highway Traffic Safety Administration				
Operations and Research -- Highway Trust Fund	2014	$118,500	$123,500	$128,500
Highway Traffic Safety Grants	2014	$561,500	$561,500	$561,500

Source: H.Rept. 113-464, pp. 128.

Rescissions and Transfers

A rescission is a provision of law that cancels previously enacted budget authority. Such provisions are used to cancel funds for programs or projects that are no longer priorities. Rescissions of unexpired budget authority carried in appropriations acts may also serve to offset increases in funding elsewhere in the bill relative to the applicable 302(a) and 302(b) allocations, as well as the statutory discretionary spending limits.[76]

As previously mentioned, a transfer occurs when funds are moved between accounts. Transfers require explicit statutory authority in order to be allowable. Such transfer authority may be provided in authorizing laws or in annual appropriations acts and may be permissive—allowing a transfer up to a certain amount or percentage—or mandate that the transfer occur.

In general, the House Appropriations Committee does not have jurisdiction over legislative language.[77] Because rescissions and transfers change existing law, they are considered to be legislative.[78] However, to provide greater flexibility in the appropriations process, the jurisdiction of the House Appropriations Committee was expanded by the Committee Reform Amendments of 1974 to include transfers and rescissions of funds previously provided in appropriations acts.[79] At

---

[75] House Committee on Rules, "Open Rules and Appropriations Bills," May 1, 2009, http://rules-republicans.house.gov/Media/PDF/BT-OpenRules.pdf.

[76] See scorekeeping rule 8 in H.Rept. 105-217.

[77] The current jurisdiction of the House Appropriations Committee is codified in House Rule X, clause 1(b).

[78] *House Manual, One Hundred Thirteenth Congress*, H. Doc. 112-161, 112th Cong., 2nd sess., compiled by Thomas J. Wickham, Parliamentarian (Washington: GPO, 2013), §1063, p. 884.

[79] H.Res. 988, 93rd Cong. The rationale for this change is discussed more extensively in H.Rept. 93-916, part II, pp. 29-
(continued...)

---

the same time, in order to provide greater transparency to Congress as to the extent to which rescissions and transfers were being proposed by the Appropriations Committee, a new House rule was adopted to require that general appropriations bills have separate headings for "Rescissions" and "Transfers of Unexpended Balances."[80] In addition, committee reports accompanying those bills must have a separate section that lists all such rescissions and transfers. This requirement is currently codified in House Rule XIII, clause 3(f)(2).

For example, in the report accompanying the FY2015 Department of Homeland Security appropriations bill, the following lists were included:

Figure 7: Rescissions and Transfers

RESCISSION OF FUNDS

Pursuant to clause 3(f)(2) of rule XIII of the Rules of the House of Representatives, the following table is submitted describing the rescissions recommended in the accompanying bill:

Account/Activity	Rescissions
Public Law 112-10, Coast Guard, AC&I—Reduction of Unobligated Balances	$2,550,000
Public Law 112-74, Coast Guard, AC&I—Reduction of Unobligated Balances	4,095,000
Public Law 113-6, Coast Guard, AC&I—Reduction of Unobligated Balances	16,892,000
Public Law 113-76, CBP, OAM—Reduction of Unobligated Balances	8,090,000
Public Law 113-76, TSA, Aviation Security, Screener PC&B	20,090,000
Public Law 113-76, Coast Guard, AC&I—Reduction of Unobligated Balances	52,905,000
S&T, Research, Development, Acquisition, & Operations (70 × 0800)	14,000,000
Treasury Asset Forfeiture Fund	200,000,000
Legacy Balances, CBP, Salaries and Expenses	1,362,000
FEMA, Disaster Relief Fund (70-X-0702)	388,511,000

TRANSFER OF FUNDS

Pursuant to clause 3(f)(2), rule XIII of the Rules of the House of Representatives, the following is submitted describing the transfer of funds provided in the accompanying bill.

The table shows, by title, department and agency, the appropriations affected by such transfers:

Appropriation Transfers Recommended in the Bill

Account to which transfer is to be made	Amount	Account from which transfer is to be made	Amount
Office of Inspector General	$24,000,000	FEMA—Disaster Relief Fund	$24,000,000

Source: H.Rept. 113-481, p. 132.

In the Senate, transfers and rescissions are also considered to be legislative language,[81] but only rescissions are in the jurisdiction of the Senate Appropriations Committee.[82] However, there is no

---

(...continued)

30.

[80] H.Res. 988, 93rd Cong., H.Rept. 93-916, part II, pp. 29-30.

[81] *Riddick's Senate Procedure*, p. 176.

[82] The current jurisdiction of the Senate Appropriations Committee is codified in Senate Rule XXV, paragraph 1(b)(2).

requirement that such provisions be separately identified in the committee report accompanying an appropriations measure.

Issues for Congress

A previous section of this report discusses the origins and purposes of the main components of appropriations report language. In some instances, these components were developed to improve the ability of Congress to control or influence the execution of budget laws by federal agencies. In others, they were intended to address the need for certain budget process information during the congressional consideration of appropriations measures each fiscal year. The choice of these components and the form they take in a particular context raise certain issues for Congress. These issues are summarized below.

Congressional Influence over Budgetary Decisionmaking

There is a long-existing tension between the executive and legislative branch over the appropriate level of detail for annual appropriations laws and related congressional directives. While some have argued that the details of budgetary decisionmaking should be left to the executive, others have asserted that Congress should have a significant role in those decisions.[83] Over the course of the 20th century, as Congress has increasingly chosen to appropriate lump sum amounts with few statutory allocations within those amounts, report language has gradually become more detailed.[84] In particular, this more detailed report language has enabled Congress—and the appropriations committees in particular—to weigh in on these spending decisions without "tying the agency's hands with inflexible statutory language."[85] This use of appropriations report language can also obviate the need for Congress to later consider laws to amend detailed statutory requirements that have subsequently been determined to be inappropriate or unworkable.[86]

In each particular instance, decisions about the appropriate level of detail to provide in the statutory text for an agency, as opposed to the accompanying committee report, are based on factors such as:

- the oversight relationship of the committee with the agency,

- the purpose and time frame of spending provided,

- the extent to which the needs that may arise during the fiscal year are readily anticipated, and

- the extent to which unforeseen circumstances have the potential to alter what is feasible or desirable for the agency from the perspective of Congress.

---

[83] For an overview of this historical debate, see Allen Schick, "Politics Through Law: Congressional Limitations on Executive Discretion," in *Both Ends of the Avenue: The Presidency, the Executive Branch, and Congress in the 1980s,* ed. Anthony King (Washington, D.C.: American Enterprise Institute, 1983), pp. 154-184; Louis Fisher, *Presidential Spending Power* (Princeton, N.J.: Princeton University Press, 1975), pp. 61-66.

[84] Stephen Horn, *Unused Power: The Work of the Senate Committee on Appropriations* (Washington, D.C.: Brookings Institution, 1970), pp. 186-192.

[85] Ibid, p. 187.

[86] Richard Munson, *The Cardinals of Capitol Hill* (New York: Grove Press, 1993), pp. 72-73.

The level of detail from year to year may also change depending on the committee's assessment of other issues. For example, the House report accompanying the FY2015 Commerce-Justice-Science appropriations bill noted (H.Rept. 113-448):

> In the absence of comity and respect for the prerogatives of the Appropriations Committees and the Congress in general, the Committee may opt to include specific program limitations and details in legislation and remove language providing the flexibility to reallocate funds. Under these circumstances, programs, projects and activities become absolutes and the executive branch shall lose the ability to propose changes in the use of appropriated funds except through legislative action. (p. 6)

The judgment of the committee that is applied in a given context takes into account both the perceived success of previous approaches to these issues and whether different circumstances are likely to materialize in the future.

The Congressional Budget Process Context for Appropriations Decisionmaking

While the report language components that are externally directed have generally been implemented at the initiative of the Appropriations Committees, both the House and the Senate have chosen to require that certain additional information also be included in the appropriations reports. This additional information tends to relate to the budget process context in which appropriations measures are considered. In some cases, the requirement for a particular component was in response to an existing budget process issue. For example, as certain Members of the House and Senate became concerned about the committee's repeated inclusion of appropriations not authorized by law in appropriations measures, both chambers ultimately adopted rules to require that such appropriations be identified in appropriations report language.[87] In other instances, requirements for appropriations report language were implemented proactively in anticipation of potential issues in the future. For example, the requirement that the applicable appropriations allocations under Section 302(b) of the Budget Act be evaluated relative to the amounts in the bill was imposed at the same time that process was first implemented.[88] Likewise, the requirement that rescissions and transfers be listed in House Appropriations Committee reports occurred concurrently with the committee gaining jurisdiction over those items.[89]

Sometimes the chambers choose to take different approaches to similar issues. For example, although House and Senate rules separating authorizations and appropriations have been in effect since the mid-19th century, legislative language was often included in the reported version of general appropriations bills.[90] In 1974, the House chose to require that legislative language included in a general appropriations measure be listed and explained in the committee report accompanying it.[91] In contrast, the Senate has not chosen to formally require that such

---

[87] For further information, see the section of this report titled "Appropriations Not Authorized by Law."

[88] For further information, see the section of this report titled "Comparison with the Budget Resolution."

[89] For further information, see the section of this report titled, "Rescissions and Transfers."

[90] For a discussion of this issue and information on the waivers of Rule XXI, clause 2, that have been routinely provided for regular appropriations measures prior to their floor consideration, see CRS Report R42933, *Regular Appropriations Bills: Terms of Initial Consideration and Amendment in the House, FY1996-FY2015*, by Jessica Tollestrup.

[91] For further information, see the section of this report titled "Language Changing Existing Law."

information be included in the committee report.[92] In such instances, divergent approaches might be due to differing levels of concern about the issue or whether requiring certain appropriations report language is the appropriate solution to it.

The extent to which the House and Senate continue the current requirements for report language or alter them in the future may depend on whether the current form of these components is judged to provide information that is adequate for its purposes. In addition, if new issues arise through the adoption of new rules and procedures—or in the exercise of those that are currently in effect—further changes in the content of appropriations report language might occur.

Author Contact Information

Jessica Tollestrup
Analyst on Congress and the Legislative Process
jtollestrup@crs.loc.gov, 7-0941

Acknowledgments

The author is grateful to Lara Chausow for her research assistance for this report.

---

[92] As previously mentioned, Senate Rule XXVI, paragraph 12, sometimes referred to as the "Cordon Rule," requires that the committee report include a comparative print of language "repealing or amending any statute." Any legislative language that would directly repeal or amend existing law would be included in that comparative display.

Overview of the Authorization-Appropriations Process

Bill Heniff Jr.
Analyst on Congress and the Legislative Process

November 26, 2012

Congressional Research Service

7-5700

www.crs.gov

RS20371

CRS Report for Congress
Prepared for Members and Committees of Congress

A primary avenue for exercising Congress's power of the purse is the authorization and appropriation of federal spending to carry out government activities.[1] While the power over appropriations is granted to Congress by the U.S. Constitution, the authorization-appropriation process is derived from House and Senate rules. The formal process consists of two sequential steps: (1) enactment of an authorization measure that may create or continue an agency, program, or activity as well as authorize the subsequent enactment of appropriations; and (2) enactment of appropriations to provide funds for the authorized agency, program, or activity.

The authorizing and appropriating tasks in this two-step process are largely carried out by a division of labor within the committee system. Legislative committees, such as the House Committee on Armed Services and the Senate Committee on Commerce, Science, and Transportation, are responsible for authorizing legislation related to the agencies and programs under their jurisdiction; most standing committees have authorizing responsibilities. The Appropriations Committees of the House and Senate have jurisdiction over appropriations measures. As discussed below, House and Senate rules generally prohibit the encroachment of these committee responsibilities by the authorizers and appropriators.

Agencies and programs funded through the annual appropriations process, referred to as *discretionary spending*, generally follow this two-step process. Not all federal agencies and programs, however, are funded through this authorization-appropriations process. Funding for some agencies and programs is provided by the authorizing legislation, bypassing this two-step process. Such spending, referred to as *direct (or mandatory) spending*, currently constitutes about 55% of all federal spending. Some direct spending, mostly entitlement programs, is funded by permanent appropriations in the authorizing law. Other direct spending (referred to as appropriated entitlements), such as Medicaid, is funded in appropriations acts, but the amount appropriated is controlled by the existing authorizing statute.

Authorizing Legislation

An authorizing measure can establish, continue, or modify an agency, program, or activity for a fixed or indefinite period of time. It also may set forth the duties and functions of an agency or program, its organizational structure, and the responsibilities of agency or program officials.

Authorizing legislation also authorizes, implicitly or explicitly, the enactment of appropriations for an agency or program. If explicit, the amount authorized to be appropriated may be specified for each fiscal year or may be indefinite (providing "such sums as may be necessary"). The authorization of appropriations is intended to provide guidance regarding the appropriate amount of funds to carry out the authorized activities of an agency.

Appropriations Measures

An appropriations measure provides budget authority to an agency for specified purposes. Budget authority allows federal agencies to incur obligations and authorizes payments to be made out of

---

[1] For further information on the authorization of appropriations specifically, see CRS Report R42098, *Authorization of Appropriations: Procedural and Legal Issues*, by Jessica Tollestrup and Brian T. Yeh.

the Treasury. Discretionary agencies and programs, and appropriated entitlement programs, are funded each year in appropriations acts.

The subcommittees of the Appropriations Committees of the House and Senate are each responsible for one of the *regular appropriations acts*. The regular appropriations acts generally provide budget authority for the next fiscal year, beginning October 1. Congress usually adopts one or more *supplemental appropriations acts* to provide additional funding for unexpected needs while the fiscal year is in progress. If the regular appropriation acts are not completed by October 1, Congress typically adopts a *continuing appropriations act*, commonly referred to as a continuing resolution, to provide stop-gap funding. In some years, instead of adopting the regular appropriation measures individually, Congress may include several in an omnibus appropriations measure, or a continuing appropriations bill providing funding for the full fiscal year.

Enforcing the Authorization-Appropriations Process

Longstanding rules of the House and Senate attempt to retain the separation between the authorization and appropriations tasks within this process, and these rules may be enforced through points of order. The application of these rules can be complicated, and the following merely summarizes their main provisions.[2] First, the House and Senate place restrictions on appropriations for agencies and activities not authorized by law. The House (Rule XXI, clause 2) prohibits any appropriation, whether in a reported appropriations bill or offered as an amendment, for an expenditure not authorized by law. The Senate (Rule XVI, paragraph 1) prohibits floor amendments proposing appropriations for an agency or activity not authorized by law, with certain exceptions. In contrast to the House, the Senate does not prohibit committee amendments or measures reported by the Appropriations Committee from including an appropriation for an agency or activity not authorized by law. Second, the House (Rule XXI, clause 2) and Senate (Rule XVI, paragraphs 2 and 4) prohibit the inclusion of legislative language (such as an authorization) in an appropriations measure. Third, the House (Rule XXI, clause 4), but not the Senate, prohibits appropriations in authorizing legislation.

While the rules are intended to encourage the adherence to this process, a point of order must be raised to enforce the rules. In addition, the rules may be waived by suspension of the rules, by unanimous consent, or, in the House, by a special rule. Further, the Senate, in some cases, may allow legislative language in an appropriations act if it determines, by an affirmative vote, that such language is germane to legislative language already in the act as passed by the House.[3] Unauthorized appropriations or legislative provision in an appropriations act signed into law would have, in most cases, full force and effect (e.g., an agency may spend the entire amount of an unauthorized appropriation), regardless of these congressional restrictions.

---

[2] For further information on the House and Senate rules, see William Holmes Brown, Charles W. Johnson, and John V. Sullivan, *House Practice: A Guide to the Rules, Precedents, and Procedures of the House* (Washington: GPO, 2011), pp. 69-151, and Floyd M. Riddick and Alan S. Frumin, *Riddick's Senate Procedure: Precedents and Practices*, 101st Cong., 2nd sess., S. Doc. 101-28 (Washington: GPO, 1992), [hereafter *Riddick's Senate Procedure*], pp. 150-213.

[3] For further information on this exception (referred to as the defense of germaneness), see *Riddick's Senate Procedure*, pp. 161-171.

Author Contact Information

Bill Heniff Jr.
Analyst on Congress and the Legislative Process
wheniff@crs.loc.gov, 7-8646

Congressional
Research Service
Informing the legislative debate since 1914

Points of Order in the Congressional Budget Process

James V. Saturno
Specialist on Congress and the Legislative Process

October 20, 2015

Congressional Research Service

7-5700

www.crs.gov

97-865

Summary

The Congressional Budget Act of 1974 (Titles I-IX of P.L. 93-344, as amended) created a process that Congress uses each year to establish and enforce the parameters for budgetary legislation. Enforcement of budgetary decisions is accomplished through the use of points of order, and through the reconciliation process. Points of order are prohibitions against certain types of legislation or congressional actions. These prohibitions are enforced when a Member raises a point of order against legislation that may violate these rules when it is considered by the House or Senate.

This report summarizes the points of order currently in effect under the Congressional Budget Act of 1974, as amended, as well as related points of order established in various other measures that have a direct impact on budget enforcement. These related measures include the budget resolution adopted by Congress in 2015 (S.Con.Res. 11, 114th Congress), as well as earlier related provisions. These include the budget resolution adopted by Congress in 2009 (S.Con.Res. 13, 111th Congress), as well as selected provisions in the Rules of the House and separate orders for the 114th Congress (H.Res. 5, 114th Congress), the Budget Enforcement Act of 1990 (P.L. 101-508), and the Statutory Pay-As-You-Go Act of 2010 (P.L. 111-139). In addition, the report describes how points of order are applied and the processes used for their waiver in the House and Senate.

These provisions have been adopted pursuant to the constitutional authority of each chamber to determine its rules of proceeding. This report will be updated to reflect any additions or further changes to these points of order.

Congressional Research Service

Points of Order in the Congressional Budget Process

Contents

Tables

Contacts

Introduction

The Congressional Budget Act of 1974P.L. 99-177P.L. 100-119 P.L. 101-508P.L. 103-66P.L. 105-33P.L. 113-67[1] established the basic framework that is used today for congressional consideration of budget and fiscal policy. The act provided for the adoption of a concurrent resolution on the budget (budget resolution) as a mechanism for coordinating congressional budgetary decision making. This process supplements other House and Senate procedures for considering spending and revenue legislation by allowing Congress to establish and enforce parameters with which those separate pieces of budgetary legislation must be consistent. The parameters are established each year when Congress adopts the budget resolution, setting forth overall levels for new budget authority, outlays, revenues, deficit, and debt.

These overall spending levels are then allocated to the various committees in the House and Senate responsible for spending legislation. The overall levels and allocations are then enforced through the use of points of order, and through implementing legislation, such as that enacted through the reconciliation process.[2] Points of order are prohibitions against certain types of legislation or congressional actions. These prohibitions are enforced when a Member raises a point of order against legislation that is alleged to violate these rules when it is considered by the House or Senate. Points of order are not self-enforcing. A point of order must be raised by a Member on the floor of the chamber before the presiding officer can rule on its application, and thus for its enforcement.

Although the congressional budget process encompasses myriad procedures dealing with spending, revenue, and debt legislation, this report focuses only on that portion of the process that stems from the Congressional Budget Act. The tables below list the points of order included in the Congressional Budget Act, as amended through the Bipartisan Budget Act of 2013 (P.L. 113-67) (**Table 1**), as well as related points of order established in various other measures. These points of order include provisions in the FY2010 budget resolution (**Table 3**); the FY2008 budget resolution (**Table 4**); the Budget Enforcement Act of 1990 (**Table 5**); the rules of the House and separate orders adopted under H.Res. 5 (114th Congress) (**Table 6**); and the provisions of the Statutory Pay-As-You-Go Act of 2010 (**Table 7**) that pertain to the consideration, contents, implementation, or enforcement of budgetary decisions.

Points of order are typically in the form of a provision stating that "it shall not be in order" for the House or Senate to take a specified action or consider certain legislation that is inconsistent with

---

[1] The Congressional Budget Act (Titles I-IX of P.L. 93-344) has been amended on a number of occasions since its enactment. The most salient of the modifications has been as a result of the Balanced Budget and Emergency Deficit Control Act of 1985 (P.L. 99-177, also known as Gramm-Rudman-Hollings or GRH); the Balanced Budget and Emergency Deficit Control Reaffirmation Act of 1987 (P.L. 100-119); the Budget Enforcement Act of 1990 (Title XIII of the Omnibus Budget Reconciliation Act of 1990,P.L. 101-508); Title XIV of the Omnibus Budget Reconciliation Act of 1993 (P.L. 103-66); Title X of the Balanced Budget Act of 1997 (P.L. 105-33), and the Bipartisan Budget Act of 2013 (P.L. 113-67). For the text of the Budget Act, as amended through 2013, see U.S. Congress, House Committee on the Budget, *Bipartisan Budget Act of 2013*, 113th Cong., 2nd sess., February 2014 (Washington: GPO, 2014), pp. 275-352.

[2] The reconciliation process is an optional procedure set forth in Section 310 of the Congressional Budget Act. First used in 1980, reconciliation is a two-step process triggered when the budget resolution includes instructions to one or more committee(s) directing them to recommend changes in revenue or spending laws necessary to achieve the overall levels agreed to. The recommendations are then considered in one or more reconciliation measures under expedited procedures. Certain features of the reconciliation process are enforced by points of order that are included in this report. For more on the reconciliation process generally, see CRS Report RL33030, *The Budget Reconciliation Process: House and Senate Procedures*, by Robert Keith and Bill Heniff Jr.

the requirements of the Budget Act. Other provisions of the act, formulated differently, establish various requirements or procedures, particularly concerning the contents and consideration of the budget resolution or reconciliation legislation. These provisions, however, are not typically enforced through points of order, and are not included here.[3]

As amended through the Bipartisan Budget Act of 2013, points of order in the Congressional Budget Act are permanent. None of the provisions listed in **Table 1** is scheduled to expire, although several points of order have limited applicability or have been rendered moot by the expiration of limits they were intended to enforce.[4] The freestanding point of order protecting the Social Security trust fund in the House established in the Budget Enforcement Act (see **Table 5**) is also permanent. However, other points of order established under recent budget resolutions have various sunset provisions or limited application.

Application of Points of Order

Most points of order in the Budget Act apply to measures as a whole, as well as to motions, amendments, or conference reports to those measures. When a point of order is sustained against consideration of some matter, the effect is that the matter in question falls.

The application of points of order in the House is clarified in Section 315 of the Budget Act. This provision states that for cases in which a reported measure is considered pursuant to a special rule, a point of order against a bill "as reported" would apply to the text made in order by the rule as original text for the purpose of amendment or to the text on which the previous question is ordered directly to passage. In this way, no point of order would be considered as applying (and no waiver would be required) if a substitute resolved the problem. In addition, the Rules of the House for the 111th Congress include a provision further specifying that for measures considered pursuant to a special rule, points of order under Title III of the Budget Act apply without regard to whether the measure considered is actually that reported from committee. Under Rule XXI, clause 8, points of order apply to the form of a measure recommended by the reporting committee where the statute uses the term "as reported" (in the case of a measure that has been reported), the form of the measure made in order as an original text for the purpose of amendment, or the form of the measure on which the previous question is ordered directly to passage.

The effect of a point of order in the Senate is clarified under Section 312(f), which provides that when a point of order against a measure is sustained, the measure is recommitted to the appropriate committee for any further consideration. This allows the Senate an opportunity to remedy the problem that caused the point of order. Section 312(d) is also designed to provide the Senate with the opportunity to remedy a problem that would provoke a point of order. This provision states that a point of order may not be raised against a measure, amendment, motion, or conference report while an amendment or motion that would remedy the problem is pending.

Section 312(e) clarifies that any point of order that would apply in the Senate against an amendment also applies against amendments between the houses. Further, this section also states

---

[3] For example, the prohibition against motions to recommit concurrent resolutions on the budget in the House under Section 305(a)(2) of the act is typically not counted as a separate point of order. Likewise, the requirement under Section 308(a) of the act for reports on legislation to include cost estimates is not formulated as a point of order, although the House has deemed it necessary to formally waive the provision on occasion.

[4] The expiration of some of the provisions of the Balanced Budget and Emergency Deficit Control Act at the end of FY2002 rendered moot a number of points of order. For example, the point of order in the Congressional Budget Act to enforce maximum deficit amounts in the Senate (Section 312(c)) has been rendered moot because no statute currently specifies such an amount.

that the effect would "be the same as if the Senate had disagreed to the amendment." This would allow the Senate to keep the underlying measure pending, and thus retain the ability to resolve their differences with the House. This provision therefore means that any resolution of the differences between the House- and Senate-passed versions of a measure, whether it is in the form of a conference report or not, must adhere to the provisions of the Budget Act.

There are exceptions to the general principle of applying points of order to a measure as a whole. The most salient is probably Section 313, the so-called Byrd Rule. This section applies to matter "contained in any title or provision" in a reconciliation bill or resolution (or conference report thereon), as well as any amendment or motion. If a point of order is sustained under this section, only the provision in question is stricken, or the amendment or motion falls.[5] Several of the points of order in the Senate subsequently established under budget resolutions have been written so that they too apply to individual provisions rather than the measure as a whole, in the same manner as provided in Section 313(e) of the Budget Act. In particular, this construction is applied to the points of order against emergency spending designations (Section 403(e)(1) of S.Con.Res. 13 (111th Congress), Section 314(e) of the Budget Act, and Section 4(g)(3) of the Statutory Pay-As-You-Go Act of 2010). These sections further provide that, if sustained, the effect of the point of order is that the provision making an emergency designation shall be stricken, and may not be offered as an amendment from the floor.

Procedures for Waiving Points of Order

The Congressional Budget Act sets forth certain procedures, under Section 904, for waiving points of order under the act. These waiver procedures apply in the Senate only. Under these procedures, a Senator may make a motion to waive the application of a point of order either preemptively before it can be raised, or after it is raised, but before the presiding officer rules on its merits.[6]

In the Senate, most points of order under the Budget Act may be waived by a vote of at least three-fifths of all Senators duly chosen and sworn (60 votes if there are no vacancies) (see **Table 1**). The three-fifths waiver requirement was first established for some points of order under the Balanced Budget and Emergency Deficit Control Act of 1985. Beginning with the Balanced Budget Act of 1997, this super-majority threshold was applied to several additional points of order on a temporary basis. These points of order are identified in Section 904(c)(2), and the three-fifths requirement is currently scheduled to expire September 30, 2025.[7] The three-fifths threshold has also been required for the Senate to waive the application of many of the related

---

[5] Section 313(d) provides a special procedure for further consideration of a measure should a point of order under this section be sustained against a provision in a conference report.

[6] In the case of points of order under Section 313 of the Budget Act (and by extension, other points of order for which this construction applies) a single point of order may be raised against several provisions. The presiding officer may sustain the point of order "as to some or all of the provisions," and a motion to waive the point of order may, likewise, be made concerning some or all of the provisions against which the point of order was raised.

[7] As originally provided in Title X of the Balanced Budget Act of 1997, the three-fifths requirement expired on September 30, 2002. The Senate subsequently adopted S.Res. 304 on October 16, 2002, renewing the three-fifths requirement for all of the points of order identified in Section 904(c)(2) (except for Section 302(f)(2)(B)) through April 15, 2003. The three-fifths requirement (including for Section 302(f)(2)(B)) was renewed through September 30, 2008, under Section 503 of H.Con.Res. 95 (108th Congress), extended through September 30, 2010, under Section 403 of H.Con.Res. 95 (109th Congress), extended through September 30, 2017, under Section 205 of S.Con.Res. 21 (110th Congress), and most recently, extended through September 30, 2025 under Section 3201(a)(1) of S.Con.Res. 11 (114th Congress).

points of order established in budget resolutions and other measures, such as the Statutory Pay-As-You-Go Act of 2010. As with other provisions of Senate rules, Budget Act points of order also may be waived by unanimous consent.

In the House, Budget Act points of order are typically waived by the adoption of special rules, although other means (such as unanimous consent or suspension of the rules) may also be used. A waiver may be used to protect a bill, specified provision(s) in a bill, or an amendment from a point of order that could be raised against it. Waivers may be granted for one or more amendments even if they are not granted for the underlying bill. The House may waive the application of one or more specific points of order, or they may include a "blanket waiver," that is, a waiver that would protect a bill, provision, or amendment from any point of order.

Table 1. Points of Order Under the Congressional Budget Act of 1974

Section	Description	Application	Senate Waiver Vote[a]
301(g)	In the Senate, prohibits consideration of a budget resolution using more than one set of economic assumptions.	Budget resolution, amendment, or conference report.	Simple majority
301(i)	In the Senate, prohibits consideration of a budget resolution that would decrease the Social Security surplus in any fiscal year covered by the resolution.	Budget resolution, amendment, motion, or conference report.	Three-fifths*
302(c)	Prohibits the consideration of any measure within the jurisdiction of the House or Senate Appropriations Committees that provides new budget authority for a fiscal year until the committee makes the suballocation required by Section 302(b).	Bill, joint resolution, amendment, motion, or conference report.	Three-fifths*
302(f)(1)	In the House, after action on a budget resolution is completed, prohibits consideration of legislation providing new budget authority for any fiscal year that would cause the applicable allocation of new budget authority made pursuant to Section 302(a) or (b) for the first fiscal year or for the total of all fiscal years to be exceeded.[b,b]	Bill, joint resolution, amendment, or conference report.	n/a
302(f)(2)(A)	In the Senate, after a budget resolution is agreed to, prohibits consideration of legislation (from any committee other than the Appropriations Committee) that would cause the applicable allocation of new budget authority or outlays made pursuant to Section 302(a) for the first fiscal year or for the total of all fiscal years to be exceeded.	Bill, joint resolution, amendment, motion, or conference report.	Three-fifths*
302(f)(2)(B)	In the Senate, after a budget resolution has been agreed to, prohibits consideration of legislation from the Appropriations Committee that would cause the applicable suballocation of new budget authority or outlays made pursuant to Section 302(b) to be exceeded.	Bill, joint resolution, amendment, motion, or conference report.	Three-fifths*
303(a)	Prohibits consideration of legislation providing new budget authority, an increase or decrease in revenues, an increase or decrease in the public debt limit, new entitlement authority (in the Senate only), or an increase or decrease in outlays (in the Senate only) for a fiscal year until a concurrent resolution for that fiscal year has been agreed to.[b,c]	Bill, joint resolution, amendment, motion, or conference report.	Simple majority[d]
303(c)	In the Senate, prohibits consideration of any appropriations measure until a concurrent resolution for that fiscal year has been agreed to, and an allocation has been made to the Committee on Appropriations under Section 302(a).[c]	Bill, joint resolution, amendment or conference report.	Simple majority[d]
305(b)(2)	In the Senate, prohibits consideration of nongermane amendments.[e]	Amendment.	Three-fifths

Section	Description	Application	Senate Waiver Vote[a]
305(c)(4)	In the Senate, prohibits consideration of nongermane amendments to amendments in disagreement to a budget resolution (Section 310(e) applies this prohibition to amendments in disagreement to reconciliation legislation as well).	Amendment in disagreement to a budget resolution (or to reconciliation legislation).	Three-fifths
305(d)	In the Senate, prohibits a vote on a budget resolution unless the figures contained in the resolution are mathematically consistent.	Budget resolution or conference report.	Simple majority
306	Prohibits consideration of matters within the jurisdiction of the Budget Committee except when it is a measure reported by the committee, or the committee is discharged from further consideration of the measure.	Bill, resolution, amendment, motion, or conference report.	Three-fifths
306(b)	Prohibits consideration of matters within the jurisdiction of the House Budget Committee except when it is a measure reported by the committee, or the committee is discharged from further consideration of the measure, or an amendment to such a measure.[f]	Bill, joint resolution, amendment, or conference report.	n/a
309	In the House, prohibits consideration of an adjournment resolution for more than three calendar days during July until the House has approved all regular appropriations bills for the upcoming fiscal year.	Resolution.	n/a
310(d)	Prohibits the consideration of amendments to reconciliation legislation that would cause a net increase in the deficit either by increasing outlays above the levels in the bill or reducing revenues below the level in the bill unless fully offset, except that in the Senate a motion to strike a provision shall always be in order.[g]	Amendment.	Three-fifths
310(e)	In the Senate, prohibits consideration of nongermane amendments to reconciliation legislation or to amendments in disagreement to reconciliation (by reference to Sections 305(b)(2) and 305(c)(4)).	Amendment.	Three-fifths
310(f)	In the House, prohibits consideration of an adjournment resolution of more than three calendar days during July until the House has completed action on any required reconciliation legislation.	Resolution.	n/a
310(g)	Prohibits the consideration of reconciliation legislation that contains recommendations with respect to Social Security.	Bill, joint resolution, amendment, motion, or conference report.	Three-fifths*
311(a)(1)	In the House, prohibits consideration of legislation that would cause new budget authority or outlays to exceed the levels set forth in the budget resolution for the first fiscal year or revenues to fall below the levels set forth in the budget resolution for the first fiscal year or for the total of all fiscal years for which allocations are made pursuant to Section 302(a)[b,h]	Bill, joint resolution, amendment, motion, or conference report.	n/a
311(a)(2)	In the Senate, prohibits consideration of legislation that would cause new budget authority or outlays to exceed the levels set forth in the budget resolution for the first fiscal year, or revenues to fall below the levels set forth in the budget resolution for the first fiscal year or for the total of all fiscal years for which allocations are made pursuant to Section 302(a).	Bill, joint resolution, amendment, motion, or conference report.	Three-fifths*

Section	Description	Application	Senate Waiver Vote[a]
311(a)(3)	In the Senate, prohibits consideration of legislation that would cause a decrease in Social Security surpluses or an increase in Social Security deficits relative to the level set forth in the budget resolution for the first fiscal year or for the total of all fiscal years for which allocations are made pursuant to Section 302(a).	Bill, joint resolution, amendment, motion, or conference report.	Three-fifths*
312(b)	In the Senate, prohibits the consideration of legislation that would cause any of the discretionary spending limits specified in Section 251(c) of the Balanced Budget and Emergency Deficit Control Act of 1985, as amended, to be exceeded.[i]	Bill, joint resolution, amendment, motion, or conference report.	Three-fifths*
312(c)	In the Senate, prohibits consideration of a budget resolution that provides for a deficit in excess of the maximum deficit amount specified in the Balanced Budget and Emergency Deficit Control Act of 1985, as amended, for the first fiscal year set forth in the resolution.[j]	Budget resolution, amendment, or conference report.	Three-fifths*
313	In the Senate, prohibits consideration of extraneous provisions in reconciliation legislation.[k]	Reconciliation bill or resolution (any title or provision), amendment, motion, or conference report.	Three-fifths
314(e)	In the Senate, provides for a point of order against the use of an emergency designation as allowed under Section 251(b)(2)(A)(i) of the Balanced Budget and Emergency Deficit Control Act.[l]	Bill, joint resolution, amendment, motion, or conference report.	Three-fifths*m
314(f)	Prohibits consideration in the House or Senate of legislation that would cause the discretionary spending limits set forth in Section 251 of the Balanced Budget and Emergency Deficit Control Act, as amended by the Budget Control Act of 2011 to be exceeded.[i]	Bill, joint resolution, amendment, motion, or conference report.	Three-fifths*n
401(a)	Prohibits consideration of legislation providing new contract authority, borrowing authority, or credit authority not limited to amounts provided in appropriations acts.[o]	Bill, joint resolution, amendment, motion, or conference report.	Simple majority
401(b)	Prohibits consideration of legislation providing new entitlement authority that is to become effective during the current fiscal year.[p]	Bill, joint resolution, amendment, motion, or conference report.	Simple majority
425(a)(1)	Prohibits consideration of legislation reported by a committee unless the committee has published a statement by CBO on the direct costs of federal mandates.	Bill or joint resolution.	Three-fifths*p

Section	Description	Application	Senate Waiver Vote[a]
425(a)(2)	Prohibits consideration of legislation that would increase the direct costs of federal intergovernmental mandates by an amount greater than the thresholds specified as in Section 424(a).	Bill, joint resolution, amendment, motion, or conference report.	Three-fifths*q
426	In the House, prohibits consideration of a rule or order that would waive the application of Section 425.	Resolution, rule, or order.	n/a

Source: The Congressional Budget Act of 1974 (P.L. 93-344), as amended. U.S. Congress, House Committee on the Budget, *Bipartisan Budget Act of 2013*, 113th Congress, 2nd session, February 2014 (Washington: GPO, 2014), pp. 275-352.

a. This column indicates the type of Senate vote (as provided under Section 904 of the Congressional Budget Act) necessary to approve a motion to waive the point of order listed. The term "simple majority" means that the provision may be waived by a majority vote of the Members voting, a quorum being present. The term "three-fifths" means that a motion to waive the provision must be approved by a vote of three-fifths of Senators "duly chosen and sworn." For those provisions marked with an asterisk (*), the three-fifths requirement is scheduled to expire on September 30, 2025, (as identified under Section 904(e) and extended under S.Con.Res. 11 (114th Congress)), reverting to simple majority after that time. See footnote 7 in the text of this report for details on previous extensions. The same voting requirement (either simple majority or three-fifths) would also apply to a vote to appeal a ruling of the chair connected with a point of order. The term "n/a" is used for those provisions that apply in the House only.

b. Section 302(g) of the Congressional Budget Act (known as the Pay-As-You-Go exception) provides that Sections 302(f)(1), 303(a) (after April 15), and 311(a), as it applies to revenues, shall not apply in the House to legislation (bill, joint resolution, amendment, or conference report) if for each fiscal year covered by the most recently agreed to budget resolution such legislation would not increase the deficit if added to other changes in revenues or direct spending provided in the budget resolution pursuant to pay-as-you-go procedures included under Section 301(b)(8). In the 109th Congress, the House adopted a provision in H.Res. 248 establishing that during the 109th Congress there would be a separate point of order in the Committee of the Whole against a motion to rise and report a general appropriations bill if that bill, as amended, were in a breach of the appropriate 302(b) allocation. This provision was subsequently readopted in the 110th-114th Congresses as a separate order of the House (see Section 3(e)(2) of H.Res. 5 (114th Congress)).

c. Section 303(b) sets forth exceptions to the prohibitions under 303(a). In the House, the point of order does not apply to (1) advance discretionary new budget authority that first become available for the first or second fiscal year after the first fiscal year covered in a budget resolution; (2) revenue legislation that is to first become effective after the first fiscal year covered in a budget resolution; (3) general appropriations bills after May 15; or (4) any bill or joint resolution unless it is reported by a committee (see also table note b above for an additional exception to 303(a) provided under Section 302(g)). In the Senate, the point of order does not apply to advance appropriations for the first or second fiscal year after the first fiscal year covered in a budget resolution. The application of this point of order to appropriations bills in the Senate is provided specifically under Section 303(c), which requires an allocation be made to the Senate Appropriations Committee under Section 302(a) as well as agreement on a budget resolution.

d. The points of order under Sections 303(a) and 303(c) were previously made subject to the three-fifths threshold under Section 403(b) of H.Con.Res. 95 (109th Congress). Section 205 of S.Con.Res. 21 (110th Congress), however, provided that Section 403 no longer apply in the Senate.

e. Section 204(g) of H.Con.Res. 290 (106th Congress) provided that for purposes of interpreting Section 305(b)(2) of the Budget Act, an amendment not be considered germane if it contains predominately precatory language (e.g., Sense of the Senate provisions), although the enforcement of this provision is not clear.

f. Prior to being amended by the Bipartisan Budget Act of 2013, this section provided a single point of order applicable in both the Senate and House. At that time, the House, by separate order, also provided that the point of order would apply to bills and joint resolutions (and amendments or conference reports thereto).

g. Under Section 310(d)(1), the budgetary impact of amendments for purposes of enforcement in the House is measured in relation to the levels in the reconciliation measure. This section was also made effective in the

Senate under Section 3206 of S.Con.Res. 11 (114th Congress). Under Section 310(d)(2), the budgetary impact in the Senate is also measured in relation to the levels provided in the reconciliation instructions which relate to the measure.

h. Section 311(c) provides that 311(a) shall not apply in the House to legislation that would not cause a committee's spending allocation under 302(a) to be exceeded.

i. The point of order in Section 312(b) was written to apply to spending limits included in Section 251(c) of the Balanced Budget and Emergency Deficit Control Act of 1985. The point of order in Section 314(f) was added to apply specifically to spending limits for FY2012-FY2021 included in Section 251(c) as amended by the Budget Control Act of 2011 (P.L. 112-25).

j. Currently no maximum deficit amounts are specified under the Balanced Budget and Emergency Deficit Control Act of 1985, as amended.

k. For more information on this provision (known as the "Byrd Rule"), see CRS Report RL30862, *The Budget Reconciliation Process: The Senate's "Byrd Rule"*, by Bill Heniff Jr.

l. See also separate points of order against the use of emergency designations in the Senate that appear at Section 403(e) of S.Con.Res. 13 (111th Congress) and 4(g)(3) of the Statutory Pay-As-You-Go Act of 2010 (P.L. 111-139).

m. The threshold for waivers and appeals for this point of order appear at Sections 314(e)(2)(A) and (B), respectively, as well as in Section 904.

n. This provision previously appeared at Section 314(e), but was redesignated as Section 314(f) under P.L. 112-78. The thresholds for waivers or appeals concerning this point of order was subsequently clarified as three-fifths of Senators "duly chosen and sworn" in the Bipartisan Budget Act of 2013, which added it to the sections enumerated in Section 904(c)(2) and 904(d)(3), respectively.

o. Section 401(d) provides that Sections 401(a) and 401(b) shall not apply to new spending authority described in those sections that flow from (1) a trust fund established under the Social Security Act or any other trust fund for which 90% or more of its expenditures are supported by dedicated revenues; (2) certain wholly owned or mixed ownership government corporations; or (3) gifts or bequests made to the United States for a specific purpose

p. Points of order under Sections 425(a)(1) and 425(a)(2) had previously been subject to the three-fifths threshold in the 109th Congress under Section 403(b) of H.Con.Res. 95 (109th Congress). Section 205 of S.Con.Res. 21 (110th Congress), however, provided that Section 403 no longer apply in the Senate. The three-fifths threshold is currently established under Section 3203 of S.Con.Res. 11 (114th Congress).

**Table 2. Points of Order Under S.Con.Res. 11 (114th Congress)
(Budget Resolution for FY2016)**

Section	Description	Application	Senate Waiver Vote[a]
2001(b)(1)	In the Senate, prohibits consideration of legislation pursuant to reconciliation instructions in this resolution that would increase the public debt limit during the period of FY2016-FY2025.	Bill, joint resolution, amendment, motion, or conference report.	Two-thirds[b]
3101(b)(1)	In the Senate, prohibits the consideration of a measure that would cause a net increase in on-budget deficits in excess of $5 billion in any of the four consecutive 10-year periods beginning with the first fiscal year that is 10 years after the budget year in the most recently agreed to budget resolution.[c]	Bill, joint resolution, amendment, motion, or conference report.	Three-fifths
3101(b)(2)	In the House, prohibits consideration of a measure that would cause a net increase in direct spending in excess of $5 billion in any of the four consecutive 10-year periods beginning with the first fiscal year that is 10 years after the budget year in the most recently agreed to budget resolution.[d]	Bill, joint resolution, amendment, motion, or conference report.	n/a
3103(b)(1)	In the Senate, prohibits consideration of a full-year appropriations measure that includes a change in a mandatory program producing a net change in direct spending that would be in excess of the amounts specified in Section 3103(b)(3) for FY2016-FY2019.[e]	Bill, joint resolution, amendment, motion, or conference report.	Three-fifths
3103(b)(2)	In the House, prohibits consideration of a provision in a full-year appropriations measure that makes a change in a mandatory program producing a net change in direct spending that would be in excess of the amounts specified in Section 3103(b)(3) for FY2016-FY2019.	Bill, joint resolution, amendment, motion, or conference report.	n/a
3104	Prohibits the consideration of a provision in a full-year appropriations measure that makes a net change in a mandatory program affecting the Crime Victims Fund that would exceed $10.8 billion.	Bill, joint resolution, amendment, motion, or conference report.	Three-fifths
3202(a)	In the Senate, prohibits consideration of advance appropriations in measures providing appropriations for FY2016 or FY2017, except as provided in Section 3202(b).[f]	Bill, joint resolution, amendment, motion, or conference report.	Three-fifths
3205(a)	In the Senate, prohibits voting on passage of any matter that requires a cost estimate under Section 402 of the Congressional Budget Act (i.e., measures reported by a committee other than the Appropriations Committee), unless that cost estimate was made publicly available not later than 28 hours before the vote.	Reported bill (except a bill reported by the Appropriations Committee).	Three-fifths

15-13

Section	Description	Application	Senate Waiver Vote[a]
3301(a)	In the House, prohibits consideration of legislation that would reduce the actuarial balance of the present value of future taxable payroll by at least 0.01% of the Federal Old-Age and Survivors Insurance Trust Fund for the 75-year period utilized in the most recent report of the Board of Trustees.[g]	Bill, joint resolution, amendment, motion, or conference report.	n/a
3304(a)	In the House, prohibits consideration of advance appropriations, except as provided in Section 3304(b).[f]	Bill, joint resolution, amendment, motion, or conference report.	n/a

Source: S.Con.Res. 11 (114th Congress).

a. This column indicates the type of Senate vote necessary to approve a motion to waive the point of order listed. The term "three-fifths" means that a motion to waive the provision must be approved by a vote of three-fifths of Senators "duly chosen and sworn." The same voting requirement would also apply to a vote to appeal a ruling of the chair connected with the point of order.

b. The threshold of two-thirds of Senators "duly chosen and sworn" for waiver of this point of order or appeals associated with it are specified in Sections 2001(b)(2) and 2001(b)(3), respectively.

c. The budget year in S.Con.Res. 11 (114th Congress) is FY2016, so the first fiscal year that is 10 years after that budget year would be FY2026.

d. The budget year in S.Con.Res. 11 (114th Congress) is FY2016, so the first fiscal year that is 10 years after that budget year would be FY2026. Under Section 3101(g), this section is scheduled to expire on September 30, 2017.

e. This point of order supersedes earlier, similar points of order in S.Con.Res. 21 (110th Congress) and S.Con.Res. 70 (110th Congress).

f. This point of order supersedes earlier, similar points of order. For more on advance appropriations generally, see CRS Report R43482, Advance Appropriations, Forward Funding, and Advance Funding: Concepts, Practice, and Budget Process Considerations, by Jessica Tollestrup.

g. Section 3(q)(2) provides that this point of order would not apply to legislation that would improve the actuarial balance of the combined balance of the Federal Old Age and Survivors Insurance Trust Fund and the Federal Disability Insurance Trust Fund over the same 75-year period. See also point of order under Separate Orders Adopted by the House, Section 3(q)(1).

Table 3. Points of Order Under S.Con.Res. 13 (111th Congress)
(Budget Resolution for FY2010)

Section	Description	Application	Senate Waiver Vote[a]
403(e)	In the Senate, provides for a point of order against the use of an emergency designation as allowed under Section 403(a) of this budget resolution to provide for exemption in the Senate from budget enforcement mechanisms specified in Section 403(b).[b]	Bill, resolution, amendment, motion, or conference report	Three-fifths
404(a)	In the Senate, prohibits the consideration of direct spending or revenue legislation that would cause a net increase in the deficit in excess of $10 billion in any fiscal year provided for in the most recently adopted budget resolution unless it is fully offset over the period of all fiscal years provided for in the most recently adopted budget resolution. [c]	Bill, joint resolution, amendment, motion, or conference report.	Three-fifths
405(a)	In the Senate, prohibits consideration of any measure or provision that extends or reauthorizes surface transportation programs that appropriates budget authority from sources other than the Highway Trust Fund. [c]	Bill, joint resolution, amendment, or conference report	Three-fifths

Source: S.Con.Res. 13 (111th Congress).

a. This column indicates the type of Senate vote necessary to approve a motion to waive the point of order listed. The term "three-fifths" means that a motion to waive the provision must be approved by a vote of three-fifths of Senators "duly chosen and sworn." The same voting requirement would also apply to a vote to appeal a ruling of the chair connected with the point of order.

b. This section concerns the use of emergency designations, but does not establish a point of order against the spending or revenue itself. It also requires committees reporting legislation that include provisions designated as emergency to include in any accompanying written report a justification for the designation. The use of an emergency designation exempts resulting new budget authority, outlays, or receipts for purposes of enforcing Sections 302 and 311 of the Budget Act, as well as Sections 401 and 404 of this budget resolution. This point of order supersedes earlier, similar points of order under H.Con.Res. 68 and H.Con.Res. 290 (both 106th Congress), H.Con.Res. 95 (108th Congress), Section 14007(b)(2) of P.L. 108-287, H.Con.Res. 95 (109th Congress), and S.Con.Res. 21 (110th Congress). No expiration date is provided for the current point of order. See also points of order against the use of emergency designations that appear at Section 314(e) of the Budget Act and Section 4(g)(3) of the Statutory Pay-As-You-Go Act of 2010.

c. The period covered in S.Con.Res. 11 (114th Congress) is FY2016-FY2025. This section was scheduled to expire on September 30, 2018, but the sunset provision in Section 404(e) was repealed by Section 3201(b)(2) of S.Con.Res. 11 (114th Congress).

Table 4. Points of Order Under S.Con.Res. 21 (110th Congress)
(Budget Resolution for FY2008)

Section	Description	Application	Senate Waiver Vote[a]
201(a)	In the Senate, prohibits consideration of any direct spending or revenue legislation that would increase or cause an on-budget deficit for the period of the current fiscal year and the five ensuing fiscal years or the period of the current fiscal year and the ten ensuing fiscal years.[b]	Bill, joint resolution, amendment, or conference report.	Three-fifths

Source: S.Con.Res. 21 (110th Congress)

a.   This column indicates the type of Senate vote necessary to approve a motion to waive the point of order listed. The term "three-fifths" means that a motion to waive the provision must be approved by a vote of three-fifths of Senators "duly chosen and sworn." The same voting requirement would also apply to a vote to appeal a ruling of the chair connected with the point of order.

b.   This point of order supersedes earlier, similar points of order provided in H.Con.Res. 67 (104th Congress), H.Con.Res. 68 (106th Congress), and H.Con.Res. 95 (108th Congress). This section was scheduled to expire on September 30, 2017, but the sunset in Section 201(d) was repealed in Section 3201(b)(1) of S.Con.Res. 11 (114th Congress). Paragraph 5 of this section specifically excludes the budget resolution or legislation that affects or continues the full funding of the deposit insurance guarantee commitment in effect on the date of enactment of the Budget Enforcement Act of 1990. Paragraph 6 of this section provides that the point of order would not apply in cases in which direct spending and revenue legislation when taken together with other direct spending and revenue legislation enacted since the beginning of the calendar year (and not accounted for in the baseline) result in a net decrease in the deficit (or increase in the surplus), although deficit reduction legislation enacted pursuant to reconciliation instructions may not be used in such calculations.

Table 5. Point of Order Under P.L. 101-508 (Budget Enforcement Act of 1990)

Section	Description	Application
13302(a)	In the House, prohibits consideration of legislation that would provide for a net increase in Social Security benefits or decrease in Social Security taxes in excess of 0.02% of the present value of future taxable payroll for a 75-year period, or in excess of $250,000,000 for the first five-year period after it becomes effective.[a]	Bill, joint resolution, amendment, or conference report.

Source: Subtitle C of the Budget Enforcement Act of 1990 (Title XIII of the Omnibus Budget Reconciliation Act of 1990).

a.   Section 13302(b) provides that the point of order would not apply to legislation that reduces Social Security taxes in excess of the threshold amounts if these reductions are offset by equivalent increases in Medicare taxes.

Table 6. Related Points of Order Under the Standing Rules and Separate Orders Adopted by the House (114th Congress)

Citation	Description	Application
Rule XXI, clause 7	In the House, prohibits consideration of a budget resolution that includes reconciliation instructions that would provide for an increase in net direct spending for the period covered by the resolution.[a]	Budget resolution, amendment, or conference report.
Rule XXI, clause 10	In the House, prohibits consideration of legislation that would have the net effect of increasing mandatory spending for the period comprising the current fiscal year, the budget year, and the four fiscal years following that budget year, or the current fiscal year, the budget year, and the nine fiscal years following that budget year.[b]	Bill, joint resolution, amendment, or conference report.
Separate Orders, Section 3(h)(1)	In the House, prohibits the consideration of a budget resolution that does not include separate presentation of means-tested and non-means-tested direct spending.	Budget resolution, amendment, or conference report.
Separate Orders, Section 3(q)(1)	In the House, prohibits consideration of legislation that would reduce the actuarial balance of the present value of future taxable payroll by at least 0.01% of the Federal Old-Age and Survivors Insurance Trust Fund for the 75-year period utilized in the most recent report of the Board of Trustees.[c]	Bill, joint resolution, amendment, or conference report.

Source: H.Res. 5 (114th Congress).

a. This point of order was first adopted as a part of the rules of the House in the 112th Congress and supersedes earlier points of order adopted as part of the rules of the House for the 110th and 111th Congresses prohibiting reconciliation instructions that would increase the deficit (or decrease the surplus) for a period comprising the current fiscal year, the budget year, and the four fiscal years following that budget year, or the current fiscal year, the budget year, and the nine fiscal years following that budget year.

b. Rule XXI, clause 10(b) provides that when a measure is considered by the House under the terms of a special order directing the Clerk to add at the end of the measure, the provisions of another measure previously passed by the House, those additional provisions are included in determining the application of this point of order. Rule XXI, clause 10(c) excludes provisions designated as an emergency for purposes of the Statutory PAYGO Act of 2010 from calculations to determine the application of this point of order. This point of order was first adopted as a part of the rules of the House in the 112th Congress and supersedes earlier points of order adopted as part of the rules of the House for the 110th and 111th Congresses prohibiting the consideration of direct spending or revenue legislation that would have the net effect of increasing the deficit (or reducing the surplus) for similar periods. For more on the House Pay-As-You-Go rule in the 110th and 111th Congresses, see CRS Report R41510, Budget Enforcement Procedures: House Pay-As-You-Go (PAYGO) Rule, by Bill Heniff Jr.

c. Section 3(q)(2) provides that this point of order would not apply to legislation that would improve the actuarial balance of the combined balance in the Federal Old Age and Survivors Insurance Trust Fund and the Federal Disability Insurance Trust Fund over the same 75-year period. See also point of order under Section 3301(a) of S.Con.Res. 11 (114th Congress).

Table 7. Points of Order Under P.L. 111-139
(Statutory Pay-As-You-Go Act of 2010)

Section	Description	Application	Senate Waiver Vote[a]
4(g)(3)	In the Senate, if a point of order is raised during consideration of legislation subject to PAYGO against an emergency designation in that measure, the provision making the designation shall be stricken.[b]	Bill, joint resolution, amendment, or conference report.	Three-fifths
13(a)	Prohibits the consideration of legislation pursuant to expedited procedures (as recommended by a task force or other commission) that contains recommendations with respect to Social Security.[c]	Bill, resolution	Three-fifths

Source: P.L. 111-139.

a. This column indicates the type of Senate vote necessary to approve a motion to waive the point of order listed. The term "three-fifths" means that a motion to waive the provision must be approved by a vote of three-fifths of Senators "duly chosen and sworn." The same voting requirement would also apply to a vote to appeal a ruling of the chair connected with the point of order.

b. Section 4(g)(4) provides that estimates made by CBO or OMB shall not include the budgetary effects of spending in PAYGO legislation designated as emergency. For more information on the Statutory Pay-As-You-Go Act of 2010, see CRS Report R41157, The Statutory Pay-As-You-Go Act of 2010: Summary and Legislative History, by Bill Heniff Jr. See also points of order against the use of emergency designations in the Senate that appear at Section 314(e) of the Budget Act and Section 403(e) of S.Con.Res. 13 (111th Congress).

c. The language in Section 13(a) was written to apply to any potential recommendations that might result from a Task Force for Responsible Fiscal Action, such as that proposed in S. 2853 (111th Congress). Although such a task force was not created, the language in Section 13(a) would appear to continue to apply to the subsequent consideration under expedited procedures of the recommendations of any task force or commission, although none appear to exist currently.

Author Contact Information

James V. Saturno
Specialist on Congress and the Legislative Process
jsaturno@crs.loc.gov, 7-2381

Congressional Research Service
Informing the legislative debate since 1914

The Budget Control Act: Frequently Asked Questions

Grant A. Driessen
Analyst in Public Finance

Megan S. Lynch
Specialist on Congress and the Legislative Process

February 23, 2018

Congressional Research Service

7-5700

www.crs.gov

R44874

Summary

When there is concern with deficit or debt levels, Congress will sometimes implement budget enforcement mechanisms to mandate specific budgetary policies or fiscal outcomes. The Budget Control Act of 2011 (BCA; P.L. 112-25), which was signed into law on August 2, 2011, includes several such mechanisms.

The BCA as amended has three main components that currently affect the annual budget. One component imposes annual statutory discretionary spending limits for defense and nondefense spending. A second component requires annual reductions to the initial discretionary spending limits triggered by the absence of a deficit reduction agreement from a committee formed by the BCA. Third are annual automatic mandatory spending reductions triggered by the same absence of a deficit reduction agreement. Each of those components is described in further detail in this report. The discretionary spending limits (and annual reductions) are currently scheduled to remain in effect through FY2021, while the mandatory spending reductions are scheduled to remain in effect through FY2027.

Congress may modify or repeal any aspect of the BCA procedures, but such changes require the enactment of legislation. Several pieces of legislation have changed the spending limits or enforcement procedures included in the BCA with respect to each year from FY2013 through FY2017. These include the American Taxpayer Relief Act of 2012 (ATRA; P.L. 112-240), the Bipartisan Budget Act of 2013 (BBA 2013; P.L. 113-67, also referred to as the Murray-Ryan agreement), the Bipartisan Budget Act of 2015 (BBA 2015; P.L. 114-74), and the Bipartisan Budget Act of 2018 (BBA 2018; P.L. 115-123).

Those laws included changes to the discretionary limits imposed by the BCA that increased deficits in each year from FY2013-FY2019. No change has been enacted for FY2020 and beyond, so the discretionary spending limits for FY2020 and FY2021 remain at the level prescribed by the BCA. Following enactment of BBA 2018, the discretionary caps in FY2018 are scheduled to be approximately $629 billion for defense activities and $579 billion for nondefense activities— higher than the levels of $551 billion and $519 billion, respectively, in FY2017. Combined, the limits for FY2018 are $138 billion higher than the FY2017 level.

This report addresses several *frequently asked questions* related to the BCA and the annual budget.

Congressional Research Service

Contents

Tables

Contacts

Congressional Research Service

1. What is the BCA?

When there is concern with deficit or debt levels, Congress will sometimes implement budget enforcement mechanisms to mandate specific budgetary policies or fiscal outcomes. The Budget Control Act of 2011 (BCA; P.L. 112-25) was the legislative result of extended budget policy negotiations between congressional leaders and President Barack Obama. These negotiations occurred in conjunction with the government's borrowing authority approaching the statutory debt limit.[1]

Budget deficits in FY2009 through FY2011 averaged 9.0% of gross domestic product (GDP) and were higher than any other year since World War II. Those deficits were due to a number of factors, including reduced revenues and increased spending demands attributable to the Great Recession and costs associated with the economic stimulus package passed through the American Recovery and Reinvestment Act of 2009 (P.L. 111-5).[2]

The BCA includes several interconnected components related to the federal budget, some of which are no longer in effect. There are five primary components:

1. An authorization to the executive branch to increase the debt limit in three installments, subject to a disapproval process by Congress. (Those provisions were temporary and are no longer in effect.)

2. A one-time requirement for Congress to vote on an amendment to the Constitution to require a *balanced budget.*[3]

3. The establishment of limits on defense discretionary spending and nondefense discretionary spending, enforced by sequestration (automatic, across-the-board reductions) in effect through FY2021.[4] Under this mechanism, sequestration is intended to deter enactment of legislation violating the spending limits or, in the event that legislation is enacted violating these limits, to automatically reduce discretionary spending to the limits specified in law.

4. The establishment of the Joint Select Committee on Deficit Reduction (often referred to as "the Joint Committee" or "the super committee"), which was directed to develop a proposal that would reduce the deficit by at least $1.5 trillion over FY2012 to FY2021.[5]

---

[1] A statutory increase had been enacted roughly once per year since its creation in 1917. For more information, see CRS Report RL31967, *The Debt Limit: History and Recent Increases*, by D. Andrew Austin.

[2] The Great Recession describes the contractionary period (which lasted from December 2007 to June 2009) and subsequent recovery of the U.S. economy.

[3] The House and Senate each voted on such an amendment. The Senate rejected two balanced budget amendments, while the House failed to achieve the necessary two-thirds vote needed for passage.

[4] The statutory limits currently included in the BCA are described in statute as security and nonsecurity. Currently, the security category is defined to include discretionary appropriations classified as budget function 050 (national defense) only, and the nonsecurity category is defined to include all other discretionary appropriations. Originally, however, the BCA caps defined the security category to include discretionary spending for the Departments of Defense, Homeland Security, and Veterans Affairs; the National Nuclear Security Administration; the intelligence community management account; and all accounts in the international affairs budget function (budget function 150) and defined the nonsecurity category to include discretionary spending in all other budget accounts. This change in category definitions occurred automatically under the BCA as part of the automatic spending reduction process that resulted from the lack of enactment of a bill reported by the Joint Committee on Deficit Reduction.

[5] While the committee was tasked with reporting legislation that would reduce the deficit by *$1.5 trillion* over the period of FY2012-FY2021, the automatic process to reduce spending was designed to be triggered only if legislation (continued...)

5. The establishment of an automatic process to reduce spending, beginning in 2013, in the event that Congress and the President did not enact a bill reported by the Joint Committee reducing the deficit by at least $1.2 trillion. (Such a bill was not enacted.) This automatic process requires annual downward adjustments of the discretionary spending limits, as well as a sequester (automatic, across-the-board reduction) of nonexempt mandatory spending programs. In this case, sequestration was included to encourage the Joint Committee to agree on deficit reduction legislation or, in the event that such agreement was not reached, to automatically reduce spending so that an equivalent budgetary goal would be achieved.

2. What components of the BCA currently affect the annual budget?

The BCA as amended has three main components that currently affect the annual budget. One component imposes annual statutory discretionary spending limits for defense and nondefense spending. A second component requires annual reductions to the initial discretionary spending limits, triggered by the absence of a deficit reduction agreement from the Joint Committee. Third are annual automatic mandatory spending reductions triggered by the same absence of a deficit reduction agreement. Each of those components is described in further detail below.

Discretionary Spending Limits

The BCA established statutory limits on discretionary spending for FY2012-FY2021.[6] (Such discretionary spending limits were first in effect between FY1991 and FY2002.)[7] There are currently separate annual limits for defense discretionary and nondefense discretionary spending.[8] The defense category consists of discretionary spending in budget function 050 (national defense) only. The nondefense category includes discretionary spending in all other budget functions.

If discretionary appropriations are enacted that exceed a statutory limit for a fiscal year, across-the-board reductions (i.e., sequestration) of nonexempt budgetary resources within the applicable category are required to eliminate the excess spending. The BCA further stipulates that some spending is effectively exempt from the limits. Specifically, the BCA specifies that the enactment of certain discretionary spending—such as appropriations designated as emergency requirements or for overseas contingency operations—allows for an upward adjustment of the discretionary limits (meaning that such spending is effectively exempt from the limits).[9]

(...continued)

reported by the committee reducing the deficit by at least *$1.2 trillion* was not enacted.

[6] Discretionary spending is controlled through the appropriations process and is generally provided annually. The appropriations committees have jurisdiction over discretionary spending programs, while authorizing committees have jurisdiction over mandatory (or direct) spending programs. For more information see CRS Report R42388, *The Congressional Appropriations Process: An Introduction*, coordinated by James V. Saturno

[7] The spending limits were part of the Budget Enforcement Act of 1990 (BEA; P.L. 101-508). For more information, see CRS Report R41901, *Statutory Budget Controls in Effect Between 1985 and 2002*, by Megan S. Lynch. During the period of FY1991-FY2002, separate caps existed and varied by year. The concept of capping defense and nondefense spending separately was discussed as early as 1984 and is often cited as "the rose garden proposal." Senator Howard Baker, Senate debate, *Congressional Record*, April 24, 1984, p. 9681.

[8] Ibid., footnote 4.

[9] For more information, see section below titled *Are some spending programs "exempt" from the BCA?*

Annual Reductions to the Discretionary Spending Limits

Another component of the BCA requires reductions to these discretionary spending limits annually. Due to the absence of the enactment of Joint Committee legislation to reduce the deficit by at least $1.2 trillion over the 10-year period (described above), the BCA requires these reductions to the statutory limits on both defense and nondefense discretionary spending for each year through FY2021.[10]

These reductions are often referred to as a sequester, but they are not a sequester per se because they do not make automatic, across-the-board cuts to programs. Instead, they lower the spending limits, allowing Congress the discretion to develop legislation within the reduced limits.

For information on the spending limit amounts, see the section below titled "10. How is discretionary spending currently affected by the BCA?"

Annual Mandatory Spending Sequester

Because legislation from the Joint Committee to reduce the deficit by at least $1.2 trillion over the 10-year period (described above) was not enacted, the BCA requires the annual sequester (automatic, across-the-board reductions) of nonexempt mandatory spending programs.[11] This sequester was originally intended to occur each year through FY2021 but has been extended to continue through FY2027.[12]

Many programs are exempt from sequestration, such as Social Security, Medicaid, the Children's Health Insurance Program (CHIP), Temporary Assistance for Needy Families (TANF), and Supplemental Nutrition Assistance Program (SNAP, formerly food stamps). In addition, special rules govern the sequestration of certain programs, such as Medicare, which is limited to a 2% reduction.[13] To see a list of direct spending programs included in the most recent sequester report, see the annual Office of Management and Budget (OMB) report to Congress on the Joint Committee sequester for FY2018.[14]

---

[10] The BCA established the Joint Select Committee on Deficit Reduction, directed to develop a proposal that would reduce the deficit by at least $1.5 trillion over FY2012 to FY2021. The BCA also established an automatic process to produce additional savings, beginning in 2013, in the event that a bill reported by the Joint Select Committee on Deficit Reduction reducing the deficit by at least $1.2 trillion was not enacted by January 15, 2012. (Such a bill was not enacted.) This automatic process requires annual downward adjustments of the discretionary spending limits, as well as a sequester of nonexempt mandatory spending programs.

[11] Ibid.

[12] The Bipartisan Budget Act of 2013 (P.L. 113-67, also referred to as the Murray-Ryan agreement) extended the mandatory spending sequester by two years to FY2023. Soon after the enactment of the Bipartisan Budget Act of 2013, a bill was enacted to "ensure that the reduced annual cost-of-living adjustment to the retired pay of members and former members of the armed forces under the age of 62 required by the Bipartisan Budget Act of 2013 will not apply to members or former members who first became members prior to January 1, 2014, and for other purposes (P.L. 113-82)." This legislation extended the mandatory spending sequester by one year to FY2024. BBA 2015 (P.L. 114-74) extended the mandatory spending sequester by one year to FY2025. BBA 2018 (P.L. 115-123) further extended the mandatory spending sequester by an additional two years through FY2027. For more information, see CRS Report R42506, *The Budget Control Act of 2011 as Amended: Budgetary Effects*, by Grant A. Driessen and Marc Labonte .

[13] These exemptions and special rules are found in Sections 255 and 256 of the Balanced Budget and Emergency Deficit Control Act of 1985 (BBEDCA, Title II of P.L. 99-177), commonly known as the Gramm-Rudman-Hollings Act. For more information, see CRS Report R42050, *Budget "Sequestration" and Selected Program Exemptions and Special Rules*, coordinated by Karen Spar.

[14] OMB, *OMB Report to the Congress on the Joint Committee Reductions for Fiscal Year 2018*, May 23, 2017, https://www.whitehouse.gov/sites/whitehouse.gov/files/omb/sequestration_reports/2018_jc_sequestration_report_may2017_potus.pdf.

For more information on the budgetary impact of the mandatory spending sequester, see the section below titled *How is mandatory spending currently affected by the BCA?*

3. What is a sequester and when will it occur?

A sequester provides for the enforcement of budgetary limits established in law through the automatic cancellation of previously enacted spending. This cancellation of spending makes largely across-the-board reductions to nonexempt programs, activities, and accounts. A sequester is implemented through a sequestration order issued by the President as required by law.

The purpose of a sequester is to enforce certain statutory budget requirements—either to *discourage* Congress from enacting legislation violating a specific budgetary goal or to *encourage* Congress to enact legislation that would fulfill a specific budgetary goal. One of the authors of the law that first employed the sequester recently stated, "It was never the objective ... to trigger the sequester; the objective ... was to have the threat of the sequester force compromise and action."[15]

As mentioned above, sequestration is currently used as the enforcement mechanism for policies established in the BCA:

- For the discretionary spending limits, a sequester will occur only if appropriations are enacted that exceed either the defense or nondefense discretionary limits. In such a case, sequestration is generally enforced when OMB issues a final sequestration report within 15 calendar days after the end of a session of Congress. In addition, a separate sequester may be triggered if the enactment of appropriations causes a breach in the discretionary limits during the second and third quarter of the fiscal year. In such an event, sequestration would take place 15 days after the enactment of the appropriation.[16]

- As mentioned above, the BCA requires reductions to these discretionary spending limits annually. These reductions are to be calculated by OMB and included annually in the *OMB Sequestration Preview Report to the President and Congress*, which is to be issued with the President's annual budget submission. The reductions would then apply to the discretionary spending limits for the budget year corresponding to the President's submission. While these reductions are often referred to as a sequester, they are not a sequester per se because they do not make automatic, across-the-board cuts to programs. Instead, they lower the spending limits, allowing Congress the discretion to develop legislation within the reduced limits.

---

[15] Oral and written testimony of the Honorable Phil Gramm, former Member of the House of Representatives from 1979 to 1985 and U.S. Senator from 1985 to 2002, before the Senate Finance Committee at the hearing on Budget Enforcement Mechanisms, May 4, 2011, https://www.finance.senate.gov/imo/media/doc/050411pgtest.pdf. The law referred to is BBEDCA (P.L. 99-177). For more information on sequestration, see CRS Report R42972, *Sequestration as a Budget Enforcement Process: Frequently Asked Questions*, by Megan S. Lynch. Sequestration was first used as an enforcement mechanism in BBEDCA (referenced above). For more information on the use of sequestration in BBEDCA and the BEA, see CRS Report R41901, *Statutory Budget Controls in Effect Between 1985 and 2002*, by Megan S. Lynch.

[16] If the enactment of appropriations causes the discretionary spending limits to be breached in the last quarter of the fiscal year, the spending limit for the following fiscal year for that category must be reduced by the amount of the breach.

- A sequester of nonexempt mandatory spending programs will take place each year through FY2025. These levels are also calculated by OMB and are included in the annual OMB report to Congress on the Joint Committee reductions, which is also to be issued with the President's budget submission. The sequester does not occur, however, until the beginning of the upcoming fiscal year.

4. What statutory changes have been made to the BCA?

Legislation has been enacted making changes to the spending limits or enforcement procedures included in the BCA for each year from FY2013 through FY2017. Some of the most significant of these changes are the following:

- The American Taxpayer Relief Act of 2012 (ATRA; P.L. 112-240) postponed the start of FY2013 sequester from January 2 to March 3 and reduced the amount of the spending reductions by $24 billion, among other things.

- The Bipartisan Budget Act of 2013 (BBA 2013; P.L. 113-67, referred to as the Murray-Ryan agreement) increased discretionary spending limits for both defense and nondefense for FY2014, each by about $22 billion. In addition, it increased discretionary spending limits for both defense and nondefense for FY2015, each by about $9 billion.[17] It also extended the mandatory spending sequester by two years through FY2023. Soon after the enactment of the Bipartisan Budget Act of 2013, a bill was enacted to "ensure that the reduced annual cost-of-living adjustment to the retired pay of members and former members of the armed forces under the age of 62 required by the Bipartisan Budget Act of 2013 will not apply to members or former members who first became members prior to January 1, 2014, and for other purposes (P.L. 113-82)." This legislation extended the direct spending sequester by one year through FY2024.

- The Bipartisan Budget Act of 2015 (BBA 2015; P.L. 114-74) increased discretionary spending limits for both defense and nondefense for FY2016, each by $25 billion. In addition, it increased discretionary spending limits for both defense and nondefense for FY2017, each by $15 billion. It also extended the direct spending sequester by one year through FY2025. In addition, it established nonbinding spending targets for Overseas Contingency Operations/Global War on Terrorism (OCO/GWOT) levels for FY2016 and FY2017 and amended the limits of adjustments allowed under the discretionary spending limits for Program Integrity Initiatives.[18]

- The Bipartisan Budget Act of 2018 (BBA 2018; P.L. 115-123) increased nondefense and defense discretionary limits in FY2018 and FY2019. In FY2018 BBA 2018 increased the defense limit by $80 billion (to $629 billion) and increased the nondefense limit by $63 billion (to $579 billion); in FY2019 it increased the defense limit by $85 billion (to $647 billion) and increased the nondefense limit by $68 billion (to $597 billion). BBA 2018 also extended the mandatory spending sequester by two years through FY2027.

---

[17] For more information, see CRS Report R43535, *Provisions in the Bipartisan Budget Act of 2013 as an Alternative to a Traditional Budget Resolution*, by Megan S. Lynch.

[18] For more information, see out of print CRS Insight IN10389, *Bipartisan Budget Act of 2015: Adjustments to the Budget Control Act of 2011*, by Grant A. Driessen, available upon request.

5. Is Congress bound by the BCA?

Congress may modify or repeal any aspect of the BCA procedures at its discretion, but such changes require the enactment of legislation. Since enactment of the BCA, subsequent legislation has modified both the discretionary spending limits and the mandatory spending sequester (as described above).

In considering the potential for Congress to reach agreement on future modifications to the BCA, particularly the discretionary spending limits, it may be worth noting the following:

- Legislation that would modify the discretionary spending limit would be subject to the regular legislative process. Such legislation would therefore require House and Senate passage, as well as signature by the President or congressional override of a presidential veto. In the House, such legislation would require the support of a simple majority of Members voting, but in the Senate, consideration of such legislation would likely require cloture to be invoked, which requires a vote of three-fifths of all Senators (normally 60 votes) to bring debate to a close.

- Previous legislative increases to the discretionary spending limits have been coupled with future spending reductions, such as extensions of the mandatory spending sequester. For example, BBA 2013 extended the mandatory spending sequester by two years (from FY2021 to FY2023).[19]

- Previous legislative increases to the discretionary spending limits have adhered to what has been referred to as the "parity principle."[20] In essence, this means that some Members of Congress have insisted that any legislation changing the limits must increase each of the two limits (defense and nondefense) by equal amounts. For example, BBA 2015 increased discretionary spending limits for both defense and nondefense for FY2016, each by $25 billion. In addition, it increased discretionary spending limits for both defense and nondefense for FY2017, each by $15 billion.[21]

6. Which types of legislation are subject to the discretionary spending limits?

Budget Resolutions

Although the budget resolution may act as a plan for the upcoming budget year, it does not provide budget authority and therefore cannot trigger a sequester for violation of the discretionary

---

[19] For more information on the Congressional Budget Office (CBO) estimates related to legislative changes to the discretionary limits, see CBO, "Frequently Asked Questions About CBO Cost Estimate," https://www.cbo.gov/about/products/ce-faq.

[20] Democratic Policy and Communications Center, "In Wake of Partisan Maneuvers to Break Budget Agreement, Senate Dem Leaders Urge GOP to Publicly Agree to Honor Core Tenets of Last Year's Bipartisan Budget Agreement to Allow Appropriations Process to Move Forward," press release, July 7, 2016, https://www.dpcc.senate.gov/?p=issue&id=594; and U.S. Senate Committee on Appropriations, "Mikulski Floor Statement on Reed-Mikulski Amendment," press release, June 8, 2016, http://www.appropriations.senate.gov/news/minority/mikulski-floor-statement-on-reed-mikulski-amendment.

[21] For more information on the parity principle, see the section below titled *How does the "parity principle" apply to the BCA?*

spending limits. Nevertheless, budget resolutions are often referred to in terms of complying with, or not complying with, the discretionary spending limits.[22]

Even if a budget resolution were agreed to that included planned levels of spending in excess of the discretionary spending limits, this would not supersede the discretionary spending limits stipulated by the BCA. While Congress may modify or cancel the discretionary spending limits at their discretion, such changes require the enactment of legislation.

Authorizations of Appropriations

Authorizations of discretionary appropriations, such as the National Defense Authorization Act (NDAA), do not provide budget authority and therefore cannot trigger a sequester for violation of the discretionary spending limits. Although authorizations often include recommendations for funding levels, budget authority is subsequently provided in appropriations legislation. It is, therefore, appropriations legislation that could trigger a sequester. Nevertheless, authorizations (the NDAA in particular) are often discussed in terms of whether or not the authorized level of funding, if appropriated, would comply with the discretionary spending limits.[23]

Even if an authorization bill were enacted that authorized appropriations at levels in excess of the discretionary spending limits, this authorization would not supersede the statutory discretionary spending limits stipulated by the BCA. While Congress may modify or cancel the discretionary spending limits at its discretion, such changes require the enactment of legislation.

Regular, Supplemental, and Continuing Appropriations

Appropriations legislation that provides budget authority for discretionary spending programs in excess of the discretionary spending limits can trigger a sequester for violation of the discretionary spending limits. This includes regular appropriations legislation, supplemental appropriations legislation, and continuing resolutions (CRs).[24]

---

[22] While it cannot trigger a sequester, a budget resolution may be subject to a point of order in the Senate created to enforce the discretionary limits. For more information on the budget resolution and discretionary spending limits, including possible points of order against a budget resolution that provides for spending in excess of the discretionary spending limits, see CRS In Focus IF10647, *The Budget Resolution and the Budget Control Act's Discretionary Spending Limits*, by Megan S. Lynch.

[23] While it cannot trigger a sequester, an authorization bill may be subject to a point of order created to enforce the discretionary limits. If an authorization bill were to authorize appropriations at levels that would breach the BCA limits, such as an amount for the defense function (050) that is higher than the spending limit for FY2018, its consideration might be subject to a point of order in the Senate under Section 312(b), which prohibits consideration in the Senate of any bill, resolution, amendment, motion, or conference report that would exceed the discretionary spending limits. (No corresponding point of order exists in the House.) It may be worth noting that the NDAA includes only the authorizations of appropriations within the jurisdiction of the House and Senate Armed Services Committees, which does not reflect all of the authorizations of appropriations within the national defense budget function (050). If such a point of order were raised, further consideration of the budget resolution might not be in order unless the point of order was waived by a vote of three-fifths of all Senators.

[24] Consideration of legislation that would provide spending in excess of the spending limits would be subject to a point or order. For example, if an appropriations bill were to provide appropriations at levels that would breach the discretionary spending limits, such as an amount for the defense function (050) that is higher than the spending limit for FY2018, its consideration would be subject to a 312(b) point of order in the Senate as well as a 314(f) point of order in either the House or the Senate. If either of those points of order were raised and sustained, further consideration of the appropriations measure would not be in order, unless the point of order was waived by a vote of three-fifths of all Senators in the Senate or in the House by a simple majority of those Members voting. For more information on those points of order, see CRS Report 97-865, *Points of Order in the Congressional Budget Process*, by James V. Saturno.

Any appropriations legislation enacted into law that provides budget authority in excess of the levels stipulated by the BCA would trigger a sequester, canceling previously enacted spending through automatic, largely across-the-board reductions of nonexempt budgetary resources within the category of the breach.

Note that the statutory limits established by the BCA as amended apply to budget authority and not outlays. Budget authority is what federal agencies are legally permitted to obligate, and it is controlled by Congress through appropriation acts in the case of discretionary spending or through other acts in the case of mandatory spending. Budget authority gives federal officials the ability to spend. Outlays are disbursed federal funds. Until the federal government disburses funds to make payments, no outlays occur. Therefore, there is generally a lag between when Congress grants budget authority and when outlays occur.

7. Is some spending "exempt" or "excluded" from the BCA?

Some spending is regarded as "exempt" from the BCA. A distinction should be noted between categories of spending that are "excluded" from the discretionary spending limits and spending programs that are "exempt" from sequestration.

- Some categories of spending are considered "exempt" or "excluded" from the discretionary spending limits, meaning that when an assessment is made as to whether the discretionary spending limits have been breached, they are not counted. (In precise terms, the BCA does not "exempt" such spending but allows for an upward adjustment of the discretionary limits to accommodate such spending.)

  For example, spending designated as emergency requirements or for OCO/GWOT is effectively excluded from the discretionary spending limits up to any amount (meaning that the designation of such spending allows for an upward adjustment of the discretionary limits to accommodate that spending).[25] The BCA does not define what constitutes this type of funding, nor does it limit the level or amount of spending that may be designated as being for such purposes.

  Similarly, "disaster funding" and spending for "continuing disability reviews and redeterminations" and "healthcare fraud and abuse control" are effectively exempt up to a certain amount (again meaning that such spending allows for an upward adjustment of the discretionary limits to accommodate that spending).

- Some programs are exempt from a sequester, such as Social Security, Medicaid, CHIP, TANF, and SNAP. In addition, special rules govern the sequestration of certain programs, such as Medicare, which is limited to a 2% reduction. These exemptions and special rules are found in Sections 255 and 256 of the BBEDCA, as amended, respectively.

  It may also be helpful to review OMB sequester reports detailing programs that have been subject to sequester. To see a list of both discretionary and direct spending programs subject to the FY2013 sequester, see the OMB report to Congress on the Joint Committee

---

[25] These adjustments are specified in Section 251(b)(2) [2 U.S.C. §901(b)(2)]. Spending designated as "emergency" or for OCO/GWOT must be designated on an account-by-account basis and must be subsequently designated so by the President.

sequestration for FY2013.[26] To see a list of direct spending programs included in the most recent sequester report, see the annual OMB report to Congress on the Joint Committee sequester for FY2018.[27]

8. Is the sequester "returning" in FY2020?

Sometimes Members of Congress, the Administration, and the press discuss the concept of the sequester "returning."[28] Generally, the term *return* is being used to describe the fact that at some point, the discretionary spending limits will again be the level prescribed by the BCA. As mentioned above, since the BCA was enacted, other legislation has been enacted to increase the discretionary spending limits.[29] The BBA 2013 increased discretionary spending limits for both defense and nondefense for FY2014 and FY2015, the BBA 2015 increased discretionary spending limits for both defense and nondefense for FY2016 and FY2017, and the BBA 2018 increased discretionary spending limits for both defense and nondefense for FY2018 and FY2019. No similar increase has been enacted for FY2020 and FY2021. The statement that the "sequester is returning in FY2020," therefore, means that the discretionary spending limits will again be the level prescribed by the BCA, as described in the section below.

9. How does the "parity principle" apply to the BCA?

The "parity principle" refers to the equality between changes made to defense and nondefense budget authority through the deficit reduction measures established by the BCA. While there has never been a statutory requirement to uphold the parity principle, budget parity has followed from deficit reduction measures imposed by the BCA and each amendment to its deficit reduction measures. However, the specific type of parity in each law has evolved over time.

The BCA and ATRA reflected parity in the budgetary impact of changes to defense and nondefense budget authority *across both discretionary and mandatory spending categories.* Subsequent BCA amendments in BBA 2013 and BBA 2015 reflected parity between defense and nondefense budget authority *for discretionary spending only*, as those laws also extended automatic mandatory deficit reduction measures that had larger budget reductions for nondefense activities than for defense programs. Finally, BBA 2018 reflected yet another type of parity, as the amended discretionary cap levels in FY2018 and FY2019 were increased by an equivalent amount relative to the initial BCA levels as established in August 2011. As compared with the caps after the automatic reductions took effect, BBA 2018 included larger increases to the defense caps than to the nondefense caps. As with BBA 2013 and BBA 2015, BBA 2018 also included an

---

[26] This was the last time that discretionary programs were subject to a sequester. OMB, *OMB Report to the Congress on the Joint Committee Sequestration for Fiscal Year 2013*, March 1, 2013, https://obamawhitehouse.archives.gov/sites/default/files/omb/assets/legislative_reports/fy13ombjcsequestrationreport.pdf.

[27] OMB, *OMB Report to the Congress on the Joint Committee Sequestration for Fiscal Year 2018*, May 23, 2017, https://www.whitehouse.gov/sites/whitehouse.gov/files/omb/sequestration_reports/2018_jc_sequestration_report_may2017_potus.pdf.

[28] For example, a press report on budget cuts related to defense stated, "Joint Chiefs Chairman Gen. Joseph Dunford, in an exchange with Sen. Lindsey Graham, R-S.C., said a return to sequestration would require a rewrite of the US national defense strategy and expose the nation to "significant risk," from Russia, China, Iran, North Korea and violent extremism, Dunford said. 'My immediate response, senator, is we would have to revise the defense strategy, if we go back to sequestration; We would not be able to do what we do right now," Dunford said.'" Joe Gould, "Sequestration Budget Cuts Pose 'Greatest Risk' to DoD," *DefenseNews*, March 17, 2016, http://www.defensenews.com/story/defense/2016/03/17/sequestration-budget-cuts-pose-greatest-risk-dod/81924766/.

[29] In the section titled *Have statutory changes been made to the BCA?*

extension to the automatic mandatory spending reductions with a larger set of reductions for nondefense programs than for defense programs.

The BCA provides for upward adjustments to the discretionary caps, sometimes called spending "outside the caps," for budget authority devoted to OCO, emergency requirements, and other purposes.[30] Budget authority for BCA upward adjustments has not reflected parity between defense and nondefense activities in any effective year of the BCA to date, as upward adjustments have allowed for more defense spending than nondefense spending in each year from FY2012 through FY2017.

For more information on the parity principle and the BCA, see CRS In Focus IF10657, *Budgetary Effects of the BCA as Amended: The "Parity Principle"*, by Grant A. Driessen.

10. How is discretionary spending currently affected by the BCA?

The BCA includes annual statutory caps that limit how much discretionary budget authority can be provided for defense and nondefense activities. These limits are in effect through FY2021 and are enforced by sequestration, meaning that a breach of the discretionary spending limit for either category would trigger a sequester of resources within that category only to make up for the amount of the breach.

A second component of the BCA makes automatic decreases to these caps annually. In the absence of the enactment of a Joint Committee bill to reduce the deficit by at least $1.2 trillion, the BCA required downward adjustments (or reductions) to the statutory limit on both defense and nondefense spending each year through FY2021. While these reductions are often referred to as sequesters, they are not technically sequesters because they do not make automatic, across-the-board cuts to programs. The reductions instead lower the spending limits, allowing Congress the discretion to develop legislation within the reduced limits. These reductions are to be calculated annually by OMB and are included in the *OMB Sequestration Preview Report to the President and Congress*, which is issued with the President's annual budget submission.

The BCA stipulates that certain discretionary funding, such as appropriations designated as OCO or for emergency requirements, allows for an upward adjustment of the discretionary limits. OCO funding is therefore sometimes described as being "exempt" from the discretionary spending limits.[31] The BCA does not define what constitutes this type of funding, nor does it limit the level of spending that may be designated as being for such purposes.

Budgetary Impact

The BCA as enacted was estimated to reduce budget deficits by a cumulative amount of roughly $2 trillion over the FY2012-FY2021 period. Subsequent modifications enacted through ATRA, BBA 2013, and BBA 2015 lessened the level of deficit reduction projected to be achieved by the BCA in selected years. ATRA reduced the BCA's deficit effect through the postponement and decreases of spending reductions in FY2013, while BBA 2013, BBA 2015, and BBA 2018 limited the deficit-reducing impact through increases in the discretionary budget authority caps in FY2014-FY2019.

---

[30] For more information, see the section above titled *Are any spending programs "exempt" or "excluded" from the BCA?*

[31] Ibid.

Table 1 shows the evolution of discretionary spending limits established by the BCA from August 2011 through February 2018. The discretionary caps in FY2018 are currently scheduled to be $629 billion for defense activities and $579 billion for nondefense activities, higher than their totals of $551 billion and $519 billion, respectively, in FY2017. The combined discretionary limit in FY2018 ($1,208 billion) is $138 billion lower than its FY2017 value.

Table 1. Discretionary Budget Authority Limits Under the BCA as Amended, August 2011-Present

(in billions of nominal dollars)

			2012	2013	2014	2015	2016	2017	2018	2019	2020	2021
BCA	Aug. 2011	Defense	*555*	*546*	*556*	*566*	*577*	*590*	603	616	630	644
		Nonde-fense	*507*	*501*	*510*	*520*	*530*	*541*	553	566	578	590
Auto. Enforce-ment	Jan. 2012	Defense	*555*	**492**	**501**	**511**	**522**	**535**	**548**	**561**	**575**	**589**
		Nonde-fense	*507*	**458**	**472**	**483**	**493**	**505**	**517**	**531**	**545**	**557**
ATRA	Jan. 2013	Defense	*555*	**518**	**497**	511	522	535	548	561	575	589
		Nonde-fense	*507*	**484**	**469**	483	494	505	518	532	545	558
BBA 2013	Dec. 2013	Defense	*555*	*518*	**520**	**521**	523	536	549	562	576	590
		Nonde-fense	*507*	*484*	**492**	**492**	493	504	516	530	543	556
BBA 2015	Nov. 2015	Defense	*555*	*518*	520	521	**548**	**551**	549	562	576	590
		Nonde-fense	*507*	*484*	492	492	**518**	**519**	516	530	543	555
BBA 2018 (Current)	Feb. 2018	Defense	*555*	*518*	520	521	548	551	**629**	**647**	576	591
		Nonde-fense	*507*	*484*	492	492	518	519	**579**	**597**	542	555

Sources: CBO, letter to the Honorable John A. Boehner and Honorable Harry Reid estimating the impact on the deficit of the Budget Control Act of 2011, August 2011; CBO, Final Sequestration Report for Fiscal Year 2012, January 2012; CBO, Final Sequestration Report for Fiscal Year 2013, March 2013; CBO, Final Sequestration Report for Fiscal Year 2014, January 2014; CBO, Final Sequestration Report for Fiscal Year 2016, December 2015; CBO, Sequestration Update Report: August 2017, August 2017; CBO, Cost Estimate for Bipartisan Budget Act of 2018, February 2018.

Notes: Spending limits apply to fiscal years. Bold figures indicate statutory changes. The BCA as amended provided for "Security" and "Nonsecurity" categories in FY2012 and FY2013: italicized figures denote CRS estimates of budget authority for defense and nondefense categories in those years. Small changes in FY2016-FY2021 budget authority shown in ATRA, BBA 2013, and BBA 2015 rows are caused by adjustments in the annual proportional allocations of automatic enforcement measures as calculated by OMB: for more information on these adjustments, see CBO, *Estimated Impact of Automatic Budget Enforcement Procedures Specified in the Budget Control Act*, September 2011.

11. How is mandatory spending currently affected by the BCA?

The absence of an agreement by the Joint Committee triggered automatic spending reductions (as provided for in the BCA) for all mandatory programs that were not explicitly exempted from FY2013 through FY2021. Notably, Social Security payments were exempted from the automatic reductions, and the effect on Medicare spending was limited to 2% of annual payments made to certain Medicare programs. Extensions of the mandatory spending reductions were included in BBA 2013, BBA 2015, and BBA 2018 and are currently scheduled to remain in place through FY2027. A recent OMB sequestration report estimated that such measures will reduce mandatory outlays by $18.14 billion in FY2018, with $17.42 billion of that total applied to nondefense programs and $0.72 billion applied to defense programs.[32]

12. Why do discretionary outlays differ from the spending limits established by the BCA?

The limits on discretionary spending established by the BCA apply to budget authority, which is the amount that federal agencies are legally permitted to obligate. Outlays, meanwhile, are disbursed federal funds: In other words, they represent amounts that are actually spent by the government. There is generally a lag between when Congress grants budget authority and when outlays occur, and that lag can vary depending on the agency and specific purpose of the obligation.[33] Furthermore, the budget may classify certain types of spending in a certain way when measuring budget authority and another way when measuring outlays. For example, much of the spending attached to the Highway Trust Fund is classified as mandatory spending when measuring budget authority and as discretionary spending when measuring outlays.[34]

13. How has federal spending changed since enactment of the BCA?

Budget deficits declined for much of the 1990s due to decreased spending, rising revenues, and an improved economy. The federal budget recorded surpluses from FY1998 through FY2001. Prior to that, the last budget surplus occurred in FY1969. Budget deficits returned starting in FY2002 and slowly increased over the next several years due to reduced revenues and increased spending. Net deficits peaked during the Great Recession from FY2009 to FY2011, as negative and low economic growth coupled with increased spending commitments provided for by the American Recovery and Reinvestment Act (P.L. 111-5) contributed to real deficits averaging 9.0% of gross domestic product (GDP) in those years.

Real deficits have declined since FY2011, due to the modifications made by the BCA, increased revenues, and the winding down of stimulus programs. However, the FY2017 deficit (3.5% of GDP, or $665 billion) remains higher than the average deficit since FY1947 (2.0% of GDP), and the CBO baseline projects that real budget deficits will increase in future years.

The budgetary measures enacted by the BCA have distinct effects on various types of federal activity. **Table 2** illustrates the division of total budgetary resources in FY2017 across major spending categories along with the effects of automatic spending reductions from the BCA in that year. Mandatory programs account for roughly two-thirds of FY2017 outlays (excluding net interest payments). The remaining third of total spending is discretionary and is split almost evenly between defense and nondefense expenditures (16% of total spending each). Meanwhile, the automatic spending cuts fall most heavily on discretionary programs. In FY2017,

---

[32] OMB, "OMB Report to the Congress on the Joint Committee Reduction for Fiscal Year 2018."

[33] See section titled *Which types of legislation are subject to the discretionary spending limits?*

[34] For more information on the budgetary treatment of the Highway Trust Fund, see CBO, *The Highway Trust Fund and the Treatment of Surface Transportation Programs in the Federal Budget*, June 2014, https://www.cbo.gov/sites/default/files/113th-congress-2013-2014/reports/45416-TransportationScoring.pdf.

discretionary spending is projected to account for 32% of budgetary resources and 83% of the automatic spending reductions. Defense discretionary spending is particularly affected, as the defense spending category received 49% of all automatic cuts but accounts for 17% of total gross budgetary resources. Across mandatory and defense categories FY2017 automatic spending cuts are equally applied to defense and nondefense programs. The BCA as amended does not directly affect the revenue side of the federal budget.

Table 2. FY2017 Budget Outcomes by Major Programmatic Area

(as a percentage of total resources or reductions)

	Budgetary Resources	BCA Spending Reductions
Defense Discretionary	16%	49%
Nondefense Discretionary	16%	34%
Defense Mandatory	2%	1%
Medicare (Nondefense Mandatory)	16%	12%
Other Nondefense Mandatory	50%	5%

Source: OMB, *OMB Report to Congress on the Joint Committee Reductions for Fiscal Year 2017*, February 2016; and CBO, *An Update to The Budget and Economic Outlook: 2017 to 2027*, June 2017.

Notes: Mandatory spending is measured on a gross basis (i.e., offsetting receipts are not netted out). The table does not include spending devoted to net interest payments.

14. How do modifications to the BCA affect baseline projections?

Modifications to the limits on discretionary spending, established by the BCA, change authorizations levels, which in turn affect outlays. Legislation that instead affects mandatory spending (or spending controlled by laws other than appropriations acts) is known as direct spending. CBO provides estimates of both discretionary spending effects and direct spending effects in its legislative cost estimates. Whether proposed legislation affects discretionary or mandatory spending may have ramifications for congressional budgetary enforcement procedures, however.

CBO's baseline projections assume that the discretionary limits imposed by the BCA as amended will proceed as scheduled through FY2021 and that subsequent discretionary spending levels will grow with the economy in subsequent years.[35] Such methodology uses the discretionary spending levels in FY2021 as the basis for discretionary spending projections for the remainder of the budget window. Therefore, new proposals that would modify discretionary spending limits in FY2020 would generate budget effects only in that year, whereas proposals that would modify FY2021 limits would generate budget effects in FY2021 and each remaining year of the 10-year baseline window.

---

[35] This methodology is consistent with Section 257 of the Deficit Control Act. For more information, see CBO, *The Budget and Economic Outlook: 2017 to 2027*, January 2017, p. 26.

Author Contact Information

Grant A. Driessen
Analyst in Public Finance
gdriessen@crs.loc.gov, 7-7757

Megan S. Lynch
Specialist on Congress and the Legislative Process
mlynch@crs.loc.gov, 7-7853

Congressional
Research
Service

Budget "Sequestration" and Selected Program Exemptions and Special Rules

Karen Spar, Coordinator
Specialist in Domestic Social Policy and Division Research Coordinator

June 13, 2013

Congressional Research Service

7-5700

www.crs.gov

R42050

CRS Report for Congress
Prepared for Members and Committees of Congress

Summary

"Sequestration" is a process of automatic, largely across-the-board spending reductions under which budgetary resources are permanently canceled to enforce certain budget policy goals. It was first authorized by the Balanced Budget and Emergency Deficit Control Act of 1985 (BBEDCA, Title II of P.L. 99-177, commonly known as the Gramm-Rudman-Hollings Act).

Sequestration is of current interest because it has been triggered as an enforcement tool under the Budget Control Act of 2011 (BCA, P.L. 112-25). Sequestration can also occur under the Statutory Pay-As-You-Go Act of 2010 (Statutory PAYGO, Title I of P.L. 111-139). In either case, certain programs are exempt from sequestration, and special rules govern the effects of sequestration on others. Most of these provisions are found in Sections 255 and 256 of BBEDCA, as amended.

Two provisions were included in the BCA that can result in automatic sequestration:

- Establishment of discretionary spending limits, or caps, for each of FY2012-FY2021. If Congress appropriates more than allowed under these limits in any given year, sequestration would cancel the excess amount.

- Failure of Congress to enact legislation developed by a Joint Select Committee on Deficit Reduction, by January 15, 2012, to reduce the deficit by at least $1.2 trillion. The BCA provided that such failure would trigger a series of automatic spending reductions, including sequestration of mandatory spending in each of FY2013-FY2021, a one-year sequestration of discretionary spending for FY2013, and lower discretionary spending limits for each of FY2014-FY2021.

In fact, the Joint Committee did not develop the necessary legislation and Congress did not meet the January 15, 2012, deadline. Thus, automatic spending cuts under the BCA were triggered, with the first originally scheduled for January 2, 2013. P.L. 112-240 subsequently delayed this until March 1, 2013, and President Obama signed a sequestration order on that date.

Under the Statutory PAYGO Act, sequestration is part of a budget enforcement mechanism that is intended to prevent enactment of mandatory spending and revenue legislation that would increase the federal deficit. This act requires the Office of Management and Budget (OMB) to track costs and savings associated with enacted legislation and to determine at the end of each congressional session if net total costs exceed net total savings. If so, a sequestration will be triggered.

Under sequestration—triggered either by the BCA or Statutory PAYGO Act—the exemptions and special rules of Sections 255 and 256 of BBEDCA apply. Most exempt programs are mandatory, and include Social Security and Medicaid; refundable tax credits to individuals; and low-income programs such as the Children's Health Insurance Program, Supplemental Nutrition Assistance Program, Temporary Assistance for Needy Families, and Supplemental Security Income. Some discretionary programs also are exempt, notably all programs administered by the Department of Veterans Affairs. Also, subject to notification of Congress by the President, military personnel accounts may either be exempt or reduced by a lower percentage.

Special rules also apply to several, primarily mandatory, programs. For example, under Section 256 of BBEDCA, Medicare may not be sequestered by more than 4%. However, under a BCA-triggered sequester, reduction of Medicare is limited to no more than 2%.

Congressional Research Service

Contents

Tables

Appendixes

Contacts

Introduction

"Sequestration" is a process of automatic, largely across-the-board spending reductions to meet or enforce certain budget policy goals.[1] It was first established by the Balanced Budget and Emergency Deficit Control Act of 1985 (BBEDCA, Title II of P.L. 99-177, 2 U.S.C. 900-922) to enforce deficit targets. In the 1990s, sequestration was used to enforce statutory limits on discretionary spending and a pay-as-you-go (PAYGO) requirement on direct spending and revenue legislation. After effectively expiring in 2002, sequestration was reestablished by the Statutory Pay-As-You-Go Act of 2010 (P.L. 111-139) to enforce a modified PAYGO requirement on direct spending and revenue legislation.

Most recently, under the Budget Control Act of 2011 (BCA, P.L. 112-25), sequestration was tied to enforcement of new statutory limits on discretionary spending and achievement of the budget goal established for the Joint Select Committee on Deficit Reduction. A sequestration was triggered by the Joint Committee's failure to achieve its goal and was originally scheduled to occur on January 2, 2013, to affect spending for FY2013. Congress enacted legislation that delayed the effective date of this sequester until March 1, 2013 (American Taxpayer Relief Act of 2012, P.L. 112-240).[2]

In general, sequestration entails the permanent cancellation of budgetary resources by a uniform percentage.[3] This uniform percentage reduction is applied to all "programs, projects, and activities" (PPAs) within a budget account.[4] However, the current sequestration procedures, as in previous iterations of such procedures, provide for exemptions and special rules. That is, certain programs and activities are exempt from sequestration, and certain other programs are governed by special rules regarding the application of a sequester. This report provides an overview of those exemptions and special rules, which are generally found in Sections 255 and 256 of BBEDCA, as amended (2 U.S.C. 905 and 906). While the report makes references to the sequestration currently in effect, triggered by failure of the Joint Committee process under the BCA, it discusses exemptions and special rules in general and should not be viewed as a comprehensive examination of the current or any future sequestration under either the BCA or the Statutory PAYGO Act.

Current Sequestration Triggers

As noted above, sequestration is tied to certain budget goals established in the Budget Control Act of 2011, as well as in the Statutory PAYGO Act of 2010. To provide some context for the

---

[1] For more information on sequestration and its historical application, see (1) CRS Report RL31137, *Sequestration Procedures Under the 1985 Balanced Budget Act*, by Robert Keith; (2) CRS Report RS20398, *Budget Sequesters: A Brief Review*, by Robert Keith; and (3) CRS Report R41901, *Statutory Budget Controls in Effect Between 1985 and 2002*, by Megan S. Lynch.

[2] President Obama issued the sequestration order on March 1, 2013. See http://www.whitehouse.gov/sites/default/files/omb/memoranda/2013/m-13-06.pdf.

[3] "Budgetary resources" include new budget authority, unobligated balances, direct spending authority, and obligation limitations, as defined in Section 250(c)(6) of BBEDCA, as amended.

[4] For accounts included in appropriations acts, "programs, projects, and activities" (PPAs) within each budget account are delineated in those acts or accompanying reports; and for accounts not included in appropriations acts, they are delineated in the most recently submitted President's budget. See Section 256(k) of BBEDCA, as amended.

exemptions and special rules applicable to these sequestration procedures, brief descriptions of the budget goals that may be enforced by sequestration are provided below. Readers also may wish to consult the following CRS reports:

- CRS Report R41965, *The Budget Control Act of 2011*, by Bill Heniff Jr., Elizabeth Rybicki, and Shannon M. Mahan

- CRS Report R42949, *The American Taxpayer Relief Act of 2012: Modifications to the Budget Enforcement Procedures in the Budget Control Act*, by Bill Heniff Jr.

- CRS Report R42972, *Sequestration as a Budget Enforcement Process: Frequently Asked Questions*, by Megan S. Lynch

- CRS Report R42675, *The Budget Control Act of 2011: Budgetary Effects of Proposals to Replace the FY2013 Sequester*, by Mindy R. Levit

- CRS Report R42051, *Budget Control Act: Potential Impact of Sequestration on Health Reform Spending*, by C. Stephen Redhead

- CRS Report R42994, *The Budget Control Act, Sequestration, and the Foreign Affairs Budget: Background and Possible Impacts*, by Susan B. Epstein

- CRS Report R43021, *Proposed Cuts to Air Traffic Control Towers Under Budget Sequestration: Background and Considerations for Congress*, by Bart Elias

- CRS Report R43065, *Sequestration at the Federal Aviation Administration (FAA): Air Traffic Controller Furloughs and Congressional Response*, by Bart Elias, Clinton T. Brass, and Robert S. Kirk

- CRS Report R42506, *The Budget Control Act of 2011: The Effects on Spending and the Budget Deficit*, by Mindy R. Levit and Marc Labonte

- CRS Report R41157, *The Statutory Pay-As-You-Go Act of 2010: Summary and Legislative History*, by Bill Heniff Jr.

Sequestration Triggers Under the Budget Control Act (BCA)

The Budget Control Act of 2011 (BCA) was enacted on August 2, 2011. It provided for increases in the debt limit and established procedures designed to reduce the federal budget deficit.[5] The BCA has two primary components that can trigger a sequestration of discretionary and/or mandatory (or direct) spending:[6]

- Title I of the BCA established discretionary spending limits, or caps, for each of FY2012-FY2021.[7] If Congress appropriates more than allowed under these

---

[5] For a comprehensive discussion of the BCA, see CRS Report R41965, *The Budget Control Act of 2011*, by Bill Heniff Jr., Elizabeth Rybicki, and Shannon M. Mahan.

[6] Discretionary spending is provided in and controlled through the annual appropriations process and represents a portion of total federal spending. The other portion, referred to as direct spending (or mandatory spending), is generally provided in or controlled by authorizing legislation that requires federal payments to individuals or entities, often based on eligibility criteria and benefit formulas set forth in statute. Some direct spending is funded in appropriations acts, referred to as appropriated entitlements, but is controlled by the authorizing statute(s).

[7] Adjustments are allowed to these discretionary spending limits for certain specified activities, such as costs associated (continued...)

spending limits in any given year, the automatic reduction process of sequestration would cancel the excess amount. For FY2012 and FY2013, the spending limits were divided into "security" and "nonsecurity" categories, with security defined broadly to include the Departments of Veterans Affairs (VA), Homeland Security (DHS), and State, in addition to the Department of Defense and certain other activities.[8] For FY2014 and subsequent years, no distinction was made between security and nonsecurity, and Title I of the law established a single discretionary spending limit for each year.[9]

- Title IV of the BCA established a bipartisan Joint Select Committee on Deficit Reduction. Failure by Congress to enact legislation by January 15, 2012, developed by the Joint Committee and reducing the deficit by at least $1.2 trillion, would trigger a series of automatic spending reductions intended to achieve that level of savings over the FY2013-FY2021 period. These automatic reductions include sequestration of mandatory spending for each of FY2013-FY2021, a one-year sequestration of discretionary spending for FY2013, and lower discretionary spending limits for each of FY2014-FY2021. Spending reductions would be divided equally between security and nonsecurity. However, *these terms are redefined*, so that "security" consists only of budget function 050 (effectively, the Department of Defense), and "nonsecurity" includes all other government spending (including the VA, DHS, and State). The distinction between security and nonsecurity (*as redefined*) remains for each of FY2014-FY2021.

The security-nonsecurity distinction is significant because sequestration is imposed within these categories. In other words, if Congress appropriated more than allowed for either category in a given year, the excess spending would be canceled in the category where the breach occurred. As noted above, security was defined broadly under Title I and spending was divided between the two categories originally for FY2012 and FY2013. However, under the automatic procedures triggered by failure of the Joint Committee, security is defined more narrowly and the separate security and nonsecurity categories remain in effect for each year through FY2021.

Because the Joint Committee did not, in fact, develop legislation to achieve the specified level of deficit reduction ($1.2 trillion) by the deadline set in the BCA, and Congress did not subsequently enact such legislation by January 15, 2012, the automatic budget enforcement procedures provided by the law were triggered.[10] The first fiscal year these procedures were intended to

---

(...continued)

with disability redeterminations, health care fraud and abuse, overseas contingency operations and the War on Terror, emergency spending, and funding for disasters.

[8] The Office of Management and Budget (OMB) determined that discretionary amounts provided for FY2012 were within the BCA spending limits, so that no sequestration was necessary for that year. See http://www.whitehouse.gov/ sites/default/files/omb/assets/legislative_reports/sequestration/sequestration_final_jan2012.pdf. OMB subsequently reported on April 9, 2013, that the discretionary spending limits for FY2013 also had not been breached and that a sequestration of discretionary spending to enforce the FY2013 limits would not be needed. See http://www.whitehouse.gov/sites/default/files/omb/assets/legislative_reports/sequestration/ sequestration_final_april2013.pdf.

[9] These provisions were amended by P.L. 112-240, to revise the amounts and categories for FY2013 and FY2014. See CRS Report R42949, *The American Taxpayer Relief Act of 2012: Modifications to the Budget Enforcement Procedures in the Budget Control Act*, by Bill Heniff Jr.

[10] For the statement of the Joint Committee co-chairs, announcing they would not meet the statutory deadline, see (continued...)

---

affect was FY2013; sequestration for that fiscal year (as outlined in the second bullet above) was originally scheduled to happen on January 2, 2013. Legislation was enacted, however, that delayed this sequester until March 1, 2013, and also reduced the total amount to be sequestered by $24 billion (American Taxpayer Relief Act of 2012, P.L. 112-240). Under the law as amended, BCA now requires a cancellation of budgetary resources equal to $85 billion in FY2013, equally divided between defense (i.e., the narrow definition of security) and nondefense.[11]

Office of Management and Budget (OMB) Calculation of March 2013 Sequestration

On March 1, 2013, President Obama signed the sequestration order triggered by failure of the Joint Committee process under the BCA, and the Office of Management and Budget (OMB) issued a report containing the percentages by which budgetary resources must be reduced in order to achieve the necessary spending reductions in FY2013.[12] OMB calculated that, in order to cancel the requisite $85 billion, annualized spending levels for each nonexempt account must be reduced by the percentages shown below in **Table 1**.

OMB noted that the spending reductions for FY2013 must be achieved over a seven-month period rather than the full fiscal year, thus making the *effective* percentage reductions higher than those shown in the table. According to OMB, the effective reductions are approximately 13% for nonexempt defense spending and 9% for nonexempt nondefense spending. Since the FY2013 appropriations process was still ongoing as of March 1, OMB generally based its calculations on the assumption that discretionary programs would be funded at the annualized level provided under the continuing appropriations resolution for FY2013 that was in effect on March 1 (P.L. 112-175),[13] plus amounts provided in the Hurricane Sandy supplemental appropriations (P.L. 113-2), plus any funding enacted as advance appropriations for FY2013. In determining the amount of mandatory spending subject to sequestration, OMB used the current law baseline amounts in the President's FY2013 budget, adjusted for any relevant legislation enacted since transmittal of the budget in February 2012.[14]

(...continued)

http://www.murray.senate.gov/public/index.cfm/2011/11/statement-from-co-chairs-of-the-joint-select-committee-on-deficit-reduction.

[11] For the mechanics of the BCA's automatic spending reduction procedures, see the section titled "Budget Goal Enforcement: Spending Reduction Trigger" in CRS Report R41965, *The Budget Control Act of 2011*, by Bill Heniff Jr., Elizabeth Rybicki, and Shannon M. Mahan, and the section titled "The Sequestration Process" in CRS Report 98-721, *Introduction to the Federal Budget Process*, coordinated by Bill Heniff Jr..

[12] See *OMB Report to the Congress on the Joint Committee Sequestration for Fiscal Year 2013*, March 1, 2013: http://www.whitehouse.gov/sites/default/files/omb/assets/legislative_reports/fy13ombjcsequestrationreport.pdf. Hereinafter referred to as *OMB Report to the Congress on the Joint Committee Sequestration for Fiscal Year 2013*, March 1, 2013.

[13] Congress subsequently passed a continuing resolution for the remainder of FY2013 (P.L. 113-6), which generally maintains programs at FY2012 levels but also includes separate measures for several departments (e.g., Agriculture, Commerce, Justice, Defense, Homeland Security, Veterans Affairs).

[14] For example, OMB took into consideration provisions of the American Taxpayer Relief Act (P.L. 112-240 that overrode the scheduled reduction in Medicare physician payments scheduled to take effect in FY2013 because of the sustainable growth rate (SGR) formula. See CRS Report R40907, *Medicare Physician Payment Updates and the Sustainable Growth Rate (SGR) System*, by Jim Hahn and Janemarie Mulvey.

Readers are referred to the OMB report for an explanation of the methodology used in making calculations, and to the report's appendix for an itemized list of budget accounts that include spending subject to sequestration, the dollar amounts that are subject to sequestration, the percentage by which they are reduced, and the dollar amount of the reduction. Readers should note, however, that OMB identifies budget accounts and not "programs, projects and activities" within these accounts.[15] The law requires sequestration to be applied uniformly at the PPA level; these applications are made by federal agencies under guidance from OMB.[16]

Table 1. OMB Calculations of FY2013 Uniform Percentage Reductions Under BCA-Triggered Sequester, Effective on March 1, 2013

Category of Funding	Defense	Nondefense
Nonexempt discretionary	7.8%	5.0%
Nonexempt mandatory (other than Medicare and selected health programs)	7.9%	5.1%
Medicare and mandatory components of selected health programs	na	2.0%

Source: OMB Report to the Congress on the Joint Committee Sequestration for Fiscal Year 2013, March 1, 2013.

Notes: "Defense" and "Nondefense" are the same as the *revised* Security and Nonsecurity categories discussed above, where Defense (or revised Security) equals budget function 050, and Nondefense (or revised Nonsecurity) equals everything else. na = not applicable. See sections, later in this CRS report, headed "Section 255 Program Exemptions" and "Section 256 Special Rules" for discussion of exemptions and special rules, including those applicable to Medicare and selected health programs.

OMB Calculation of FY2014 Sequestration

On April 10, 2013, OMB issued a report to Congress on the automatic spending reductions for FY2014 under the terms of the BCA.[17] The law requires that $109 billion in spending—divided equally between defense and nondefense—must be reduced in FY2014 (and each subsequent fiscal year through FY2021) as a result of the failure of the Joint Committee process. As explained in the second bullet on p. 3 of this report, spending reductions in FY2014 through FY2021 will occur through a reduction of the discretionary spending limits established under Title I of the BCA and a sequestration of nonexempt mandatory spending.

---

[15] The Sequestration Transparency Act (P.L. 112-155) directed the President to issue a report on the impact of sequestration as it was originally scheduled to occur on January 2, 2013. In that report, the President was to identify all exempt and nonexempt accounts at the program, project, and activity level. The report was issued in September 2012, but did not provide information by PPA, stating that "additional time is necessary to identify, review, and resolve issues associated with providing information at this level of detail." See *OMB Report Pursuant to the Sequestration Transparency Act of 2012 (P.L. 112-155)*, September 2012: http://www.whitehouse.gov/sites/default/files/omb/assets/legislative_reports/stareport.pdf. Hereinafter referred to as *OMB Report Pursuant to the Sequestration Transparency Act*, September 2012.

[16] Many executive branch agencies have posted their final FY2013 budgets, reflecting the effects of sequestration, on their websites. However, there is currently no single authoritative governmentwide source for this information.

[17] OMB released a corrected version of its April 10 report on May 20, 2013. See *OMB Sequestration Preview Report to the President and Congress for Fiscal Year 2014 and OMB Report to the Congress on the Joint Committee Reductions for Fiscal Year 2014*, http://www.whitehouse.gov/sites/default/files/omb/assets/legislative_reports/fy14_preview_and_joint_committee_redu ctions_reports_05202013.pdf.

Accordingly, the OMB report indicates that the $109 billion in spending reductions for FY2014 will be achieved through lowering the discretionary spending limits by about $91 billion ($53.9 billion in the defense category and $36.6 billion in the nondefense category)[18] and sequestering $18 billion in nonexempt mandatory spending. OMB calculates the FY2014 sequestration percentages will equal 2% for nonexempt Medicare spending, 7.3% for nonexempt nondefense mandatory spending, and 9.8% for nonexempt defense mandatory spending. As noted above, sequestration in FY2014 and later years will affect *mandatory spending only,* unless the lowered discretionary spending limits are breached. Because defense spending is largely discretionary, sequestration in FY2014 will primarily affect nondefense spending.

Readers may consult the OMB report's appendix for an itemized list of budget accounts that include mandatory spending that would be subject to sequestration in FY2014, the dollar amounts that would be subject to sequestration (based on OMB's current law baseline), the percentage by which they would be reduced, and the dollar amount of the reduction.

Sequestration Trigger Under Statutory PAYGO

The Statutory Pay-As-You-Go Act of 2010 was enacted on February 12, 2010, as Title I of P.L. 111-139.[19] It established a permanent budget enforcement mechanism intended to prevent mandatory (i.e., direct) spending and revenue legislation that would increase the deficit from being passed and signed into law. (Statutory PAYGO does not apply to discretionary spending.) The act requires various scorekeeping procedures, including 5-year and 10-year scorecards that track costs and savings associated with enacted legislation. At the end of each congressional session, OMB generally must determine whether the net effect of direct spending and revenue legislation enacted during the session has increased the deficit, and if so, a sequestration will be triggered. Certain costs and savings are not counted toward Statutory PAYGO, including designated emergency spending, debt service costs, costs associated with a shift in timing of certain outlays, and net savings from the CLASS Act.[20]

Program Exemptions and Special Rules for Sequestration

Certain programs are exempt from sequestration, and special rules govern the sequestration of others. For the most part, these provisions are found in Sections 255 and 256 of the Balanced Budget and Emergency Deficit Control Act (BBEDCA), as amended. These provisions apply to sequestration orders that occur under either the BCA or the Statutory PAYGO Act. However, the

---

[18] Congress will determine the specific impact of the $91 billion in reduced discretionary spending allowable for FY2014 through the normal appropriations process. This means that reductions will not necessarily be made equally across-the-board, as under sequestration. Moreover, there are no statutory exemptions or special rules that govern these decisions; the reductions may be allocated however Congress and the President choose, within the statutory discretionary spending limits for each category (defense and nondefense).

[19] For a detailed discussion of the Statutory PAYGO Act, see CRS Report R41157, *The Statutory Pay-As-You-Go Act of 2010: Summary and Legislative History*, by Bill Heniff Jr.

[20] The CLASS Act was anticipated but not yet enacted at the time P.L. 111-139 was enacted. It has since been repealed. See CRS Report R40842, *Community Living Assistance Services and Supports (CLASS): Overview and Summary of Provisions*, by Kirsten J. Colello and Janemarie Mulvey.

---

application of these rules for certain programs might differ, depending on the specific provision that triggers the sequestration.

Questions about the impact of sequestration on any particular program or account cannot be answered strictly from reading the relevant provisions of law. As noted earlier, under a sequestration, all nonexempt "programs, projects, and activities" must be reduced by a uniform percentage (unless provided otherwise under special rules; see "Section 256 Special Rules"). However, numerous factors potentially affect the sequestration process, including the amount of budgetary resources subject to sequestration and the interpretation of statutory requirements as they apply to specific programs and activities.

Section 255 of BBEDCA (codified at 2 U.S.C. 905) identifies programs that are exempt from sequestration, and Section 256 of BBEDCA (codified at 2 U.S.C. 906) establishes special rules. Readers should note that these sections have been amended as recently as February 2010 under the Statutory PAYGO Act; however, until the most recent action on March 1, an actual sequestration had not occurred since the early 1990s.[21] CRS cannot say with certainty how these provisions will be interpreted and applied in any particular sequestration, or how potential ambiguities in language may be resolved. The following should be considered as a general description of the law and not an attempted interpretation. Ultimately, the execution and impact of any automatic spending reduction triggered under provisions of the BCA or Statutory PAYGO depend in large part on the legal interpretations and actions taken by OMB.

As noted above, OMB issued a report on March 1, which identifies budget accounts that include spending subject to sequestration in FY2013 under the BCA. In addition, OMB's September 2012 report, issued in response to the Sequestration Transparency Act, gave preliminary information on the "sequestrable" or "exempt" classification of budgetary resources, and provided citations for the provisions in BBEDCA that determined these classifications. Readers are referred to those documents for more specific information on OMB's interpretation and implementation of the law in the case of the March 1 Joint Committee- triggered sequester.[22] *However, readers should note that the sequester percentages and amounts shown in the September 2012 OMB report are obsolete, since that report was prepared before the American Taxpayer Relief Act of 2012 (P.L. 112-240) delayed the FY2013 sequestration from January 2 to March 1, 2013, and reduced the amount of resources to be sequestered.*

Section 255 Program Exemptions[23]

Section 255 contains a list of programs and activities that are exempt from sequestration.[24] Most are mandatory, although a few are discretionary, most notably programs administered by the

---

[21] See CRS Report RS20398, *Budget Sequesters: A Brief Review*, by Robert Keith, dated March 8, 2004.

[22] See *OMB Report to the Congress on the Joint Committee Sequestration for Fiscal Year 2013*, March 1, 2013; and *OMB Report Pursuant to the Sequestration Transparency Act of 2012 (P.L. 112-155)*, September 2012. Also, some federal agencies have posted information on implementation of sequestration for specific programs; see individual agency or program websites to determine whether such information has been made available.

[23] See **Appendix** for the complete statutory language of Section 255 of BBEDCA.

[24] For a table showing some of the largest programs exempt from sequestration, including their FY2010 budgetary authority and discretionary/mandatory status, see Table 4 in CRS Report R42013, *The Budget Control Act of 2011: How Do the Discretionary Caps and Automatic Spending Cuts Affect the Budget and the Economy?*, by Marc Labonte and Mindy R. Levit.

Department of Veterans Affairs (VA). In many cases, specific budget accounts are provided, so readers are referred to the statute for precise identification of exempted programs and activities (see **Appendix**). While the law provides a list of programs and types of spending that are exempt from sequestration, it provides no definitive list of programs or types of spending that absolutely *are* subject to sequestration. As stated above, the impact of sequestration on any given program depends on the actions and interpretations of OMB. The following are selected programs and types of spending identified in Section 255 as exempt from sequestration:

- Social Security benefits (old-age, survivors, and disability) and Tier 1 Railroad Retirement benefits.

- All programs administered by the VA, and special benefits for certain World War II veterans.[25]

- Net interest (budget function 900).

- Payments to individuals in the form of refundable tax credits.[26]

- Unobligated balances, carried over from prior years, for nondefense programs.

- At the President's discretion (subject to notification to Congress), military personnel accounts may be exempt entirely, or a lower sequestration percentage may apply.[27]

- A list of "other" budget accounts and activities; readers should consult the statute for a complete list. A few selected examples include

    - activities resulting from private donations, bequests or voluntary contributions, or financed by voluntary payments for good or services;

    - advances to the Unemployment Trust Fund;[28]

    - payments to various retirement, health care, and disability trust funds;

    - certain Tribal and Indian trust accounts; and

    - Medical Facilities Guaranty and Loan Fund.

- Specified federal retirement and disability accounts and activities (consult the statute for the complete list).

- Prior legal obligations of the federal government in specified budget accounts (consult the statute for the complete list).[29]

---

[25] In its report issued pursuant to the Sequestration Transparency Act, OMB stated that the exemption for VA programs would also apply to the agency's administrative expenses. Also, see discussion of special rules in the "Veterans' Medical Care" section, below.

[26] These include the Earned Income Tax Credit and the refundable portion of the Child Tax Credit (sometimes referred to as the Additional Child Tax Credit). In addition, the Patient Protection and Affordable Care Act (ACA, P.L. 111-148, as amended) established a refundable tax credit for individuals and families with incomes between specified levels to help them purchase health insurance coverage; this tax credit also is exempt. See CRS Report R42051, *Budget Control Act: Potential Impact of Sequestration on Health Reform Spending*, by C. Stephen Redhead.

[27] On July 31, 2012, then-Acting OMB Director Jeffrey Zients notified Congress of the President's intent to exempt military personnel accounts from sequestration: http://www.whitehouse.gov/sites/default/files/omb/legislative/letters/military-personnel-letter-biden.pdf.

[28] Also see discussion of special rules in the "Unemployment Compensation" section, below.

Budget "Sequestration" and Selected Program Exemptions and Special Rules

- Low-income programs, including
  - Academic Competitiveness/Smart Grant Program;[30]
  - mandatory funding under the Child Care and Development Fund;
  - Child Nutrition Programs (including School Lunch, School Breakfast, Child and Adult Care Food, and others, but excluding Special Milk);
  - Children's Health Insurance Program (CHIP);
  - Commodity Supplemental Food Program;
  - Temporary Assistance for Needy Families (TANF) and the TANF Contingency Fund;
  - Family Support Programs;[31]
  - Federal Pell Grants;
  - Medicaid;
  - Foster Care and Permanency Programs;
  - Supplemental Nutrition Assistance Program (SNAP, formerly food stamps); and
  - Supplemental Security Income (SSI).
- Medicare Part D low-income premium and cost-sharing subsidies; Medicare Part D catastrophic subsidy payments; and Qualified Individual (QI) premiums.[32]
- Specified economic recovery programs, including GSE Preferred Stock Purchase Agreements, the Office of Financial Stability, and the Special Inspector General for the Troubled Asset Relief Program.
- The following "split-treatment" programs, to the extent that the programs' budgetary resources are subject to obligations limitations in appropriations bills:
  - Federal Aid-Highways;
  - Highway Traffic Safety Grants;
  - Operations and Research NHTSA and National Driver Register;
  - Motor Carrier Safety Operations and Programs;
  - Motor Carrier Safety Grants;

(...continued)

[29] Programs on the list include the Federal Crop Insurance Corporation Fund; the exemption of prior legal obligations for agriculture is similar to a special rule under Section 256 of BBEDCA for the Commodity Credit Corporation (discussed below).

[30] Due to sunset provisions, no grants can be made under this program after June 30, 2011.

[31] This account includes the Child Support Enforcement program. See discussion of special rules in the "Child Support Enforcement" section, below.

[32] These programs are not listed in Section 255, but instead Section 256(d) identifies them as programs exempt from sequestration "in addition to" the programs listed in Section 255. See the "Medicare" section, below.

Congressional Research Service 9

- Formula and Bus Grants; and
- Grants-in-Aid for Airports.

Section 256 Special Rules

In addition to the exemptions in Section 255 of BBEDCA, Section 256 establishes special rules for sequestration of certain programs or types of spending. Most Section 256 special rules apply to mandatory programs, although some discretionary programs are included (e.g., certain health programs). Once again, the effect of sequestration on any given program is subject to the interpretation of the law's provisions by OMB. The discussions below provide some information on interpretations made in implementing the March 1 sequestration order.

The following is a list of programs included in Section 256 (they are discussed in greater detail below):

- student loans under Title IV-B and IV-D of the Higher Education Act;
- Medicare;
- community and migrant health centers, Indian health services and facilities, and veterans' medical care;
- Child Support Enforcement;
- federal pay;
- federal administrative expenses;
- Unemployment Compensation; and
- Commodity Credit Corporation.

Student Loans[33]

Special sequestration rules (Section 256(b)) apply to federal student loans made under the William D. Ford Federal Direct Loan program during the period when a sequestration order is in effect. Origination fees on Direct Loans made during a period of sequestration must be increased by the uniform percentage specified in the sequestration order.[34] Loan origination fees are calculated as a proportion of the loan principal borrowed and are deducted proportionately from each disbursement of the loan proceeds to the borrower. The origination fee helps offset the costs of federal loan subsidies.

---

[33] This section was prepared by David Smole, dsmole@crs.loc.gov, 7-0624.

[34] Sections 251A(8) and 256(b) of BBEDCA. The William D. Ford Federal Direct Loan program is authorized under Title IV, Part D of the Higher Education Act of 1965 (HEA), as amended. BBEDCA, §256(b) references federal student loans made under HEA, Title IV, Part B and Part D, during the period when a sequestration order is in effect. With the enactment of the SAFRA Act, part of the Health Care and Education Reconciliation Act of 2010 (HCERA; P.L. 111-152), student loans are no longer being made under HEA, Title IV, Part B (the Federal Family Education Loan (FFEL) program). As such, the special rule applies only to student loans made under HEA, Title IV, Part D (i.e., Direct Loans).

Four types of federal student loans are made under the Direct Loan program: Direct Subsidized Loans, Direct Unsubsidized Loans, Direct PLUS Loans, and Direct Consolidation Loans.[35] In general, for Direct Loans made on or after July 1, 2010, the origination fee on Direct Subsidized Loans and Direct Unsubsidized Loans is 1%, and the origination fee on Direct PLUS Loans is 4%. The Department of Education (ED) does not currently charge an origination fee on Direct Consolidation Loans.

Under a sequestration order applicable to direct spending programs, origination fees on Direct Loans made during the sequestration period are required to be increased by the uniform percentage amount. As illustrated in **Table 1**, OMB has calculated a uniform percentage amount of 5.1% for nonexempt nondefense mandatory programs, under the March 1, 2013, sequestration triggered by the BCA. Thus, the 1% origination fee on Direct Subsidized Loans and Direct Unsubsidized Loans and the 4% origination fee on Direct PLUS Loans will each be increased by 5.1%. The Department of Education has announced that it will implement the origination fee increase for loans on which the first disbursement is made on or after July 1, 2013. According to ED, for these loans the loan origination fee will be 1.051% for Direct Subsidized Loans and Direct Unsubsidized Loans, and will be 4.204% for Direct PLUS Loans.[36]

Medicare[37]

Enacted in 1965, the Medicare program provides hospital and supplementary medical insurance to Americans age 65 and older and to certain disabled persons, including those with end-stage renal disease. Medicare enrollment has increased from 19 million in 1966 to about 52 million beneficiaries in FY2013. CBO estimates that by 2023, the number of Medicare enrollees will increase by about a third, to almost 69 million.[38]

Medicare consists of two parts financed through separate trust funds. Hospital Insurance (Part A) pays health care providers for inpatient care that beneficiaries receive at hospitals; it also pays for care at skilled nursing facilities, some home health care, and hospice services. Supplementary Medical Insurance (Parts B and D) pays for physicians' services, outpatient services at hospitals, home health care, and outpatient prescription drugs. (Payments to private insurance plans under Part C are financed by a blend of funds from the two trust funds.) Medicare is administered by the Centers for Medicare & Medicaid Services (CMS), within the Department of Health and Human Services (HHS).

CBO estimates that in FY2013 gross Medicare outlays will reach $592 billion.[39] Most of this spending (about 99%) is comprised of mandatory spending that is primarily used to cover benefit payments (i.e., payments to health care providers for their services). CBO projects that spending

---

[35] For additional information on DL program loans, see CRS Report R40122, *Federal Student Loans Made Under the Federal Family Education Loan Program and the William D. Ford Federal Direct Loan Program: Terms and Conditions for Borrowers*, by David P. Smole.

[36] U.S. Department of Education, Federal Student Aid, Electronic Announcement, "Update: Impact of Sequestration on the Title IV Student Aid Programs," April 5, 2013.

[37] This section was prepared by Patricia Davis, pdavis@crs.loc.gov, 7-7362.

[38] Congressional Budget Office, May 2013 Medicare Baseline, http://www.cbo.gov/sites/default/files/cbofiles/attachments/44205_Medicare_0.pdf.

[39] Congressional Budget Office, May 2013 Medicare Baseline, http://www.cbo.gov/sites/default/files/cbofiles/attachments/44205_Medicare_0.pdf.

---

on Medicare benefits will increase from \$583 billion in FY2013 to about \$1 trillion in FY2023,[40] an annual growth rate of about 6%.

About 0.5% of Medicare mandatory outlays are used for administrative purposes, such as funding quality improvement organizations, for certain activities against fraud and abuse, and payments of Part B premiums for Qualifying Individuals.[41] A small portion of Medicare spending is discretionary (about \$6 billion in FY2013). This portion is used almost entirely for program management activities, such as payments to contractors to process providers' claims, funding for beneficiary outreach and education, and the maintenance of Medicare's information technology (IT) infrastructure.

Sequestration Rules for Medicare

Section 256(d) of BBEDCA contains special rules for the Medicare program in case of a sequestration. However, while BBEDCA ordinarily limits reduction of certain Medicare spending to 4% under a sequestration order (which would apply in the case of a Statutory PAYGO sequestration), the BCA limits the size of this reduction to 2%.

As stated earlier, sequestration requires that all nonexempt programs must be reduced by a uniform percentage. This percentage is calculated by OMB, based on the necessary amount of spending reduction that must occur overall. Under a sequestration triggered by the BCA, if the uniform percentage is less than 2%, it will be applied to all nonexempt accounts, including Medicare. If the percentage is greater than 2%, then a 2% reduction will be made in Medicare spending, and the uniform reduction percentage for the remaining programs will be recalculated and increased by the amount necessary to achieve the total level of reductions needed. If sequestration were triggered by Statutory PAYGO, the process would be the same but Medicare sequestration would be limited to 4%.

As explained earlier in this report, OMB has calculated that the uniform reduction percentage for nondefense mandatory spending under the March 1 BCA sequester is more than 2%; thus, Medicare sequestration is limited to 2% and remaining nondefense mandatory spending is being reduced by 5.1%. CBO estimates that Medicare benefit spending will be reduced by about \$90 billion over the nine-year sequestration period.[42]

Under sequestration, Medicare's benefit structure generally remains unchanged (i.e., beneficiaries will not see a change in their Medicare coverage). Additionally, spending for certain Medicare programs and activities are exempt from sequestration and are therefore not reduced under a sequestration order. These include (1) Part D low-income subsidies;[43] (2) the Part D catastrophic subsidy (reinsurance); and (3) Qualified Individual (QI) premiums.[44]

---

[40] Congressional Budget Office, May 2013 Medicare Baseline, http://www.cbo.gov/sites/default/files/cbofiles/attachments/44205_Medicare_0.pdf.

[41] The Qualifying Individual Program (QI) is one of the Medicare Savings Programs and covers the Part B premium for eligible individuals. To be eligible for the QI program, one must be entitled to Medicare Part A, have an income of at least 120% of the Federal Poverty Level (FPL) but less than 135% of FPL with resources not exceeding twice the limit for SSI eligibility, and not be otherwise eligible for Medicaid benefits. Mandatory funding is provided through 2013.

[42] Congressional Budget Office, May 2013 Medicare Baseline, http://www.cbo.gov/sites/default/files/cbofiles/attachments/44205_Medicare_0.pdf.

[43] See CRS Report R40425, *Medicare Primer*, coordinated by Patricia A. Davis and Scott R. Talaga for an overview of (continued...)

For Medicare Parts A and B services or discharges occurring on or after April 1, 2013, the percentage reductions are to be made to individual payments to providers for services (e.g., hospital and physician services). According to guidance provided by CMS,[45] the provider payment adjustments are to be made to claims after determining coinsurance, any applicable deductible, and any applicable Medicare Secondary Payer adjustments. In other words, the 2% reduction only applies to the portion of the payment paid to providers by Medicare; the beneficiary cost-sharing amounts, and amounts paid by other insurance, are not reduced.[46]

In the case of inpatient services, the services are considered to be furnished on the date of the individual's discharge from the inpatient facility. For services paid on a reasonable cost basis,[47] the reduction is to be applied to payments for such services incurred at any time during each cost reporting period during the sequestration period, for the portion of the cost reporting period that occurs during the effective period of the order. For Part B services provided under assignment,[48] the reduced payment is to be considered *payment in full* and the Medicare beneficiary will not pay higher copayments to make up for the reduced amount.[49]

In the case of Parts C and D, reductions are to be made to the monthly payments to the private plans that administer these parts of Medicare. Reductions are to be made at a uniform rate and are not to exceed 2%. CMS has indicated that Medicare Advantage Organizations (MAOs) and Prescription Drug Plan sponsors may not modify their current benefit or cost-sharing structures, including increasing premiums or cost sharing, to offset lower payments resulting from sequestration.[50] CMS also provided instructions regarding the treatment of contract and non-

(...continued)

the Medicare Part D benefit.

[44] The report issued by OMB in September 2012, pursuant to the Sequestration Transparency Act, indicated that certain additional Medicare-related funds would also be exempt from sequestration under Section 255(g)(1)(A) of BBEDCA. Mandatory spending for Quality Improvement Organizations and discretionary spending for the Office of Medicare Hearings and Appeals would be exempt as intragovernmental payments; and mandatory payments to health care trust funds are specifically listed as exempt in Section 255(g)(1)(A).

[45] CMS, Medicare FFS Provider e-News, March 8, 2013, *Monthly Payment Reductions in the Medicare Fee-for-Service (FFS) Program – "Sequestration,"* http://www.cms.gov/Outreach-and-Education/Outreach/FFSProvPartProg/Downloads/2013-03-08-standalone.pdf.

[46] For example, if the total allowed payment for a particular service is $100 and the beneficiary has a 20% co-pay, the beneficiary would be responsible for paying the provider the full $20 in co-insurance. The remaining 80% that is paid by Medicare would be reduced by 2%; in this instance, $80 minus 2% of $80 ($1.60) would equal $78.40. Therefore, the provider would be paid $20 (beneficiary portion) plus $78.40 (Medicare portion) for a total payment of $98.40.

[47] Most providers are paid under a prospective payment system or fee schedule. Some types of providers, such as Critical Access Hospitals, are paid on a reasonable cost basis under which payments are based on actual costs incurred. Reasonable cost is defined at Social Security Act §1861(v).

[48] Assignment is an agreement by a doctor, provider, or supplier to be paid directly by Medicare, to accept the payment amount Medicare approves for the service, and not to bill the beneficiary for any more than the Medicare deductible and coinsurance (if applicable). Providers that don't accept assignment may charge more than the Medicare-approved amount.

[49] Medicare's payment to beneficiaries for unassigned claims is subject to the 2% payment reduction. See CMS Medicare FFS Provider e-News, March 8, 2013, *Monthly Payment Reductions in the Medicare Fee-for-Service (FFS) Program – "Sequestration"*, http://www.cms.gov/Outreach-and-Education/Outreach/FFSProvPartProg/Downloads/2013-03-08-standalone.pdf.

[50] CMS sequestration guidance to Medicare Advantage organizations and Part D drug plans are contained in a March 22, 2013, memorandum from Cheri Rice of CMS, *Medicare Advantage Prescription Drug System (MARx) April 2013 Payment – Information,* in the section entitled "Mandatory Payment Reductions in the Medicare Advantage and Part D Programs – Sequestration," and a May 1, 2013 memorandum from Cheri Rice and Danielle Moon of CMS entitled *Additional Information Regarding the Mandatory Payment Reductions in the Medicare Advantage, Part D, and Other* (continued...)

contract providers who provide services under Parts C and D. Specifically, "whether and how sequestration might affect an MAO's payments to its contracted providers are governed by the terms of the contract between the MAO and the provider."[51] Similarly, a Part D plan sponsor's payment to its network pharmacy providers is governed by the payment terms in their contracts. Non-contracted providers, however, must accept as payment in full the fee-for-service payment amounts; therefore, MAOs may be able to reduce payments to non-contracted providers by 2%.

Section 256(d) of BBEDCA specifies that the Secretary may not take into account any reductions in payment amounts under sequestration for purposes of computing any adjustments to Medicare payment rates, including the Part C growth percentage, the Part D annual growth rate, and the determination of Medicare Part D risk corridors.[52] In other words, annual provider and plan payment updates are to be determined as if the reductions under sequestration had not taken place.

Special Considerations Regarding Medicare

The budgetary baseline that must be used in implementing a sequestration has special implications with regard to Medicare. For direct spending, the baseline is to be calculated by assuming that the laws providing or creating direct spending will operate in the manner specified, and that funding for entitlement authority is adequate to make all required payments.[53]

Specifically, CBO's May 2013 projections of Medicare spending incorporated the assumption that Medicare spending would be constrained beginning in 2014 by the sustainable growth rate (SGR) mechanism used to calculate the fees paid for physicians' services.[54] Those fees are scheduled to be reduced by about 24% beginning in January 2014 and by additional amounts in subsequent years; however, in prior years Congress has almost always taken action to prevent these cuts from occurring. CBO estimates that it would cost at least $139 billion over the next 10 years to eliminate these reductions.[55]

There have been some concerns that although Medicare benefits are not to be reduced under sequestration, reductions in provider payments could discourage some providers from accepting Medicare patients. For instance, there have been reports of cancer clinics turning away Medicare patients because of the impact of sequestration on Medicare's reimbursement for chemotherapy drugs.[56] Additionally, there is concern that costs could be shifted to other third-party payers or

---

(...continued)

Programs.

[51] May 1, 2013, memorandum from Cheri Rice and Danielle Moon, CMS, *Additional Information Regarding the Mandatory Payment Reductions in the Medicare Advantage, Part D, and Other Programs.*

[52] Information on Medicare provider payments and the determination of updates may be found in CRS Report RL30526, *Medicare Payment Updates and Payment Rates*, coordinated by Paulette C. Morgan.

[53] BBEDCA §257(b)(1).

[54] See CRS Report R40907, *Medicare Physician Payment Updates and the Sustainable Growth Rate (SGR) System*, by Jim Hahn and Janemarie Mulvey.

[55] Congressional Budget Office, *An Analysis of the President's 2014 Budget*, May 2013, p. 10, http://www.cbo.gov/sites/default/files/cbofiles/attachments/44173-APB_0.pdf.

[56] For example, see the Community Oncology Alliance statement at http://www.communityoncology.org/site/blog/detail/2013/05/09/may-9-2013-sequestration-cuts-threaten-seniors-au-cancer-care-while-increasing-medicare-costs.html.

---

beneficiaries to make up for the additional decrease in payments. For instance, private payers could see increased costs or Medicare Advantage or Prescription Drug Sponsors could design their plans in future years so that Medicare enrollees pay higher premiums and/or increased cost sharing. Finally, some of the administrative functions, including fraud and abuse and quality oversight activities, that do not qualify as "Medicare benefits" are subject to reductions higher than 2% (5.0% and 5.1% for discretionary and mandatory funding respectively in FY2013). There is some concern that reduced funding for such activities could result in increased costs to the program and/or reduced quality of care.

Health Centers, Indian Health, and Veterans' Medical Care

Health Centers[57]

Community and migrant health centers are two types of federally funded health centers: nonprofit entities that receive grants to provide primary care to people who experience financial, geographic, cultural, or other barriers to health care. They are administered by the Health Resources and Services Administration (HRSA) within the Department of Health and Human Services (HHS). In addition to these two types of health centers, HRSA provides grants to support health centers for the homeless and health centers for residents of public housing.

Section 256(e) of BBEDCA limits the amount of funding that can be reduced from community and migrant health centers under a sequestration to 2%. At the time of BBEDCA's enactment in 1985, there were four separate health center programs administered by HRSA and funded under HRSA's budget account. The Health Centers Consolidation Act of 1996 (P.L. 104-299) combined the four health center programs—community health centers, migrant health centers, health centers for the homeless, and health centers for residents of public housing—into Section 330 of the Public Health Service Act, which receives a single discretionary appropriation as part of the HRSA budget.

With regard to the sequester that took effect March 1, 2013, OMB determined that this special rule for community and migrant health centers applies only to mandatory health center funds (i.e., funds appropriated for the health center program under the ACA from FY2011 through FY2015).[58] It further determined that the 2% limit applies to that portion (90.1%) of the mandatory appropriation that is allocated specifically for community and migrant health centers. The remaining 9.9% of the mandatory appropriation and the discretionary portion of health centers funding is subject to the full sequestration amount (5.1% for nondefense mandatory and 5.0% for nondefense discretionary spending).

---

[57] This section was prepared by Elayne Heisler, eheisler@crs.loc.gov, 7-4453. For more information on health centers, see CRS Report R42433, *Federal Health Centers*, by Elayne J. Heisler.

[58] See discussion on pp. 4-5 of *OMB Report Pursuant to the Sequestration Transparency Act*, September 2012. For information on these funds, see CRS Report R41301, *Appropriations and Fund Transfers in the Patient Protection and Affordable Care Act (ACA)*, by C. Stephen Redhead.

Indian Health Service[59]

The Indian Health Service (IHS) in HHS is responsible for providing comprehensive medical and environmental health services for approximately 2.0 million American Indians and Alaska Natives who belong to 566 federally recognized tribes.[60] Health care is provided through a system of facilities and programs operated by IHS, tribes and tribal groups, and urban Indian organizations. IHS is funded by two discretionary budget accounts—Indian Health Services and Indian Health Facilities. However, IHS also receives reimbursements from Medicare, Medicaid, and CHIP for services provided at IHS facilities for beneficiaries eligible for these programs, and IHS also receives mandatory appropriations for diabetes programs.[61]

Under Section 256(e) of BBEDCA, sequestration may only reduce funding for the two IHS accounts by 2% in any fiscal year. With regard to the sequester that took effect on March 1, 2013, however, OMB determined that this special rule (i.e., the 2% limit) applies only to mandatory funds that IHS receives (i.e., diabetes program funding). The IHS discretionary appropriation thus is fully sequestrable.[62] OMB did not include reimbursements that IHS receives from other federal programs, or rent that IHS receives from renting staff quarters in the amount that could be sequestered from the IHS budget (i.e., it exempted these amounts from sequestration).

Veterans' Medical Care[63]

The VA, through the Veterans Health Administration (VHA), operates the nation's largest integrated direct health care delivery system.[64] Veterans' medical care is a discretionary program, and eligibility for VA medical care is based on veteran status, presence of service-connected disabilities or exposures, income, and/or other factors, such as status as a former prisoner of war or receipt of a Purple Heart.[65]

Under current law, and as originally enacted, Section 256(e) of BBEDCA allows a maximum 2% reduction in budget authority for VA medical care for any fiscal year. However, Section 255 of BBEDCA, as amended in 2010 (P.L. 111-139), specifically excludes from sequestration *all* programs administered by the VA, which includes veterans' medical care. This apparent discrepancy between the two sections of the law raised questions about whether VA will be totally exempt from sequestration or whether medical care will be subject to a maximum permissible 2% reduction in budget authority, under a BCA-triggered sequestration. On April 23, 2012, OMB issued a letter stating that "all programs administered by the VA, including Veterans' Medical

---

[59] This section was prepared by Elayne Heisler, eheisler@crs.loc.gov, 7-4453.

[60] Department of Health and Human Services, Indian Health Service, "IHS Year 2013 Profile," January 2013, http://www.ihs.gov/factsheets/index.cfm?module=dsp_fact_profile.

[61] Appropriated under P.L. 111-309.

[62] See discussion on pages 4 and 5 of *OMB Report Pursuant to the Sequestration Transparency Act*, September 2012.

[63] This section was prepared by Sidath Panangala, spanangala@crs.loc.gov, 7-0623.

[64] U.S. Department of Veterans Affairs, *FY 2010 Performance and Accountability Report*, Washington, DC, November 17, 2008, p. I-20. Established on January 3, 1946, as the Department of Medicine and Surgery by P.L. 79-293, succeeded in 1989 by the Veterans Health Services and Research Administration, renamed the Veterans Health Administration in 1991.

[65] For more information on eligibility for VA health care, see CRS Report R42747, *Health Care for Veterans: Answers to Frequently Asked Questions*, by Sidath Viranga Panangala and Erin Bagalman.

Care, are exempt from sequestration under Section 255(b)."[66] In its report issued pursuant to the Sequestration Transparency Act, OMB further clarified that administration accounts (which include, among others, construction projects, general administration, and information technology systems) are exempt.[67] In other words, all accounts of the Department of Veterans Affairs are exempt from sequestration.

Child Support Enforcement[68]

The Child Support Enforcement (CSE) program is a mandatory spending program that seeks to enhance the well-being of children by obtaining child support, including financial and medical support, from noncustodial parents through services and activities that locate noncustodial parents, establish paternity, establish child support obligations, and collect and monitor child support payments. The CSE program is a federal-state program, administered by HHS. The federal government reimburses each state for 66% of all expenditures on CSE activities and also provides states with an incentive payment to encourage them to operate effective CSE programs.

Section 256(f) of BBEDCA stipulates that any required reduction in CSE program expenditures or CSE incentive payments must be accomplished by reducing the federal matching rate for state CSE program costs. However, subsequent to enactment of this provision, Section 255 was amended (in 1997, by P.L. 105-33), and specifically excludes from sequestration Family Support Programs, which include the CSE program.

Federal Pay[69]

In general, for purposes of sequestration, Section 256(g) provides that federal pay under a statutory pay system—the General Schedule (GS), Foreign Service (FS) pay schedule, and Department of Medicine and Surgery at the Department of Veterans Affairs (VA) pay schedule—is subject to reduction in the same manner as other administrative expense components of the federal budget (see "Federal Administrative Expenses," immediately below).[70] Likewise, elements of military pay[71] are subject to such reduction. Such an order may not, however, reduce or have the effect of reducing the rate of pay an employee is entitled to under the GS, FS, or VA pay systems or any increase in special pay rates authorized by 5 U.S.C. Section 5305. The order also may not reduce or have the effect of reducing the rate of any element of military pay an

---

[66] Letter from Steven D. Aitken, Deputy General Counsel Office of Management and Budget (OMB), to Julia C. Matta, Assistant General Counsel for Appropriations and Budget, U.S. Government Accountability Office, April 23, 2012, http://www.murray.senate.gov/public/_cache/files/f8868d52-eec0-43a5-b5c8-9cecbff4596e/VASequesterQuestion.pdf.

[67] *OMB Report Pursuant to the Sequestration Transparency Act,* September 2012, pp. 160-165.

[68] This section was prepared by Carmen Solomon-Fears, csolomonfears@crs.loc.gov, 7-7306.

[69] This section was prepared by Barbara Schwemle, bschwemle@crs.loc.gov, 7-8655.

[70] Budgetary resources available for federal pay, which are subject to sequestration as part of the reduction of administrative expenses, are detailed in the September 2012 OMB report issued pursuant to the Sequestration Transparency Act under the "Salaries and Expenses" function for each account.

[71] The term "elements of military pay" means the monthly basic pay adjustments for members of the uniformed services authorized by 37 U.S.C. §1009, allowances provided to members of the uniformed services under 37 U.S.C. §§403a and 405, and cadet pay and midshipman pay under 37 U.S.C. §203(c). The term "uniformed services" means the Army, Navy, Air Force, Marine Corps, Coast Guard, National Oceanic and Atmospheric Administration, and Public Health Service.

individual is entitled to or any increase in rates of pay authorized by 37 U.S.C. Section 1009, or any other provision of law.

The conference report (H. Rept. 99-433) that accompanied the original BBEDCA explained the provision as follows:

> The conference agreement provides that rates of pay for civilian employees (and rates of basic pay, basic subsistence allowances and basic quarters allowances for members of the uniformed services) may not be reduced pursuant to a sequestration order. The agreement retains the House position that a scheduled pay increase may not be reduced pursuant to an order and the Federal pay be treated as other components of administrative expenses. The conferees urge program managers to employ all other options available to them in order to achieve savings required under a sequestration order and resort to personnel furloughs only if other methods prove insufficient.[72]

An employee may experience a pay cut when placed "in a temporary nonduty, nonpay status because of lack of work or funds, or other nondisciplinary reasons." This action occurs under an administrative furlough that "is a planned event by an agency which is designed to absorb reductions necessitated by downsizing, reduced funding, lack of work, or any other budget situation other than a lapse in appropriations."[73]

In another matter related to federal pay, an OMB Memorandum issued by Controller Danny Werfel on February 27, 2013, advised executive department and agency heads that "issuing discretionary monetary awards to employees ... should occur only if legally required until further notice."[74]

Federal Administrative Expenses[75]

In general, under Section 256(h) of BBEDCA, federal administrative expenses are subject to sequestration, regardless of whether they are incurred in connection with a program, project, activity, or account that is otherwise exempt or subject to a special rule.[76] As an example, while Supplemental Security Income (SSI) is exempt from sequestration, the federal administrative expenses associated with this program would generally not be exempt. With regard to the sequester that took effect on March 1, 2013, however, OMB determined that the special rule for federal administrative expenses applies only to mandatory funds and not discretionary funds.[77] This means, according to OMB, that mandatory administrative expenses for an otherwise exempt

---

[72] *Congressional Record*, vol. 131, December 10, 1985, p. 35776.

[73] U.S. Office of Personnel Management, *Guidance for Administrative Furloughs* (Washington: OPM, March 8, 2013), p. 1, available at http://www.opm.gov/policy-data-oversight/pay-leave/furlough-guidance/guidance-for-administrative-furloughs.pdf. See especially the section on "Pay," which begins on p. 5.

[74] U.S. Office of Management and Budget, Memorandum for Executive Department and Agency Heads from Danny Werfel, Controller, *Agency Responsibilities for Implementation of Potential Joint Committee Sequestration*, M-13-05, February 27, 2013, p. 3, available at http://www.whitehouse.gov/sites/default/files/omb/memoranda/2013/m-13-05.pdf.

[75] The BBEDCA does not define administrative expenses. For purposes of the March 1 sequestration, OMB states that "'administrative expenses' for typical government programs are defined as the object classes for personnel compensation, travel, transportation, communication, equipment, supplies, materials, and other services."

[76] The statute lists several federal financial services entities that would not be covered by this section (e.g., Comptroller of the Currency, Federal Deposit Insurance Corporation, and others).

[77] See discussion on pp. 4-5 of *OMB Report Pursuant to the Sequestration Transparency Act*, September 2012, or p. 2 of *OMB Report to the Congress on the Joint Committee Sequestration for Fiscal Year 2013*, March 1, 2013.

program are subject to sequestration, but that discretionary administrative expenses for an exempt program are not. Therefore, since federal administrative expenses for SSI are discretionary (although program benefits are mandatory), they are not subject to sequestration under the Joint Committee-triggered automatic reduction provisions, despite the special rule described above.[78]

Section 256 also states that federal payments to state and local governments that match or reimburse these governments for their administrative costs are not considered "federal administrative expenses" and are subject to sequestration *only* to the extent that the relevant federal program is subject to sequestration. In other words, if a program is exempt under Section 255, then federal payments to states for the costs of administering that program also are exempt. (However, certain unemployment compensation payments are not covered by this provision, as noted below.)

Unemployment Compensation[79]

Section 256(i) of BBEDCA reiterates the exemption from sequestration (provided under Section 255) of federal loans to the states for payment of unemployment benefits. Additionally, Section 256(i) exempts regular unemployment compensation (UC) benefits from sequestration. This exemption is extended to UC for former federal workers (UCFE) and UC for former servicemembers (UCX). Generally, these benefits have a duration of up to 26 weeks and are paid by state unemployment taxes. However, Section 256 specifically does not exempt administrative grants to the states and the federal share of the permanently authorized extended benefit (EB) program from sequestration. States are required to continue to pay their share of EB payments. If a state's unemployment insurance law allows it, the state may reduce the EB benefit amount by a percentage that does not exceed the percentage by which the federal share of EB has been reduced. The authorization of the temporary emergency unemployment compensation (EUC08) benefit ends at the end of calendar year 2013; the EUC08 benefit is subject to sequestration.[80]

On March 8, 2013, the U.S. Department of Labor released the details on how the sequester reductions to administrative grants, unemployment benefits, and other types of unemployment benefit expenditures will occur.[81] The reductions to UI expenditures will generally begin the week beginning on or after March 31, 2013. No unemployment benefits already paid to individuals will be recovered to satisfy the sequestration reductions.

Commodity Credit Corporation[82]

The Commodity Credit Corporation (CCC) is the funding mechanism for the mandatory spending of the U.S. Department of Agriculture (USDA) for farm commodity support and certain conservation programs. The CCC is a wholly owned government corporation that has the legal

---

[78] For more discussion of administrative expenses of the Social Security Administration, which administers the SSI program, see the section titled "Sequestration of SSA Administrative Funds" in CRS Report R41716, *Social Security Administration (SSA): Budget Issues*, by Scott Szymendera.

[79] This section was prepared by Julie Whittaker, jwhittaker@crs.loc.gov, 7-2587.

[80] For more information, see section headed "Unemployment Benefits and the Sequester" in CRS Report R42936, *Unemployment Insurance: Legislative Issues in the 113th Congress*, by Julie M. Whittaker and Katelin P. Isaacs.

[81] Employment and Training Administration, U.S. Department of Labor, Unemployment Insurance Program Letter (UIPL) 13-13, March 8, 2013, http://wdr.doleta.gov/directives/attach/UIPL/UIPL_13_013_Acc.pdf.

[82] This section was prepared by Jim Monke, jmonke@crs.loc.gov, 7-9664.

authority to borrow up to $30 billion at any one time from the U.S. Treasury. Its borrowing authority is replenished annually in the Agriculture appropriations bill by a "such sums as are necessary" appropriation. Most spending for these programs was authorized by the 2008 farm bill (P.L. 110-246).

Section 256(j) says that sequestration should not restrict the CCC's authority to discharge its primary duties. Specifically, it states that commodity loan contracts entered into before the sequestration order shall not be reduced.[83] Section 256 says, though, that loan contracts after the sequestration order shall be reduced. The farm commodity programs have evolved to include other support mechanisms than the loan program, and the loan program is no longer the primary outlay.

In fact, the Joint Committee sequestration applies to many CCC-funded programs, including the direct payment program, disaster payments, the Milk Income Loss Contract (MILC) program, and conservation programs (except the Conservation Reserve Program), as well as other farm bill programs that use CCC funds.[84] Outlays of the federal crop insurance program are not funded under the CCC but instead have their own mandatory funding mechanism, addressed in Section 255, that exempts the prior legal obligations of the Federal Crop Insurance Fund from sequestration.

---

[83] Commodity loans are one part of the farm support program that makes government loans to farmers at farm-bill specified support prices per unit of commodity. Farmers can use these loans as financing to pay their expenses and, if market prices are below the support price, can benefit financially by the difference between the support price and the market price.

[84] See section titled "Budget Sequestration" in CRS Report R42484, *Budget Issues Shaping a Farm Bill in 2013*, by Jim Monke.

     17-23

Appendix. Section 255 of the Balanced Budget and Emergency Deficit Control Act, as Amended

SEC. 255. (2 U.S.C. 905) EXEMPT PROGRAMS AND ACTIVITIES.

(a) SOCIAL SECURITY BENEFITS AND TIER I RAILROAD RETIREMENT

BENEFITS.—Benefits payable under the old-age, survivors, and disability insurance program established under title II of the Social Security Act (42 U.S.C. 401 et seq.), and benefits payable under section 231b(a), 231b(f)(2), 231c(a), and 231c(f) of title 45 United States Code, shall be exempt from reduction under any order issued under this part.

(b) VETERANS PROGRAMS.—The following programs shall be exempt from reduction under any order issued under this part:

All programs administered by the Department of Veterans Affairs.

Special Benefits for Certain World War II Veterans (28–0401–0–1–701).

(c) NET INTEREST.—No reduction of payments for net interest (all of major functional category 900) shall be made under any order issued under this part.

(d) REFUNDABLE INCOME TAX CREDITS.—Payments to individuals made pursuant to provisions of the Internal Revenue Code of 1986 establishing refundable tax credits shall be exempt from reduction under any order issued under this part.

(e) NON-DEFENSE UNOBLIGATED BALANCES.—Unobligated balances of budget authority carried over from prior fiscal years, except balances in the defense category, shall be exempt from reduction under any order issued under this part.

(f) OPTIONAL EXEMPTION OF MILITARY PERSONNEL.—

(1) IN GENERAL.—The President may, with respect to any military personnel account, exempt that account from sequestration or provide for a lower uniform percentage reduction than would otherwise apply.

(2) LIMITATION.—The President may not use the authority provided by paragraph (1) unless the President notifies the Congress of the manner in which such authority will be exercised on or before the date specified in section 254(a) for the budget year.

(g) OTHER PROGRAMS AND ACTIVITIES.—

(1)(A) The following budget accounts and activities shall be exempt from reduction under any order issued under this part:

Activities resulting from private donations, bequests, or voluntary contributions to the Government.

Activities financed by voluntary payments to the Government for goods or services to be provided for such payments.

Administration of Territories, Northern Mariana Islands Covenant grants (14–0412–0–1–808).

Advances to the Unemployment Trust Fund and Other Funds (16–0327–0–1–600).

Black Lung Disability Trust Fund Refinancing (16–0329–0–1–601).

Bonneville Power Administration Fund and borrowing authority established pursuant to section 13 of Public Law 93–454 (1974), as amended (89–4045–0–3–271).

Claims, Judgments, and Relief Acts (20–1895–0–1–808).

Compact of Free Association (14–0415–0–1–808).

Compensation of the President (11–0209–01–1–802).

Comptroller of the Currency, Assessment Funds (20–8413–0–8–373).

Continuing Fund, Southeastern Power Administration (89–5653–0–2–271).

Continuing Fund, Southwestern Power Administration (89–5649–0–2–271).

Dual Benefits Payments Account (60–0111–0–1–601).

Emergency Fund, Western Area Power Administration (89–5069–0–2–271).

Exchange Stabilization Fund (20–4444–0–3–155).

Farm Credit Administration Operating Expenses Fund (78–4131–0–3–351).

Farm Credit System Insurance Corporation, Farm Credit Insurance Fund (78–4171–0–3–351).

Federal Deposit Insurance Corporation, Deposit Insurance Fund (51–4596–0–4–373).

Federal Deposit Insurance Corporation, FSLIC Resolution Fund (51–4065–0–3–373).

Federal Deposit Insurance Corporation, Noninterest Bearing Transaction Account Guarantee (51–4458–0–3–373).

Federal Deposit Insurance Corporation, Senior Unsecured Debt Guarantee (51–4457–0–3–373).

Federal Home Loan Mortgage Corporation (Freddie Mac).

Federal Housing Finance Agency, Administrative Expenses (95–5532–0–2–371).

Federal National Mortgage Corporation (Fannie Mae).

Federal Payment to the District of Columbia Judicial Retirement and Survivors Annuity Fund (20–1713–0–1–752).

Federal Payment to the District of Columbia Pension Fund (20–1714–0–1–601).

Federal Payments to the Railroad Retirement Accounts (60–0113–0–1–601).

Federal Reserve Bank Reimbursement Fund (20–1884–0–1–803).

Financial Agent Services (20–1802–0–1–803).

Foreign Military Sales Trust Fund (11–8242–0–7–155).

Hazardous Waste Management, Conservation Reserve Program (12–4336–0–3–999).

Host Nation Support Fund for Relocation (97–8337–0–7–051).

Internal Revenue Collections for Puerto Rico (20–5737–0–2–806).

Intragovernmental funds, including those from which the outlays are derived primarily from resources paid in from other government accounts, except to the extent such funds are augmented by direct appropriations for the fiscal year during which an order is in effect.

Medical Facilities Guarantee and Loan Fund (75–9931–0–3–551).

National Credit Union Administration, Central Liquidity Facility (25–4470–0–3–373).

National Credit Union Administration, Corporate Credit Union Share Guarantee Program (25–4476–0–3–376).

National Credit Union Administration, Credit Union Homeowners Affordability Relief Program (25–4473–0–3–371).

National Credit Union Administration, Credit Union Share Insurance Fund (25–4468–0–3–373).

National Credit Union Administration, Credit Union System Investment Program (25–4474–0–3–376).

National Credit Union Administration, Operating fund (25–4056–0–3–373).

National Credit Union Administration, Share Insurance Fund Corporate Debt Guarantee Program (25–4469–0–3–376).

National Credit Union Administration, U.S. Central Federal Credit Union Capital Program (25–4475–0–3–376).

Office of Thrift Supervision (20–4108–0–3–373).

Panama Canal Commission Compensation Fund (16–5155–0–2–602).

Payment of Vietnam and USS Pueblo prisoner-of-war claims within the Salaries and Expenses, Foreign Claims Settlement account (15–0100–0–1–153).

Payment to Civil Service Retirement and Disability Fund (24–0200–0–1–805).

Payment to Department of Defense Medicare-Eligible Retiree Health Care Fund (97–0850–0–1–054).

Payment to Judiciary Trust Funds (10–0941–0–1–752).

Payment to Military Retirement Fund (97–0040–0–1–054).

Payment to the Foreign Service Retirement and Disability Fund (19–0540–0–1–153).

Payments to Copyright Owners (03–5175–0–2–376).

Payments to Health Care Trust Funds (75–0580–0–1–571).

Payment to Radiation Exposure Compensation Trust Fund (15–0333–0–1–054).

Payments to Social Security Trust Funds (28–0404–0–1–651).

Payments to the United States Territories, Fiscal Assistance (14–0418–0–1–806).

Payments to trust funds from excise taxes or other receipts properly creditable to such trust funds.

Payments to widows and heirs of deceased Members of Congress (00–0215–0–1–801).

Postal Service Fund (18–4020–0–3–372).

Radiation Exposure Compensation Trust Fund (15–8116–0–1–054).

Reimbursement to Federal Reserve Banks (20–0562–0–1–803).

Salaries of Article III judges.

Soldiers and Airmen's Home, payment of claims (84–8930–0–7–705).

Tennessee Valley Authority Fund, except nonpower programs and activities (64–4110–0–3–999).

Tribal and Indian trust accounts within the Department of the Interior which fund prior legal obligations of the Government or which are established pursuant to Acts of Congress regarding Federal management of tribal real property or other fiduciary responsibilities, including but not limited to Tribal Special Fund (14–5265–0–2–452),

Tribal Trust Fund (14–8030–0–7–452),

White Earth Settlement (14–2204–0–1–452), and Indian Water Rights and Habitat Acquisition (14–5505–0–2–303).

United Mine Workers of America 1992 Benefit Plan (95–8260–0–7–551).

United Mine Workers of America 1993 Benefit Plan (95–8535–0–7–551).

United Mine Workers of America Combined Benefit Fund (95–8295–0–7–551).

United States Enrichment Corporation Fund (95–4054–0–3–271).

Universal Service Fund (27–5183–0–2–376).

Vaccine Injury Compensation (75–0320–0–1–551).

Vaccine Injury Compensation Program Trust Fund (20–8175–0–7–551).

(B) The following Federal retirement and disability accounts and activities shall be exempt from reduction under any order issued under this part:

Black Lung Disability Trust Fund (20–8144–0–7–601).

Central Intelligence Agency Retirement and Disability System Fund (56–3400–0–1–054).

Civil Service Retirement and Disability Fund (24–8135–0–7–602).

17-27

Budget "Sequestration" and Selected Program Exemptions and Special Rules

Comptrollers general retirement system (05–0107–0–1–801).

Contributions to U.S. Park Police annuity benefits, Other Permanent Appropriations (14–9924–0–2–303).

Court of Appeals for Veterans Claims Retirement Fund (95–8290–0–7–705).

Department of Defense Medicare-Eligible Retiree Health Care Fund (97–5472–0–2–551).

District of Columbia Federal Pension Fund (20–5511–0–2–601).

District of Columbia Judicial Retirement and Survivors Annuity Fund (20–8212–0–7–602).

Energy Employees Occupational Illness Compensation Fund (16–1523–0–1–053).

Foreign National Employees Separation Pay (97–8165–0–7–051).

Foreign Service National Defined Contributions Retirement Fund (19–5497–0–2–602).

Foreign Service National Separation Liability Trust Fund (19–8340–0–7–602).

Foreign Service Retirement and Disability Fund (19–8186–0–7–602).

Government Payment for Annuitants, Employees Health Benefits (24–0206–0–1–551).

Government Payment for Annuitants, Employee Life Insurance (24–0500–0–1–602).

Judicial Officers' Retirement Fund (10–8122–0–7–602).

Judicial Survivors' Annuities Fund (10–8110–0–7–602).

Military Retirement Fund (97–8097–0–7–602).

National Railroad Retirement Investment Trust (60–8118–0–7–601).

National Oceanic and Atmospheric Administration retirement (13–1450–0–1–306).

Pensions for former Presidents (47–0105–0–1–802).

Postal Service Retiree Health Benefits Fund (24–5391–0–2–551).

Public Safety Officer Benefits (15–0403–0–1–754).

Rail Industry Pension Fund (60–8011–0–7–601).

Retired Pay, Coast Guard (70–0602–0–1–403).

Retirement Pay and Medical Benefits for Commissioned Officers, Public Health Service (75–0379–0–1–551).

Special Benefits for Disabled Coal Miners (16–0169–0–1–601).

Special Benefits, Federal Employees' Compensation Act (16–1521–0–1–600).

Special Workers Compensation Expenses (16–9971–0–7–601).

Congressional Research Service   25

Tax Court Judges Survivors Annuity Fund (23–8115–0–7–602).

United States Court of Federal Claims Judges' Retirement Fund (10–8124–0–7–602).

United States Secret Service, DC Annuity (70–0400–0–1–751).

Voluntary Separation Incentive Fund (97–8335–0–7–051).

(2) Prior legal obligations of the Government in the following budget accounts and activities shall be exempt from any order issued under this part:

Biomass Energy Development (20–0114–0–1–271).

Check Forgery Insurance Fund (20–4109–0–3–803).

Credit liquidating accounts.

Credit reestimates.

Employees Life Insurance Fund (24–8424–0–8–602).

Federal Aviation Insurance Revolving Fund (69–4120– 0–3–402).

Federal Crop Insurance Corporation Fund (12–4085–0–3–351).

Federal Emergency Management Agency, National Flood Insurance Fund (58–4236–0–3–453).

Geothermal resources development fund (89–0206–0–1–271).

Low-Rent Public Housing—Loans and Other Expenses (86–4098–0–3–604).

Maritime Administration, War Risk Insurance Revolving Fund (69–4302–0–3–403).

Natural Resource Damage Assessment Fund (14–1618–0–1–302).

Overseas Private Investment Corporation, Noncredit Account (71–4184–0–3–151).

Pension Benefit Guaranty Corporation Fund (16–4204–0–3–601).

San Joaquin Restoration Fund (14–5537–0–2–301).

Servicemembers' Group Life Insurance Fund (36–4009–0–3–701).

Terrorism Insurance Program (20–0123–0–1–376).

(h) LOW-INCOME PROGRAMS.—The following programs shall be exempt from reduction under any order issued under this part:

Academic Competitiveness/Smart Grant Program (91–0205–0–1–502).

Child Care Entitlement to States (75–1550–0–1–609).

Child Enrollment Contingency Fund (75–5551–0–2–551).

Child Nutrition Programs (with the exception of special milk programs) (12–3539–0–1–605).

Children's Health Insurance Fund (75–0515–0–1–551).

Commodity Supplemental Food Program (12–3507–0–1–605).

Contingency Fund (75–1522–0–1–609).

Family Support Programs (75–1501–0–1–609).

Federal Pell Grants under section 401 Title IV of the Higher Education Act.

Grants to States for Medicaid (75–0512–0–1–551).

Payments for Foster Care and Permanency (75–1545–0–1–609).

Supplemental Nutrition Assistance Program (12–3505–0–1–605).

Supplemental Security Income Program (28–0406–0–1–609).

Temporary Assistance for Needy Families (75–1552–0–1–609).

(i) ECONOMIC RECOVERY PROGRAMS.—The following programs shall be exempt from reduction under any order issued under this part:

GSE Preferred Stock Purchase Agreements (20–0125–0–1–371).

Office of Financial Stability (20–0128–0–1–376).

Special Inspector General for the Troubled Asset Relief Program (20–0133–0–1–376).

(j) SPLIT TREATMENT PROGRAMS.—Each of the following programs shall be exempt from any order under this part to the extent that the budgetary resources of such programs are subject to obligation limitations in appropriations bills:

Federal-Aid Highways (69–8083–0–7–401).

Highway Traffic Safety Grants (69–8020–0–7–401).

Operations and Research NHTSA and National Driver Register (69–8016–0–7–401).

Motor Carrier Safety Operations and Programs (69–8159–0–7–401).

Motor Carrier Safety Grants (69–8158–0–7–401).

Formula and Bus Grants (69–8350–0–7–401).

Grants-In-Aid for Airports (69–8106–0–7–402).

(j) IDENTIFICATION OF PROGRAMS.—For purposes of subsections (b), (g), and (h), each account is identified by the designated budget account identification code number set forth in the Budget of the United States Government 2010–Appendix, and an activity within an account is designated by the name of the activity and the identification code number of the account.

Congressional Research Service   27

SEC. 256. (2 U.S.C. 906) [excerpt]

(7) EXEMPTIONS FROM SEQUESTRATION.—In addition to the programs and activities specified in section 255, the following shall be exempt from sequestration under this part:

(A) PART D LOW-INCOME SUBSIDIES.—Premium and cost-sharing subsidies under section 1860D–14 of the Social Security Act.

(B) PART D CATASTROPHIC SUBSIDY.—Payments under section 1860D–15(b) and (e)(2)(B) of the Social Security Act.

(C) QUALIFIED INDIVIDUAL (QI) PREMIUMS.—Payments to States for coverage of Medicare cost-sharing for certain low-income Medicare beneficiaries under section 1933 of the Social Security Act.

Author Contact Information

Karen Spar, Coordinator
Specialist in Domestic Social Policy and Division
Research Coordinator
kspar@crs.loc.gov, 7-7319

Patricia A. Davis
Specialist in Health Care Financing
pdavis@crs.loc.gov, 7-7362

Elayne J. Heisler
Analyst in Health Services
eheisler@crs.loc.gov, 7-4453

Jim Monke
Specialist in Agricultural Policy
jmonke@crs.loc.gov, 7-9664

Sidath Viranga Panangala
Specialist in Veterans Policy
spanangala@crs.loc.gov, 7-0623

Barbara L. Schwemle
Analyst in American National Government
bschwemle@crs.loc.gov, 7-8655

David P. Smole
Specialist in Education Policy
dsmole@crs.loc.gov, 7-0624

Carmen Solomon-Fears
Specialist in Social Policy
csolomonfears@crs.loc.gov, 7-7306

Julie M. Whittaker
Specialist in Income Security
jwhittaker@crs.loc.gov, 7-2587

Acknowledgments

The coordinator of this report appreciates the helpful comments received from Bill Heniff Jr., Analyst on Congress and the Legislative Process, and Todd Tatelman, former Legislative Attorney at CRS.

17-31

Congressional
Research Service
Informing the legislative debate since 1914

Continuing Resolutions: Overview of Components and Recent Practices

James V. Saturno
Specialist on Congress and the Legislative Process

Jessica Tollestrup
Specialist on Congress and the Legislative Process

January 14, 2016

Congressional Research Service
7-5700
www.crs.gov
R42647

Summary

Congress uses an annual appropriations process to fund the routine activities of most federal agencies. This process anticipates the completion of 12 *regular appropriations bills* to fund these activities before the beginning of the fiscal year. Over the past half century, the timing of congressional action on regular appropriations bills has varied considerably, but enactment after the start of the fiscal year has been a recurring issue. Until regular appropriations for a fiscal year are enacted, one or more continuing appropriations acts (commonly known as *continuing resolutions* or CRs) can be used to provide funding for a specified period of time.

Under recent congressional practice, CRs typically include as many as six main components. First, CRs provide funding for certain activities, which are typically specified with reference to the prior fiscal year's appropriations acts. This is referred to in this report as the CR's *coverage*. Second, CRs provide budget authority for a specified *duration* of time. This duration may be as short as a single day or as long as the remainder of the fiscal year. Third, CRs typically provide funds based on an overall *funding rate*. Fourth, the use of budget authority provided in the CR is typically prohibited for *new activities* not funded in the previous fiscal year. Fifth, the duration and amount of funds in the CR, and purposes for which they may be used for specified activities, may be adjusted through *anomalies*. Sixth, *legislative provisions*—which create, amend, or extend other laws—have been included in some instances.

Between FY1977 and FY2016 (excluding the four fiscal years in which all appropriations were enacted on time), over half of the regular appropriations bills for a fiscal year were enacted on time in only one instance (FY1978). In all other fiscal years, fewer than six regular appropriations acts were enacted on or before October 1. In addition, in 14 out of the 40 years during this period, none of these regular appropriations bills were enacted prior to the start of the fiscal year. Nine of these fiscal years have occurred in the interval since FY2001. For further information, see **Table 1**.

In the interval since FY1997—the most recent fiscal year that all regular appropriations bills were completed on time—CRs have been enacted on average almost six times per fiscal year. During this period, CRs provided funding for an average of almost five months each fiscal year. For further information, see **Table 2** and **Figure 1**.

Congress has employed full-year CRs on a number of occasions. For each of the 11 fiscal years covering FY1978-FY1988, Congress enacted a full-year CR covering at least one regular appropriations act. Three years later, Congress enacted another full-year CR for FY1992. Most recently, full-year CRs were enacted for FY2007, FY2011, and FY2013. The budget authority in these full-year CRs was also provided in different forms. The 10 full-year CRs for FY1980 through FY1984, FY1992, FY2007, FY2011, and FY2013 included formulaic provisions that provided funding for at least one of the covered appropriations acts. The full-year CRs for FY1985 through FY1988, by contrast, did not use formulaic provisions but instead specified amounts for each account. For further information, see **Table 3**.

For a list of all continuing resolutions enacted since FY1977, see **Table 4** at the end of this report.

This report will be updated after the annual appropriations process for a fiscal year has concluded.

Contents

Figures

Tables

Contacts

Introduction

Congress uses an annual appropriations process to fund the routine activities of most federal agencies.[1] This process anticipates the enactment of 12 *regular appropriations bills* to fund these activities before the beginning of the fiscal year.[2] When this process is delayed beyond the start of the fiscal year, one or more continuing appropriations acts (commonly known as *continuing resolutions* or CRs)[3] can be used to provide funding until action on regular appropriations is completed.

Over the past half century, the timing of congressional action on regular appropriations bills has varied considerably, but their enactment after the start of the fiscal year has been a recurring issue. During the 25-year period covering FY1952-FY1976, when the fiscal year began on July 1, at least one regular appropriations bill was enacted after the fiscal year began. At the end of this period, the start of the fiscal year was moved from July 1 to October 1 by the Congressional Budget Act of 1974 (P.L. 93-344; 88 Stat. 297).[4] When the act was fully implemented for FY1977, all of the regular appropriations bills for that fiscal year were enacted on time. Since FY1977, however, all of the regular appropriations bills were enacted before the beginning of the fiscal year in only three additional instances (FY1989, FY1995, and FY1997).[5]

Agencies are generally prohibited from obligating or expending federal funds[6] in the absence of appropriations.[7] When appropriations for a particular project or activity are not enacted into law, a

---

[1] The congressional budget process distinguishes between discretionary spending, which is controlled through appropriations acts, and direct (or mandatory) spending, which is controlled through permanent law. For further information on the types of spending in the congressional budget process, see CRS Report 98-721, *Introduction to the Federal Budget Process*, coordinated by James V. Saturno. For further information on the appropriations process, see CRS Report R42388, *The Congressional Appropriations Process: An Introduction*, by Jessica Tollestrup.

[2] Several key terms in this report are italicized for emphasis. Under current practice, each House Appropriations subcommittee typically drafts one regular appropriations bill for the activities under its jurisdiction, for a total of 12 bills each fiscal year. Consolidated appropriations measures—sometimes referred to as "omnibus bills," where two or more of the regular bills are combined into one legislative vehicle—have also been used for consideration and enactment. For further information, see CRS Report RL32473, *Omnibus Appropriations Acts: Overview of Recent Practices*, by Jessica Tollestrup.

[3] Continuing appropriations acts are commonly referred to as "continuing resolutions" because they usually provide continuing appropriations in the form of a joint resolution rather than a bill. Continuing appropriations are also occasionally provided through a bill.

[4] §501 of P.L. 93-344 (88 Stat. 321); July 12, 1974. This section was later replaced by the Federal Credit Reform Act of 1990, but the start of the fiscal year remains October 1 (see 31 U.S.C. 1102).

[5] FY1977 marked the first full implementation of the congressional budget process established by the Congressional Budget Act of 1974, which moved the beginning of the fiscal year to October 1.

[6] Appropriations bills provide agencies *budget authority*, which is authority provided by federal law to enter into contracts or other financial *obligations* that will result in immediate or future expenditures (or *outlays*) involving federal government funds. For explanations of these terms, see U.S. Government Accountability Office (GAO), *A Glossary of Terms Used in the Federal Budget Process*, GAO-05-734SP, September 2005, pp. 20-21, http://www.gao.gov/.

[7] These prohibitions are contained in the Antideficiency Act (31 U.S.C. §1341-1342, §1511-1519). Exceptions are made under the act, including for activities involving "the safety of human life or the protection of property" (31 U.S.C. 1342). The Antideficiency Act is discussed in CRS Report RL30795, *General Management Laws: A Compendium*, by Clinton T. Brass et al. In addition, the GAO provides information about the act online at http://www.gao.gov/ada/antideficiency.htm.

"funding gap" occurs until such appropriations are provided. When a funding gap occurs, federal agencies must begin a "shutdown"[8] of the affected projects and activities.[9]

To prevent the occurrence of funding gaps after the start of the fiscal year until the annual appropriations process is completed, a CR can be used to provide temporary funding. Such funding is provided for a specified period of time, which may be extended through the enactment of subsequent CRs. During the 25 fiscal years covering FY1952-FY1976, one or more CRs were enacted for all but one fiscal year (FY1953).[10] Since FY1977, all of the regular appropriations acts were completed before the start of the fiscal year in only four instances—FY1977, FY1989, FY1995, and FY1997.[11] Consequently, one or more CRs were needed to prevent a funding gap each of the other fiscal years during this period. In total, 175 CRs were enacted into law during the period covering FY1977-FY2016, ranging from zero to 21 in any single fiscal year. On average, about four CRs were enacted each fiscal year during this interval.

The purpose of this report is to provide an overview of the components of CRs and a longitudinal analysis of recent congressional practices. Consequently, the data and analysis in this report are inclusive of all appropriations acts entitled or otherwise designated as providing continuing appropriations.[12] The first section of this report explains six of the possible main components of CRs: coverage, duration, funding rate, restrictions on new activities, anomalies, and legislative provisions. The second section discusses the enactment of regular appropriations prior to the start of the fiscal year and the number of regular appropriations bills enacted through a CR since FY1977. The third section analyzes variations in the number and duration of CRs enacted each fiscal year since FY1997, the most recent fiscal year that all regular appropriations were enacted on time. Finally, the fourth section of this report discusses the features of the 15 CRs that provided funding through the remainder of the fiscal year since FY1977. A list of all CRs enacted between FY1977 and FY2016 is provided at the end of this report in **Table 4**.

Main Components of Continuing Resolutions

Under recent congressional practice, CRs typically include as many as six main components. First, CRs provide funding for certain activities, which are typically specified with reference to the prior or current fiscal year's appropriations acts. This is referred to in this report as the CR's *coverage*. Second, CRs provide budget authority for a specified *duration* of time.[13] This duration

---

[8] For further information on shutdowns, see CRS Report RL34680, *Shutdown of the Federal Government: Causes, Processes, and Effects*, coordinated by Clinton T. Brass.

[9] Funding gaps and shutdowns should be distinguished, however, because a full shutdown may not occur in some instances, such as when a funding gap is of a short duration over a weekend. For a further discussion of this issue, as well as a list of all funding gaps that have occurred since FY1977, see CRS Report RS20348, *Federal Funding Gaps: A Brief Overview*, by Jessica Tollestrup.

[10] Although regular appropriations for FY1953 were enacted into law after the start of the fiscal year, no continuing appropriations were provided. §1414 of P.L. 82-547 (July 15, 1952), a supplemental appropriations measure for FY1953, resolved the legalities arising from the tardy enactment of appropriations for that year.

[11] Although regular appropriations for FY1977 were enacted into law before the start of the fiscal year, CRs were also enacted to fund certain unauthorized programs whose funding had not been included in the regular appropriations acts. §1414 of P.L. 82-547 (66 Stat. 661) made regular appropriations enacted later than the beginning of the fiscal year available retroactively as of July 1, 1952 (the first day of FY1953) and ratified any obligations incurred before their enactment.

[12] In some instances, such acts might alternatively be characterized by some observers as "omnibus appropriations acts." For a further discussion of this issue, see the section titled "Funding Rate" and CRS Report RL32473, *Omnibus Appropriations Acts: Overview of Recent Practices*, by Jessica Tollestrup.

[13] Appropriations bills provide agencies with *budget authority*, which is defined as authority provided by federal law to (continued...)

may be as short as a single day or as long as the remainder of the fiscal year. Third, CRs typically provide funds based on an overall *funding rate*. Fourth, the use of budget authority provided in the CR is typically prohibited for *new activities* not funded in the previous fiscal year. Fifth, the duration and amount of funds in the CR, and purposes for which they may be used for specified activities, may be adjusted through *anomalies*. Sixth, *legislative provisions*—which create, amend, or extend other laws—have been included in some instances.

Although this section discusses the above components as they have been enacted in CRs under recent practice, it does not discuss their potential effects on budget execution or agency operations. For analysis of these issues, see CRS Report RL34700, *Interim Continuing Resolutions (CRs): Potential Impacts on Agency Operations*, by Clinton T. Brass.

Coverage

A CR provides funds for certain activities, which are typically specified with reference to other pieces of appropriations legislation or the appropriations acts for a previous fiscal year. This is referred to in this report as the CR's "coverage." Most often, the coverage of a CR is defined with reference to the activities funded in prior fiscal years' appropriations acts for which the current fiscal year's regular appropriations have yet to be enacted. For example, in Section 101 of P.L. 111-68 (the first CR for FY2010), the coverage included activities funded in selected regular and supplemental appropriations acts for FY2008 and FY2009:

> Sec. 101. Such amounts as may be necessary... under the authority and conditions provided in such Acts, for continuing projects or activities (including the costs of direct loans and loan guarantees) that are not otherwise specifically provided for in this joint resolution, that were conducted in fiscal year 2009, and for which appropriations, funds, or other authority were made available in the following appropriations Acts:
>
> *(1) Chapter 2 of title IX of the Supplemental Appropriations Act, 2008 (P.L. 110-252).*
>
> (2) Section 155 of division A of the Consolidated Security, Disaster Assistance, and Continuing Appropriations Act, 2009 (P.L. 110-329), except that subsections (c), (d), and (e) of such section shall not apply to funds made available under this joint resolution.
>
> (3) Divisions C through E of the Consolidated Security, Disaster Assistance, and Continuing Appropriations Act, 2009 (P.L. 110-329).
>
> *(4) Divisions A through I of the Omnibus Appropriations Act, 2009 (P.L. 111-8), as amended by section 2 of P.L. 111-46.*
>
> *(5) Titles III and VI (under the heading `Coast Guard') of the Supplemental Appropriations Act, 2009 (P.L. 111-32).* [emphasis added]

Less frequently, CRs specify coverage with reference to regular appropriations bills for the current fiscal year that have yet to be enacted.[14] In these instances, it is possible that an activity covered in the corresponding previous fiscal year's appropriations bill might not be covered in the CR. Alternatively, a CR might stipulate that activities funded in the previous fiscal year are covered only if they are included in a regular appropriations bill for the current fiscal year. For

---

(...continued)

enter into contracts or other financial *obligations* that will result in immediate or future expenditures (or *outlays*) involving federal government funds. For explanations of these terms, see GAO, *Glossary*, pp. 20-21. For the purposes of this report, the terms "budget authority" and "funding" are used interchangeably.

[14] See, for example, §101 of P.L. 105-240.

example, Section 101 of P.L. 105-240, the first CR for FY1999, provided that funding would continue only under such circumstances.

> SEC. 101. (a) Such amounts as may be necessary under the authority and conditions *provided in the applicable appropriations Act for the fiscal year 1998* for continuing projects or activities including the costs of direct loans and loan guarantees (not otherwise specifically provided for in this joint resolution) which were conducted in the fiscal year 1998 *and for which appropriations, funds, or other authority would be available in the following appropriations Acts*:
>
> (1) the Agriculture, Rural Development, Food and Drug Administration, and Related Agencies Appropriations Act, 1999....
>
> (8) the Departments of Labor, Health and Human Services, and Education, and Related Agencies Appropriations Act, 1999, the House and Senate reported versions of which shall be deemed to have passed the House and Senate respectively as of October 1, 1998, for the purposes of this joint resolution, unless a reported version is passed as of October 1, 1998, in which case the passed version shall be used in place of the reported version for purposes of this joint resolution;
>
> (9) the Legislative Branch Appropriations Act, 1999.... [emphasis added]

CRs may be enacted as stand-alone legislative vehicles or as provisions attached to a regular appropriations bill or an omnibus bill.[15] In instances in which one or more regular appropriations bills are near completion, Congress may find it expeditious to include a CR in that same legislative vehicle to cover activities in the remaining regular bills that are not yet enacted. In such instances, some activities may be covered by reference while funding for others is provided through the text of the measure. For example, Division D of P.L. 112-55, the third CR for FY2012, provided continuing appropriations through December 16, 2011, by referencing the FY2011 regular appropriations acts, while the other parts of P.L. 112-55 contained the full text of the FY2012 Agriculture, Commerce-Justice-Science, and Transportation-Housing and Urban Development regular appropriations acts.

Duration

The duration of a CR refers to the period for which budget authority is provided for covered activities. The period ends either upon the enactment of the applicable regular appropriations act or on an expiration date specified in the CR, whichever occurs first. When a CR expires prior to the completion of all regular appropriations bills for a fiscal year, one or more additional CRs may be enacted to prevent funding gaps and secure additional increments of time to complete the remaining regular appropriations bills. The duration of any further CRs may be brief, sometimes a single day, to encourage the process to conclude swiftly, or it may be weeks or months to accommodate further negotiations or congressional recesses. In some cases, CRs have carried over into the next session of Congress.

In most of the fiscal years in which CRs have been used, a series of two or more have been enacted into law.[16] Such CRs may be designated by their order (e.g., "first" CR, "second" CR) or, after the initial CR has been enacted, designated as a "further" CR. When action on the regular appropriations bills is not complete by the time when the first CR expires, subsequent CRs will

---

[15] Two or more regular appropriations bills are sometimes packaged into a single or "omnibus" legislative vehicle prior to enactment. For a discussion of this practice, see CRS Report RL32473, *Omnibus Appropriations Acts: Overview of Recent Practices*, by Jessica Tollestrup.

[16] For further information, see **Table 1** and **Table 4** in this report.

18-7

often simply replace the expiration date in the preceding CR with a new expiration date. For example, Section 1 of the second CR for FY2004, P.L. 108-104 (117 Stat. 1200), stated that "Public Law 108-84 is amended by striking the date specified in Section 107(c) and inserting 'November 7, 2003.'" This action extended the duration of the preceding CR by seven days.

Funds provided by a CR will not necessarily be used by all covered activities through the date the CR expires. In practice, the budget authority provided by a CR may be superseded by the enactment of subsequent appropriations measures or the occurrence of other specified conditions. In an instance in which a regular appropriations bill was enacted prior to the expiration of a CR, the budget authority provided by the regular bill for covered activities would replace the funding provided by the CR. All other activities in the CR, however, would continue to be funded by the CR unless they were likewise superseded or the CR expired. The duration of funds for certain activities could also be shortened if other conditions that are specified in the CR occur. For example, Section 107 of P.L. 108-84, the first CR for FY2004, provided funds for 31 days or fewer:

> Sec. 107. *Unless otherwise provided* for in this joint resolution or in the applicable appropriations Act, appropriations and funds made available and authority granted pursuant to this joint resolution shall be available until (a) enactment into law of an appropriation for any project or activity provided for in this joint resolution, or *(b) the enactment into law of the applicable appropriations Act by both Houses without any provision for such project or activity, or (c) October 31, 2003, whichever first occurs.* [emphasis added]

In this instance, funding for all other activities not subject to these conditions would continue under the CR until it expired or was otherwise superseded.

When a CR is attached to a regular appropriations bill, the activities covered by regular appropriations are funded through the remainder of the fiscal year, whereas the activities covered by the CR are funded through a specified date. Congress may also single out specific activities in a CR to receive funding for a specified duration that differs from the vast majority of other accounts and activities. This type of variation in duration is discussed in the "Exceptions to Duration, Amount, and Purposes: Anomalies" section.

As an alternative to the separate enactment of one or more of the regular appropriations bills for a fiscal year, a CR may provide funds for the activities covered in such bills through the remainder of the fiscal year. This type of CR is referred to as a *full-year* CR. Full-year CRs may provide funding for all bills that have yet to be enacted or include the full text of one or more regular appropriations bills. For example, Division A of P.L. 112-10 contained the text of the FY2011 Defense Appropriations Act, whereas the programs and activities covered by the 11 remaining regular appropriations bills were funded by the full-year CR in Division B.

Funding Rate

CRs usually fund activities under a formula-type approach that provides budget authority at a restricted level but not a specified amount. This method of providing budget authority is commonly referred to as the "funding rate." Under a funding rate, the amount of budget authority for an account[17] is calculated as the total amount of budget authority annually available based on a reference level (usually a dollar amount or calculation), multiplied by the fraction of the fiscal

---

[17] Regular appropriations bills contain a series of unnumbered paragraphs with headings, generally reflecting a unique budget "account." Elements within budget accounts are divided by "program, project or activity" based upon the table "Comparative Statement of New Budget Authority" in the back of the report accompanying the appropriations bill.

year for which the funds are made available in the CR.[18] This is in contrast to regular and supplemental appropriations acts, which generally provide specific amounts for each account.

In previous years, many CRs have provided funding across accounts by reference to the amount of budget authority available in specified appropriations acts from the previous fiscal year. For example, Section 101 of P.L. 110-329, the first CR for FY2010, provided the following funding rate:

> Such amounts as may be necessary, *at a rate for operations as provided in the applicable appropriations Acts for fiscal year 2008* and under the authority and conditions provided in such Acts, for continuing projects or activities (including the costs of direct loans and loan guarantees) that are not otherwise specifically provided for in this joint resolution, that were conducted in fiscal year 2008, and for which appropriations, funds, or other authority were made available in the following appropriations Acts: *divisions A, B, C, D, F, G, H, J, and K of the Consolidated Appropriations Act, 2008 (P.L. 110-161).* [emphasis added]

Other CRs have provided funding by reference to the levels available in the previous fiscal year, with either an increase or decrease from the previous fiscal year's level. For example, Section 101(a) and (b) of P.L. 112-33, the first CR for FY2012, provided the following funding rate:

> (a) Such amounts as may be necessary, at a rate for operations as provided in the applicable appropriations Acts for fiscal year 2011 and under the authority and conditions provided in such Acts, for continuing projects or activities (including the costs of direct loans and loan guarantees) that are not otherwise specifically provided for in this Act, that were conducted in fiscal year 2011, and for which appropriations, funds, or other authority were made available in the following appropriations Acts....
>
> (b) *The rate for operations provided by subsection (a) is hereby reduced by 1.503 percent.* [emphasis added]

Although these examples illustrate the most typical types of funding rates provided in recent years, other types of funding rates have sometimes been used when providing continuing appropriations. For example, P.L. 105-240, the first CR for FY1999, provided a variable funding rate for covered activities. Specifically, the CR provided funds derived from three possible reference sources: the House- and Senate-passed FY1999 regular appropriations bills, the amount of the President's budget request, or "current operations" (the total amount of budget authority available for obligation for an activity during the previous fiscal year), whichever was lower. In instances where no funding was provided under the House-and Senate-passed FY1999 appropriations bills, the funding rate would be based on the lower of the President's budget request or current operations. In addition, while the first CR for a fiscal year may provide a certain funding rate, subsequent CRs sometimes may provide a different rate.

CRs have sometimes provided budget authority for some or all covered activities by incorporating the actual text of one or more regular appropriations bills for that fiscal year rather than providing funding according to the rate formula.[19] For example, P.L. 112-10 provided funding for the Department of Defense through the incorporation of a regular appropriations bill in Division A, whereas Division B provided formulaic funding for all other activities for the

---

[18] For a discussion of how funding rates are calculated, see GAO, Office of the General Counsel, *Principles of Federal Appropriations Law*, vol. II, 3rd ed. (2004), at 8-10 to 8-14.

[19] From a functional perspective, CRs that do not include any formulaic provisions but instead provide appropriations only by using the full text of acts (including by cross-reference) are sometimes regarded as omnibus appropriations acts rather than CRs, even if they are entitled an act "making continuing appropriations" or "making further continuing appropriations."

remainder of the fiscal year.[20] In this type of instance, the formula in the CR applies only to activities not covered in the text of the incorporated regular appropriations bill or bills.

Purpose for Funds and Restrictions on New Activities

CRs that provide a funding rate for activities typically stipulate that funds may be used for the purposes and in the manner provided in specified appropriations acts for the previous fiscal year. CRs also typically provide that the funds provided may be used only for activities funded in the previous fiscal year. In practice, this is often characterized as a prohibition on "new starts." In addition, conditions and limitations on program activity from the previous year's appropriations acts are typically retained by language contained within the resolution's text. An example of such language, from P.L. 112-33, is below:

> Sec. 103. Appropriations made by section 101 shall be available *to the extent and in the manner* that would be provided by the pertinent appropriations Act. [emphasis added]

> Sec. 104. Except as otherwise provided in section 102, no appropriation or funds made available or authority granted pursuant to section 101 shall be used *to initiate or resume any project or activity* for which appropriations, funds, or other authority were not available during fiscal year 2011. [emphasis added]

This language prevents the initiation of new activities with the funds provided in the CR. Agencies may use appropriated funds from prior fiscal years that remain available, however, to initiate new activities in some circumstances.[21]

Exceptions to Duration, Amount, and Purposes: Anomalies

Even though CRs typically provide funds at a rate, they may also include provisions that enumerate exceptions to the *duration, amount,* or *purposes* for which those funds may be used for certain appropriations accounts or activities. Such provisions are commonly referred to as "anomalies." The purpose of anomalies is to preserve Congress's constitutional prerogative to provide appropriations in the manner it sees fit, even in instances when only short-term funding is provided.[22]

Duration

A CR may contain anomalies that designate a duration of funding for certain activities that is different from the overall duration provided. For example, Section 112 of P.L. 108-84 provided an exception to the expiration date of October 31, 2003, specified in Section 107(c) of the CR:

> For entitlements and other mandatory payments whose budget authority was provided in appropriations Acts for fiscal year 2003, and for activities under the Food Stamp Act of 1977, activities shall be continued at the rate to maintain program levels under current

---

[20] The formulaic funding for many of the accounts funded in Division B was modified by anomalies. For a discussion of this practice, see the "Anomalies" section of this report.

[21] Although appropriations bills most commonly provide budget authority that is available for obligation for only one fiscal year, budget authority for an activity may be provided for more than one year ("multiyear") or indefinitely ("no-year"). In instances where funds provided in previous years are still available for the purpose of initiating a new project or activity, such funds may generally be used for this purpose, even though funds for the current fiscal year are provided by a CR. GAO, *Glossary*, p. 22.

[22] Article 1, §9, of the U.S. Constitution grants Congress the "power of the purse" by prohibiting expenditures "but in Consequence of Appropriations made by Law."

law, under the authority and conditions provided in the applicable appropriations Act for fiscal year 2003, to be continued through the date specified in section 107(c): *Provided, That notwithstanding section 107, funds shall be available and obligations for mandatory payments due on or about November 1 and December 1, 2003, may continue to be made.* [emphasis added]

Amount

Anomalies may also designate a specific amount or rate of budget authority for certain accounts or activities that is different than the funding rate provided for the remainder of activities in the CR.[23] Typically, such funding is specified as an annualized rate based upon a lump sum. For example, Section 120 of P.L. 112-33 provided the following anomaly for a specific account, which was an exception to the generally applicable rate in Section 101:

> Notwithstanding section 101, amounts are provided for "Defense Nuclear Facilities Safety Board—Salaries and Expenses" at a rate for operations of $29,130,000. [emphasis added]

Funding adjustments can also be provided in anomalies for groups of accounts in the bill. For example, Section 121 of P.L. 112-33 provided a different rate for certain funds in a group of accounts:

> Notwithstanding any other provision of this Act, except section 106, the District of Columbia may expend local funds under the heading "District of Columbia Funds" for such programs and activities under title IV of H.R. 2434 (112th Congress), as reported by the Committee on Appropriations of the House of Representatives, *at the rate set forth under "District of Columbia Funds—Summary of Expenses" as included in the Fiscal Year 2012 Budget Request Act of 2011* (D.C. Act 19–92), as modified as of the date of the enactment of this Act. [emphasis added]

Further, anomalies may provide exceptions to amounts specified in other laws. For example, Section 121 of P.L. 110-329 provided that funds may be expended in excess of statutory limits up to an alternative rate.

> Notwithstanding the limitations on administrative expenses in subsections (c)(2) and (c)(3)(A) of section 3005 of the Digital Television Transition and Public Safety Act of 2005 (P.L. 109-171; 120 Stat. 21), the Assistant Secretary (as such term is defined in section 3001(b) of such Act) may expend funds made available under sections 3006, 3008, and 3009 of such Act for additional administrative expenses of the digital-to-analog converter box program established by such section 3005 *at a rate not to exceed $180,000,000* through the date specified in section 106(3) of this joint resolution. [emphasis added]

Purpose

CRs may also use anomalies to alter the purposes for which the funds may be expended. Such anomalies may allow funds to be spent for activities that would otherwise be prohibited or prohibit funds for activities that might otherwise be allowed. For example, Section 114 of P.L. 108-309, the first CR for FY2005, prohibited funds from being available to a particular department for a certain activity:

---

[23] Regular appropriations bills contain a series of unnumbered paragraphs with headings, generally reflecting a unique budget "account." Elements within budget accounts are divided by "program, project or activity" (GAO, *Glossary*, p. 80). When a CR provides funds for activities in the prior year's regular appropriations acts, anomalies reflect the account structure in such acts.

18-11

Notwithstanding any other provision of this joint resolution, except sections 107 and 108, amounts are made available for the Strategic National Stockpile ("SNS") at a rate for operations not exceeding the lower of the amount which would be made available under H.R. 5006, as passed by the House of Representatives on September 9, 2004, or S. 2810, as reported by the Committee on Appropriations of the Senate on September 15, 2004: *Provided, That no funds shall be made available for the SNS to the Department of Homeland Security under this joint resolution....* [emphasis added]

Legislative Provisions

Substantive legislative provisions, which have the effect of creating new law or changing existing law, have also been included in some CRs. One reason why CRs have been attractive vehicles for such provisions is that they are often widely considered to be must-pass measures to prevent funding gaps. Legislative provisions previously included in CRs have varied considerably in length, from a short paragraph to more than 200 pages.

House and Senate rules restrict the inclusion of legislative provisions in appropriations bills, but such restrictions are applicable in different contexts. Although House rules prohibit legislative provisions from being included in general appropriations measures (including amendments or any conference report to such measures), these restrictions do not apply to CRs.[24] Senate rules prohibit non-germane amendments that include legislative provisions either on the Senate floor or as an amendment between the houses.[25] While these Senate restrictions do apply in the case of CRs, there is considerable leeway on when such provisions may be included, such as when the Senate amends a legislative provision included by the House.[26] The rules of the House and Senate are not self-enforcing. A point of order must be raised and sustained to prevent any legislative language from being considered and enacted.[27]

Substantive provisions in CRs have included language that established major new policies, such as an FY1985 CR, which contained the Comprehensive Crime Control Act of 1984.[28]

More frequently, CRs have been used to amend or renew provisions of law. For example, Section 140 of P.L. 112-33 retroactively renewed import restrictions under the Burmese Freedom and Democracy Act of 2003 (P.L. 108-61):

(a) Renewal of Import Restrictions Under Burmese Freedom and Democracy Act of 2003.—

(1) In general.—Congress approves the renewal of the import restrictions contained in section 3(a)(1) and section 3A (b)(1) and (c)(1) of the Burmese Freedom and Democracy Act of 2003.

---

[24] House Rule XXI, clause 2, prohibits such language in general appropriations measures and applicable amendments. House Rule XXII, clause 5, in effect, generally extends the House Rule XXI, clause 2, prohibition to conference reports. CRs, however, are not considered to be general appropriations bills. W[illia]m Holmes Brown, Charles W. Johnson, and John V. Sullivan, *House Practice: A Guide to the Rules, Precedents and Procedures of the House*, 112th Cong., 1st sess. (Washington: GPO, 2011), ch. 4, §6, pp. 76-77.

[25] Senate Rule XVI, paragraphs 2-6.

[26] For further information on House and Senate restrictions on legislation in appropriations, see CRS Report R41634, *Limitations in Appropriations Measures: An Overview of Procedural Issues*, by Jessica Tollestrup.

[27] For further information on points of order, see CRS Report 98-307, *Points of Order, Rulings, and Appeals in the House of Representatives*, by Valerie Heitshusen; and CRS Report 98-306, *Points of Order, Rulings, and Appeals in the Senate*, by Valerie Heitshusen.

[28] P.L. 98-473, 98 Stat. 1837.

(2) Rule of construction.—This section shall be deemed to be a ``renewal resolution" for purposes of section 9 of the Burmese Freedom and Democracy Act of 2003.

(b) Effective Date.—This section shall take effect on July 26, 2011.

CRs have also contained legislative provisions that temporarily extended expiring laws. For example, Section 118 of P.L. 111-242 provided a temporary extension of a section in the FY2006 National Defense Authorization Act:

The authority provided by section 1202 of the National Defense Authorization Act for Fiscal Year 2006 (P.L. 109-163), as most recently amended by section 1222 of the National Defense Authorization Act for Fiscal Year 2010 (P.L. 111-84; 123 Stat. 2518), shall continue in effect through the date specified in section 106(3) of this Act.

Legislative provisions that temporarily extend expiring laws are effective through the date the CR expires, unless otherwise specified.

The Enactment of Regular Appropriations Bills and Use of CRs, FY1977-FY2016

As mentioned previously, regular appropriations were enacted after October 1 in all but four fiscal years between FY1977 and FY2016. Consequently, CRs have been needed in almost all of these years to prevent one or more funding gaps from occurring.[29]

Table 1 provides an overview of the enactment of regular appropriations bills and the use of CRs between FY1977 and FY2016. Excluding the four fiscal years that all appropriations were enacted on time (FY1977, FY1989, FY1995, and FY1997), over half of the regular appropriations bills for a fiscal year were enacted on time in only one instance (FY1978). In all other fiscal years, fewer than six regular appropriations acts were enacted on or before October 1. In addition, in 14 out of the 40 years during this period, no regular appropriations bills were enacted prior to the start of the fiscal year. Nine of these fiscal years have occurred in the interval since FY2001.

Table 1. The Enactment of Regular Appropriations Bills and Use of Continuing Resolutions (CRs), FY1977-FY2016

Fiscal Year	Number of Regular Appropriations Bills[a]	Regular Appropriations Bills Enacted on or Before October 1	CRs Enacted[b]
1977	13	13	(2)[c]
1978	13	9	3
1979	13	5	1
1980	13	3	2
1981	13	1	3
1982	13	1	4

---

[29] For further information on the funding gaps that occurred during this period, see CRS Report RS20348, *Federal Funding Gaps: A Brief Overview*, by Jessica Tollestrup.

Continuing Resolutions: Overview of Components and Recent Practices

Fiscal Year	Number of Regular Appropriations Bills[a]	Regular Appropriations Bills Enacted on or Before October 1	CRs Enacted[b]
1983	13	1	2
1984	13	4	2
1985	13	4	5
1986	13	0	5
1987	13	0	6
1988	13	0	5
1989	13	13	0
1990	13	1	3
1991	13	0	5
1992	13	3	4
1993	13	1	1
1994	13	2	3
1995	13	13	0
1996	13	0	13
1997	13	(13)[d]	0
1998	13	1	6
1999	13	1	6
2000	13	4	7
2001	13	2	21
2002	13	0	8
2003	13	0	8
2004	13	3	5
2005	13	1	3
2006	11	2	3
2007	11	1	4
2008	12	0	4
2009	12	(3)[e]	2
2010	12	1	2
2011	12	0	8
2012	12	0	5
2013	12	0	2
2014	12	0	4
2015	12	0	5
2016	12	0	3

Sources: U.S. Congress, Senate Committee on Appropriations, *Appropriations, Budget Estimates, Etc.,* 94th Congress, 2nd session-104th Congress, 1st session (Washington: GPO, 1976-1995). U.S. Congress, House of Representatives, *Calendars of the U.S. House of Representatives and History of Legislation,* 104th Congress, 1st session-113th Congress, 1st session (Washington: GPO, 1995-2012). CRS appropriations status tables (FY1999-FY2016), http://www.crs.gov/pages/AppropriationsStatusTable.aspx.

a. Between the 95th and 108th Congresses, there were 13 House and Senate Appropriations subcommittees responsible for one regular appropriations bill each. During the 109th Congress, due to subcommittee realignment, the total number of regular appropriations bills was effectively reduced to 11 during each year of the Congress. Beginning in the 110th Congress, subcommittee jurisdictions were again realigned for a total of 12 subcommittees, each of which is currently responsible for a single regular appropriations bill. For further information on subcommittee realignment during this period, see: CRS Report RL31572, *Appropriations Subcommittee Structure: History of Changes from 1920 to 2015,* by James V. Saturno and Jessica Tollestrup.

b. For further information on each of these CRs, see **Table 4**.

c. Although all 13 FY1977 regular appropriations bills became law on or before the start of the fiscal year, two CRs were enacted. These CRs generally provided funding for certain activities that had not been included in the regular appropriations acts.

d. This number reflects six regular acts being combined to form an omnibus appropriations act and the other seven bills being enacted individually.

e. Three regular appropriations bills were packaged into a single act that also included the initial FY2010 CR (P.L. 110-329).

CRs were enacted in all but three of these fiscal years (FY1989, FY1995, and FY1997). In FY1977, although all 13 regular appropriations bills became law on or before the start of the fiscal year, two CRs were enacted to provide funding for certain activities that had not been included in the regular appropriations acts.

Duration and Frequency of Continuing Resolutions, FY1998-FY2016

In the interval since FY1997 (the most recent fiscal year that all regular appropriations bills were completed on time), CRs have been a significant element of the annual appropriations process. As shown in **Table 2**, a total of 106 CRs were enacted into law during this period. While the average number of such measures enacted per year was about six (5.6), the number enacted ranged from two measures (for FY2009, FY2010, and FY2013) to 21 (for FY2001).

During the past 18 fiscal years, Congress provided funding by means of a CR for an average of almost five months (137.5 days) each fiscal year. Taking into account the total duration of all CRs for each fiscal year, the period for which continuing appropriations were provided ranged from 21 days to 365 days. On average, each of the 106 CRs lasted for about 25 (24.6) days; 51 of these were for seven days or fewer.[30] Three full-year CRs were used during this period, for FY2007, FY2011, and FY2013.

In the first four instances (FY1998-FY2001), the expiration date of the final CR was set in the first quarter of the fiscal year on a date occurring between October 21 and December 21. The expiration date in the final CR for the next three fiscal years (FY2002-FY2004), however, was set in the following session of Congress on a date occurring between January 10 and February 20. In six of the next 12 fiscal years (FY2005, FY2006, FY2008, FY2010, FY2012, and FY2016), the expiration dates were in the first quarter of the fiscal year on a date occurring between December

---

[30] The fifth CR enacted for FY2004, P.L. 108-185, did not change the expiration date of January 31, 2004, set in the preceding CR.

18-15

8 and December 31. For the remaining fiscal years, the final CRs were enacted during the next session of Congress. In one instance, the final CR for the fiscal year expired during the month of January (FY2014). In two instances, the final CR expired in March (FY2009 and FY2015). Three other final CRs—for FY2007, FY2011, and FY2013—provided funding through the end of the fiscal year.

Table 2. Number and Duration of Continuing Resolutions (CRs): FY1998-FY2016

Fiscal Year	Number of CRs	Total Duration in Days[a]	Average Duration for Each Act	Final Expiration Date[b]
1998	6	57	9.5	11-26-1997
1999	6	21	3.5	10-21-1998
2000	7	63	9.0	12-02-1999
2001	21	82	3.9	12-21-2000
2002	8	102	12.8	01-10-2002
2003	8	143	17.9	02-20-2003
2004	5[c]	123	24.6	01-31-2004
2005	3	69	23.0	12-08-2004
2006	3	92	30.7	12-31-2005
2007	4	365	91.3	09-30-2007
2008	4	92	23.0	12-31-2007
2009	2	162	81.0	03-11-2009
2010	2	79	39.5	12-18-2009
2011	8	365	45.6	9-30-2011
2012	5	84	16.8	12-23-2011
2013	2	365	182.5	9-30-2013
2014	4[d]	110[d]	27.5	01-18-2014
2015	5	156	31.3	03-06-2015
2016	3	83	27.7	12-22-2015
Total	**106**	**2,613**	—	—
Annual Average	**5.6**	**137.5**	**24.6**	—

Sources: Prepared by the Congressional Research Service using data from the Legislative Information System; Congressional Research Service, appropriations status tables (various fiscal years), available at http://crs.gov/Pages/appover.aspx; and various other sources.

a. Duration in days is measured, in the case of the first CR for a fiscal year, from the first day of the year (October 1). For example, a CR enacted on September 30 that provided funding through October 12 would be measured as having a 12-day duration. For subsequent CRs for a fiscal year, duration in days is measured from the day after the expiration of the preceding CR.

b. The final expiration date is the date the CR expired. In some of these instances, the CR had previously been superseded by the enactment of the remaining regular appropriations acts for that fiscal year. For example, in FY2014, the expiration date of P.L. 113-73, the fourth CR for FY2014, was January 18, 2014. However, final regular appropriations were enacted the previous day in the Consolidated Appropriations Act, 2014 (P.L. 113-76).

c.   The fifth CR for FY2004 did not change the expiration date of January 31, 2004, established in the preceding CR.

d.   A total of four CRs were enacted for FY2014. This count includes two CRs that provided funding for only specific programs and activities during the FY2014 funding gap. The Pay Our Military Act (P.L. 113-39) was enacted on September 30, 2013. The Department of Defense Survivor Benefits Continuing Appropriations Resolution, 2014 (P.L. 113-44), was enacted on October 10, 2013. The funding provided by both of these CRs was terminated on October 17, 2013, through the enactment of at third CR, P.L. 113-46, which broadly funded the previous fiscal year's activities through January 15, 2014. The funding provided by this third CR was extended through January 18 through the enactment of a fourth CR (P.L. 113-73). Section 118 of P.L. 113-46 provided that the time covered by that act was to have begun on October 1, 2013. To preserve counting consistency, the FY2014 duration of days for the purposes of this table and Figure 1 begins on October 1 and ends on January 18, 2014. For further information on the FY2014 funding gap and congressional action on CRs, see CRS Report RS20348, *Federal Funding Gaps: A Brief Overview*, by Jessica Tollestrup.

Figure 1 presents a representation of the duration of CRs for FY1998-FY2016. As the figure shows, there is no significant correlation between these two variables. For example, six CRs were enacted for both FY1998 and FY1999, but the same number of measures lasted for a period of 57 days for FY1998 and only 21 days for FY1999. The largest number of CRs enacted for a single fiscal year during this period—21 for FY2001—covered a period lasting 82 days at an average duration of 3.9 days per act. The smallest number enacted—two each for FY2009, FY2010, and FY2013—covered 162 days, 79 days, and 365 days, respectively.

Figure 1 also shows considerable mix in the use of shorter-term and longer-term CRs for a single fiscal year. For example, for FY2001, 21 CRs covered the first 82 days of the fiscal year. The first 25 days were covered by a series of four CRs lasting between five and eight days each. The next 10 days, a period of intense legislative negotiations leading up to the national elections on November 7, 2000, were covered by a series of 10 one-day CRs. The next 31 days were covered by two CRs, the first lasting 10 days and the second lasting 21 days. The first of these two CRs was enacted into law on November 4, the Saturday before the election, and extended through November 14, the second day of a lame-duck session. The second CR was enacted into law on November 15 and expired on December 5, which was 10 days before the lame-duck session ended. The remaining five CRs, which ranged in duration from one to six days, covered the remainder of the lame-duck session and several days beyond (as the final appropriations measures passed by Congress were being processed for the President's approval).[31]

Table 4 provides more detailed information on the number, length, and duration of CRs enacted for FY1977-FY2016. As indicated previously, this represents the period after the start of the federal fiscal year was moved from July 1 to October 1 by the Congressional Budget Act.

---

[31] For further information on the appropriations context for FY2001, see "Longest Appropriations Cycle in Five Years Ends with Omnibus Spending Bill," *Congressional Quarterly Almanac*, 106th Cong., 2nd sess. (2000), vol. LVI, pp. 2-3 through 2-6.

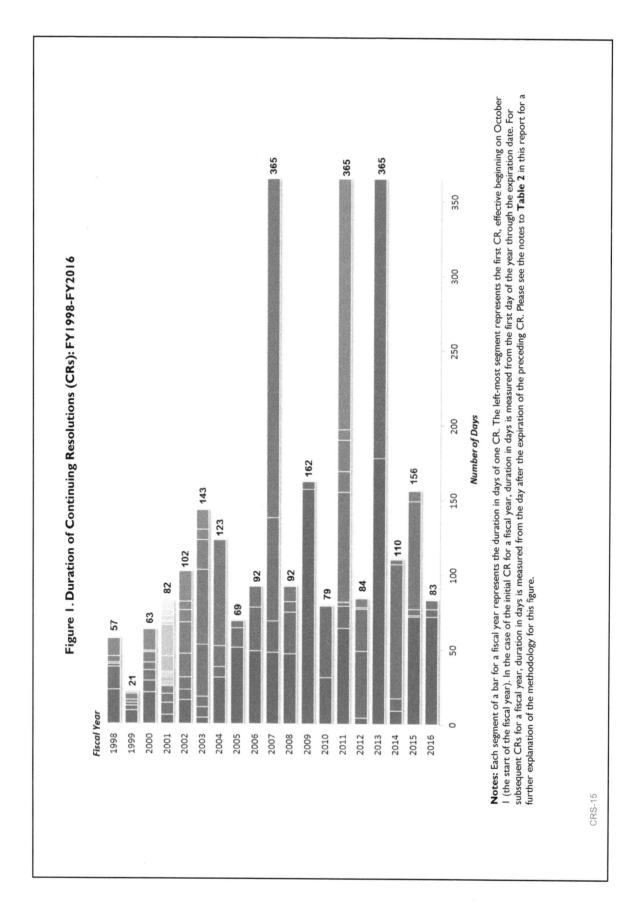

Figure 1. Duration of Continuing Resolutions (CRs): FY1998–FY2016

Notes: Each segment of a bar for a fiscal year represents the duration in days of one CR. The left-most segment represents the first CR, effective beginning on October 1 (the start of the fiscal year). In the case of the initial CR for a fiscal year, duration in days is measured from the first day of the year through the expiration date. For subsequent CRs for a fiscal year, duration in days is measured from the day after the expiration of the preceding CR. Please see the notes to **Table 2** in this report for a further explanation of the methodology for this figure.

CRS-15

Features of Full-Year CRs, FY1977-FY2016

Full-year CRs have been used to provide annual discretionary spending on a number of occasions. Prior to the full implementation of the Congressional Budget Act in FY1977, full-year CRs were used occasionally, particularly in the 1970s. Full-year CRs were enacted into law for four of the six preceding fiscal years (FY1971, FY1973, FY1975, and FY1976).[32] Following the successful completion of all 13 regular appropriations acts prior to the start of FY1977, full-year CRs were used in each of the 11 succeeding fiscal years (FY1978-FY1988) to cover at least one regular appropriations act. Three years later, another full-year CR was enacted for FY1992. Most recently, full-year CRs were enacted for FY2007, FY2011, and FY2013.

Table 3 identifies the 15 full-year CRs enacted for the period since FY1977. Nine of the 15 full-year CRs during this period were enacted in the first quarter of the fiscal year—three in October, two in November, and four in December. The six remaining measures, however, were enacted during the following session between February 15 and June 5.

The full-year CRs enacted during this period also varied in terms of length and the form of funding provided. Full-year CRs prior to FY1983 were relatively short measures, ranging in length from one to four pages in the *Statutes-at-Large*. Beginning with FY1983 and extending through FY1988, however, the measures became much lengthier, ranging from 19 to 451 pages (averaging 244 pages). The greater page length of full-year CRs enacted for the period covering FY1983-FY1988 may be explained by two factors. First, full-year CRs enacted prior to FY1983 generally established funding levels by formulaic reference. Beginning with FY1983, however, Congress began to incorporate the full text of some or all of the covered regular appropriations acts, thereby increasing its length considerably. None of the full-year CRs enacted between 1985 and 1988 used formulaic funding provisions. Secondly, the number of regular appropriations acts covered by full-year CRs increased significantly during the FY1983-FY1988 period. For the period covering FY1978-FY1982, the number of regular appropriations acts covered by CRs for the full fiscal year ranged from one to six (averaging about three). Beginning with FY1983 and extending through FY1988, the number of covered acts ranged from five to 13, averaging 10.2.

The next two full-year CRs, for FY1992 and FY2007, returned to the earlier practice of using formulaic references and anomalies to establish funding levels. Both CRs provided funding only through this means. As a consequence, the length of these measures was considerably shorter than the FY1983 through FY1988 full-year CRs.

The two most recent full-year CRs, for FY2011 and FY2013, in some respects were a hybrid of the earlier and recent approaches. The FY2011 full-year CR provided funding for 11 bills through formulaic provisions and anomalies. It also carried the full text of one regular appropriations bill in a separate division of the act (the FY2011 Department of Defense Appropriations Act). Similarly, the FY2013 CR contained the texts of five regular appropriations bills in Divisions A through E of the act—the FY2013 Agriculture, Rural Development, Food and Drug Administration, and Related Agencies Appropriations Act; the Commerce, Justice, Science, and Related Agencies Appropriations Act; the Department of Defense Appropriations Act; the Department of Homeland Security Appropriations Act; and the Military Construction and Veterans Affairs and Related Agencies Appropriations Act. In addition, Division F was characterized as providing continuing appropriations for the remaining seven regular

---

[32] The full-year CR for FY1976, P.L. 94-254, provided funding through the end of the fiscal year (June 30, 1976) as well as through the end of a "transition quarter" (September 30, 1976). The additional quarter of funding was necessary to facilitate the change in the start of the federal government fiscal year from July 1 to October 1.

appropriations bills through formulaic provisions and anomalies. Unlike previous years, the formula for providing continuing appropriations was based on the amount provided in FY2012 rather than a rate.

Table 3. Appropriations Acts Containing Full-Year Continuing Resolutions (CRs), FY1977-FY2016

Fiscal Year	Public Law Number	Enactment Date	Page Length (Statutes-at-Large)	Included Formulaic Funding Provision(s)?	Number of Appropriations Acts Covered or Contained in the Act[a]
1978	P.L. 95-205	12-09-1977	2	No	2/13[b]
1979	P.L. 95-482	10-18-1978	4	No	1/13
1980	P.L. 96-123	11-20-1979	4	Yes	6/13[c]
1981	P.L. 97-12	06-05-1981	2[d]	Yes	5/13[d]
1982	P.L. 97-161	03-31-1982	1	Yes	3/13[e]
1983	P.L. 97-377	12-21-1982	95	Yes	7/13
1984	P.L. 98-151	11-14-1983	19	Yes	5/13[f]
1985	P.L. 98-473	10-12-1984	363	No	9/13[g]
1986	P.L. 99-190	12-19-1985	142	No	8/13[h]
1987	P.L. 99-591	10-30-1986	391	No	13/13
1988	P.L. 100-202	12-22-1987	451	No	13/13
1992	P.L. 102-266	04-01-1992	8	Yes	1/13[i]
2007	P.L. 110-5	02-15-2007	53	Yes	9/11[j]
2011	P.L. 112-10	04-15-2011	98	Yes	12/12[k]
2013	P.L. 113-6	03-26-2013	240	Yes	12/12[l]

Sources: Prepared by the Congressional Research Service using data from the Legislative Information System; Congressional Research Service, appropriations status tables (various fiscal years), available at http://crs.gov/Pages/appover.aspx; and various other sources.

a. Between the 95th and 108th Congresses, there were 13 House and Senate Appropriations subcommittees responsible for one regular appropriations bill each. During the 109th Congress, due to subcommittee realignment, the total number of regular appropriations bills was effectively reduced to 11 during each year of the Congress. Beginning in the 110th Congress, subcommittee jurisdictions were again realigned for a total of 12 subcommittees, each of which is currently responsible for a single regular appropriations bill. For further information on subcommittee realignment during this period, see CRS Report RL31572, *Appropriations Subcommittee Structure: History of Changes from 1920 to 2015*, by James V. Saturno and Jessica Tollestrup.

b. This full-year continuing appropriations for the District of Columbia provided by this act were later superseded by a standalone regular appropriations act (P.L. 95-288).

c. Some of the appropriations acts covered by this full year CR were later superseded by standalone regular appropriations acts for Interior and Related Agencies (P.L. 96-126); Military Construction (96-130); Department of Defense (P.L. 96-154); and Transportation (P.L. 96-131).

d. This full-year CR was contained within the FY1981 Supplemental Appropriations and Rescissions Act 1981 (P.L. 97-12, see Title IV, "Further Continuing Appropriations"). Title IV extended through the end of the fiscal year the expiration of P.L. 96-536, which covered the appropriations acts that had not yet been enacted for Foreign Assistance; the Legislative Branch; Departments of Labor, Health and Human Services, Education, and Related Agencies; Departments of State, Justice, and Commerce, the Judiciary, and Related Agencies; the Treasury, Postal Service and General Government.

e. This full-year CR extended through the end of the fiscal year the expiration date of P.L. 97-92, which covered the appropriations acts that had not yet been enacted for the Treasury, Postal Service and General Government; Departments of Commerce, Justice, and State, the Judiciary; and Departments of Labor, Health and Human Services, Education, and Related Agencies.

f. Some of the appropriations acts covered by this full-year CR were later superseded by standalone regular appropriations acts for the Department of Defense (P.L. 98-121); Commerce, Justice, and State, the Judiciary, and Related Agencies (P.L. 98-166); and the Treasury, Postal Service and General Government (P.L. 98-151).

g. The full-year continuing appropriations for the Departments of Labor, Health and Human Services, Education, and Related Agencies that were provided by this act were later superseded by a standalone regular appropriations act (P.L. 98-619).

h. The Departments of Labor, Health and Human Services, Education, and Related Agencies provided by the CR were superseded by the enactment of P.L. 99-178.

i. This full-year CR extended through the end of FY1992 the expiration date of P.L. 102-163, which covered appropriations that had not yet been enacted for Foreign Operations, Export Financing, and Related Programs.

j. Despite the reorganization of the House and Senate Appropriations subcommittees at the beginning of the 110th Congress, the FY2007 CR (P.L. 110-5), which was enacted on February 15, 2007, reflected the subcommittee jurisdictions in the 109th Congress.

k. P.L. 112-10, Division B, provided continuing appropriations through the end of the fiscal year for Agriculture, Rural Development, Food and Drug Administration, and Related Agencies; Commerce, Justice, Science, and Related Agencies; Energy and Water Development and Related Agencies; Financial Services and General Government; Department of Homeland Security; Department of the Interior, Environment, and Related Agencies; Departments of Labor, Health and Human Services, Education, and Related Agencies; Legislative Branch; Military Construction and Veterans Affairs and Related Agencies; Department of State, Foreign Operations, and Related Programs; and Transportation, Housing and Urban Development, and Related Agencies. Division A contained the text of the Department of Defense Appropriations Act.

l. P.L. 113-6, Division F, provided continuing appropriations for FY2013 for Energy and Water Development and Related Agencies; Financial Services and General Government; Department of the Interior, Environment, and Related Agencies; Departments of Labor, Health and Human Services, Education, and Related Agencies; Legislative Branch; Department of State, Foreign Operations, and Related Programs; and Transportation, Housing and Urban Development, and Related Agencies. Divisions A through E contained the texts of the Agriculture, Rural Development, Food and Drug Administration, and Related Agencies Appropriations Act; Commerce, Justice, Science, and Related Agencies Appropriations Act; the Department of Defense Appropriations Act; Department of Homeland Security Appropriations Act; and Military Construction and Veterans Affairs and Related Agencies Appropriations Act.

Table 4. Number, Page Length, and Duration of Continuing Resolutions (CRs): FY1977-FY2016

Fiscal Year	Number of Acts by Fiscal Year	Number of Acts Cumulatively	Public Law Number	Statutes-at-Large Citation	Page Length	Enactment Date	Expiration Date	Duration in Days[a]
1977	1	1	P.L. 94-473	90 Stat. 2065-2067	3	10-11-1976	03-31-1977	183
	2	2	P.L. 95-16	91 Stat. 28	1	04-01-1977	04-30-1977	30
1978	1	3	P.L. 95-130	91 Stat. 1153-1154	2	10-13-1977	10-31-1977	31
	2	4	P.L. 95-165	91 Stat. 1323-1324	2	11-09-1977	11-30-1977	30
	3	5	P.L. 95-205	91 Stat. 1460-1461	2	12-09-1977	09-30-1978	304
1979	1	6	P.L. 95-482	92 Stat. 1603-1605	3	10-18-1978	09-30-1979	365
1980	1	7	P.L. 96-86	93 Stat. 656-663	8	10-12-1979	11-20-1979	51
	2	8	P.L. 96-123	93 Stat. 923-926	4	11-20-1979	09-30-1980	315
1981	1	9	P.L. 96-369	94 Stat. 1351-1359	9	10-01-1980	12-15-1980	76
	2	10	P.L. 96-536	94 Stat. 3166-3172	7	12-16-1980	06-05-1981	172
	3	11	P.L. 97-12[b]	95 Stat. 95-96	2	06-05-1981	09-30-1981	117
1982	1	12	P.L. 97-51	95 Stat. 958-968	11	10-01-1981	11-20-1981	51
	2	13	P.L. 97-85	95 Stat. 1098	1	11-23-1981	12-15-1981	22
	3	14	P.L. 97-92	95 Stat. 1183-1203	21	12-15-1981	03-31-1982	106

Fiscal Year	Number of Acts by Fiscal Year	Number of Acts Cumulatively	Public Law Number	Statutes-at-Large Citation	Page Length	Enactment Date	Expiration Date	Duration in Days[a]
	4	15	P.L. 97-161	96 Stat. 22	1	03-31-1982	09-30-1982	183
1983	1	16	P.L. 97-276	96 Stat. 1186-1205	20	10-02-1982	12-17-1982	78
	2	17	P.L. 97-377	96 Stat. 1830-1924	95[c]	12-17-1982	09-30-1983	287
1984	1	18	P.L. 98-107	97 Stat. 733-743	11	10-01-1983	11-10-1983	41
	2	19	P.L. 98-151	97 Stat. 964-982	19	11-14-1983	09-30-1984	321
1985	1	20	P.L. 98-441	98 Stat. 1699-1701	3	10-03-1984	10-03-1984	3
	2	21	P.L. 98-453	98 Stat. 1731	1	10-05-1984	10-05-1984	2
	3	22	P.L. 98-455	98 Stat. 1747	1	10-06-1984	10-09-1984	4
	4	23	P.L. 98-461	98 Stat. 1814	1	10-10-1984	10-11-1984	2
	5	24	P.L. 98-473	98 Stat. 1837-1976	140[d]	10-12-1984	09-30-1985	354
1986	1	25	P.L. 99-103	99 Stat. 471-473	3	09-30-1985	11-14-1985	45
	2	26	P.L. 99-154	99 Stat. 813	1	11-14-1985	12-12-1985	28
	3	27	P.L. 99-179	99 Stat. 1135	1	12-13-1985	12-16-1985	4
	4	28	P.L. 99-184	99 Stat. 1176	1	12-17-1985	12-19-1985	3
	5	29	P.L. 99-190	99 Stat. 1185-1326	142[e]	12-19-1985	09-30-1986	285
1987	1	30	P.L. 99-434	100 Stat. 1076-1079	4	10-01-1986	10-08-1986	8
	2	31	P.L. 99-464	100 Stat. 1185-1188	4	10-09-1986	10-10-1986	2

Fiscal Year	Number of Acts by Fiscal Year	Number of Acts Cumulatively	Public Law Number	Statutes-at-Large Citation	Page Length	Enactment Date	Expiration Date	Duration in Days[a]
	3	32	P.L. 99-465	100 Stat. 1189	1	10-11-1986	10-15-1986	5
	4	33	P.L. 99-491	100 Stat. 1239	1	10-16-1986	10-16-1986	1
	5	34	P.L. 99-500[f]	100 Stat. 1783 through 1783-385	386	10-18-1986	09-30-1987	349
	6	35	P.L. 99-591[f]	100 Stat. 3341 through 3341-389	390	10-30-1986	[n/a][f]	—
1988	1	36	P.L. 100-120	101 Stat. 789-791	3	09-30-1987	11-10-1987	41
	2	37	P.L. 100-162	101 Stat. 903	1	11-10-1987	12-16-1987	36
	3	38	P.L. 100-193	101 Stat. 1310	1	12-16-1987	12-18-1987	2
	4	39	P.L. 100-197	101 Stat. 1314	1	12-20-1987	12-21-1987	3
	5	40	P.L. 100-202	101 Stat. 1329 through 1329-450	451[g]	12-22-1987	09-30-1988	284
1989	[none]	—	—	—	—	—	—	—
1990	1	41	P.L. 101-100	103 Stat. 638-640	3	09-29-1989	10-25-1989	25
	2	42	P.L. 101-130	103 Stat. 775-776	2	10-26-1989	11-15-1989	21
	3	43	P.L. 101-154	103 Stat. 934	1	11-15-1989	11-20-1989	5
1991	1	44	P.L. 101-403	104 Stat. 867-870	4[h]	10-01-1990	10-05-1990	5
	2	45	P.L. 101-412	104 Stat. 894-897	4	10-09-1990	10-19-1990	14
	3	46	P.L. 101-444	104 Stat. 1030-1033	4	10-19-1990	10-24-1990	5

Fiscal Year	Number of Acts by Fiscal Year	Number of Acts Cumulatively	Public Law Number	Statutes-at-Large Citation	Page Length	Enactment Date	Expiration Date	Duration in Days[a]
	4	47	P.L. 101-461	104 Stat. 1075-1078	4	10-25-1990	10-27-1990	3
	5	48	P.L. 101-467	104 Stat. 1086-1087	2	10-28-1990	11-05-1990	9
1992	1	49	P.L. 102-109	105 Stat. 551-554	4	09-30-1991	10-29-1991	29
	2	50	P.L. 102-145	105 Stat. 968-871	4	10-28-1991	11-14-1991	16[i]
	3	51	P.L. 102-163	105 Stat. 1048	1	11-15-1991	11-26-1991	12
	4	52	P.L. 102-266	106 Stat. 92-99	8	04-01-1992	09-30-1992	183
1993	1	53	P.L. 102-376	106 Stat. 1311-1314	4	10-01-1992	10-05-1992	5
1994	1	54	P.L. 103-88	107 Stat. 977-980	4	09-30-1993	10-21-1993	21
	2	55	P.L. 103-113	107 Stat. 1114	1	10-21-1993	10-28-1993	7
	3	56	P.L. 103-128	107 Stat. 1355	1	10-29-1993	11-10-1993	13
1995	[none]	—	—	—	—	—	—	—
1996	1	57	P.L. 104-31	109 Stat. 278-282	5	09-30-1995	11-13-1995	44
	2	58	P.L. 104-54	109 Stat. 540-545	6	11-19-1995	11-20-1995	7
	3	59	P.L. 104-56	109 Stat. 548-553	6	11-20-1995	12-15-1995	25
	4	60	P.L. 104-69	109 Stat. 767-772	6	12-22-1995	01-03-1996	19
	5	61	P.L. 104-90	110 Stat. 3-6	4	01-04-1996	01-25-1996	22

Fiscal Year	Number of Acts by Fiscal Year	Number of Acts Cumulatively	Public Law Number	Statutes-at-Large Citation	Page Length	Enactment Date	Expiration Date	Duration in Days[a]
	6	62	P.L. 104-91	110 Stat. 10-14	5	01-06-1996	09-30-1996	290[i]
	7	63	P.L. 104-92	110 Stat. 16-24	9	01-06-1996	09-30-1996	290
	8	64	P.L. 104-94	110 Stat. 25	1	01-06-1996	01-26-1996	42
	9	65	P.L. 104-99	110 Stat. 26-47	22	01-26-1996	03-15-1996	49[i]
	10	66	P.L. 104-116	110 Stat. 826	1	03-15-1996	03-22-1996	7
	11	67	P.L. 104-118	110 Stat. 829	1	03-22-1996	03-29-1996	7
	12	68	P.L. 104-122	110 Stat. 876-878	3	03-29-1996	04-24-1996	26[i]
	13	69	P.L. 104-131	110 Stat. 1213	1	04-24-1996	04-25-1996	1
1997	[none]	—	—	—	—	—	—	—
1998	1	70	P.L. 105-46	111 Stat. 1153-1158	6	09-30-1997	10-23-1997	23
	2	71	P.L. 105-64	111 Stat. 1343	1	10-23-1997	11-07-1997	15
	3	72	P.L. 105-68	111 Stat. 1453	1	11-07-1997	11-09-1997	2
	4	73	P.L. 105-69	111 Stat. 1454	1	11-09-1997	11-10-1997	1
	5	74	P.L. 105-71	111 Stat. 1456	1	11-10-1997	11-14-1997	4
	6	75	P.L. 105-84	111 Stat. 1628	1	11-14-1997	11-26-1997	12
1999	1	76	P.L. 105-240	112 Stat. 1566-1571	6	09-25-1998	10-09-1998	9
	2	77	P.L. 105-249	112 Stat. 1868	1	10-09-1998	10-12-1998	3
	3	78	P.L. 105-254	112 Stat. 1888	1	10-12-1998	10-14-1998	2
	4	79	P.L. 105-257	112 Stat. 1901	1	10-14-1998	10-16-1998	2

CRS-23

Fiscal Year	Number of Acts by Fiscal Year	Number of Acts Cumulatively	Public Law Number	Statutes-at-Large Citation	Page Length	Enactment Date	Expiration Date	Duration in Days[a]
	5	80	P.L. 105-260	112 Stat. 1919	1	10-16-1998	10-20-1998	4
	6	81	P.L. 105-273	112 Stat. 2418	1	10-20-1998	10-21-1998	1
2000	1	82	P.L. 106-62	113 Stat. 505-509	5	09-30-1999	10-21-1999	21
	2	83	P.L. 106-75	113 Stat. 1125	1	10-21-1999	10-29-1999	8
	3	84	P.L. 106-85	113 Stat. 1297	1	10-29-1999	11-05-1999	7
	4	85	P.L. 106-88	113 Stat. 1304	1	11-05-1999	11-10-1999	5
	5	86	P.L. 106-94	113 Stat. 1311	1	11-10-1999	11-17-1999	7
	6	87	P.L. 106-105	113 Stat. 1484	1	11-18-1999	11-18-1999	1
	7	88	P.L. 106-106	113 Stat. 1485	1	11-19-1999	12-02-1999	14
2001	1	89	P.L. 106-275	114 Stat. 808-811	4	09-29-2000	10-06-2000	6
	2	90	P.L. 106-282	114 Stat. 866	1	10-06-2000	10-14-2000	8
	3	91	P.L. 106-306	114 Stat. 1073	1	10-13-2000	10-20-2000	6
	4	92	P.L. 106-344	114 Stat. 1318	1	10-20-2000	10-25-2000	5
	5	93	P.L. 106-358	114 Stat. 1397	1	10-26-2000	10-26-2000	1
	6	94	P.L. 106-359	114 Stat. 1398	1	10-26-2000	10-27-2000	1
	7	95	P.L. 106-381	114 Stat. 1450	1	10-27-2000	10-28-2000	1
	8	96	P.L. 106-388	114 Stat. 1550	1	10-28-2000	10-29-2000	1
	9	97	P.L. 106-389	114 Stat. 1551	1	10-29-2000	10-30-2000	1
	10	98	P.L. 106-401	114 Stat. 1676	1	10-30-2000	10-31-2000	1
	11	99	P.L. 106-403	114 Stat. 1741	1	11-01-2000	11-01-2000	1
	12	100	P.L. 106-416	114 Stat. 1811	1	11-01-2000	11-02-2000	1
	13	101	P.L. 106-426	114 Stat. 1897	1	11-03-2000	11-03-2000	1

CRS-24

Fiscal Year	Number of Acts by Fiscal Year	Number of Acts Cumulatively	Public Law Number	Statutes-at-Large Citation	Page Length	Enactment Date	Expiration Date	Duration in Days[a]
	14	102	P.L. 106-427	114 Stat. 1898	1	11-04-2000	11-04-2000	1
	15	103	P.L. 106-428	114 Stat. 1899	1	11-04-2000	11-14-2000	10
	16	104	P.L. 106-520	114 Stat. 2436-2437	2	11-15-2000	12-05-2000	21
	17	105	P.L. 106-537	114 Stat. 2562	1	12-05-2000	12-07-2000	2
	18	106	P.L. 106-539	114 Stat. 2570	1	12-07-2000	12-08-2000	1
	19	107	P.L. 106-540	114 Stat. 2571	1	12-08-2000	12-11-2000	3
	20	108	P.L. 106-542	114 Stat. 2713	1	12-11-2000	12-15-2000	4
	21	109	P.L. 106-543	114 Stat. 2714	1	12-15-2000	12-21-2000	6
2002	1	110	P.L. 107-44	115 Stat. 253-257	5	09-28-2001	10-16-2001	16
	2	111	P.L. 107-48	115 Stat. 261	1	10-12-2001	10-23-2001	7
	3	112	P.L. 107-53	115 Stat. 269	1	10-22-2001	10-31-2001	8
	4	113	P.L. 107-58	115 Stat. 406	1	10-31-2001	11-16-2001	16
	5	114	P.L. 107-70	115 Stat. 596	1	11-17-2001	12-07-2001	21
	6	115	P.L. 107-79	115 Stat. 809	1	12-07-2001	12-15-2001	8
	7	116	P.L. 107-83	115 Stat. 822	1	12-15-2001	12-21-2001	6
	8	117	P.L. 107-97	115 Stat. 960	1	12-21-2001	01-10-2002	20
2003	1	118	P.L. 107-229	116 Stat. 1465-1468	4	09-30-2002	10-04-2002	4
	2	119	P.L. 107-235	116 Stat. 1482	1	10-04-2002	10-11-2002	7
	3	120	P.L. 107-240	116 Stat. 1492-1495	4	10-11-2002	10-18-2002	7
	4	121	P.L. 107-244	116 Stat. 1503	1	10-18-2002	11-22-2002	35

CRS-25

Fiscal Year	Number of Acts by Fiscal Year	Number of Acts Cumulatively	Public Law Number	Statutes-at-Large Citation	Page Length	Enactment Date	Expiration Date	Duration in Days[a]
	5	122	P.L. 107-294	116 Stat. 2062-2063	2	11-23-2002	01-11-2003	50
	6	123	P.L. 108-2	117 Stat. 5-6	2	01-10-2003	01-31-2003	20
	7	124	P.L. 108-4	117 Stat. 8	1	01-31-2003	02-07-2003	7
	8	125	P.L. 108-5	117 Stat. 9	1	02-07-2003	02-20-2003	13
2004	1	126	P.L. 108-84	117 Stat. 1042-1047	6	09-30-2003	10-31-2003	31
	2	127	P.L. 108-104	117 Stat. 1200	1	10-31-2003	11-07-2003	7
	3	128	P.L. 108-107	117 Stat. 1240	1	11-07-2003	11-21-2003	14
	4	129	P.L. 108-135	117 Stat. 1391	1	11-22-2003	01-31-2004	71
	5	130	P.L. 108-185	117 Stat. 2684	1	12-16-2003	[n/a]k	—
2005	1	131	P.L. 108-309	118 Stat. 1137-1143	7	09-30-2004	11-20-2004	51
	2	132	P.L. 108-416	118 Stat. 2338	1	11-21-2004	12-03-2004	13
	3	133	P.L. 108-434	118 Stat. 2614	1	12-03-2004	12-08-2004	5
2006	1	134	P.L. 109-77	119 Stat. 2037-2042	6	09-30-2005	11-18-2005	49
	2	135	P.L. 109-105	119 Stat. 2287	1	11-19-2005	12-17-2005	29
	3	136	P.L. 109-128	119 Stat. 2549	1	12-18-2005	12-31-2005	14
2007	1	137	P.L. 109-289k	120 Stat. 1311-1316	6	09-29-2006	11-17-2006	48
	2	138	P.L. 109-369	120 Stat. 2642	1	11-17-2006	12-08-2006	21
	3	139	P.L. 109-383	120 Stat. 2678	1	12-09-2006	02-15-2007	69
	4	140	P.L. 110-5	121 Stat. 8-60	53	02-15-2007	09-30-2007	227

CRS-26

Fiscal Year	Number of Acts by Fiscal Year	Number of Acts Cumulatively	Public Law Number	Statutes-at-Large Citation	Page Length	Enactment Date	Expiration Date	Duration in Days[a]
2008	1	141	P.L. 110-92	121 Stat. 989-998	10	09-29-2007	11-16-2007	47
	2	142	P.L. 110-116[l]	121 Stat. 1341-1344	4	11-13-2007	12-14-2007	28
	3	143	P.L. 110-137	121 Stat. 1454	1	12-14-2007	12-21-2007	7
	4	144	P.L. 110-149	121 Stat. 1819	1	12-21-2007	12-31-2007	10
2009	1	145	P.L. 110-329	122 Stat. 3574-3716	143	09-30-2008	03-06-2009	157
	2	146	P.L. 111-6	123 Stat. 522	1	03-06-2009	03-11-2009	5
2010	1	147	P.L. 111-68[m]	123 Stat. 2043-2053	11	10-01-2009	10-31-2009	31
	2	148	P.L. 111-88[n]	123 Stat. 2972-2974	3	10-30-2009	12-18-2009	48
2011	1	149	P.L. 111-242	124 Stat. 2607-2616	10	09-30-210	12-03-2010	64
	2	150	P.L. 111-290	124 Stat. 3063	1	12-04-2010	12-18-2010	15
	3	151	P.L. 111-317	124 Stat. 3454	1	12-18-2010	12-21-2010	3
	4	152	P.L. 111-322[o]	124 Stat. 3518-3521	4	12-22-2010	03-04-2011	73
	5	153	P.L. 112-4	125 Stat. 6-13	8	03-02-2011	03-18-2011	14
	6	154	P.L. 112-6	125 Stat. 23-30	8	03-18-2011	04-08-2011	21
	7	155	P.L. 112-8	125 Stat. 34-35	2	04-09-2011	04-15-2011	7
	8	156	P.L. 112-10[p]	125 Stat. 102-199	98	04-15-2011	09-30-2011	168

CRS-27

Fiscal Year	Number of Acts by Fiscal Year	Number of Acts Cumulatively	Public Law Number	Statutes-at-Large Citation	Page Length	Enactment Date	Expiration Date	Duration in Days[a]
2012	1	157	P.L. 112-33	125 Stat. 363-368	6	09-30-2011	10-04-2011	4
	2	158	P.L. 112-36	125 Stat. 386-391	6	10-05-2011	11-18-2011	45
	3	159	P.L. 112-55q	125 Stat. 710	1	11-18-2011	12-16-2011	28
	4	160	P.L. 112-67	125 Stat. 769	1	12-16-2011	12-17-2011	1
	5	161	P.L. 112-68	125 Stat. 770	1	12-17-2011	12-23-2011	6
2013	1	162	P.L. 112-175	126 Stat. 1313	12	09-28-2012	03-27-2013	178
	2	163	P.L. 113-6	127 Stat. 198-437	240	03-26-2013	09-30-2013	(365)[s]
2014	1	164	P.L. 113-39	127 Stat. 532-533	2	09-30-2013	[n/a][t]	(17)[t]
	2	165	P.L. 113-44	127 Stat. 555-556	2	10-10-2013	12-15-2013[t]	(8)[t]
	3	166	P.L. 113-46	127 Stat. 558-571	14	10-17-2013	01-15-2013	(107)[t]
	4	167	P.L. 113-73	128 Stat. 3	1	01-15-2013	01-18-2013	3
2015	1	168	P.L. 113-164	128 Stat. 1867	11	09-19-2014	12-11-2014	72
	2	169	P.L. 113-202	128 Stat. 2069	1	12-12-2014	12-13-2014	1
	3	170	P.L. 113-203	128 Stat. 2070	1	12-13-2014	12-17-2014	4
	4	171	P.L. 113-235	128 Stat. 2767	1	12-16-2014	2-27-2015	72
	5	172	P.L. 114-3	129 Stat. 38	1	02-27-2015	03-06-2015	7
2016	1	173	P.L. 114-53	129 Stat. 502-512	11	09-30-2015	12-11-2015	72
	2	174	P.L. 114-96	129 Stat. 2193	1	12-11-2015	12-16-2015	5
	3	175	P.L. 114-100	129 Stat. 2202	1	12-16-2015	12-22-2015	6

CRS-28

Sources: Prepared by the Congressional Research Service using data from the Legislative Information System; Congressional Research Service, appropriations status tables (various fiscal years), available at http://crs.gov/Pages/appover.aspx; and various other sources.

a. Duration in days is measured, in the case of the initial CR for a fiscal year, from the first day of the year (October 1) through the expiration date. For subsequent CRs for a fiscal year, duration in days is measured from the day after the expiration of the preceding CR. In several instances, as appropriate, the number of days reflects an extra day in a leap year (every fourth year beginning with calendar year 1976). Several CRs provided continuing appropriations for mixed periods of time. For example, three CRs—P.L. 96-86 (for FY1980), P.L. 97-51 (for FY1982), and P.L. 97-276 (for FY1983)—were enacted in November or December of the applicable year for periods covering 51 days, 51 days, and 78 days, respectively, but they also included continuing appropriations for the remainder of that fiscal year for activities covered by the Legislative Branch Appropriations Act. (See also the discussion of actions for FY1996 under footnote j.) In these instances, the "Duration in Days" column reflects the time period that applied to the greatest number of activities funded by the measure.

b. Title IV (95 Stat. 95-96) of P.L. 97-12, the Supplemental Appropriations and Rescission Act for FY1981, provided continuing appropriations for FY1981; the other titles of the act (95 Stat. 14-95) are excluded from the page count.

c. P.L. 97-377 incorporated the full text of various regular appropriations acts.

d. Title I (98 Stat. 1837-1976) of P.L. 98-473 provided continuing appropriations for FY1985; the other title, Title II (98 Stat. 1976-2199), set forth the Comprehensive Crime Control Act of 1984 and is excluded from the page count.

e. P.L. 99-190 incorporated the full text of various regular appropriations acts.

f. P.L. 99-591 superseded P.L. 99-500 and corrected enrollment errors in the earlier act; both laws originated as H.J.Res 738.

g. P.L. 100-202 incorporated the full text of various regular appropriations acts.

h. Title I (104 Stat. 867-870) of P.L. 101-403 provided continuing appropriations for FY1991; Titles II and III (104 Stat. 871-874) provided supplemental appropriations and are excluded from the page count.

i. Section 106(c) of P.L. 102-145 provided that, as an exception to the general expiration date, continuing appropriations for the Foreign Operation Appropriations Act would expire on March 31, 1992 (a duration of 154 days).

j. A total of 13 CRs were enacted for FY1996 (and one was vetoed). Two funding gaps occurred, the first in mid-November 1995 and the second from mid-December 1995 until early January 1996. The CRs for this year may be divided into two categories depending on whether their coverage was generally comprehensive or partial. Nine of the CRs enacted for FY1996 generally provided short-term funding for all activities under the regular appropriations acts that had not yet been enacted, while the other four provided funding only for selected activities within certain acts. The four acts in the latter category included the following:

(1) P.L. 104-69, which funded the Aid to Families With Dependent Children (AFDC) and Foster Care and Adoption Assistance programs, programs of the District of Columbia, and certain veterans' programs;

(2) P.L. 104-90, which funded programs of the District of Columbia;

(3) P.L. 104-91, Title I, which funded a variety of programs, including ones pertaining to the Peace Corps, the Federal Emergency Management Agency, the Federal Bureau of Investigation, trade adjustment assistance benefits, and the National Institutes of Health, among others; and

(4) P.L. 104-92, which funded a variety of programs, including ones pertaining to nutrition services for the elderly, visitor services in the National Park System, certain veterans' programs, and programs of the District of Columbia, among others.

Activities under two of the regular appropriations acts for FY1996 were funded through the end of the fiscal year (September 30, 1996) in CRs: (1) Title IV of P.L. 104-92 provided such funding for activities covered by the District of Columbia Appropriations Act; and (2) Title III of P.L. 104-99 provided such funding for activities covered by the Foreign Operations Appropriations Act. In addition, other selected activities were funded through the remainder of the fiscal year in P.L. 104-91, P.L. 104-92, and P.L. 104-122. Action on the regular appropriations acts for FY1996 was concluded with the enactment of P.L. 104-134, the Omnibus Consolidated Rescissions and Appropriations Act of 1996, on April 26, 1996 (110 Stat. 1321 through 1321-381), which provided funding for the remainder of the fiscal year for activities covered by five of the regular appropriations acts.

Three of the CRs had mixed periods of duration. The duration shown in the table was determined as follows:

(1) Most of the funding provided in P.L. 104-92 was for the remainder of the fiscal year, so a duration of 290 days was used;

(2) While the funding provided in P.L. 104-99 for activities covered by the Foreign Operations Appropriations Act was for the remainder of the fiscal year, the funding provided for activities covered by four other regular appropriations acts was through March 15, 1996, so a duration of 49 days was used; and

(3) Most of the funding provided in P.L. 104-122 was through April 24, while only one account was funded through the remainder of the fiscal year, so a duration of 26 days was used.

In the case of P.L. 104-91, a measure requiring the Secretary of Commerce to convey to the Commonwealth of Massachusetts the National Marine Fisheries Service laboratory located on Emerson Avenue in Gloucester, Massachusetts, Title I (110 Stat. 10-14) of the act provided continuing appropriations for selected activities for the remainder of FY1996; Section I (110 Stat. 7-10) and Title II (110 Stat. 14-15) pertained to other matters and are excluded from the page count. Section 110 of the act made the funding effective as of December 16, 1995.

k. P.L. 108-185 contained provisions affecting funding levels for two specified programs but did not contain a provision affecting the expiration date of January 31, 2004, established in the preceding CR (P.L. 108-135).

l. Continuing appropriations for FY2007 were provided by Division B (120 Stat. 1311-1316) of P.L. 109-289, the Defense Appropriations Act for FY2007; the other portions of the act (120 Stat. 1257-1311) are excluded from the page count.

m. Continuing appropriations for FY2008 were provided by Division B (121 Stat. 1341-1344) of P.L. 110-116, the Defense Appropriations Act for FY2008; the other portions of the act (121 Stat. 1295-1341) are excluded from the page count.

n. Continuing appropriations for FY2010 were provided by Division B (123 Stat. 2043-2053) of P.L. 111-68, the Legislative Branch Appropriations Act for FY2010; the other portions of the act (123 Stat. 2023-2043) are excluded from the page count.

o. Continuing appropriations for FY2010 were provided by Division B (123 Stat. 2972-2974) of P.L. 111-88, the Interior, Environment, and Related Agencies Appropriations Act for 2010; the other portions of the act (123 Stat. 2904-2972) are excluded from the page count.

p. Continuing appropriations for FY2011 were provided by Division A (124 Stat. 3518-3521) of P.L. 111-322, the Continuing Appropriations and Surface Transportation Extensions Act for 2011; the other portions of the act (124 Stat. 3522-3531) are excluded from the page count.

q. Full-year continuing appropriations for FY2011 were provided by Division B (125 Stat. 102-199) of P.L. 112-10, the Department of Defense and Full-Year Continuing Appropriations Act for 2011; the other portions of the act (125 Stat. 38-102, 199-212) are excluded from the page count.

r. Continuing appropriations for FY2012 were provided by Division D (125 Stat. 710) of P.L. 112-55, the Consolidated and Further Continuing Appropriations Act for 2012; the other portions of the act (125 Stat. 552-709) are excluded from the page count.

s. In P.L. 113-6, both the full text (Divisions A through E) and continuing (Division F) appropriations were for the entire fiscal year (FY2013) and superseded the continuing appropriations provided by P.L. 112-175

t. A total of four CRs were enacted for FY2014. This count includes two CRs that provided funding for only specific programs and activities during the FY2014 funding gap. The Pay Our Military Act (P.L. 113-39) was enacted on September 30, 2013, and provided funding for FY2014. The Department of Defense Survivor Benefits Continuing Appropriations Resolution, 2014 (P.L. 113-44), was enacted on October 10, 2013, and expired on December 15, 2013. However, the funding provided by both of these CRs was terminated on October 17, 2013, through the enactment of a third CR, P.L. 113-46, which broadly funded the previous fiscal year's activities through January 15, 2014. The funding provided by this third CR was extended through January 18 by the enactment of a fourth CR (P.L. 113-73). Section 118 of P.L. 113-46 provided that the time covered by that act was to have begun on October 1, 2013. For the purposes of this table, the duration in days for the first two CRs is considered to have ended on October 17, 2013. The third CR is considered to have begun on October 1, 2013, and expired on January 15, 2014. For further information on the FY2014 funding gap and congressional action on associated CRs, see CRS Report RS20348, *Federal Funding Gaps: A Brief Overview*, by Jessica Tollestrup.

Author Contact Information

James V. Saturno
Specialist on Congress and the Legislative Process
jsaturno@crs.loc.gov, 7-2381

Jessica Tollestrup
Specialist on Congress and the Legislative Process
jtollestrup@crs.loc.gov, 7-0941

Resources from TheCapitol.Net

Federal Budget Links and Research Tools, Laws, Web Sites, and Books
<TCNBudget.com>

Custom On-Site Training

Understanding Congressional Budgeting and Appropriations
<TCNUCBA.com>

Advanced Federal Budget Process
<TCNAFBP.com>

Congressional Dynamics and the Legislative Process
<TCNCDLP.com>

Capitol Learning Audio Courses™
<CapitolLearning.com>

Appropriations Process in a Nutshell with James Saturno,
ISBN 1-58733-043-1

Authorizations and Appropriations in a Nutshell with James Saturno,
ISBN 1-58733-029-6

The Federal Budget Process with Philip Joyce,
ISBN 1-58733-083-0

Index

A

References are to chapter and page number (e.g., 6-2 refers to page 2 in chapter 6).

References are to chapter and page number (e.g., 6-2 refers to page 2 in chapter 6).

References are to chapter and page number (e.g., 6-2 refers to page 2 in chapter 6).

References are to chapter and page number (e.g., 6-2 refers to page 2 in chapter 6).

References are to chapter and page number (e.g., 6-2 refers to page 2 in chapter 6).

References are to chapter and page number (e.g., 6-2 refers to page 2 in chapter 6).

Printed in the USA
CPSIA information can be obtained
at www.ICGtesting.com
CBHW081707270124
3748CB00039B/972

9 781587 332937